From Diplomacy to *Resistance*

D1257626

Translated from the Hebrew by ALTON M. WINTERS

The Jewish Publication Society of America

Philadelphia   5730/1970

Yehuda Bauer

From Diplomacy to *Resistance*

A History of Jewish Palestine
1939–1945

English translation Copyright © 1970 by The Jewish Publication
Society of America
Original Hebrew edition printed in Israel by Sifriat Poalim, 1966
First Edition   All rights reserved
Library of Congress Catalog Card Number: 70-105065
Manufactured in the United States of America
Designed by Adrianne Onderdonk Dudden

THE TRANSLATION OF THIS BOOK
INTO ENGLISH WAS MADE POSSIBLE THROUGH
A GRANT FROM THE ADOLF AMRAM FUND

To the living memory of my friends,
members of the Palmakh,
Daniel Reich, *who fell on January 16, 1948,*
and
David Goldenfun, *who fell on February 12, 1948,*
so that Israel may live

Preface

A book dealing with the history of Palestine during the period of the Second World War raises all the problems of contemporary history generally. There is no real answer to the argument that the contemporary historian is running greater risks than those dealing with earlier periods. Up to a point he is a participant in the events he recounts, and his objectivity will be suspect. All he can do, therefore, is lessen the danger by as careful a study of available sources as possible. Yet he can hardly avoid having his own view on what happened and how and why it happened. Indeed, without such a view it would hardly be worthwhile writing a book or, most probably, reading it. Provided he avoids falling victim to his own preconceived notions, provided his conclusions are based as solidly as possible on his source material, he cannot and must not avoid imparting to the reader his own view of the events he describes. If that is not done, he becomes a chronicler rather than a historian.

The major problem in contemporary history is of course that of the available sources. Fortunately, I enjoyed the full help and cooperation of Dr. Alex Bein of Central Zionist Archive and

Israel's chief archivist. Dr. Michael Hyman of the CZA and his staff were also extremely helpful in allowing me to roam freely through their archives. The Hagana Archives (ATH) in Tel Aviv were opened to me by Mr. Shaul Avigur and Lt. Col. Gershon Rivlin, and my special thanks are due to my friend Dr. Yehuda Slutsky, author of the authoritative history of the Hagana, who spared neither help nor constructive criticism. Thanks are also due to Mr. Boris Guriel, late of the Weizmann Archive, for his great help and to Mr. Berele Teitz of the Histadrut Archive for making large amounts of material available to me. Much of the material is based on oral interviews, some of which were collected by ATH and some of which I added and deposited there; the many persons who gave me of their time and patiently answered my questions are in a way co-authors of this book, without of course being in any way responsible for its contents.

It is a special pleasure to offer thanks again to my teacher and colleague Prof. Israel Halperin, who guided me through this research until its publication in Hebrew in 1963. I was fortunate in having as a translator Rabbi Dr. Alton M. Winters of Glen Cove, New York, a man thoroughly versed in both languages, who became a friend and a colleague in the process of translating this work. Last but not least, my kibbutz, Kibbutz Shoval in the Israeli Negev, whose members showed not only patience and interest but who wholeheartedly supported and continue to support my work, are living proof of the worth of labor done in a communal social environment.

Y.B.

March 1969
Kibbutz Shoval
Negev, Israel

Contents

From Diplomacy to *Resistance*

Introduction

Anyone who wishes to examine Zionist diplomacy and the military policy of the Zionist movement during World War II is confronted by the question, What caused the change that occurred in British policy toward Palestine during the years of the Arab rebellion, 1936–1939? The accomplishment of such a change was the goal of the leaders of the rebellion, to whom the Jewish immigration of the years 1933–1936 signified peril for the Palestine Arab national movement. During those years 164,267 Jews entered the country. And from 1936 to 1942 an additional 68,287 Jews arrived. Most of them came from Eastern Europe, while a quarter of their number were rescued from the direct domination of German nazism.

During that period (1932–1937) the Jewish birthrate also temporarily approached that of the Moslems, surpassing the birthrate of Palestinian Christians. There were, apparently, British statesmen who felt that the time would come when Arab superiority in this area would be wholly erased. It was easy to figure out that if immigration continued at the rate of 62,000 per year (as in 1935, the peak year of Jewish immigration) the day

would not be far off when the Jews would become the majority
of the population of Palestine. The Arab leadership, with its fear
of loss of Arab numerical superiority, sought to halt immigration and Jewish land acquisition while there was still time. This
was accompanied by a strident demand for the preservation of
the Arabic character of Palestine by turning the land into an
independent state. According to democratic principles, the Arab
majority would govern it. These items took the form, in November 1935, of a series of demands presented by an Arab mission to High Commissioner Arthur Wauchope. Arab pressure
mounted and speedily became a combined political, economic,
and military pressure.[1]

It must be said that, notwithstanding inner vacillations and
numerous contradictions, a fundamental line of clear encouragement, or at least noninterference, toward the growth and development of the Jewish national home is discernible in British
Palestine policy until the years of the rebellion. This proceeded
from the assumption that the Arabs would ultimately reconcile
themselves to the establishment of the national home and would
reach a compromise agreement with Zionism. It was not clear
beforehand what Britain's reaction might be if these hopes were
not realized. When the Arabs did not make peace with the idea
of a Jewish national home and, on the contrary, made plain
their decided opposition to the possibility of losing the numerical majority—and thus the chance of governing the country—
Britain stood at a difficult crossroads and was forced to redeter-
mine her policy.

We shall not concern ourselves here with the stages of the
Arab general strike of 1936 (April 22 to October 12) or the
rebellion of 1937–1939. Pointing out several decisive turning
points that accompanied the dramatic developments in Palestine
will suffice. In October 1936 the independent and semi-inde-
pendent Arab states (Saudi Arabia, Iraq, Yemen, and Transjordan) were asked by the British to intervene in Palestine to
stop the Arab strike, which had by then been going on for half
a year. And indeed, the heads of those governments addressed

the Arab Higher Committee in Palestine and requested that they halt the strike, with the promise that Britain would render a just decision concerning the country. Thus it was made possible for the Arab Higher Committee—which was confronted with the imminent collapse of the strike if it were to be substantially prolonged—to retreat from open conflict with Britain at that level without losing face. At that time, Britain recognized, in fact, the right of the Arab governments to intervene in the affairs of a British mandate, an act without parallel or precedent. Also, Britain perforce recognized the pan-Arab character of the Palestine conflict and the vital interest of the overall Arab national movement in Palestine.

On November 5, 1936, the British colonial secretary announced in Parliament that the high commissioner had been requested "to take a conservative view of the economic absorptive capacity of the country." The economic absorptive capacity had been designated, following the Churchill White Paper of 1922, as the guiding principle for the purpose of setting the Jewish immigration quotas. This doctrine attempted to link immigration with an apparently objective, scientific determinant and ruled out, by its very nature, the limiting of immigration for political purposes. The colonial secretary's announcement signified an about-face on this British position: it meant the limitation of immigration for political reasons, namely, Arab opposition. The appointment of the Peel Commission in November 1936 clearly indicated the possibility of a fundamental change as the result of a thorough and exhaustive report, after the consideration of all the possibilities, on the heels of the Arab strike.

The significance of these steps was no mystery to the Jewish leadership. Even in November 1936, at an informal Hagana leadership meeting, Ben-Gurion stated that

we are about to receive a heavy blow. The Arab uprising has frightened England. We must anticipate a drastic reduction of *aliyah* and possibly severe restrictions on land acquisition as well. . . . [If England does not protect the Yishuv due to her military weakness, there awaits the Yishuv the danger of] extermination, because the attackers will be not only the Arabs of Palestine but the people of Iraq and Saudi Arabia, who have airplanes and artillery. We must prepare ourselves in earnest to become a substantial force in the country, capable of withstanding a massive assault and also able to talk with the English in a different language.[2]

The international situation itself did not make a solution of the Palestine question any easier for England. Both her power and her prestige had been weakened in the eyes of the Arab world as a result of the Ethiopian conflict and German rearmament. Also, it is well to recall, British imperial tradition never left movements of revolt unexamined and uninvestigated. For when they were over—after the rebellion was militarily crushed —England would often acquiesce in those areas where rebel demands seemed vital. The statesmen feared that crushing by force alone—and England was capable of that despite her military weakness in the thirties—would not solve the problem; they had to strive for a political solution.

The recommendations of the Peel Commission contained two parts: a temporary solution, the whole principle of which was a diminution of immigration and a cessation of Jewish settlement; and a permanent solution, which was to be the partitioning of the country into two states and a British zone. The two states were to be bound to the British Empire by treaties that would guarantee her strategic and economic interests. The borders of the Jewish state were, in fact, to be identical with the boundaries of Jewish settlement. The Arab-Jewish conflict was defined as a disagreement between one just cause and another. And the conclusion was that the mandate, and with it the integrity of the country, as well as any chance for Jewish-Arab agreement, could no longer be considered realizable.

From what is known, there is substance to the view that the government assumed that the Arabs would accept this plan, which would have assured them a barrier against the development of Jewish immigration and settlement and guaranteed the confinement of the Jews to a relatively small area of the country. The program was well received in Amman. An English historian[3] who had at least partial access to British sources claims that the British government consulted the independent Arab states on the matter of the partition plan, and the idea became crystallized that this plan would be received by them as sufficient proof of the British will to do justice. Therefore, the government obligated itself (on July 7, 1937, the very day the Peel Commission report was published) to implement the report, by the government's overall agreement with its text and conclusions.[4]

How great, then, was the surprise when it became clear that no Arab country, including Transjordan, was prepared to support the plan publicly in the face of the determined opposition of the mufti of Jerusalem, the recognized leader of Palestinian Arabs, to the entire plan. In a debate that took place in the British Parliament on July 30, the government was attacked by both the Arab supporters and a segment of the Jews' supporters. In the vote at the conclusion of the discussion, the government majority had shrunk drastically. The Jewish reaction was also quite mixed. Only rather laboriously was the Zionist Executive able to achieve a majority for its compromise motion at the Twentieth Zionist Congress in August 1937. According to the compromise, the Zionist Executive was empowered to continue to conduct negotiations with Britain on the partition plan on the condition that the final decision on the matter be brought before a special congress.

It is not surprising, therefore, that as early as the summer of 1937 the British government began to seek ways to withdraw from the partition plan. The steps it took turned the debate in the Zionist Congress into an empty discussion. Even in August 1937 the Mandates Committee of the League of Nations— apparently with British inspiration—proposed that the mandate be continued at least until the two states were able to stand on their own. On September 16, the council adopted in principle the resolution in favor of partition, preserving for itself, however, the right to accept or reject concrete proposals that might come before the league. Anthony Eden stated, in the name of Britain, that she would consult the Jews and the Arabs and would advance proposals at the proper time.

On December 23, 1937, a directive sent by the government to the newly appointed high commissioner, Sir Harold Mac-Michael, was published. It was stated there that the government did not see itself as bound by the Peel partition plan and rejected absolutely the idea of forcibly moving the Arab population out of the Jewish state, an idea included in the commission's recommendations. On February 28, 1938, a seemingly practical technical commission was appointed, the Woodhead Commission. It was not until November 9, 1938, that the new commission published its conclusions. In the meantime, the rumor spread that the government intended to withdraw from partition. Thus the report of the Woodhead Commission, which turned the partition plan into an absurdity, was no surprise at all.

With the publishing of the Peel Commission report in the summer of 1937, the Arab struggle was renewed, and this time in sharper form: a mass armed revolt. The factors that operated in the outbreak of the strike and the rebellion of the national and nationalistic movement of the Arabs of Palestine have still not been sufficiently explored. Apparently economic growth and social progress (a by-product of Jewish colonization activity, among other causes) had given rise to a class of Arab intelligentsia within a population where aristocratic families of estate owners, local dignitaries, and religious leaders still ruled. The same development raised the level of interest of a portion of the Arab simple folk above narrow local events and facilitated the rooting of national ideas—without diminishing the powerful hold of the patriarchal and traditionalist religious elements.

It must be emphasized that the renewed Arab terror was not the only, indeed not even the chief, cause of the changed

British position—though it served as a pretext for that change. At that moment Britain was being subjected to the ever-growing threat of the Rome-Berlin Axis. In British ruling circles the idea was gaining currency that the security of the lines of communication of the empire in the Middle East depended upon the degree of tranquillity that reigned in the Arab world. Moreover, the opinion had also gained favor that the Arab national movement was destined to be the dominant factor in the region and that an overall compromise with it had to be made. The British tried, of course, to come to an understanding, not with the extremist wing of the movement but with the feudal forces, whom the British felt most responsive. Leaving the Jews to the mercy of Arab nationalism was a logical conclusion of these deliberations. These ideas had never been foreign to British thinking, but the riots now gave them more validity than ever.

There was no lack of programs and proposals for handling the Palestine question. The Peel Commission report itself, in its interim proposals, pointed to one possible solution, in the wake of which immigration and colonization could be expected to diminish drastically. These proposals meant acquiescence, albeit temporary, to the Arab demands.

But various proposals were brought forth outside the Peel Commission as well. Thus Lord Samuel, the first British high commissioner in the country—a Jew of considerable influence in both Jewish and non-Jewish circles in England and particularly in his own Liberal party—suggested that the Jews agree that, over a very protracted period, their proportion of the general population not rise above "perhaps 40 percent." Palestine would become part of a "federation of the Fertile Crescent," which would include Saudi Arabia, and the Arabs would receive the right to prohibit land sales to those not of their nation. The government of Palestine would remain under British control and would be based on a central council in which the Jewish and Arab communities would be represented according to their ratio of the population. Over against this, the Jews—up to 40 percent—would be permitted to settle in Transjordan.[5]

On October 9, 1937, something similar was suggested by Colonel Newcombe, a friend of the Arabs, with the support of Albert Hyamson, a well-known English Jew. According to this proposal, the Jews were to be allowed to attain up to 50 percent of the population of Palestine on both sides of the Jordan. The suggestion was examined by the Jewish Agency, but it was rejected when it became clear that the Arabs (meaning, in this instance, the mufti's representative—in a meeting with the Jewish Agency on January 12, 1938) were not prepared to reconcile themselves to any additional Jewish immigration.[6] In October 1938 the foreign minister of Iraq, Taufik es-Sawidi, visited London. He offered the British a proposal in the name of his chief, Nuri Said Pasha, by which the Jews would be enabled to achieve regional-municipal and cultural autonomy within the framework of a Palestinian state that would comprise a part of a "federation of the Fertile Crescent."[7]

All these proposals shared several assumptions. One axiom was that the growth of the Jewish national home would be halted, or else so limited that the Jews would remain a minority in a Palestine ruled, in whatever form decided upon, by the Arab majority. Another assumption was that the vital interests of the empire would be preserved in any arrangements whatsoever, whether it be an independent or autonomous Palestine, or a federation. In the federation plans the role of guardian was reserved for Britain.

In August 1938 Malcolm MacDonald, the colonial secretary, paid a call to Jerusalem in order to consult with the new high commissioner. The latter returned the visit in London on October 10. There is no doubt that in these discussions the British political line concerning the near future of Palestine was summarized, and the means to its implementation were outlined.[8] It appears that this new line had two aspects—the military and the political. England could make no political concessions to the Arabs while the rebellion was still raging in the country. That would have seriously damaged her prestige among the Arabs.

The first result of the consultations in Jerusalem and London was, therefore, a crushing attack by the British Army against the rebels, with the aid of reinforcements that had been brought in for the purpose. And, indeed, within two months, by the end of 1938, most of the areas held by the rebels had fallen into British hands, along with the major cities.

However, the other side of the coin was the decision to effect a qualitative change in British Palestine policy. As a start in that direction, a roundtable conference was called in London, the purpose of which was to discuss the entire problem. The conference was set up by MacDonald on November 23, 1938, and convened on February 7, 1939, in the Palace of Saint James. One gets the impression from the discussion that the conclusions of the government at the close of the talks were, at least in general terms, clear to the government at the very time of the conference's preparation.

Now there began a far-reaching transformation of the security concepts of Zionism as well. The official position of the institutions of the Jewish community in Palestine during the period of the rebellion was that one must take a line of restraint in regard to the Arab terror. At first, this line was interpreted as meaning a completely defensive passivity. If there were active responses, they were outbursts on the part of individuals or one-time operations of retaliation for especially serious acts. But as the disturbances continued, an alteration of the meaning of "restraint" occurred.

The passivity line had been the child of an effort for cooperation with the British that had seemed at once possible and vital. One markedly positive result of this policy was the Supernumerary Police Force (starting in May of 1936). In July 1936 approximately 22,000 Supernumeraries were appointed (including city and village special policemen), organized in legal formations. The Supernumerary Police Force served as a legal cover for the activities of the Hagana, and with the assistance of the British instructors of the Supernumeraries, the level of training of Hagana members was also raised. The Supernumerary Police Force represented to some extent the idea of the "legal Hagana" which Jabotinsky* had preached. But it was not intended to guard the frontiers of the country as Jabotinsky had anticipated. It was designed to be a militia concentrated chiefly on the Hebrew village, protecting the goat, cow, and life of the settler.

Beginning in the fall of 1937, Mobile Guards employing armored vehicles were organized within the framework of the Supernumerary Police Force. They moved beyond the limitations of static defense and made a substantial contribution to the realization of the idea of a countrywide Jewish mobile force. But the Mobile Guards, being clearly legal formations, could never have taken on the military-political significance that would adhere, after a time, to the independent mobile units of the Hagana. The first revolutionary step was made in this direction, as early as the middle of 1936, with the organization of *Hanodedet* ("the flying column") in the hills of Jerusalem by Yitzhak Sadeh and Eliyahu Cohen. This unit abandoned passive defense and began to develop a method of attacking the attackers. With this, the idea of restraint took on a new meaning (a change of form, though not a change in quality): not to answer the Arabs in their own manner, by indiscriminately assaulting innocent bystanders, but to attack the gangs in their lairs and to hit the guilty alone. This change in policy also answered an internal need. Members of the Hagana had begun to rebel against the notion of passivity, and there was a threat of serious dissension within the ranks of the Hagana unless a more active policy was pursued.

This method attained particular expression with the organization of the Field Squads and the Special Night Squads. These latter were strongly influenced by the personality, methods, and

* Vladimir Ze'ev Jabotinsky, founder of the Revisionist movement, which in the late thirties stood in opposition to the official Zionist organization. Jabotinsky hoped for an arrangement with Britain whereby a Jewish force ("legion" or "legal Hagana"), under British command, would guard the security of Palestine.

ideas of a remarkable Englishman, Charles Orde Wingate. Under British auspices he trained mixed British-Jewish mobile units for war against the Arab marauders. In his brief period of activity—from May to the end of September 1938—Wingate wielded a most profound influence over his Jewish charges. From many points of view, it must be said that Wingate was one of the chief molders of the Hebrew fighting force in Palestine. His basic innovation was not in military tactics alone, although in that area he wrought mightily. His major contribution was his insistence that the leaders of Zionism and the Hagana render political aid to the military arm.

Wingate, the British patriot, was among those who proposed that the Hagana undertake more active methods of struggle than it had previously done. At the same time he hoped (as did most of the Zionist leaders) that the Jewish people, renewing itself in its own land, would find its place within the framework of the British Empire. Certainly the Hagana was already striding toward new concepts before the appearance of Wingate. But it was he who sped this development along and lent it a powerful, dynamic drive.[9]

The Field Squads were organized at the beginning of 1938. But they only attained regular status in November 1938, shortly before their dissolution—a status stamped with the seal of compromise between the need for a countrywide mobile force, with a specialized structure, and the demands of the Hagana districts for local control over that force. What was involved here was a struggle between a philosophy of overall centralization, most of whose advocates were numbered in the Histadrut camp, and one of decentralized local autonomy. According to the compromise, command of the Field Squads was not taken out of the hands of the local authority, but the Hagana High Command was permitted to employ that force in time of emergency. The Field Squads had no commander, but Eliyahu Cohen and Yitzhak Sadeh were virtually responsible for all the squads' activities, in spite of the limitations we have cited.

From various clues we learn that the liquidation of the Field Squads in February of 1939 came, first of all, because of right-wing opposition in the Yishuv to the existence of a unit, numbering some 2,500 men, composed solely of the members of the Histadrut and employing military doctrines not identical with those of the Right. Nevertheless, the seed of the idea of a national mobile force as a security arm for the purpose of realizing a definite political line was sown in the days of the Field Squads.

The line of restraint was broken by another Jewish element, the Revisionist Etzel. This underground organization had been founded in 1931 as a breakaway group from the Hagana. Its leaders were not Revisionists, but in time the Revisionist element came to predominate. It had a generally right-wing hue and stressed militarism, as against the more egalitarian-minded Hagana. In April 1937 half of Etzel, also known as "Irgun B," returned to the ranks of the Hagana, including those of its members who belonged to right-wing or religious Zionist groups. The remaining half, composed chiefly of Revisionists, now constituted a new Etzel organization. During the period of command over Etzel by Moshe Rosenberg and David Raziel, a great many assaults (some of them en masse) were carried out against Arab bystanders and shoppers: men, women, and children (November 1937–July 1939). These were acts of terror on the Arab pattern.

It would appear that these operations had no known restraining influence on the Arab terror. On the contrary, they caused the Jews great damage by driving moderate Arabs into the ranks of the extremists. Isolated acts of retaliation were carried out here and there by the people of the Hagana as well, some launched with the confirmation of the supreme national institutions, some without approval (but the latter were few and far between and of limited extent).

The difference between the actions of the two organizations was that the operations of Etzel flowed out of political considerations, uninfluenced by public opinion except for that of the

Revisionist party. Furthermore, the influence of that party over Etzel was, at times, rather doubtful. In contrast, the Hagana was subject to the authority of the Zionist movement, and its policy of restraint was flexible and could be altered to meet the needs of the hour. It never stood for retaliation as a method, and the operations cited above were only rare exceptions. The Hagana High Command explicitly forbade "the murder of women, children, passersby, and innocent Arabs."[10]

The organization of the Hagana reflected its popular character. After the summer of 1938, its National Command was composed of proportional representatives of the Right and Left, with Professor Yohanan Rattner, a neutral, at its head. This command was subject to the authority of a civilian committee made up of representatives of the Vaad Leumi and the Agency Executive (The Committee of Eight). Monetary matters were placed chiefly in the hands of the president of the Kofer Hayishuv (Community Fund). The latter was also constituted according to a party formula, and from its inception in the fall of 1938 it covered most of the expenditures for security purposes. The scattering of authority into the hands of various elements, whose attitude toward one another was not marked by excellence and who were submerged in a continual political struggle over the image of Zionism, disrupted the activities of the Hagana more than once.

In sum, the end of the period of the Arab rebellion was also the end of the era of cooperation between Great Britain and the Zionist movement—albeit an unsteady cooperation full of pitfalls—that had lasted since the days of Balfour. A change of values occurred. The Hagana ceased to be a localized militia and gradually became a single military organization, the security arm of a national movement. New forms of organization and methods of action were evolved—*Hanodedet,* the Field Squads, the Special Night Squads, the Mobile Guards, and so on. The White Paper of 1939 nurtured new concepts both in matters of diplomacy and defense.

1 ⚑ *The White Paper Policy and the Beginning of the Struggle*

⚑ *The Saint James Conference*

The parties were invited to the London Conference. After the precedent of the intervention of the Arab states in ending the Arab strike in October 1936, their representatives were invited to the discussions on this occasion. Thus the representatives of Iraq, Saudi Arabia, Egypt, Transjordan, and Yemen arrived in London at the beginning of 1939. Britain sought to influence the Palestinian Arab extremists through the mediation of the Arab governments whose attitude toward the Palestine question seemed moderate.

The main difficulty arose over the composition of the Palestinian Arab delegation. The British government could not invite the mufti himself, the escaped leader of the armed rebellion against England, without losing face. On the other hand, it was clear to the British that any negotiations on Palestine affairs without the participation of the mufti would have no practical value. A compromise solution was found by inviting the lieutenant and kinsman of the mufti, Jamal el-Husseini, to head the Palestine Arab delegation. Also invited was a delegation from the well-known Nashashibi family, who opposed the mufti

—so that in reality two Palestine Arab delegations participated in the London discussions. But in fact this caused no difficulties, because the Nashashibis preferred to keep silent throughout the course of the discussions; they went along like a shadow with all the acts and omissions of the mufti delegation.

The Jewish delegation was in harmony despite grave fears during its preparation for the discussions. The Jewish Agency and the Agudath Israel took part in the conference, as did a number of dignitaries of British Jewry. (The representatives of the agency nicknamed the latter "the Lords," because several of them bore titles of British nobility.) But of the Jewish political elements of some importance, representatives of the New Zionist Organization (Revisionist) were missing. They had not been invited by the agency to take part.

The mission consisted of forty-two persons ("the panel"); they had an advisory role only. In practice political decisions were made by the Agency Executive, which convened frequently in the course of the talks. The executive was advised by the panel and even undertook to involve representatives of various colorations in the negotiations themselves. A detailed report on the course of the conversations was also delivered to the panel. Under these conditions the non-Zionists on the panel agreed to the Agency Executive's sole power of decision on political matters. The appearance of unity within the mission was made possible throughout the talks because the various segments were united in their regard for the personality of Dr. Weizmann, chairman of the entire delegation. In fact, the formal aspect was perhaps less important than the influence of several Zionist leaders who, by mutual consultation, determined what the Jewish line should be. Chief among these were Dr. Chaim Weizmann, David Ben-Gurion, Moshe Sharett, Berl Katznelson, and Rabbi Stephen S. Wise.

The very decision to take part in these discussions came only after hard perplexities. The affirmative resolution was adopted in the Agency Executive itself, after a stormy debate, by a vote

of six to three (Rabbi Yehuda Leib Maimon, Yitzhak Gruenbaum, and Mrs. Rose Jacobs).* An even more difficult struggle
developed in the Smaller Zionist Actions Committee in Palestine.† In its session on December 20, 1938, opinions were
evenly divided (eleven each), until a compromise was found
according to which the final determination was to be left to
the executive. However viewed, it was clear that there were
numerous opponents, especially in Palestine, to participation
in these talks. It was being said that as long as the government
had run out on the mandate anyway, and was about to abandon
Jewish interests to their fate, there was no sense in negotiations
with England; it would be better if the job of surrendering to
the mufti were done without the presence of the Jews. Of course,
the government had announced, through the mouth of Lord
Dufferin (in the House of Lords on December 8, 1938) that
in the scheduled discussions it would show itself bound by the
Balfour Declaration and the mandate. But even this pronouncement included a passage according to which the government
reserved its right to alter this formula should such seem vital
to the government during the course of the discussions.[1]

Six days after the announcement, Weizmann could already
report that the administration sought to halt immigration and
land sales. On a similar occasion the threat of an Arab veto
power over immigration (that is, an arrangement by which
Jewish immigration would be permitted only with the consent
of the Arabs[2]) was also noted.

Another episode in December also aroused profound reverber-
ations among the Jews. The government absolutely rejected a
Jewish proposal for the immediate rescue of ten thousand Jewish children from Germany and Austria by immigration into

* Maimon was the representative of the Mizrahi, the religious Zionist
party; Gruenbaum represented liberal Zionism, especially in Poland; and
Mrs. Jacobs was a representative of American Zionism.
† The Smaller Zionist Actions Committee was composed of those members of the Zionist Actions Committee elected by the Zionist Congress
who resided in Palestine.

Palestine. (However, it accepted more than nine thousand refugee children into England itself from the end of 1938 until the outbreak of the war.) This was interpreted as an omen of British policy in Palestine. Even so, the heads of Zionism felt that "Britain will not abandon us altogether and will refuse to establish an Arab state" in Palestine.[3] The decisive factor in favor of Jewish participation in the talks was, in the last analysis, negative. The fear was expressed that in the absence of the Jews, an Arab-British conspiracy could be plotted and that public opinion, that indefinite but potent ally of the Jewish cause, might see in Jewish nonparticipation a sign of political immaturity and lack of willingness to engage in a dialogue with the Arabs.

What were, ultimately, the motives for the change in British policy, and can we single one factor out of these motives as the chief or central cause?

The Jewish representatives did not have many doubts on this matter. At the session of the panel on February 5, 1939, just two days before the opening of the discussions, Weizmann analyzed the problem of Britain's strategic considerations in the Middle East. In his judgment, there were differences of opinion in the government between those who sought to freeze the situation in Palestine until the storm should pass (that is, until war broke out or the existing international tension abated) and those who sought to put a stop, once and for all, to the further development of Zionism. Several cabinet members felt, according to Weizmann, that in any future war the Jews would not be able to refrain from fighting on the side of Britain against the Axis powers. One British writer confirms Weizmann's report with his claim that the Jews could not but oppose their German persecutors and hope for an improvement in their own position in future.[4] On the other hand, the British considered that with the enmity of the Arab world, no matter how ineffective it might be from a purely military viewpoint, there was implied a profound threat to the vital position of Great Britain in the Middle East.[5]

What, then, were the strategic considerations that brought the British to the conclusion that it was better to sacrifice the Jews than to be imperiled by Arab hostility? The matter was most plainly stated by the British themselves at a session in the Saint James Palace (February 14, 1939). At that meeting, Malcolm MacDonald asserted that the safety of British forces in the Middle East and the lines of communication to India and the Far East were dependent in large measure on the British ability to convince the Egyptian government, and other governments in that part of the world, to fulfill their treaty obligations (where such existed) or at any rate to hold a position of sympathetic neutrality. He continued by stating that Egypt, for example, dominated the sea and air routes to the East and the air and land routes to the Sudan and Africa, that Egypt contained the land base for the defense of Suez and the only naval base (Alexandria) suitable for the defense of the eastern Mediterranean. He further averred that Iraq controlled the land and air routes eastward and served as a center for important oil interests there and in Iran. He felt that Saudi Arabia was weighing her capability of threatening the avenues of communication through Transjordan to Iraq and the Aden Protectorate. The opinion of experts in His Majesty's government was that in the event of war Ibn Saud would be capable, even without help, of bringing about a most uncomfortable situation, if he wished to; and he could cause very serious damage if he were supported by a hostile power.[6]

It was made plain in MacDonald's words, then, that the British government had very little doubt that war would soon come to the world. In that event, Britain would have to do everything in order to preserve her interests in the Middle East. The conclusion to be drawn was clear enough—there was no escaping the sacrifice of the Jewish cause on the altar of preparations for a second world war. His words about the government's advisors had reference to the British chiefs of staff, and it was they who had issued the gravely explicit warning. MacDonald's intent was spelled out at the end of his remarks when he formulated his conclusion: Since the Jews were interested in a British victory, they must willingly accept political concessions to the Arab position. We find language identical to MacDonald's at Saint James in a book by the official British historian, I. S. O. Playfair. Playfair specifies that the advisors who counseled the government on this matter were none other than the chiefs of staff. He also states that the land route claimed special attention from the chiefs of staff because of the fear that the sea and air routes would be cut off by the Italian army and navy, which were operating bases in Eritrea and Ethiopia. That route then led from Palestine (by way of the desert station Rutba, on the Transjordan-Iraq border) to Habbaniya, the British airfield, and from there to the Persian Gulf. This route was quite vulnerable to raids by irregular forces, for only in 1941 was a paved road laid down there.[7]

The Jewish answer to these military assertions was based on the words of Wingate, as he wired them from Palestine to London[8] (February 12, 1939). In the main they stated that the Arabs were poorer soldiers than the Jews and that with the mobilization of a large number of Jews into the army, it would be possible not only to preserve the tranquillity of the Middle East but also to give Britain appreciable aid in her war. In addition, Wingate stated that no step of the government would appease the Arabs successfully; only the full might of the empire in the region would prevent rebellion on their part. He also said that the creation of an industrial-military base in Palestine was preferable to one in Egypt, by reason of the skill of the workers and other factors. Wingate expressed the feeling that a pro-Arab stand by Britain would offend anti-Arab Turkey and also cause damage in the United States, where the Jews had a powerful influence.

Weizmann employed the Turkish argument in his response

to MacDonald with his assertion that, from any point of view, the chain of countries comprising Turkey, Iran, and Afghanistan was more important for Great Britain than were the Arab lands. But, in fact, these same three states identified themselves with the Arab stand in the Palestine dispute in September 1938, as that position emerged in the form of Iraq's opposition to British policy on the floor of the League of Nations. Ben-Gurion dwelt, for the most part, on Arab reaction to British victory or defeat. He averred that, in the event of retreat or defeat, the Arabs would rebel against Britain no matter what the British policy in Palestine might be; Arab neutrality would be observed only if Britain were sufficiently strong in the area. "If Iraq does take sides against the British Empire in time of war, she will do so in any case, even if the British government decides to expel all the Jews from Palestine."

MacDonald was not at all impressed by the Jewish arguments. In the eyes of the British it made no sense to mobilize thousands of Jews to suppress a potential Arab rebellion—which would break out because of that very mobilization. He stood by his opinion of the destructive effect a pro-Zionist policy would have on what he termed "public opinion" in Saudi Arabia and Iraq. Ultimately, the words were spoken explicitly and even with a certain crudeness: If it came to a choice between Arab and Jewish support, he did not believe that, valuable as Jewish assistance would be, it would make up for what would be lost by the lack of the vital support of the Arab and Moslem world. The goal of the conference was, in his opinion, this: Without sacrificing the Jewish cause more than they thought proper, to meet the Arabs and get their consent and goodwill for what was going on in Palestine.

This position was reinforced by Chamberlain himself in an interview with the Jewish leaders on February 16. Chamberlain expressed his opinion that "if some measure of appeasement is achieved now, then the chances for satisfactory development in the future will be much improved." He added that since

September 1938, the Munich period, a fundamental change had occurred in Britain's military status. If in the fall England had viewed any worsening of the international situation with real dread because she was not prepared for war, now, in February of 1939, it would be possible to greet any development "without any undue worry."[9]

A perusal of the minutes of the Saint James Conference raises some questions about the general evaluation of British world policy at the beginning of 1939, which are widespread even today. The accepted view is that the British government persisted in what was called appeasement until the taking of Prague by the Germans (March 15, 1939). Just three days after that date, on March 18, Chamberlain delivered his famous speech in Birmingham in which he announced a change in British policy toward Germany and noted Britain's ironclad decision not to concede anything further to the German dictator. But here in this "colonial" conference, as if in passing, a somewhat different picture emerges. One gets the impression that as early as December 1938, and in a most explicit form in February 1939, British policy was operating on the assumption that there was no avoiding war with the Axis powers. It is typical that these considerations were not brought before the Arab delegations (at any rate, we find no mention of them in the official minutes).

The opinion given by Chamberlain, quoted above, only strengthens the feeling that long before Prague—but it is not clear exactly when—the top ranks in the British government reached the conclusion that the war was apparently not to be prevented, that everything must be done to put Britain in a comfortable position, in all respects and on all fronts, should such a war break out. Therefore it is no surprise that precisely here, on the military question, one can sense the center of gravity of the entire conference. One can say without exaggeration that that was the focal problem about which the London talks revolved. And the solution presented in May, in the form of the White Paper of 1939, was stamped with signs of the military imperative as understood at that moment by the British.

The Jewish answer to that central question was very weak, measured against the British appraisal of British interests. The Jews could not speak from a position of strength, real or imaginary, as had been done in 1917. The Jews no longer had any choice other than to identify with the British struggle against the Axis powers. In Europe the Jews were turned into actual or potential refugees, and they no longer possessed any political influence. In contrast to the Arab threat—actual or not, it made no difference—even Jewish influence in the United States seemed a secondary factor, for there too the Jew had no choice but to support any step taken against the Axis powers. The Jews, therefore, appeared in a position of weakness, a result of the drastic change that had occurred in their position since the advent of the great world economic crisis of 1929 and Hitler's rise to power. The actual strength of Zionism in Palestine and the bond between the Yishuv and the Diaspora were unappreciated factors, still ungrasped and undiscerned in 1939.

It is true that there were officers in the top echelon of the British military whose view was different from that of the chiefs of staff. One of them was doubtlessly Sir Edmund Ironside, at that time commander of British forces in the Middle East, with headquarters in Gibraltar. But it appears that it was not their opinion that prevailed.[10]

The foregoing should not create the impression that the Jews did not also employ threats, both implicit and explicit. Thus Moshe Sharett observed (February 13) that the government would have to take the existing reality into consideration, and this included a large Jewish community in Palestine. "I cannot venture here into an inquiry as to what, in light of history, generally happens in the long run as a result of such a clash" between reality and a policy which does not take the reality into account, he said. Weizmann saw no other way than to acknowledge the British statement that the Jews had, as a matter of course, no alternative except to support the British; but with this he pointed out the doubtful morality of such a position. In addition, he noted (February 8) that if war were indeed to come, there was no sense in final arrangements; the future war would overturn any arrangement now determined. On February 13 he added that without Jewish consent any Arab state in Palestine would be forced to depend on British bayonets; and on the 17th he further stated that there was also a limit to the degree of pressure which the Jews would be able to bear. The Jews were not threatening His Majesty's government. But if the government gave in to the Arabs, then those whose friendship with Britain had always been the cornerstone of their policy would not be able to carry on with their roles—an allusion to Weizmann's resignation in 1931 in a somewhat similar situation (during the regime of Ramsay MacDonald, the father of the colonial secretary of 1939).

When these words, too, were of no avail, Weizmann informed Malcolm MacDonald (February 24) in an unofficial talk, that there would be no tranquillity in Palestine if they tried to downgrade the Jews to the rank of a minority. These and similar statements were voiced several times during the talks by various Jewish leaders. But these were only bloodless words, as opposed to the constant, grave threat of an Arab rebellion. The only one who felt that it was possible to speak from a position of strength, even under such conditions, was Rabbi Stephen Wise, who warned the British about a step that might cause them damage on the American scene. But again, in British eyes the Arab threat was more serious than the Jewish.

Another interesting aspect of the Saint James discussions is the light they shed on the state of Jewish-Arab relations at that stage. The Arabs refused to sit at the same table as the Jews; therefore when the talks were officially opened (February 7,

1939), there were actually two sets of discussions: between the British and Jews, and between the British and Arabs.

One of the goals of the agency delegation was promotion of direct negotations with the Arabs, in an attempt to arrive at a dialogue with them. David Ben-Gurion formulated this at the beginning of February when he said, at a session of the Zionist Executive, that one must break through to an understanding with the Arabs, even if the chances of that were slim, and that he was "prepared to accept less from the Arabs than from the government." From his words on the Arab federation in that same session, one can learn of the minimum hinted at (the federation was one of the ideas that had captured attention at that time in the area of the political world of the Middle East). He said he recognized the "difficulties involved in this idea; but the desire for such a federation exists. It is a historic imperative, and sooner or later it will become a reality. . . . A Jewish state is slowly developing in Palestine. We cannot prevent the realization of the Arab federation, and if the Arabs are prepared to accept the historic imperative of the Jewish people for a state in Palestine, as a part of the federation," it would be possible to arrive at an agreement. He further stated that in order to attain a minimal understanding with the Arabs, the Arab recognition of the Jewish right of immigration into the country would suffice. If the Arabs would recognize that, one could hope for fruitful negotiations with them.[11]

These words expressed the position of the Agency Executive and especially that of Weizmann. The Agency Executive was convinced that one should not reject out of hand the possibility, even though remote, of a Jewish-Arab agreement on immigration quotas without British mediation. This stood out against a background of information regarding the conclusions which the government had arrived at even prior to the beginning of the talks. In Weizmann's interviews with government ministers in December and January, it became clear beyond the shadow of a doubt that the government's intention in the discussions

was to press the Jewish side to make concessions—in a seemingly willing fashion—to Arab demands for the independence of
the country, the cessation of immigration, and the diminution
of colonization.

In light of these facts, the first stage of the talks (February
7–14) consisted of a kind of shadowboxing, with an atmosphere
of absolutely abstract argumentation far distant from any actual
political reality. During this first stage, the Jews based their
case on international law, the mandate and the Balfour Declaration, an appeal to the conscience of the British government, and
the tradition of British law and justice in England's relationship
with other nations. MacDonald took it upon himself to present
the Arab position. He argued that the government had a double
obligation, to Jews and Arabs alike. In his opinion, it was
stamped into all the historic documents on which the British
delegation based itself.

In the parallel talks between the Arabs and the British, the
image was inverted. There the Arabs argued their democratic
right to rule Palestine. They theorized that the continually
strengthening independence of the Arab peoples was in no way
an excuse for negating such independence for the Arabs of
Palestine, and they threatened a continuation of the rebellion
if their desires were not granted. In those talks MacDonald presented the Jewish case, but in a tone much more patient than
the one he had employed as advocate of the Arab cause against
the Jews.

One gets the impression—and it grows stronger with the
testimonies of British personalities after the event—that not
just a political interest and a new line of policy were operating
here, but also a matter-of-fact inclination to view the Arab
cause as more logical and correct. Thus, MacDonald argued
against the Jews that they must not underrate the power of the
Arab opposition, which now also included the Arab states. The
Arabs were a majority. They had been the masters of Palestine
for a long time. One could not use force to thrust a regime of

alien migrants on them; it would even be unjustified to do so. Their claim to political independence was not inferior to that of other Arab nations.

In the last analysis, however, these arguments were not the basis of the British position, though one should not discount them. Lord Halifax, the British foreign minister, expressed this nicely in his statement (at the meeting on February 14) that there are times when cold political calculation comes before all pronouncements on justice and morality. He recalled a meeting with Gandhi in which a clash between administrative necessity and spiritual rights was apparent. He had had to admit the validity of Gandhi's claim, but had successfully pleaded administrative necessity. He would suggest now that the Jews should, "of their own free will, dispose of their rights by offering terms of conciliation."

This first stage of the talks ended when MacDonald asked whether the Jews seriously intended to say that the Arabs must be forced to accept Jewish immigration. The problem of consent became uppermost. Weizmann retorted (February 13) with particular sharpness: "Are the British in Palestine with the consent of the Arabs?"

The second stage, the phase of British proposals, opened on February 15, with the government's proposals on the issue of immigration. These were actually a sort of rewording of Lord Samuel's proposal of the summer of 1937. A strong desire to achieve Arab consent to this solution caused MacDonald to specify a percentage that would form a sort of "ceiling" or upper limit for Jewish immigration; this proposed quota would continue for several years without Arab consent. After the allotted number of years, additional immigration would depend on Arab consent. (This would allay the Arabs' fears and open an opportunity for further negotiations for the purpose of attaining Arab consent to the expansion of the Palestine Jewish community.) Moreover, MacDonald followed Samuel's suggestion even on the matter of Transjordan and expressed the opinion that Trans-jordan would open her doors to the Jews.

At the decidedly negative response of the Jews to this pro-posal, the minister answered that if the Jewish position was as described by Mr. Ben-Gurion, then a British withdrawal from Palestine would mean a civil war whose result no one could foresee. In other words, the British threatened to withdraw from the country and abandon the Jews to superior Arab power if the Jews did not accept the British proposals. To the British this seemed, in those days (and later), a very convincing argu-ment, because they viewed the Jewish community as dependent upon them, for better or for worse. "As long as the Jews have the British government behind them, they will never meet the Arabs halfway," declared MacDonald on March 11.

There is evidence for the hypothesis that even from the start of their regime in Palestine, Mandatory officials and members of influential circles in London were of the opinion that the mandate was unfulfillable and that England should keep her hands off direct rule of Palestine, securing her interests there in another manner.

The Jews were not then interested in a British departure and thereby reinforced MacDonald's position even further. In 1939 Ben-Gurion stated in a private conversation with the colonial secretary (February 18):

> I know that for your own reasons—and I know they are valid reasons—you must remain in Palestine. And I can tell you that for the same reasons we are anxious to have you remain there. We have an interest in the British Empire, and that not only as Jews, but as part of humanity.

Even if there were no immigration, Ben-Gurion said, the Arabs would still fight the British because they did not want their rule. If there were no reasons of empire (which were also important to the Jews), if it were only a question of Jews and Arabs in Palestine, the Jews would not need Britain to remain in any form, not for defense and not for immigration. Even though the Jews were a minority, they could care for themselves in an attack by the Arabs of Palestine and could also organize *aliyah* for themselves. "Even though the Arabs are twice your number?" asked the minister. Ben-Gurion answered with an unqualified yes. But it is completely clear that the government looked on these words as mere boasting, that they did not believe that the Jews could stand up to the Arabs without British aid.[12]

After the rejection of their proposals of February 15, the British advanced a slightly revised proposal on the 20th, in which the number of immigrants was fixed at fifteen to thirty thousand per year for a period of ten years (that is, an *aliyah* of up to 35 to 40 percent of the country's population). After ten years, an Arab veto over immigration would take effect. An alternative proposal also was made, according to which immigration would be more restricted but the Arabs would not receive the veto; instead, the entire problem would be restudied later. As to legislative proposals, the government rejected both partition and a Jewish-Arab federal arrangement with parity of powers and proposed independence. It is clear that the British sought to bring about a Jewish-Arab compromise solution, weighted in favor of the Arab position, by granting the Arabs a veto over Jewish immigration in exchange for a Jewish veto over independence for Palestine.

This latter matter obtruded more, of course, in the parallel British-Arab talks. The Arab demand (February 20) for an "immediate, clear-cut, and final" solution was based, first of all, on the Arab threat that the relationship of the Arab states to Britain would be determined not a little by her policy in Palestine. Once again, the suggestion came that if the government could not see its way to making concessions, this time to the Arabs, it could leave the country; then the Jews would present no problem whatsoever. "Failing decisive assurances from the British government, it will be a matter of war." MacDonald's answer matched the spirit of his words to the Jews: "If the Jews should refuse to cooperate [with British plans] then I can say, with fair certainty, that they will be dropped."

The principal Arab demand was, of course, for independence. The British agreed in principle, and the debate revolved about the fate of the Jewish minority. Would it be an "ordinary" minority, as the Arabs insisted (the Iraqi foreign minister tried to draw an analogy between the rights of the Kurds in his country and the future status of the Jews in the Palestinian state); or an "extraordinary" minority, as the British advocated, that is, a minority possessed of definite special rights guaranteed under the law of the land. In order to save time, it was suggested to the Arabs (and the Jews) that they postpone the negotiations on the details of the constitutional proposals until the autumn of 1939.

The Jews had quite authentic information on the course of the proceedings between the Arabs and British. This further strengthened the inclination of the Zionist Executive to try to achieve direct contact with the Arab delegation. Then the British suggested something of the sort, in the form of an unofficial meeting with the delegations of the Arab states (with the exception of the Palestine Arab missions). The Jews responded willingly, and three such meetings were held on February 23 and 24 and on March 7.

These talks made plain the vast distance between the two parties. In one of these discussions (March 7), Weizmann reached the point of declaring that he would be willing to speak about a reduction in immigration if only he could achieve a dialogue with the other side. These words, a slip of the tongue by the Zionist leader, were immediately exploited by the British (who were present in all these meetings) to try to extort their main objective from the Jewish delegation—abdication of the right to free immigration. But the Arabs held to the position that the entry of Jews into Arab states, including Palestine, was at most a humanitarian question of Arab aid in the solution of the refugee problem, not a question of a Jewish right to any immigration whatsoever. On this basis it was impossible to reach an agreement. The importance of the talks lay in that here, for the first time since the Faisal-Weizmann agreement, Jews and Arabs met for a quiet consideration of the question of the two peoples' relations. The inflexible stand of the Arabs prevented any progress at that stage.

In his memoirs, as well as in his address to the Twenty-first Zionist Congress, Dr. Weizmann claimed that the details of the British legislative proposals, which were formulated on February 24, were known to him—through a clerical "error" by a British official who was supposed to transmit the proposals to the Arabs and instead made them available to the Jews. In Weizmann's opinion, this dishonorable form of diplomatic negotiation contributed not a little to the ugly atmosphere between the British and Jews. If we are to judge by Weizmann's words, this was one of the focal occurrences, if not *the* focal one, of the Saint James discussions. Our sources do not confirm this version.

It is clear that on February 24 an unofficial talk was held between Weizmann, Sharett, and MacDonald; and the next day (the Sabbath) MacDonald again met with Weizmann, Sharett, and Ben-Gurion. In those talks, MacDonald suggested that a round-table conference be held in the fall on matters of legal structure. They discussed various possibilities, immigration figures and connected items. MacDonald proposed an immigration of sixty thousand persons for five years, with or without an Arab veto on the continuation of immigration. The government's intention of announcing the granting of independence to Palestine was spoken of, as was its desire to cast temporary constitutional patterns—even before convening the fall conference—for turning over the remainder of responsibility for rule to the Jewish and Arab representatives.

The minutes of the talk were sent to the Jews on Sunday, February 26. A formal proposal came along with these minutes, repeating MacDonald's words in the talks two days earlier and actually adding nothing new beyond that. It was that formulated proposal which comprised the famous letter against which Weizmann's indignation gushed forth. It is doubtful whether the formulation was intended for either the Jews or the Arabs; it was, apparently, in the nature of an inside British memorandum. A clerk in the Colonial Office included this memorandum in an envelope of reports on the previous talks. Lord Rothschild, a member of the panel and the Jewish delegation, saw the mail on Sunday (in the absence of Zionist office personnel) and summoned Weizmann up to London. A council was set up at Weizmann's house in which Ben-Gurion, Sharett, Sir Simon Marks, and Lord Reading took part. MacDonald also came to the meeting and explained to those present that the proposals sent by accident to the Jews were not finally crystallized proposals and that he was sorry for what had happened. Indeed, the Jews exploited this British tactical error by submitting a memorandum (February 27) that also related to issues of legal structure and rejected the British suggestions in the sharpest fashion, with the motive of thus bringing the talks to an end; but it is difficult to ascribe to this event the importance that Weizmann did.[13]

The possibility of stopping the talks was discussed by the Jewish mission more than once during their course. It was clear that the talks would end in failure; the problem was to find a suitable pretext, from a public relations point of view, for adjourning negotiations. The British slip, on which we have dwelt, provided that pretext—but the British were not yet ready for an end to the discussions. The government sought to appear, for public opinion, as an impartial judge forced to use coercive power, after all efforts to make peace between litigants came to nought. The British, therefore, informed the Jewish delegation that their suggestions were neither final nor the sole basis for continuing negotiations; if the Jews would present alternative proposals, the government would consider them seriously. Even

Chamberlain intervened and assured the Jews that, if they continued the discussions, they would find the government a good listener.

The third stage of talks was therefore reached. It went on from the beginning of March until the 12th. At this stage, what might be called unofficial contacts took place between the Jews and the British, while on the British-Arab side of Saint James Palace a political subcommittee met, the role of which was to confer on the details of British and Arab proposals. The discussion, on both wings, revolved chiefly about legal questions. The British position held that the transitional period to independence "cannot end until the Jews and Arabs cooperate in practice"; of course, the first question was what "in practice" meant. After protracted argumentation it became clear that the British intent was that independence not be established without explicit Jewish consent; that is, the agreement of recognized institutions or a substantial segment of the Jewish population. Along with this, it was emphasized that Jewish confirmation was not needed for the first steps on the road to independence—the quasi-independent institutions of the transitional era could be set up even without Jewish agreement.

Meanwhile, the suggestion for a fall conference dropped out of the agenda because of fierce opposition on the part of the Arabs, who averred that if Britain had called the current conference to put the Palestine problem in order, then it made no sense to postpone the main deliberation until the autumn. The British, therefore, proposed several alternatives for a legislative arrangement and requested the parties' comments:

(a) The partition of Palestine into cantons mutually bound in a federation;

(b) Parity of parliamentary representatives elected by nationality groups, but no parallel parity in the government;

(c) A bicameral system, with the lower house to be chosen by proportional representation and the upper to preserve representational parity. In this event it was proposed that certain ("reserved") questions be decided only by a two-thirds majority in the two houses jointly convened;

(d) A unicameral system with the "reserved" questions requiring a separate majority among both Jewish and Arab members;

(e) A constitution whereby elections would be held in "weighted" districts; that is, the Jews would receive a larger quota of legislators than would normally come to them by their proportion of the population; and

(f) An arrangement whereby the right of decision on "reserved" items would remain in the hands of the British high commissioner. This last proposal, the actual meaning of which was continued British rule of Palestine even in formal matters, disappeared forthwith from the discussions.

On March 6 a revised list of British proposals was handed the Jews. Only the first four of those cited above were on it. According to these proposals, Britain was undertaking to waive all further direct intervention in the affairs of an independent Palestine and to protect her interests there by means of special treaties, as MacDonald had stressed in his February 18 talk with Ben-Gurion.

The proposals were rejected by both sides. The Jews were prepared to discuss parity in representation and governmental regime on the basis of agreed-upon immigration arrangements, while the Arabs were not ready to forgo control by right of their majority. They agreed to discuss "ordinary" Jewish minority rights of the type that comprised parts of the national constitutions of certain countries of Eastern Europe between the two world wars.[14]

In this situation, with the British suggesting what were most grave proposals from the Jewish point of view, the Jews could only advance alternative proposals from their side. The question had already been brought up on February,[15] in a caucus of

the Mapai members of the mission, in which Ben-Gurion stated
—with a certain deviation from his public pronouncements—
that it was impossible to pressure England into remaining in
Palestine if she did not wish to do so. Hence the logical remedy
was partition.

But at this point the old debate between those in Mapai who
were for and those against partition flared up. Things came
to the point where Berl Katznelson announced that if such a
proposal were to be made publicly, "it would bring a split in
the party and the Zionist movement." But of course, Katznelson
stated, such a proposal would be absurd. The State would not
rise through the British because the Arabs objected to it, and,
he went on, the Jews could see with their own eyes that this
was the compelling basis of British policy. Sharett's view was
that it was plain that someday a Jewish state in a part of Palestine would be attained but that could not be the content of an
announced policy. "This will not come by the force of our
demands on the government. It will come either by lack of any
other way out or as a result of our own political activity. A condition is possible in the country where we may reach that point,
not only because of our political but also because of our security
needs. But a proclamation by us to that effect can only do damage." If partition was not turned into a matter of slogans, Berl
Katznelson and his followers could support a Zionist struggle,
toward the outcome of which each might entertain his own
concepts. Even Ben-Gurion finally agreed to this formulation.
"I do not propose the slogan of a Jewish state or any such announced policy. I am talking about our actual policy. Even at
this moment my ultimate objective is not the establishment of
a state in only a part of the country."

The Mapai position, in reality, was in every respect identical
with Weizmann's. The accepted formulation for all of them was,
then, Jewish independence, or more exactly a Jewish state—or
at least an arrangement that would place the primary attributes
of independence, especially the immigration question, in Jewish

hands. "Our fight during the next era will be nonsensical if you do not see the sole aim for which we must strive and battle in the new phase (which is in no way the last and final phase): independence for the Jews of Palestine, that is, a Jewish state." In the "last phase," any type of federative framework was feasible, whether within the framework of an Arab federation or a Jewish-Arab federation in Palestine only, on the basis of a regime of parity.

During March 7–9 these proposals were worded, and they were sent to the government on the 10th[16] in a document signed by Dr. Weizmann. Two main articles were included: (1) "the establishment of a Jewish state in a part of Palestine with an area adequate to allow for further immigration and land settlement on a substantial scale" or (2) "the setting up of an administration for Palestine based on a federal arrangement with full Jewish control over immigration, and with federal institutions based on parity, always allowing for the adequate growth of the Jewish national home." To these two proposals, partition or a binational parity state with free immigration, there was unofficially added another proposal that had first been suggested to MacDonald by Ben-Gurion (with the knowledge of the delegation, of course) at that session of February 18 which we have already mentioned several times: to fix a certain number of immigrants for the next five years and to leave all the other problems for further discussion after that period. This was the most moderate of all the Jewish proposals, and the closest of all to those of the British. But the British did not accept it, apparently out of the knowledge that the Arabs would not agree to it.

After receiving the Jewish answer, MacDonald made one last try (on March 11) to convince the Jews that they should accept the doctrine of concessions which he had sought, on the basis of the Jewish proposals of March 10, in which Weizmann had written that no independent Palestinian state could rise without the agreement of both Jews and Arabs. The colonial secretary declared that he could not, indeed, agree to the legal force of the principle of immigration according to economic absorptive capacity alone. On this alone did he disagree in principle with "most of the Jewish delegation"; but if Weizmann were prepared to stand by that section of his note which implied that an independent Palestine could be established with Jewish consent, it would still be possible to find a compromise. It was immigration that had caused the Arab rebellion and the disquiet in the region; led to the persecution of the Jews of Egypt, Iraq, and other countries; and increased anti-Semitism in Britain. "This was the last thing desired by the British government, who wished to remain the friend of the Jews. The British government would be reluctant in the extreme to adopt a policy in Palestine which would lead to a severance of that friendship."

On the basis of a Jewish concession, MacDonald was prepared to discuss the matter of limited immigration, with or without an Arab veto; on the basis of that section of Weizmann's note, he suggested to the Jews that the unified state be established in Palestine by mutual consent. Let the Jews accept one of the British constitutional proposals, and then he could discuss the matter with the Arabs. That would have been the Jewish concession, and in exchange MacDonald was ready to ask for limited immigration from the Arabs. The Jews, including the group nicknamed "the Lords," rejected the proposal, and thereby brought the discussions to a crisis.

MacDonald's answer came during that very session, after he had heard the Jewish reaction. He said he had "entered on the present conference disliking the idea of an Arab veto on immigration, but Mr. Ben-Gurion and Mr. Shertok [Sharett] had made him feel that this was the only way to secure Jewish cooperation with the Arabs. Mr. Ben-Gurion and Mr. Shertok [Sharett] had conveyed the impression that, so long as the Jews had the British government behind them, they would never meet the Arabs halfway." The way that seemed right to MacDonald in respect to the Jews' lack of readiness for concessions was to

place limitations on both parties: Arab independence would depend on Jewish consent, and Jewish immigration on Arab consent. Meanwhile, to anticipate matters a bit, the first phases of
the gift of self-rule for Palestinians would be carried out even
without Jewish agreement; and a restricted immigration would
be allowed without Arab agreement. With this, the fourth and
final phase of the talks was opened.

The ultimate British proposals were presented to the parties
on March 15 (see Appendix IV). There the establishment of an
independent Palestinian state, perhaps in the form of a federation (which was, of course, to be sheltered by the British Empire), was spoken of. That state would be neither Jewish nor
Arab, and its constitution would be determined by a national
constituent assembly. Britain would take care that this constitution should guarantee: (1) preservation of the holy places;
and (2) protection of various ethnic groups, the Jewish national home, and foreign interests. There would be a transition
period during which British rule would continue. Its extent was
not specified, but the hope was expressed that it would not last
longer than ten years.

During the transition period, the country would progress
toward independence according to the customary procedure for
such cases in the British Empire. Elections for the constituent
assembly, it was hoped, would be held within two years. An
immigration of 75,000 more Jews would be permitted in the
course of the next five years; thereafter, further immigration
would depend upon Arab consent. A war of annihilation would
be waged against illegal immigration, and limitations would be
placed on land sales to Jews. The Jewish veto over the rise of
an independent state found expression in the statement that
His Majesty's government could not contemplate relinquishing
all responsibility for the government of Palestine unless they
were assured that the measure of agreement between the
communities in Palestine was such as to make good government possible.

These proposals did not satisfy the parties. The Arabs felt cheated, inasmuch as their hoped-for independence was, once more, pushed off into the obscure regions of the future and was conditional on Jewish consent, which would surely be unobtainable. Meanwhile, immigration was going to continue, and who could know what might happen five years from now? The uncompromising struggle of the mufti's movement had yielded only a lean harvest.

From the Jewish side, things looked more serious. Formally, the government had not given up its Mandatory basis in that its stated position was that its promises had been fulfilled. The Jewish national home, with its own language, culture, and political institutions, had been established under British rule. The structure was completely finished, and nothing was to be added to it except for the proposed 75,000 immigrants. The British intention of forcing the Jews to accept the yoke of Arab rule in Eretz Israel (the Land of Israel) was especially grave. On the distant horizon, the possibility of a struggle with weapons in hand appeared. This feeling was strengthened because of the Arabs' reasons for rejecting British proposals. Among other things, the Arabs demanded the setting of a terminal date for the granting of independence. There were also announcements, like that of Jamal el-Husseini that the Arabs had not "modified their view that the present population [of Palestine] is larger than the country can support" (March 17).[17]

It must be said that from the tactical viewpoint none of the delegations gained a political victory in the Saint James talks. The British party might claim that a sincere attempt to solve the Palestine problem failed because of the refusal of the two other parties to make the slightest concessions. The Arabs and Jews claimed, each from their own point of view, that the English had gone back on their promises and had made proposals that were completely unreasonable. But when it became clear that, in comparison with the previous situation, the Jewish position had worsened the most, and when the Jews' supporters in British public life viewed government policy as a direct outgrowth of the general appeasement line of the prime minister, the Jewish stand won a certain sympathy in the two main British political parties. Jewish pressure and attempts to influence public opinion flowed, more than a little, from the profound feeling of the disaster that was coming on like a raging storm with the approaching world war. It was obvious that the war would bring down trouble and pain on the Jews of Europe and create a serious refugee problem, though no one thought in terms of a cataclysm in the sense of physical extermination. It was the Jewish sense of helplessness in the face of these events, and the desire to find a solution to this situation, that moved many people during the years 1937–1939 to support the program for the establishment of a Jewish state, even if in only a small part of the country, so that the Jews could be a factor in determining the fate of their brethren in Europe. There were Englishmen —not many—who comprehended this coinciding of the humanitarian factor with the proposed political solution, and they were among the chief battlers against British policy after Saint James.

It was and is widely accepted that the White Paper was part of the Munich appeasement policy which abandoned small peoples to the tender mercies of the great powers.[18] But one must not ignore the difference between the two matters. The prime characteristic of the Munich policy was the desire to preserve peace under any conditions. The discarding of Czechoslovakia was the product of the nearly hysterical wish to hold back the war. This was not so in the case of Palestine. The White Paper was the child of the recognition that war was near, that therefore the British forces for total war against the Axis powers had to be strengthened. It must also be kept in mind that the promulgation of the White Paper came after the English government had officially renounced the appeasement policy, after the fall of Prague.

The captains of Zionism, who looked upon the White Paper

as an outgrowth of appeasement policy, hoped for its cancellation in wartime, when any policy of appeasement is inapplicable.
But since there was no compelling tie between the White Paper
and appeasement, there was no room for those hopes. The
White Paper flowed from a certain viewpoint, a rather consis-
tent one, on affairs of empire. The validity of that viewpoint
did not wane, either during the war years or after. On the contrary, it gathered force with the increased flaring up of the Arab
nationalist movement during those years. In brief, some of
Britain's leaders came to the conclusion that insofar as Zionism
disrupted an understanding with the Arab world (which contained the sources of oil and the main avenues of communication
of the empire), the abandonment of the policy of implementing
Zionism was inescapable.

Two months passed between the close of the London talks
and publication of British policy in the form of a White Paper
(May 17, 1939). During this period, desperate efforts were
made to prevent or delay the publication of the White Paper.
Political and paramilitary preparations were also made for battle
against the new policy. And political discussion was carried on
in order to formulate an alternative policy to the White Paper.

Leading the action to prevent the publication of the White
Paper was Dr. Weizmann, who reached Palestine with Ben-
Gurion on April 3. Telegrams were sent to Chamberlain (April
18), Churchill, the influential Conservative M.P., Leo S. Amery,
and finally Roosevelt (May 8). Likewise, many discussions were
held and an interpretative effort was made, by means of the press
and so forth. One central point was stressed: that the resolute
opposition of the Jews of Palestine to the White Paper policy
would bring to nought the government's chief objective, to
bring peace to the Holy Land after three years of riots and to
assure tranquillity in the future zone of operation of the Royal
forces. The usefulness of such direct pressure—and threats—
against the helmsmen of British diplomacy was doubtful, even
in the view of its initiators (although there were some who

hoped for liquidation of the new policy if it could be delayed until after the outbreak of war). An attempt was also made to get the American ambassador in London, Joseph Kennedy, to intervene in favor of the Jews. The truth of the matter is that it was clear that Roosevelt was not prepared to quarrel with Britain over the Palestine issue; he had even handed England a note in that spirit. But the very approach hinted at the growing importance of United States Jewry in Zionist policy.[19]

Apparently, the threat of retaliation with force on the part of the Jews did not hit the mark. The British knew that it would be impossible for the Jews to conduct a struggle against Britain while an Anglo-German war raged. And, as has been said, the White Paper came into the world when appeasement was already bankrupt, and the change in policy toward the Jews was made in order to reinforce Britain's position in the coming war.

Not only Jewish pressure was exerted against the British government. The Arab governments also applied pressure—they were interested in calming their peoples down so as to put the brakes on jingoistic, extremist anti-British sentiment. They sought to achieve concessions that would make it possible for the mufti to accept the new British policy officially. It seems that the alterations in language between the first proposals, advanced by the British in London in the middle of March, and the final version of the White Paper were introduced under that Arab pressure.[20]

At that time, discussions were being conducted in the Jewish community in Palestine on the line of Zionist policy. During April and May, Ben-Gurion formulated his views. He spoke of three periods of Zionism: Hibbat Zion (Love of Zion), Political Zionism, and Fighting Zionism. Another formulation, in a lecture he delivered on April 24, consisted of the Infiltration Period, the Mandate Period, and the Period of Zionist fulfillment, on the basis of a regime of Jewish sovereignty. A continuation of Zionist activity would be made possible only by struggle with Britain. Indeed, there was the possibility, if all other means were exhausted, that an armed encounter between the Jews and British would occur. But the goal was not anti-British, because it was not in line with Zionist interests to drive the British out of the country.[21]

The Zionist aim was again formulated by Ben-Gurion at the Twenty-first Zionist Congress in August 1939, and especially in the labor bloc's caucus there. Ben-Gurion asserted that the mandate had ceased to exist, that it was necessary to stop talking about a mandate and demand the establishment of a Jewish state. "A portion of us—and I am counted among them—say that we are fighting for a Jewish state in a part of Palestine. That does not mean partition, even if I believe that that would be the best solution." The allusion to a solution other than partition apparently meant the federation program (see above), with a Jewish autonomous zone in western Palestine, a program that had also been brought up in March at the London conference.

Ben-Gurion returned to this proposal for a binational arrangement at the Mapai Central Committee meeting (July 5, 1939). He stated that "we do not have to fix the ultimate aim at this moment. We need a goal for this period." Federative arrangement meant "Jewish sovereignty over immigration and an autonomous area sufficient for broadening the national home, and parity in the federative regime. A possible favorable arrangement is a Jewish state, not necessarily according to the Peel proposal, either by area or constitution, but on a federative basis."[22]

We learn from this that the political programs of the Zionist Executive in 1939 made three fundamental assumptions. First, there was no sense in demanding a resumption of the mandate. Second, it was necessary to struggle for Jewish independence in any form whatsoever—within the framework of the British Empire and, if possible, on the basis of an agreement with the Arabs. And third, the time had not yet come to proclaim these ambitions publicly.

Was opposition in principle to these concepts also expressed?

Various elements, like Mizrahi and a substantial segment of Mapai (with Berl Katznelson at its head), opposed partition (even from the time of the Peel Commission); but they agreed to the vague formulation of Jewish independence as it found expression in the programs of Weizmann and Ben-Gurion on the eve of the war. Fundamental opposition came from the Hashomer Hatzair, which asserted, out of a different evaluation of the changes that had occurred in British policy, that the mandate was still alive and valid. It was also said that Britain would not leave the country (this was the opinion of the Zionist Executive also). If you could hope to get a Jewish state from England, then by the same token you could seek the restoration of the Zionist articles of the mandate, which is what Hashomer Hatzair proposed.

What was the attitude of the leaders of Zionist policy to the question of the agreement with the Arabs? There is no doubt that they wanted such an agreement, on the basis of the right of Jewish immigration, but one gets the impression that they usually conceived of such an agreement as coming through the mediation, consent, and blessing of the British government. It seemed to them that the only real chance for obtaining Arab consent to the basic aspirations of Zionism was by British coercion or pressure on the Arabs. They were undeterred by the fact that those with overriding influence hadn't the slightest desire to coerce the Arabs into this kind of compromise. At times, the attitude of Zionist leaders to the Arabs and British bordered on naïveté. Thus, for example, Weizmann journeyed to Egypt on April 10, 1939, (on the heels of the London meetings) to speak with Mohammed Mahmud, head of the Egyptian government. Weizmann stressed to him two reasons for rejecting the White Paper. One, Britain now needed the help of the United States, where there existed a powerful Jewish influence, and it was not worthwhile for Britain to quarrel with America over this issue; and second, the Jews would never agree to the limitations of the White Paper.

This is not the place to trace out the intricate political negotiations, two- and three-sided, which the Agency Executive conducted with Arab personages during the period of World War II. We will just point out in a general way that those negotiations were much more serious than those who leveled criticism at the executive thought, and that at the time, the character of the negotiations was limited by the executive's expectation of the consent and encouragement of the "third party," without whom the formulation of any agreement was looked upon as unrealistic.

Though a certain degree of obscurity prevailed in the area of "grand policy," there was a considerable measure of unanimity and clarity about the immediate reaction to the White Paper. In the White Paper[23] it was stated that five years after the establishment of peace and order in the country, the beginning of the creation of an independent Palestinian state should be made. And if, five years after the promulgation of the White Paper, cooperation between the Jewish and Arab communities had not come into being to make the establishment of the state possible, further consultation would be held with the purpose of granting the country independence at the earliest possible time. It was further stated in the White Paper that in the course of the ensuing five years an immigration of 75,000 Jews was to be permitted, 25,000 of them refugees. At the close of that period, any additional immigration would depend upon Arab consent (Arab veto over immigration). The reduction of immigration was condoned on the grounds of the fear of Jewish domination that nested in the Arab breast, a fear that had brought on violent events. In order to prevent the embittering of relations between the two communities, immigration would be diminished; laws would be promulgated limiting land purchase by Jews in areas where large amounts of Arab land had already been bought and where there was a danger that the Arab population would be dislodged from its soil. (It is proper to point out that the land law, which was promulgated on February 27, 1940, forbade the Jews to buy land in the areas where they had not so far done so, and purchase was permitted precisely in those areas where most of the land was already in Jewish hands.)

In response to the White Paper, some spoke in the Jewish right-wing press in Palestine about "nonsurrender," in the sense of spiritual passive resistance, and the right-wing members of the Agency Executive expressed such a position in their words. In contrast to them, Ben-Gurion saw in the White Paper an end (at least temporarily) to cooperation with the British, though at the very same time he urged on England the continuation of the political orientation of Zionism. As early as March 22, 1939, he formulated his position in a letter to the Agency Executive: (1) uncompromising war against the White Paper, and pro-British orientation in the grappling of world powers (with apparent reference to the approaching war); (2) an increase in the strength of the Yishuv; and (3) armed opposition to Arab terror, side by side with an attempt at understanding with the Arabs. (It is proper to stress that in this program, active resistance was spoken of, and not just "nonsurrender" to British policy; this active slogan found implementation in the Yishuv with the return of Weizmann and Ben-Gurion from London on April 3, 1939.)

The various provisions of this "activistic" program underwent numerous transformations; not all the versions agree, but the main articles were:

(1) The Jews would not participate in governmental institutions intended to implement the White Paper.

(2) The Jews would break laws whose purpose was the disruption of the rebuilding of Palestine, especially laws pertaining to immigration and settlement. This article also demanded the organizing and strengthening of unofficial immigration.

(3) The Jews would offer forceful resistance to being disarmed.

(4) The Jews would develop a thalassic capability, set up

Jewish fortified positions in the environs of Haifa, and establish a defense industry ("for ourselves and for the British").

(5) They would train their youth under a central authority.

(6) They would encourage aviation.

(7) They would separate the Supernumerary Police Force, then called the "legal" Hagana, from the "illegal" Hagana and intensify Hagana organization.

(8) They would institute a secret press.

(9) They would establish a Jewish community-wide administrative organization with the aim of taking power in Palestine by force, "if the government does not, in the course of time, desist from the new policy."

After a time, paragraphs advocating the following were added: (10) Jewish rule in the municipality of Jerusalem and cessation of British administrative interference in Tel Aviv; (11) encouragement of local manufacture; (12) consolidation of the Yishuv, particularly the youth and the community leadership, to wage war on the White Paper; and (13) general mobilization, agricultural and military, of the youth.[24]

Articles five and nine were stamped with the seal of a new doctrine that struck a response in the Zionist camp. It was somewhat reminiscent of the "pressure doctrine" of Vladimir Jabotinsky. Its main point was that the British were conspiring against the Jews because of their desire to have quiet in Palestine. That fact obliged the Jews to break the quiet. The sole means of bringing the British to make concessions was political, economic, and military pressure, along with the mobilization of British and American public opinion. It is possible to see here the beginning of the anti-British struggle of 1945–1948, though the wording still contained a pro-British touch that gradually disappeared between 1945 and 1947. This version differed somewhat from the Jabotinsky concept, first of all, in the stress here on immigration and settlement as a central means of the struggle, as against the statist and diplomatic view of Jabotinsky. There is no doubt that the chief line of Zionist policy from 1939 on is embodied in this program.[25]

If we thus interpret the struggle of the spring and summer of 1939, there is room for the view that the Zionist policy of the World War II period was a long and important episode which temporarily diverted the development of the political struggle against Britain. At the close of the war, the struggle was renewed on the lines described here. At the same time it seems correct to say that this is hindsight, and one may doubt whether the struggle against Britain was unavoidable. (Quite the contrary—the reader will see, subsequently, to what degree the British came near, in this era of war, to political and military decisions that would have substantially changed the picture of the struggle during the years of 1945 to 1947.) But with hindsight one can discern a sort of line of struggle, beginning with the promulgation of the White Paper, temporarily ending or drawing back with the outbreak of the war, and reappearing with the shaping of Labour government policy after the victory over Germany.

One of the weightiest inner problems that came up was the interpretation to be given the article which spoke of national mobilization and centralization of leadership. Thus, for example, Yosef Supraski, a rightist, proposed (in the Smaller Zionist Actions Committee) a sort of restricted administration with a right-wing majority and dictatorial powers. Rabbi Maimon and Dr. Emil Shmorak supported the motion, and it is possible that discussions were carried on about it.

In the end, the proposal was not accepted, though there is no sign that David Ben-Gurion opposed it.[26] During the fight over this issue, Ben-Gurion developed vigorous activity in order to achieve the support of the youth, organized in various movements, to establish a unified youth movement for purposes of the struggle. The movements indeed responded to the idea of the struggle itself, but Ben-Gurion failed in his efforts to establish a set, unified framework. At work here, apparently, was the fear of dictatorial tendencies and of a threat to the independence of the various movements.

What was the position of the various circles on the idea of the struggle itself? In the executive, the moderate Dr. Werner Senator and Dr. Emil Shmorak (representative of the "B" General Zionists) disassociated themselves from it. They were alarmed to hear of the possibility of armed rebellion against England, hinted at in Ben-Gurion's remarks in the Smaller Zionist Actions Committee. Of course, at that time Ben-Gurion had no such actual intent. But the thought that had been brought out in a practical way by Wingate took on flesh and sinew with the suggestion of increasing independent Jewish power, and (as a result of mass immigration) of attaining a position where revolt against England—if there were no escaping it—would not be in the category of a mere dream.[27] In Mapai itself, and in Hashomer Hatzair as well, this idea encountered resistance. In the labor bloc caucus at the Twenty-first Congress, Pinhas Lavon and Shmuel Dayan (father of Moshe Dayan) of Mapai took issue with a policy of taking on the British by force, whereas Mordekhai Oren (Hashomer Hatzair) favored civil disobedience and armed resistance to protect constructive pioneering projects.

One can cast doubt on the degree of realism in the idea of armed revolt in 1939, but one should not underestimate its propaganda value in the storm of emotions into which the Yishuv was plunged with the publication of the White Paper. It is possible that even to Ben-Gurion this was more of a slogan than practical politics, for there then existed no small similarity between the position of Ben-Gurion and that of Weizmann. The latter was advocating a policy that would force the English to use force against the Jews and not a policy of Jewish initiative in the matter. Indeed, Ben-Gurion was sitting on the fence. Side by side with slogans of revolt, he also voiced words in the spirit of Weizmann and even in the very same forms.

Yet there existed a difference between the concepts of the two men on the issue of the use of force. To Weizmann it was a matter of political principle not to resort to armed revolt against the British. But Ben-Gurion spoke first and foremost of the goal, which was independence in any form; and he sought to prepare for any required means in order to achieve that goal. The end was the main thing; the means—a matter for practical consideration.

🦅 *The Hagana and the White Paper*

The development that led to the proclamation of the White Paper brought changes in Zionism's political outlook, and thus also in the area of internal security. Ben-Gurion, who went back to Palestine at the beginning of April, exerted great effort to introduce organizational changes into the Hagana structure, changes made necessary by the new situation.

The Hagana's internal condition at that moment was unsatisfactory. The National Command did not function as a coordinated body. The dividing line ran not only between the nonsocialist representatives (Yitzhak Sitkov, Dov Gefen, and Uri Nadav) and the Histadrut representatives (Eliyahu Golomb, Israel Galili, and Meir Rutberg). Even the Histadrut representatives—who, by force of reality, bore more responsibility in matters of security than any other section of the Yishuv—were not united.

Golomb ceased his activity in the command in March 1939, asserting that without a reorganization of the Hagana, the parity arrangement between the left and right wings was a stumbling block. By force of his moral authority, Golomb practically served as the overall commander in the eyes of the Hagana officers; and thus a situation was created where the High Command was turned into a body competing with Golomb for control of the organization. The right wing was not ready to reconcile itself to this. It attacked the chief of the National Command, Professor Yohanan Rattner, and Israel Galili of Mapai, who were forced to answer for and explain away Golomb's departure from the command. The tangle grew unbearable, and even Galili threatened to resign. Rattner had tendered his resignation to the Political Department of the agency on March 23. He was to insist on his wish to resign several times during the summer.

The zonal division of the Hagana into regions and districts also had not been completed. Trained members of the Hagana numbered no more than two thousand, about half of them in legal formations, (that is, under British command). The Field Squads had finally been disbanded in April, with their remaining personnel (about one hundred men) retained as a police unit, with money from the Kofer Hayishuv for a short additional period. A mobile Field Force, the establishment of which was being discussed at the time of the demobilization of the Field Squads, had not come into existence because of budgetary difficulties.

The most serious deficiency in the Hagana organization was the lack of a professional staff that would work on technical and special skill problems while the National Command confined itself to administrative, monetary, and political control. There was much talk of this, but for a long time it was never more than a mere projected program.

Ben-Gurion, who took upon himself the burden of security problems on his return from London, tried first of all to convince Rattner to continue his role; he also tried to bring Golomb back to the command. These efforts delayed the crisis, but they did not put an end to it. At the same time, Ben-Gurion attempted to persuade the people involved in the matter—mainly the right-wingers in the command—to agree to the proposals being made by Golomb, Rattner, and Galili, who were trying to turn the operations section (which was a technical planning section) into a real General Staff. This proposal was accepted after several months and on September 19, 1939, the National Command announced the formation of a General Staff, at the head of which Yaakov Dori, the commander of Haifa, was placed.

Ben-Gurion, who considered this realm of activity very important, tried to place the Hagana under the control of the

Agency Executive, (more exactly, under his own control). But in this he met with many difficulties, heaped up by the right wing. The Vaad Leumi,* an important partner in the ordering of Hagana matters, transferred some of its powers in these matters to the presidium of the Kofer Hayishuv at its creation in 1938; great influence was held in this body by Yitzhak Rokakh, mayor of Tel Aviv, who represented the middle-class position with great forcefulness. Then Ben-Gurion brought into the open the demand for separation of the Supernumeraries (the "legal" Hagana) from the "illegal" Hagana organization (at the session of the Smaller Zionist Actions Committee on May 3). Only the illegal Hagana would remain under the control of the National Command.

It was immediately apparent that, with this, there had been brought up the idea of distinguishing between the static-passive Hagana and the rest of the security functions, in order to bypass in this fashion the intervention of the impotent National Command and the rightist-controlled Kofer Hayishuv—even though these elected bodies represented community democracy and the community's control over its security institutions. Ben-Gurion's intention was to gain control over the most important branches of the Hagana. The Supernumeraries were separate from Hagana command anyway and were administered by the agency political division. Aliyah Bet (unofficial immigration), the all-important arm of the anti-British struggle, was under the Histadrut's authority. Since 1938 Shaul Avigur had stood at the head of the Aliyah Bet "Immigration Bureau" (Mosad), possessed of seniority and authority; he had functioned for years as head of the Hagana directorate. The Field Force, too, was about to be wrenched away from the National Command.

But for carrying on the anti-British struggle an additional branch was needed, a more active one, that would be under the

* The elected National Council of the Yishuv.

political jurisdiction of the chairman of the Agency Executive. Ben-Gurion determined that this formation (the Special Squads) should be directly subject to him. Thus he bypassed the National Command altogether. There arose, therefore, an underground within the underground, in which those who opposed the new "activist" line were given no role. The Special Squads were composed of Mapai people (or political independents who supported the activist doctrine), except that even in Mapai there was no dearth of internal differences of opinion on this issue. The party as a party refused to discuss the Special Squads and left it to him who was prepared to do it.

The creation of the Special Squads broke the camel's back as far as Rattner was concerned. As chief of the National Command he was held responsible (by the right wing of the Command) for actions which he had not directed—though he knew of them and apparently agreed to them. In August, they began to look for a replacement after Rattner had, for all practical purposes, left his job and had not returned to it, even after an end was put to the Special Squads' actions with the outbreak of the war.

In the spring of 1939, with the disbanding of the Field Squads, the idea of a national mobilized force gained in Mapai. Eliyahu Golomb stated his findings (at a session of the Histadrut Actions Committee on March 30, 1939) that the Night Squads held "the capability of creating the cadre of a Jewish army" and that the Yishuv was obliged to create such a Hebrew force for defense against an Arab *putsch,* as well as against police and military regulations. "It is plain that the present situation, in the world and the country, obligates us to see to the formation of a Hebrew force upon which we shall be able to depend for defense of the land, in case we are left to our own resources." A cadre of five thousand men was essential.

Golomb suggested keeping eight hundred to one thousand men in permanent encampments. They would spend half their time training; during the other half they would serve in active defense roles. The retention of this force would cost £150,000 —an enormous sum in those days, equal to the total income of the Kofer Hayishuv from its inception until the end of September 1939. Golomb knew that the right wing would oppose the formation of a force of this kind which "would be composed in its overwhelming majority of Histadrut forces," even though its initiators might try to make it a thoroughly all-encompassing national force. Golomb also visualized the dangers bound up within the establishment of this kind of formation:

It is the essence of such a force that it will begin to regard itself as an elite; of its nature that it will begin to form a special discipline within itself; of its essence that it should become aggressive. But these are no reasons to do without this kind of force.

To the debate that developed in the Actions Committee, Ben-Zion Israeli of Kibbutz Kinneret brought the experience he had gained in the Jordan Valley. There, in the spring of 1939, a local unit had been established in which men served who worked in their home areas for most of the year and alternated on set tours of duty. Israeli requested the formation of a "central national force in this manner: to turn our agricultural settlements into points of departure for this force." He told of the unit of two hundred men that had been decided on for the Jordan Valley. He spoke in terms of an "infantry force, an assault squad, a motorized squad, etc. and also of ten to fifteen men who would be under Yitzhak [Yitzhak Sadeh—an allusion to special actions]. For this purpose, we decided that every man of military age would be bound to serve in a military unit for at least one year. At the end of the year, the first group would enter the reserves and the second group would take its place. Each man would receive concentrated training for two months and during the other ten would continue his training from time to time." Israeli pictured fifteen thousand men for the entire country; in fact this was the plan for a Field Force whose units would remain in their own localities but be subject to overall command when necessary.

Yitzhak Sadeh had a less extensive plan for seven thousand men, but he put special stress on wrenching the unit away from district jurisdiction. In this plan, the concentrated encampment was reduced to two weeks.

In this debate, it appears that Israeli represented military maximalism, but it is probable that his intention was otherwise. Such a large military force could not be self-sustaining in underground conditions. He was suggesting this force (on July 28, 1939, in a session of the Histadrut Actions Committee) as a replacement for the British Army in guarding the country. Even though there was no hint in his words as to why and how the British might agree to be replaced in guarding Palestine by a Jewish force, one may guess that he—like many others—saw an opportunity in the approaching war to go back to full cooperation with the British. And indeed, this was Israeli's position even after the outbreak of the war.

Golomb too, in that session, withdrew his demand for an underground army. He stated that "the problem now is not how to create an independent Jewish force (though I would very much like that) but how to attain our most desirable result, and that is a Jewish force connected with England."

The opinion of Hashomer Hatzair was not as clear as it might have been. Its leader, Meir Ya'ari—who feared most of all the political aspect, that is, the connection of the overall force with England—explicitly dissociated himself from the program. Whereas Yaakov Hazan specified that from purely military considerations "a force must rise whose role is not just standing guard down by the fence, but the defense of the Jewish community in Palestine."

Even while the talks were going on, the first skeleton of the Field Force was formed during the months of May, June, and July 1939 under the command of Yitzhak Sadeh, approximately along the lines of Israeli's suggestion. At the same time, a new unit was created, the Special Squads. In many respects it was the link that joined the Night Squads and the Field Squads to the Palmakh.

✍ *The Special Squads and Their Place within the Hagana*

In its June 5, 1939, session, in keeping with Professor Rattner's proposal, the Agency Executive decided to establish a special unit—the Special Squads; this unit was subject solely to Ben-Gurion and received its budget from the Agency Executive. An advisory committee operated alongside Yitzhak Sadeh; participating in it were Rattner, Dov Hos, Galili, Golomb, and Dori. The tasks of the Special Squads were: actions in response to those of Arab terrorists, punishment actions against Jewish informers, and various anti-British actions, including training for unofficial immigration operations. A rather extended course in seamanship was instituted in Tel Aviv for unofficial immigration activities. The Special Squads operated in three areas: the north under Levi Avrahami, Tel Aviv and the south under Tsvi Spector, and Jerusalem, under Shelomo Shamir.

The buds of the northern detachment were formed on the initiative of Levi Avrahami and Dori even before the framework of the Special Squads was organized. A small group of men punished Bedouins of the Arab Zubeidat (near Haifa) for the murder of a Jew in Tivon (February 15, 1939) in an operation that was not confirmed by the high command. Later the Special Squads were officially established and operated in the north against the villages of Balad es-Sheik (June 13) and Sasa (July 29). In Lubia (June 20) several houses in the village were demolished. David Shaltiel, Yigal Allon, Tsvi Brenner, and others took part. The action was not taken within the organized framework of the Special Squads, but was taken in its spirit.

The remaining units in the country did not, apparently, operate chiefly against Arabs. The southern group prepared an attempt (never carried out) on the life of a high British official and also carried out operations of punishment against Jewish informers. In the north, anti-British actions were also taken. On August 9, 1939, Israel Norden, a member of Avrahami's unit, sank the police boat *Sindbad II* which had done "excellent" work in action against unofficial immigrant ships.

In the middle of July, the oil pipeline in the vicinity of Sarid was damaged by a Special Squads detachment and further demolition acts were planned against oil pipelines and refineries. These plans were frustrated by the activity of Yitzhak Meromi, a Hashomer Hatzair man (of Kibbutz Mizra), who opposed them. Meromi informed Hazan and Ya'ari about the action, and they immediately demanded a hearing in the Histadrut bodies. At that session, Ben-Gurion demanded (according to the testimony of Hazan, in vain) that the Hashomer Hatzair people reveal to him the source of their information. The plan was eventually postponed after Yosef Shprinzak, a moderate leader of Mapai, also opposed it. The Hashomer Hatzair people had already stated that they were ready for any military action in defense of immigration, settlement, and Hagana arms; but not for what seemed to them mere acts of provocation.

In Jerusalem, a small unit went into action against the automobiles of the C.I.D.,* but fortune did not smile on it. It accidentally set fire to some Jewish cars as well; and for that its commander was tried before a Hagana court-martial. The same unit also planned attacks on several English senior officials and raids on the government printing house, the high commissioner's palace, the Russian compound area, the police buildings and garages, and other targets. All these programs were canceled before they reached the operational stage. The Second World War broke out, and the campaign against the British was interrupted.

* Civil Investigation Department—the political police.

It must be reemphasized that the Special Squads actions were not aimed at driving the British out of the country. The goal was to make the enforcement of the White Paper difficult for them. Ben-Gurion thought it was imperative to encourage an atmosphere of rebellious action against the English. He believed that if this was not done, certain sections of the Yishuv would make peace with the White Paper, while a portion of the youth would probably develop unorganized, "wild" means of action for themselves.

This latter danger showed itself clearly in the disturbance that broke out among the students of the Haifa Technion (technical college). They were demanding sabotage raids and even organized a demonstration unapproved by the official bodies on the day of the White Paper's publication. One gets the impression that only intervention by Golomb and Ben-Gurion in this case, and by Golomb in similar cases, prevented the development of the seeds of rebellion against the Jewish Agency.

With all the internal political importance of the Special Squads, one should not conceal their ineffectiveness in combat with the British. The roots of this deficiency lay in inexperience, not in lack of devotion or enthusiasm. But to the Special Squads must be assigned a consumate historical importance. It was an embryonic military force on a countrywide scale, acting according to political directives, and divorced from all local obligation. It served as the operating arm of a certain policy, even though that section of the policy had not been agreed upon within the higher bodies whose very role was to direct the struggle as a whole. Nevertheless, it seems that the activist doctrine that found its expression in the operations of the Special Squads was an imperative, in one form or another, of that reality which prevailed under the conditions of the struggle with the British regime (although one may debate about certain types of such operations). The Special Squad activities, though they were fragmentary and even pitifully ineffective, hinted at a continuation which never came because of the outbreak of the war.

The war postponed the continuation of the battle until 1945.

To what degree was the activity of the Special Squads divergent from what had been acceptable until then—in the Field Squads, for example? Now, attempts were being planned on the lives of anti-Jewish officials. In this respect, there was, doubtless, a signpost on a path not different from that of Lehi (the so-called Stern Gang) in the coming years. Of course, the Hagana courts were very careful in pronouncing sentence. Except for informers, no one was ever executed by the Hagana. But Galili tells that even Berl Katznelson, the great labor leader, pressed for the execution of Jardin, an English official of the Government Land Department known for his enmity to the Jews. Within the Hagana, moods that favored personal terror were apparently widespread. But in the end, the opinion of personalities like Ben-Gurion, Galili, and others who opposed this manner of warfare with all their might won out. By Ben-Gurion's intervention, the execution of Jardin was prevented, as was the assassination of the mufti.

Special Squads activity was halted in the second half of September. If we can depend upon a sizable number of witnesses, a part of the unit's personnel remained as a special nucleus at the order of the High Command, for carrying out special operations. But the Special Squads, as a military element and a countrywide body, was dissolved.

In the face of World War II, the leaders of the Yishuv sought to renew, partially at least, cooperation with the British. The disbanding of the Special Squads was one sign of that change.

✍ Other Means of Struggle

The most important means of struggle against the White Paper were not chiefly those which we have delineated up to this point, but rather the activities which had long been the foundation of the Zionist structure: immigration and settlement. There is danger in overemphasizing the types of activity engaged in by the Special Squads. In truth, they were only buds for future development. And even when their time came, they matured only because of immigration and settlement. The fact is that it was the open struggle for immigration in all its forms, and for free settlement, that determined the character of Zionism's battle.

In 1934, the first attempt was made to transport "illegal" immigrants to Palestine, on the ship *Velos,* by operatives of the Histadrut. This experiment failed after an initial success. During 1937–1938, the Revisionists and their associates[28] operated in the area of unofficial immigration, as did some private individuals for their own profit. The people of Betar (Revisionist Youth) and Etzel kept organizing this type of *aliyah;* the rest of the Zionist elements still believed in the possibility of legal immigration on the basis of close cooperation with the British. Beginning with the start of 1938, the "Immigration Bureau" (Mosad) of the Histadrut, under Shaul Avigur, organized unofficial immigration. From that time until the outbreak of the war, it was conducted in three streams: the Mosad, Etzel, and private parties. About 6,100 immigrants were brought into Palestine by the Mosad. During the same period, the Revisionists also brought in between 5,000 and 6,000 persons.[29]

Contrary to claims that were frequently heard from British sources, the unofficial immigration required no propaganda. It attempted nothing except the transfer to Palestine of a part of the multitudes of Jews who had been driven out of or uprooted from their homes. The need for unofficial immigration became especially urgent after the annexation of Austria, and after the November 1938 pogroms in Germany and the capture of Prague in March 1939.

The struggle at the Zionist summit about unofficial immigration raged mainly with Weizmann and some of the right-wing people. This debate was needlessly exposed to public view in the Twenty-first Congress at Geneva in August 1939. Weizmann, who feared the response of English public opinion to violations of the law on the part of the Jews, was not pleased by the public debate on unofficial immigration. He tried to turn the main emphasis of the struggle against the White Paper to settlement questions. But the debate burst onto the floor of the Congress with Rabbi Abba Hillel Silver's open opposition to unofficial immigration. Then Berl Katznelson sharply answered the opposers and the hesitaters, expressing the stand of the labor bloc and others. Weizmann, as representative of an official body—the Jewish Agency, with its seat in London—saw himself in an unbearable position when parties which participated in the Agency Executive sided in public with an illegal action. The heavy pressure of the labor bloc in the congress, and of bodies and personalities from other wings (the liberal Yitzhak Gruenbaum), finally moved Weizmann to make his peace with the public demand for unofficial immigration. The policy of support for unofficial immigration won out in the congress.

From February 1939 on, unofficial immigration became a political question.[30] In the beginning, most of the ships of the Mosad succeeded in reaching the coast of Palestine without being detected by the British. Other ships, the *Cattina* and the *Astir* of the Revisionists, and the private vessels *Aspia, Hagios Nikoloros*, and *Liesel* were taken and turned back. A few of them were later able to reapproach the shore and disembark immigrants.

As the organization of unofficial immigration improved, so did the means of fighting it. From the beginning of June 1939, the British began to hinder it seriously—with the help of police boats, searchlights, planes, and secret agents. The authorities did not know how to deal with the immigrants who were caught. Until April 1939 they tried to return them to their ports of origin. On April 22 the vessel *Assimi* (240 persons) was expelled from Haifa. It had been organized by private individuals and "adopted" by the Hagana. As a reaction to this, a demonstration and strike were organized by the Hagana in Haifa by order of Ben-Gurion. This protest apparently had an effect. About 160 unofficial immigrants of the *Panagia Conasteriu,* arriving at that time, were permitted to land and placed in internment at Sarafand.[31]

Then the government found a way out of the tangle. On July 13 Colonial Secretary MacDonald informed Parliament that any further "illegals" captured on the shores of Palestine would be deducted from the White Paper quota. Over against this policy, the Zionist line crystallized; it planned to: (1) bring in a maximum number of refugees; (2) demolish the underpinnings of the White Paper by demonstrating the full right of Jews to enter their national home; and (3) break the government's immigration quota. The government decided to halt legal immigration for the half-year of October 1939 to March 1940 and began to "stretch out" the quota of 75,000 immigrants, in order to put off the time when it would have to determine by what means it would prevent further immigration. The Jews, of course, were interested in "finishing" the quota business at the earliest date, in order to place the government in the fundamental political dilemma.[32]

A fresh problem arose. Was it preferable to rescue a maximal number of refugees by bringing them in secretly, and hope for public opinion to be in sympathy with the national and humanitarian disaster that was theirs? Or was it better to bring in the refugees in the light of day, with mobilized Hagana cover, as a political demonstration, in order to make the British confront the Jews' claim to *aliyah* face to face? Ben-Gurion favored the latter policy. But most of his associates opposed it with the argument that taking on the British directly was fraught with peril, its results were predictable, and it would depress the spirits of the Yishuv. The destruction of the Yishuv's security machine by its careless use seemed to be threatened by such a course. And indeed, there is substance to the supposition that the Hagana would have endangered its very existence by such political displays.

But the question can be asked, Why did Ben-Gurion view it as imperative to employ the force of arms in order to protect a demonstrative *aliyah* action? It is a fact that in the case of the vessels *Parita* (in August) and *Tiger Hill,* immigrants were brought in by civilians as a demonstrational action, in broad daylight and without the use of arms. In this instance, Weizmann's words were truly fulfilled. He had said that the English would be forced to shoot Jews because of the White Paper policy. However, real political results were not destined for these actions. While the immigrants of *Tiger Hill* crossed the shoreline on September 2, Hitler's armies were invading Poland. The worldwide conflagration overshadowed, in the world's heart, the struggle of a small people in a corner of the Mediterranean Sea.

The other principal means of struggle was *hityashvut* (settlement). Until the publishing of the White Paper, it was customary (though it was not a legal obligation) to inform the authorities about the establishment of new points of settlement. But after its promulgation, the agency departed from that practice and began settlements in frontier areas without giving such notification. Dan and Dafna were founded in the north (May 3, 1939), and six settlements were then created in various corners of the country. This action did not bring on any substantial encounter with the British, inasmuch as they had been warned not to go beyond the level of political pressure and not to come into direct contact with the settlers. Thus, for example, the British threatened to remove a portion of the arms that were in the hands of the settlement police, as a punishment for the creation of these points, but the threat was never carried out. It must be pointed out that the British government used immense caution in respect to Jewish bitterness. The hope that influential supporters of the White Paper would turn up among the Jews still nestled in many British hearts; and until the clarification of the international picture, the government was not interested in a deterioration of relations—already tense—with the Jews.

At the same time, even after the publication of the White Paper, Jewish political activity did not stop. Its effect was discernible in a debate conducted in Parliament on May 22 and 23, in which Churchill, Leo S. Amery, P. Noel-Baker, Tom Williams (Labour), and others participated. The government sustained a moral defeat when its normal majority of 220 shrank to a mere 89. But this did not prevent the confirmation of its policy.

In the debate, MacDonald based his stand on arguments from international law, and the government even submitted the White Paper for the examination of the Mandates Commission in Geneva. This caused an additional diplomatic worry for Britain's government. The commission ruled unanimously that the White Paper did not correspond with the interpretation thus far given the mandate, and a majority of its members thought that it could not be reconciled with any other possible interpretation of the mandate (June 1939). The commission did not summarize its decisions in an official report, but turned over its members' opinion to the council of the League of Nations. In reply to this, the British government proclaimed that it would request the League of Nations to adjust the wording of the mandate to the new political reality.[33] In this struggle within the League of Nations, the chances for Zionism were very slim; no one doubted England's ability to muster a majority that would support her policy in the league. But neither was the British government's position comfortable, at least from the moral standpoint. Things never came to an open battle on international law, however, because the war relieved England of further trial before the League of Nations. Then at the close of the war, with the creation of the United Nations, England regarded herself as free in practice from all the old international obligations, except for that of consulting with the government of the United States.

One of the problems brought up during the struggle was that of noncooperation with the British. Was the young Jewish community of half a million capable of denying cooperation, in the areas of economy and administration, to the country's government? Ben-Gurion demanded noncooperation in limited areas, to be determined by the Jews. With this in mind, a Community Committee was appointed, one of the tasks of which was to clarify suitable means of implementation.

In a certain sense, the idea of a "state within a state" was now evolving—"We must govern ourselves as if we were the State in Eretz Israel," Ben-Gurion proclaimed at the Twenty-first Congress.[34] When it came to the noncooperation program, the activists, of all colorations, encountered resistance on the part of various mutually conflicting factions, within the Histadrut and especially outside it. It became clear that this whole plan, which had roused such raging fury, was nothing but a scheme stillborn. When all was said and done, not a twig of it sprouted, and the work of the Community Committee brought no practical results. The bitter truth was that the Yishuv in 1939 was still too dependent on the favors of outsiders to be able to oppose the government by these means.[35]

Among the leaders of the Palestine Jewish community were some who understood the psychological tempest that was raging in the Yishuv. This Yishuv, the vast majority of which participated neither in the Hagana nor in unofficial immigration, nor even in settlement, was looking for an outlet for its emotions. The demonstrations that came as a response to the publication of the White Paper provided that outlet. They encompassed all the cities of Palestine. The efforts of the national bodies to control them did not always succeed. Etzel (the Irgun), which was not subject to control of the Yishuv's institutions, and even many members of the Hagana tended to burst the bonds of discipline. Government offices were attacked in Tel Aviv and Jerusalem. A British policeman was shot to death by a Hagana member acting on his personal initiative. The police, who did not employ firearms, beat many Jewish citizens cruelly, including even several people of the Magen David Adom (equivalent to the Red Cross).[36]

This reply of demonstrations, burnings, and the like was not in line with the thinking of the agency leaders because it lacked the political weight carried by acts of *aliyah,* settlement, preservation of Hebrew arms, or planned activities of response. The mass outbursts did not arouse a positive reaction from world public opinion or among the friends of Zionism. Nevertheless, the Zionist heads were now given the opportunity to point once again at the peril of the new policy and to threaten a sharp Jewish response.[37]

In summary: The struggle of the spring and summer of 1939 had no effect on the British. It was too short, too fragmentary, and demonstrated a lack of experience and maturity. It did not appear to the British government to be an organized battle by a people for its rights. Nor did it leave anything but the vaguest memories in the consciousness of the Yishuv. Nevertheless, this struggle had some importance, in that it showed the way to means of battle, some possible and some impossible; some successful, some not.

The struggle did not take up in 1945 at the point at which it left off in 1939. But it may be said that the line of anti-British action, with its various forms, the beginnings of which are recognizable in 1939, continued in an attenuated fashion during the interim period of World War II, influenced by the varying turns of political reality—and was renewed in an altered shape at the end of the war.

¾ Struggles and Political Goals at the Beginning of the War

If there were Zionist leaders who were hoping that, with the outbreak of the war, changes in British policy would take place, they were due for a bitter disappointment. MacDonald continued to serve as colonial secretary and Sir Harold MacMichael as high commissioner in Palestine. They were both firmly of the opinion that the implementation of the White Paper (at any rate in its two chief provisions, immigration and land) was vital for the tranquillity of the empire. Regarding the "third phase," the constitutional stage of which the White Paper spoke—the advance of the country toward independence under the domination of an Arab majority—the government was subjected to Arab pressure (chiefly voiced, apparently, by Nuri Said). On December 3, 1939, the high commissioner announced his refusal to grant clemency to Arab terrorists (who were under sentence in Palestine). This was interpreted as the breakdown of Arab-British negotiations. The mere existence of such negotiations was only being surmised in Zionist circles. Later, Mac-Donald informed the British cabinet that the "third phase" would be postponed for the time being, until an opportune moment came.[1]

During the first year of World War II, Zionism's political struggle took on a distinctly defensive character. It was necessary to demand a maximum number of immigration certificates for refugees from occupied Europe, and it was imperative to do battle against the tendency toward the promulgation of the land law referred to in the White Paper. At the same time, discussions were also taking place within the Zionist camp on political goals and directions.

The agency seized on every opportunity to squeeze additional certificates out of rigid ministers. Its representatives met with a wall of indifference and resentment, and their efforts mostly came to nothing. In the half-year from October 1939 to March 1940, no permits whatsoever were given. The British tactics were aimed at postponing the time when the quota of immigration permits, as provided in the White Paper, would be ended.

On the issue of the land law, it appeared at first that there was a chance of reversing the decision. Labour, Churchill, and some Conservative statesmen vigorously opposed the law. But MacMichael informed Ben-Gurion and Sharett in September that it would be adopted. Several efforts were made to avoid it. And in October 1939 Foreign Secretary Lord Halifax calmed Weizmann by telling him not to expect such a law at that time.[2] Weizmann, therefore, decided to go to the United States in order to prepare the ground there for large-scale political activity and to organize American Jewry in a pro-British spirit. One gets the impression that there was no fear that the law would be promulgated during his absence from London (Butler, at that time Halifax's assistant, stated on December 4, 1939, that there was no danger that the law would be passed soon).

But on the eve of Weizmann's departure (December 19, 1939), a letter written at the Foreign Office was received from Halifax, a letter that upset the apple cart. The letter "promised" that there was no change in British policy and that the White Paper would be carried out. At that stage (Weizmann was then absent) Churchill, then already a member of the government, intervened. The damage seemed to have been repaired in his talk with Halifax. Churchill also wrote a memorandum against the land law to the cabinet. As a result of these actions, Mac-Donald was forced to present the law to the entire cabinet, which he did on January 16, 1940.

The new land law was, in fact, based on the partition plan of the Woodhead Commission (a narrow coastal strip for the Jews, a British mandate and an Arab state in the remaining areas of Palestine); but it contradicted the quasi-humanitarian goal of the legislation, as expounded at the time by MacDonald in Parliament: to prevent the uprooting of Arabs in regions where they lived in high density and where the Jews had already purchased large amounts of land. The new law allowed unhampered land purchase precisely in the most populated areas (5 percent of the country) where most of the land was already in Jewish hands; while, in contrast, purchase was prohibited in none other than the wilderness zones.

The cabinet appointed a special committee (Chamberlain, MacDonald, Churchill, and Halifax) which discussed the law only about two weeks before its promulgation. We can suppose that Churchill was in the minority on the committee; it decided that the law should be adopted. This became known to the agency on February 13, and it turned urgently to people of the Labour party. In a talk with Labour representatives, Mac-Donald stated on February 22 that the decision had not been firmly taken; when it was, he would notify them. But the Labour representatives were quickly invited back and information was delivered to them on the decision (which had already existed for at least a week!). Labour saw that it had been duped. It determined to have a parliamentary debate, which for tactical reasons the agency was not interested in at that moment.

On February 27, the date when the land law was to be adopted, a further intervention by Attlee and Greenwood occurred. It was returned to the prime minister for additional consideration, but the next day it was publicly promulgated.[3] The "Jewish national home" was turned into a ghetto made up of

5 percent of the area of western Palestine. Cooperation between Zionism and Great Britain was struck another crippling blow.

The Yishuv's reaction to the land law was not long in coming. Inspired by the Hagana, demonstrations and strikes broke out all over the country (February 29–March 2, 1940), an illegal radio broadcast was started (called Kol Israel), and the events of May 1939 were reenacted. In Jerusalem, a youth, Menahem Prywes, was beaten to death by British policemen (March 3, 1940). The police also ran wild in Petah-Tiqva and the ortho-dox neighborhoods of Jerusalem. In the latter, an aged rabbi was injured, among others. The agency responded sharply, de-manding an investigation. But the British self-investigation "bore no fruit," and the murder of Prywes became an official "mys-tery."[4]

Of course, political actions were also taken. Ben-Gurion sent a protest on the law to the high commissioner. In it he recalled the Jewish Pale of Settlement in czarist Russia, to which the Land of Israel was now to bear a resemblance. He proclaimed that only in the Nazi lands was there such racist and national discrimination.

The chief justification for the enactment of White Paper policy was unaltered. The government wished to conclude the business of the Jewish national home in order to obtain Arab friendship. It seemed to Britain that the slightest deviation from her obligation to the Arabs meant uprisings and riots. Even at the end of the war, Britain kept her position. The noted histo-rian George Kirk pleads the case of the White Paper by agreeing with precisely this argument. He states that because of bitterness over Palestine, the Arabs of Iraq revolted and Britain held on there with the remnant of her forces. Furthermore, Kirk argues for a connection between the Palestine issue and French obedience to German instructions (in 1941) in Syria. However, we know that the revolt broke out in Iraq after the White Paper and the land law had already been promulgated—a sure sign that the satisfaction of Arab claims in the Palestine issue had not the slightest connection with the Iraqi rebellion. And just what had the business of the French in Syria to do with Arab demands in regard to Palestine?[5] But such was the British rationalization. No wonder that a report of the Palestine C.I.D. could relate with great satisfaction that the land law had frustrated the efforts of German propaganda broadcasts in Arabic.[6]

After the war broke out, a definite change took place in Zionist policy. The widely accepted slogan of the time—to fight the White Paper as if there were no war, and to fight Hitler as if there were no White Paper—was certainly a nice motto, but a very difficult one to put into effect. In fact, the active struggle against the White Paper ceased with the start of the war, and immense efforts were put forth to create Hebrew units within the framework of the British Army. The war seemed to provide an opportunity for the liquidation of the White Paper—in the course of time, if not at once. The view was widely held that the mobilization of tens of thousands of Jews would turn Zionism into a substantial international factor, while in the area of mobilization the Arabs would fail. The main point was that Jewish troubles in Europe would, of course, worsen as a result of Nazi conquests. An urgent solution would be required for masses of homeless refugees. In time, there would be an end to the influence of Zionism's opponents (many of whom belonged to the "Munich" branch of the Conservative party), while pro-Zionist forces would come to power. Thus, approximately, ran the hopes of the groups represented in the Agency Executive.

Zionist political thought was discussed and formulated primarily in London, in Dr. Weizmann's circle. "Chaim voices our demand—a state in all of western Palestine." And Professor Louis B. Namier, who was then working in the political office of the Jewish Agency in London, "sets forth, at the central office, the problem of Jewish refugees, which will deteriorate as a result of the war. . . ." Namier saw the possibility for the fulfillment of the Jewish demand in the surrender by France of Syria to the English and the Arabs. Sharett accepted the idea of Palestine as a Jewish state at the level of a political step, a goal to be demanded—whether or not it was possible of achievement. One gets the impression that at the start Weizmann, and apparently Sharett as well, viewed this as a maximal program.[7]

In November 1939 Ben-Gurion joined Weizmann and Sharett (Sharett had remained in London since the beginning of October). For Ben-Gurion, the main thing was to undermine White Paper policy, and he had misgivings as to the value of discussing Zionist "war aims." Fixed in his attention was the question of how to exert powerful pressure upon Britain to retreat from its policy. He had not despaired of an active struggle against it, even for the war period—and, even so, on the basis of a British "orientation." "We have no desire to drive the British out of Palestine by force—I suppose that in this gathering there is not one person who is thinking of that. One may think that we must fight them with force; that is quite another matter." The English were interested in having peace prevail in the country, but it "cannot be our ideal to make the implementation of the White Paper possible."

Ben-Gurion was still striving for partition or binational federation in some form or other—he apparently meant these goals even when he was speaking of a Jewish state. His words were informed with a sharp perception of Zionist reality. But they sometimes appeared in company with his own typical political fantasies, for example, the creation of the Jewish state by force, against the British or without their support, even while the war was still raging.[8] Ben-Gurion accepted the idea of the whole of western Palestine as a Jewish state only to a degree; and, in his opinion, that was dependent from the start upon Britain's attitude. "If there is hope for help, it can only be from England. If there is no hope for help, we shall have to fight and stand on our own, but it would be better if things did not come to that." But indeed, was there hope for a "change of heart" on the part of the British government? Weizmann's answer was: There is hope. Chamberlain would step down, and Churchill or Halifax would take his place.

Weizmann recognized the tremendous importance of the

United States, both of its Jewish citizens and its government. He sent his aide, Joseph Cohen, there in order to prepare public opinion for a program of turning western Palestine over to the Jews, resettling the Arabs in Arab countries, financing the plan with a large American loan, and gaining the political support of America. However, Ben-Gurion remained unconvinced and continued to look upon this program as that of Weizmann's alone.[9]

This situation—Weizmann voicing the demand for the whole of Palestine as a Jewish state while Ben-Gurion and his associates were still prepared to discuss other solutions—lasted at least until Ben-Gurion's departure for England and the United States (April 25, 1940) and, for some of his associates, until his return (February 16, 1941).

On May 9, 1940, Ben-Gurion wrote from London that Weizmann "had rediscovered America—Jewish power and the huge Zionist potentialities of American Jewry. The distance between us is far smaller than that between myself and some of the Zionists in Jerusalem (and Tel Aviv)." And if Ben-Gurion still could speak in the Agency Executive (February 16, 1940) of two possible solutions—partition or a binational solution ("complete equality for the two peoples in rule over the land") —after that date, we do not find Ben-Gurion mentioning any solution other than that of a Jewish state—a slogan whose contents approached nearer and nearer the Weizmann program.

We have seen that, with the adoption of the land law, the issue of the anti-British struggle reawoke. This aroused bitter differences of opinion. And Ben-Gurion found himself in a minority among his comrades in Zionist work. His program for the fight after the promulgation of the law (February 28, 1940) was based upon the assumption that "for us, war on the White Paper now takes precedence over anything else"[10]; the view that only the Arabs could hurt the government had to be smashed. The aides of the executive's chairman were then being restrained from any improvement in relations with the Arabs in order to prevent the slightest impression that, under a White Paper regime, peace and understanding would prevail in the country.[11]

In Ben-Gurion's view, opposition to the White Paper meant doing all possible injury to the government. Ben-Gurion rejected the argument that such a struggle would give aid to Hitler. His line of reasoning was: If the government becomes convinced that our fight causes it damage, it will repent. Ben-Gurion emphasized that he was a "patriot of the British Empire, a great anglophile, and may our lot always fall with the British Empire." But he was first of all a Jew, and "the problem of the Jewish people comes before anything else." In this vein, Ben-Gurion formulated what he labeled "clandestine policy—serious and protracted unrest in the country . . . fine for fine, punishment for punishment."[12]

There could be no two ways about it—these words could only mean a full return to the Special Squads policy. But of all the members of the Agency Executive, only Rabbi Maimon and Menachem Ussishkin (the latter, serving *ex officio* as chairman of the Zionist Actions Committee, had no vote) lent their support. The others including Sharett were, for various reasons, in opposition. It was difficult to imagine a forceful struggle against Britain during the war with Hitler—taking into consideration world public opinion as well as British, and even Jewish, public opinion. Nor were there many chances for success in such a fight while all the forces of the empire were mobilized. The severe economic crisis in Palestine (sixteen thousand unemployed) did not make the situation any easier.

It was also clear that any action taken in the country, against the wishes of the government, would be met by the military censor with silence or distortion. The demonstrations against the land law served as quite a convincing example of this. Very likely, the idea of battling the British could have come only during the period of the *Sitzkrieg,* the "tranquil" initial phase of the war between September 1939 and April 1940. During the later stages of the war, even Ben-Gurion did not repeat his demand for a sharp struggle. Eliezer Kaplan, the agency treasurer, expressed the opposition opinion with his remark that "the new path that has been proposed is, in my opinion, after long consideration, a shortcut, not to victory, but to the liquidation of our endeavors in this land" (Agency Executive session of April 8, 1940).

It appears that the religious party was divided on the issue of resistance to the British, and the secularist right-wingers tended to oppose the struggle. In Mapai, Ben-Gurion found himself in the middle of a stormy debate. Mapai contained one fiery advocate of the struggle, Berl Katznelson, who demanded nothing less than a Jewish state on both sides of the Jordan. Even his manner of presenting the issue was marked by a clearly military ring: We must learn from the Maccabees. Why did they win? Because the thing against which they fought struck at the apple of their eye, because they stressed that they were defending the dearest of all things. That is how the Jews must conduct themselves now. "You cannot say we shall have cooperation with the Arabs and the British. You do not defend the dearest of all things in that way!"[13]

Mapai's opposition in the Histadrut came mainly from Hashomer Hatzair, which had always been against "activism." In a session of the Actions Committee of Histadrut on April 25, 1940, Meir Ya'ari stated that they did not accept gloomy conclusions in regard to England; their role, he said, was to protect the Yishuv and wait for a better opportunity. At the present time there was no reason for a revolt—not only the English and the Arabs would fight against them, but a large portion of the Yishuv as well.

In contrast, Hashomer Hatzair proposed "responses connected with the entire upbuilding machinery," by which was meant defense of "illegal" immigration, settlement, and protection of weaponry.[14] This was also the opinion of Sharett.

In these circumstances, with opposition to his plans stirred up on every side and in order to confront his comrades with a decisive public act, Ben-Gurion took a grave step. He suddenly rose at the meeting of the Zionist Actions Committee (February 29, 1940) and, without having previously informed the executive, announced his resignation. At the executive session (held that very day) he said that his view was determined and his decision final, that a certain task had been placed upon him, and in light of the situation his conscience would not permit him to continue in office. In his opinion, Zionism, as it had been so far, no longer existed; he had his own Zionism. He was a soldier, ready to take on any duty assigned to him, but his membership on the Agency Executive could no longer be a subject for discussion.

We do not know the details of the negotiations that took place to make Ben-Gurion withdraw his resignation. At any rate, the Agency Executive formally rejected it; as a result, great efforts were exerted to appease Ben-Gurion. Despite his sudden announcement, Ben-Gurion continued to take part in several further clarification sessions with the executive (March 12, April 8, April 14), but these only served to deepen the disagreement. Ben-Gurion finally decided to go to London to gain an understanding of the details of Zionist policy there. He did not actually go to London as a member of the executive (from which he had resigned), but we may guess that he himself recognized the error he had committed. He did not refer again to the resignation announcement.

In the executive it was agreed to pass over the entire matter to the day's agenda, particularly since circumstances had suddenly undergone a fundamental change which made the idea of the struggle utterly unrealistic. This is quite clear from the very date on which Ben-Gurion arrived in London, May 1, 1940— about two weeks after the German invasion of Denmark and Norway and ten days before the invasion of the Low Countries. On May 10 Churchill came to power in England. Labour joined the government ("Morrison, Bevin, and several other friends of ours"), the "appeasers" went, and in their place came those with a supposedly different policy. Under these circumstances, new hopes in regard to England blossomed, even in Ben-Gurion's heart. On May 15, 1940, Weizmann and Ben-Gurion were received by Lord Lloyd, the new colonial secretary. Lloyd informed them that the White Paper remained in full force, but the two leaders, who stayed on in London, did not give up hope on him.

The summer months of 1940 were a difficult time to carry on real political activity in the beleaguered capital of Great Britain. It was just at that time, apparently, that the background of the quarrel between Weizmann and Ben-Gurion, to which the latter referred in a letter to his associates in Palestine, developed. At the beginning of September, Ben-Gurion went to the United States to see with his own eyes what could be done there in Zionist affairs. He left England with great anxiety in his heart.

Even in England Ben-Gurion had not yet accepted Weizmann's program. On July 15 he wrote against the federation concept that he had previously supported:

> I doubt if the time is right for "final" arrangements. In my opinion, there is one basic concern at present: Victory . . . the participation of the maximum Jewish force in the defense of Palestine and in bringing about Hitler's defeat—that, to my way of thinking, has to be our whole program of activity until the victory.[15]

Since February, a decisive turnabout had taken place in Ben-Gurion's position; from the view that one must fight against England during the time of war itself, his opinion had now become that cooperation with England at this time was, in and of itself, the be-all and end-all of a Zionist political program. This was Ben-Gurion's view until his second visit to the West, as we shall see later. Even when he accepted the program of a Jewish state in all western Palestine, Ben-Gurion looked upon the military problem as primary, while he considered the political program of lesser importance.

❧ *The Yishuv's Open Military Effort, 1939–1941*

In the cooperation of the Jews with the British Army during the period 1936–1939, friendly relations between the Yishuv and Britain reached their high point in Palestine. No wonder, then, that the Zionist leadership hoped to undermine the White Paper precisely by means of military cooperation with Britain during time of war. There is no doubt that many officers in the British Army saw the military value of the mobilization of the Jews of Palestine. But this was basically a Jewish matter—to the British it was nothing more than a matter of secondary importance, at best. In contrast, Jewish motives for military mobilization were many. There were three chief reasons:

First, the desire of many Jews to wreak their people's vengeance on the Nazi foe, plus the wish to protect Palestine from a Nazi invasion and an Arab uprising. Second, an armed Jewish force, even under British command, would add weight to the Zionist political battle and obligate the British to a certain reconsideration of the Jews at the end of the war. And third, a Jewish force would serve as a further stage in the process of military self-emancipation of the Yishuv. Military skill acquired in the war would certainly not be forgotten by the young people who had been mobilized.

From every point of view, therefore, there was deep Jewish interest in mobilization, especially since considerations of neutrality—which had given birth to not a few controversies during World War I—did not exist now. No Jew could be neutral in a war between Hitler and his enemies (except for the tiny Palestine Communist party).

As early as the period of the Arab rebellion, the idea of mobilizing Jews for the British Army poked up its head from time to time. At the time of the Saint James Conference (March 8, 1939), there was a conversation between the man who was responsible under the agency for the Jewish Settlement Police and General Barker, commander of British forces in Palestine. Barker was interested in the creation of a Jewish force of three battalions with about 3,600 men in all. The conversation got some attention in agency circles at the time, but it appears to have involved no more than information-gathering on the part of the government. There were witnesses to similar conversations even in 1938.

With the promulgation of the White Paper, even these hopes seemed to have been trampled. Yet Moshe Sharett pointed to the possibility of breaking through the wall of enmity precisely by military cooperation. Although the chiefs of the General Staff significantly influenced the crystallization of the White Paper policy, there was little opposition to mutual military effort with the Jews in London. Opposition centered in British military and civilian circles in Egypt and the Middle East in general.

Jewish military thought on the eve of the war turned in two directions. One was the organization of Palestinian units for local and regional defense; the other aimed for the creation of some sort of Jewish legion that would be placed under British authority. A program to mobilize Jewish volunteers from the United States for such a legion drew heavy opposition, even in Jewish circles. But this line of thought enchanted Weizmann and his associates because it had a basis in precedent from World War I and had been suggested to the British at the time of the Saint James negotiations.

After the Twenty-first Zionist Congress in August 1939, steps were taken to bring the aforementioned Jewish proposals before the responsible authorities in London and Jerusalem. It is interesting that the proposals advanced in the two places differed from one another. In a letter dated August 25, 1939, and sent one day earlier, Sharett in London suggested to the operations officer of the Imperial General Staff that forty thousand Jews be mobilized in Palestine for the defense of the country. He further proposed the creation of a unit of volunteers from all free Jewish communities, for service wherever needed, and the training of a cadre of officers for them (to be composed mostly of Palestinian Jews). Over against this, Dov Joseph and Dov Hos in Jerusalem made an offer to General Barker (August 29) to establish a Jewish unit for Palestine only. The British response was also different in each place. It was made clear to Sharett, in his talk with General Ironside, the chief of the Imperial General Staff, that there was no fundamental opposition to his program, but that its enactment would be postponed for a time. An entirely different impression was received in Jerusalem. There, Barker listened to the proposal and then

> asked us to take a look at the map hanging on the wall of his room. He pointed to Lebanon and Syria and said: "Here in the north are the French. I think you will agree that they are not going to attack us. Around Palestine there are all these Arab countries. Ibn Saud feels that it is not healthy for him, for the present at least, to assault us. As for [Amir] Abdullah here in Transjordan, we can safely go even further. In Iraq the situation is the same as in Saudi Arabia."

If a Jewish force were assembled in Palestine—and the British (Barker claimed) had neither arms nor equipment for such a force—they would be forced to employ it immediately to put down an Arab uprising that would certainly break out because of it.

> If that's how it would work out, we would be fighting one great war, another war against the Arabs all around Palestine, and a third war against the revolting Arabs of the country. Gentlemen, three wars at once are too much for me. One is enough. Last night Nashashibi came to offer me the service of Arabs in the British Army. What would you say if we had mobilized ten Arab battalions?

Finally, he stated that he did not know whether or not there would be a war and if there were, what position Italy would assume in it. If there were need for Jewish forces, he would know to whom to turn. And, at any rate, he was grateful for the suggestion.[16]

This conversation makes the position of British higher officialdom in the East eminently clear. For what is the meaning of Barker's words? He is saying: It is possible that we will need you. If it turns out that way, there is no doubt that you will respond to our demands because, look, you have no other choice. However, we are afraid of Arab reactions if a Jewish unit is established; therefore we have no interest in one.

This concept of the generals contained much of the over-simplification characteristic of the attitudes inherited from the celebrated Lawrence of Arabia. From that point of view, it seemed that there were millions of heroic Arab fighters with their thoughts centered on nothing but the problem of the Jews in Palestine, ready to attack Britain the moment she created a Jewish military unit. Barker's approach was marked, also, by a measure of complacency and misplaced self-confidence that, naturally, waned during the course of the war. From Barker's words one could gather—and the words were uttered repeatedly afterward—that Jewish units were a vital matter for the Jews but were of no vital military (to say nothing of political) interest to the British Army.

Two days before the outbreak of war, Weizmann wrote Chamberlain a letter in which he offered the services of the Jewish people in the approaching conflict. Chamberlain's reply was rather noncommittal and vague. Immediately thereafter, negotiations began on the mobilization of Jewish refugees in England into special Jewish units. The negotiations ended in complete failure. Similar was the fate of another discussion, carried on by Dr. Nahum Goldmann with the French government for the creation of a Jewish force in France. This was to be composed of refugees and volunteers from the United States (although American neutrality statutes heaped difficulties in the way of assembling volunteers in the United States).

At that time, propaganda emphasizing the war against Hitler was carried on in the Jewish community in Palestine, as if the White Paper did not exist. In September 1939 a popular muster was organized in which more than 136,000 men and women were enrolled, demonstrating the potential power of the Yishuv. This muster had no results. The masses who signed up had expected that their willingness would be turned to some use or that some actions would be taken, but these were slow in coming.

In the fall of 1939, three proposals were made to the Jewish Agency for Palestine on military matters. The proposals expressed the intent of the authorities to pursue the White Paper policy even in the matter of military mobilization by not recognizing Jews, but only "Palestinians." It was suggested that mixed local Jewish-Arab units be created; the establishment of mixed units of trench diggers ("Pioneers") to be sent to the western front was proposed; and the proposal was also made to enlist technicians and skilled workers as replacements for British units that were not up to strength. On the issue of mixed units and trench diggers, negative responses were received from Weizmann, Wingate, and Sharett in London. In Palestine opinions were divided. There were some who were inclined to accept these proposals.

The Pioneer unit was finally raised by the British, without agency participation. The severe economic crisis in Palestine affected many people, and the unit was formed, partly of unemployed. It contained various elements, among others a great many Revisionists. It was sent to France, and dug fortifications there until the invasion of the German armies in May and June 1940. Most of the unit, still largely unarmed, managed to obtain some arms, and it was ordered to defend the approaches to St. Malo harbor as long as it could. Under cover of this "noncombatant" unit, French and British soldiers left St. Malo, leaving the Jews to fight at the perimeter (June 17/18) until they, too, extricated themselves and boarded small craft; most of them managed to reach Britain. There the unit was reorganized and sent to the Middle East, where some of its men (including a large number of Revisionist members) transferred to the Fifty-first Commando unit in the Middle East. This unit fought valiantly in key battles in Eritrea (1941).

Enlistment for the technical units was carried out by the agency, beginning October 17, 1939. The agency hoped that these units might, in the course of time, develop into large Jewish formations. However, in the meantime, there were only the beginnings. The requirements of the official Jewish bodies in this direction were still unfulfilled.

At that time, there began in London the exertion of pressure on government elements in order to advance the cause of the Jewish fighting force. On August 19, 1939, Weizmann met with Churchill. The latter had now been appointed first lord of the admiralty. Churchill earnestly agreed to the arming of the Jews of Palestine and asked that a memorandum be handed him on the subject.

There arose the serious question of sending Palestinians— both the Pioneers and the proposed larger Jewish formation— to the western front. In the top echelon of the Yishuv, opinions were divided. After a fierce debate and under pressure from Sharett, a resolution not to prevent the stationing of Palestinian Jews on the western front was accepted in the Agency Executive. In Mapai, Golomb shared Sharett's opinion; for while it would not do to send a large force outside the borders of the country, it was desirable to discuss a "smaller nucleus." But Katznelson, Hashomer Hatzair, and the Left within Mapai were all among the bitter opponents of the idea.

It was finally decided not to send men from Palestine to fronts in the west. As a result of the decision, Sharett wrote General Barker expressing the willingness of the agency to mobilize Jews for the defense of Palestine and adjacent areas, but emphatically opposing their transfer to the west (except for the men of the technical units, on whose status negotiations were then being conducted). The agency markedly softened its stand when the first positive echoes arrived from London about the Jewish Pioneer units that had been sent to the western front. At the beginning of November, the Agency Executive agreed, by a majority vote, to the sending of the nucleus of a Palestinian unit to the western front, within the framework of a broader program for a large unit of Diaspora Jews that would be fighting there.

What was this broader program? As early as the beginning of October when Sharett went to London, the opinion was expressed in the executive (especially by Professor Namier) that the political attack on the military issue must be renewed. Namier proposed bringing the demand out in the open. The demand would be supported by the pressure of public opinion on the part of all pro-Zionist elements in the Western world. Its basic concept would be the sending of a large Palestinian force to the west. The second part of the idea encountered stiff opposition from Ben-Gurion (who reached London on November 13). We have seen that even the Agency Executive in Jerusalem gave its consent only for a Palestinian nucleus around which others would assemble.

The influence of Wingate and Sharett was decisive. They were demanding an aggressive Palestinian policy. In the middle of November the program received its final form. It contained several provisions: the raising of a Jewish force in Palestine for the defense of the country; the raising of a volunteer Jewish force from all the free and neutral lands of the world (this to compose a Jewish division in which a Palestinian nucleus would serve); and the training of a cadre of officers for this division (their number was set by Wingate at a minimum of' five hundred men).

One could argue that this division, proposed as a general

service unit to be employed on any front where needed, presented an insufficient guarantee for the security of the Jewish community of Palestine. To that Wingate replied that the main thing was the creation of the unit. A division in existence would not be easily demobilized, but on the other hand forces would gather to prevent its creation. At the British pace of action, in Wingate's opinion, the unit would come into being just about the time the war reached the Middle East, and then they would employ it there.

In the middle of November meetings were held between Weizmann and Ironside, together with the latter's aide, Colonel MacLeod. They both showed great understanding for the cause, but they held out for one qualitative change in the Jewish proposal: the negotiations should not be accompanied by any publicity whatsoever. The executive agreed, and in so doing, practically negated the whole point of Namier's plan. On December 1, 1939, the agency presented a memorandum containing the proposals for the raising of a division from Palestine and the Diaspora for general service and the preparation of cadres (mostly from Palestine) in England.[17] The second part of the program—the creation of a Palestinian force for the defense of that country—was not mentioned in the document.

A positive reply was received from Colonel MacLeod on the memorandum. However, the difficulty of carrying out the plan for a division became apparent in a talk between Weizmann and General Wavell in London (December 8, 1939). Wavell, who was not to be counted among the anti-Zionists, voiced doubts and fears based on a dread of "what will the Arabs say?" The measure of that terror's influence is already well known to us. In the middle of December Weizmann left England, and there was no progress on the division issue until the spring of 1940. The wheels of the British military machine inched along throughout those last months of the "phoney war."[18]

With the Nazi invasion of the Low Lands and the fall of France, the political situation underwent a fundamental change.

Churchill came to power in England. MacDonald's place as colonial secretary was taken by Lord Lloyd, who was a friend of Churchill's, a pro-Arab but not an anti-Zionist extremist. More important than the change of characters on the political stage was the shifting of entire sets. The debate over a division that would fight on the western front became an academic quibble, for no such front existed any longer. Italy's entry into the war (June 10, 1940) placed Palestine on the front line and increased the military value of the Jewish element in Palestine. But the event also made the danger of an Arab uprising more apparent.

Weizmann, who had returned from the United States, was joined by Ben-Gurion, who went to London from Palestine at the beginning of May. The two leaders' activity bore fruit. On May 31 Lloyd informed the Jews of Britain's agreement in principle to the creation of a large Jewish unit outside Palestine. On June 15 Lloyd wrote Weizmann that there would be no opposition on Lloyd's part to the plan for a division, should Weizmann place such a plan before the War Office.[19] At this point, the first negotiations were closed. Despite Zionist efforts to hasten the decision, there was no further progress until the fall.

In the meanwhile, the Zionist Executive continued to press for military units in Palestine. Once more it was Weizmann who represented Jewish demands in a letter to Lloyd (June 15). In addition to the demand for a home guard in Palestine, further requests were expressed:

(a) To organize a maximum number of Jewish units through the official Jewish bodies and to supply them with arms on the responsibility of those bodies;

(b) To permit the agency to obtain help of all types from the Jews of the Diaspora for the Yishuv; and

(c) To instruct the government of Palestine to look upon the Jewish community there as an ally of Britain and encourage mutual cooperation in the country's defense.

Ben-Gurion in his talk with Lloyd (July 3), and Weizmann

in a letter to Churchill (August 6), repeated this demand. But it was far easier for the anti-Zionist officialdom to agree to a unit made up mostly of Jews from the neutral countries (whose area of service would not be predetermined) than to lend a hand in arming the Jews of Palestine. In both official and unofficial talks the excuse was also raised that, after the end of the war, the Jews might use the weapons given them for evil. This was a reference to the possibility of a Jewish revolt against England or to Jewish domination over Palestine by force, or the two things together. Such aims were, indeed, not foreign to the thinking of numerous sections of the Yishuv. But in London an attempt was, of course, made to explain to Lord Lloyd that his fears were groundless.

Nevertheless, those very fears constituted a turning point in British thinking. We have seen that at the time of Saint James, the British derided the notion of Palestine as a military factor. It was hinted that there was nothing to fear in the threats of revolt that were then being uttered by the Jewish representatives. Now the picture had changed. From 1940 on, British dread of the actions of the Jewish underground would continually grow stronger. The British assumption that there was nothing to fear from the Jews had had an effect on the establishment of the White Paper policy. Jewish opposition, or a reappraisal that looked upon such as a serious factor, once again brought about a change in the basic assumptions of British policy in Palestine. Here, for the first time, we meet with that reappraisal in such a striking form.

We do not know exactly what moved various English elements to make concessions in this matter during the summer of 1940. One gets the impression that the grave war situation and Churchill's pressure were among the decisive factors. In his memoirs Churchill publishes a good many documents (letters to Anthony Eden, June 6, 1940; Lloyd, June 25; and Wavell, August 12, among others) which testify that efforts were made on his part to put arms into the hands of the Jews of Palestine. How they answered him and how the program to arm the Jews of Palestine was transformed into a pitiful plan to raise two battalions (one Jewish and one Arab, on a "parity" basis, within the framework of a British regiment), there is no knowing for the time being.[20] At any rate, it is a fact that on August 6, 1940, the war secretary informed Parliament of the creation of such units within the Kentish regiment of the Royal Fusiliers (the Buffs).

The Jews did not accept Ben-Gurion's demand to reject this British proposal and refuse to participate in the enlistment. In September in Jerusalem, Sharett succeeded in extracting a promise from General Neame, the G.O.C. in Palestine, that these units would remain in Palestine and not be sent beyond the borders of the country (September 14). After the announcement on the establishment of the Buffs battalions, the effort for the division was renewed. To Weizmann and Ben-Gurion it seemed the most important matter and the most likely opportunity. On September 3 Weizmann met with Churchill. The latter agreed to support a five-point program formulated by Weizmann. By this plan, the division was transferred, in practice, to the Middle East—through a provision to train the officers in Egypt. The program spoke also of the establishment of "desert units" in keeping with Wingate's suggestion. The term "commando" was not yet used, but the intent was for a unit that would operate behind enemy lines. Wingate saw himself as future commander of this unit. This plan was never carried out. Although units of this type were created, and Jews even had a role in them, the original aim was not attained.[21]

Progress was once more made through Churchill's influence —not, to be sure, in the direction of creating Jewish units in Palestine, but in line with the original policy: the raising of a division for general service. On September 13 (and again on the 18th) Anthony Eden, the British war secretary, announced his agreement to the plan. On October 17 Lloyd wrote Weizman that the program had been accepted.

In these talks there was agreement that the proposed division be designated for service in Palestine and adjacent areas; it appeared that the boldest hopes of the leaders of Zionism were about to be fulfilled. The remaining steps seemed nothing more than mere formalities. On December 31 a commanding officer was appointed for the division, and he vigorously began the necessary preparations. At the same time, negotiations went forward on the wording of the public announcement of the units formation, questions of pay, kosher food, flags, anthems, marching songs, and many more such items. Details of future steps to be taken to enlist Jews in neutral countries for the unit were also specified.[22]

It seemed highly probable, therefore, at the end of 1940 and the beginning of 1941, that the formation of the division would go through; it was as good as certain. In light of Eden's promise on its locality of service, the fear that the Palestinian section of the unit would leave for some distant front was automatically refuted. The great hope for large-scale cooperation with Britain was about to be realized. And the line that affirmed cooperation seemed to claim a brilliant victory. Once more it had been demonstrated that one must not utterly despair of England. (And, indeed, if the program had been carried through, political conditions absolutely different from those actually created would have been brought into existence.)

The two outstanding aspects of the situation were the nearness of political victory and the utter secrecy that surrounded the entire program. The general public knew nothing of the chain of events, and the second rank of the leadership took a sort of doubtful attitude about the matter because it had no idea how near the program was to enactment.

It is interesting that it was Lord Lloyd's death (February 4, 1941) that upset the plan. On February 8, Lord Moyne, an anti-Zionist, was named colonial secretary. Of him it may be said, "He knew not Joseph." While Lloyd had supported the program and, in practice, had become its patron, Moyne tended to accept the arguments of officials and officers in the Middle East who opposed the division—or indeed any Jewish force. The disagreements were brought before Churchill precisely during the period in which he was pressing General Wavell to accept the program of defending Greece from the Nazi invasion. Wavell opposed that program. And Churchill refrained from worsening relations with him on an additional point—like the creation of a Jewish division designed to serve in the Middle East, Wavell's region of command. Churchill gave in to pressure under protest—to which he gave voice in a letter to Moyne (March 1, 1941).[23]

Churchill demanded that Weizmann not be told the true reason for the postponement of the plan and that he be promised that in four months it would be reexamined. And, indeed, a letter in that vein was sent Weizmann on April 3, 1941. In the meantime, Wavell and Miles Lampson, the British ambassador in Egypt, pressed energetically for a final cancellation of the program. An exchange of telegrams between Cairo and London which fell into the hands of the agency shows clearly the focal point of opposition to the division program.[24]

On August 28 Moyne wrote Weizmann a second letter in which he gave notice of the program's postponement and noted that the program itself was impractical at the moment. As a result of this development and the protracted delays, Weizmann demanded, in a conversation with Moyne (September 1), a conclusive answer to his proposals. To reinforce his arguments he wrote another memorandum to Churchill (September 10), in which he again put forward all the reasons for the establishment of the division. The memorandum bore no fruit. On October 15 the final answer was received. It stated that after a fundamental discussion in the cabinet, it had been decided to cancel the program altogether.

On November 9, 1941, Weizmann held a press conference on the failure of the negotiations. This was the first time that the Jewish community had heard any authoritative announcement about this vital business, which had been going on for two years behind the scenes.

The sad affair had a sad end. On November 25 a debate on the Jewish army took place in the House of Lords. Moyne claimed that the program had been agreed upon only in principle. Important questions had remained to be discussed. And Weizmann's impulsiveness (his desire to have an answer in the fall of 1941) was what brought on the final negative reply. Moyne rehashed the reasons (as he had detailed them in a letter of October 15, 1941) which had compelled him to say nay: difficulties of supply and equipment, lack of shipping (due to obligations to the Soviet Union), and so on. As a result of this pronouncement, an exchange of letters developed between Moyne and Weizmann. Weizmann charged him with distortion of the facts and asserted that the plan had been on the verge of practical implementation. Weizmann charged that its cancellation constituted a gross breach of faith. Naturally, Lord Moyne refused to admit all this. High hopes ended in bitter disappointment.[25]

At this point it is proper to mention another matter which was unknown at the time, even to many within the Zionist leadership itself—the relationship between the two leading Zionist statesmen, Weizmann and Ben-Gurion. We are aware that as early as 1940 and 1941, relations between them were deteriorating. Dr. Weizmann was the recognized representative of Zionism in London; and Ben-Gurion, of necessity, took second place. The president was not always fastidiously candid even with his friends. At times his most intimate friends did not know of business he was carrying on. Of course, similar assertions were uttered by various elements about Ben-Gurion as well, and certainly with no less justification.

Ben-Gurion claimed in three memorandums[26] that Weizmann did not place sufficient stress on demands for the creation of a Jewish unit in Palestine. But the truth is that the demands for the division and for a Palestinian force were generally being voiced at one and the same time. Ultimately, the two demands converged in the drive for the establishment of a division for the Middle East. Ben-Gurion participated in Weizmann's negotiations for a Jewish formation in Palestine in the spring of 1940, and he shared in the accomplishment that resulted (the Buffs). His second complaint centered on the general slovenliness which, in his opinion, marked the political activity in London.

Insofar as these claims can be checked today, it is hard to see anything substantial to them. One might say that both personal differences of opinion and the sense of helplessness of the Jewish delegation in the face of intransigent British hostility were what deeply embittered the relationship between the two Zionist leaders.

Another point in Ben-Gurion's criticism of Weizmann was that it was a mistake not to give publicity to the division demand and not to turn the issue of the Jewish force into a *cause célèbre* against the government (perhaps because of Weizmann's political relations with British government personalities). In this case, there may have been substance to the arguments against Weizmann. Whether in response to this criticism or not, Weizmann did accept the policy of political action coordinated with publicity and public influence—after the failure of negotations in October 1941.

In light of the grave events in the area (the losses of Greece, Crete, and North Africa), a policy crystallized in London whereby nothing likely to determine the future of Palestine was to be done until the end of the war. Eden delivered a comprehensive speech in London on May 29, 1941. He supported the idea of Arab unity and called upon the Arabs to work in that direction. But he avoided mentioning the Palestine problem. Moyne, himself, related[27] that pressure was being exerted on him to carry out all the provisions of the White Paper to the letter—in order to win the friendship of the Arab extremists.

It would seem that the establishment of the division had been pictured to him as a change in the status quo, and he expressed satisfaction at having successfully "frozen" the Palestine problem—he postponed both the implementation of the White Paper and the formation of the Jewish division. Thus he considered that he had thereby observed the British tradition of statesmanship without favoritism.

Meanwhile, voluntary enlistment continued in Palestine, encouraged with all the propaganda means within the power of the agency. Up to the end of 1941, 10,881 Jewish soldiers were enlisted for all services of the British forces.

We shall not follow the development of the mobilization for the British Army, or the problems it stirred up, in any detail. But we may not ignore the debate over the place of this mobilization in the overall field of Zionist policy.

Hashomer Hatzair, the opposition party to Mapai in the Histadrut, asserted that Jewish soldiers should not be taken outside Palestine as long as the country's security was not assured. This position was summarized on July 7, 1940, in a Hashomer Hatzair draft resolution in Histadrut which required "the creation of independent Jewish units and the broadening of the Supernumerary Police Force, to be ready, in cooperation with the British, to defend the Yishuv and the country. After defense of the land and the Yishuv is guaranteed, the Histadrut shall be prepared to consider the sending of certain auxiliary units to nearby countries" (for the air force, and so on).

If the intent was to defend Palestine, then from a strategic point of view there was no possibility of so doing within the borders of the country, unless the front approached those borders (as happened in 1942). There were opinions, even in Hashomer Hatzair, which would have set a policy of this type. Meir Ya'ari stated that he would not oppose sending soldiers to foreign soil on the condition that they be given weapons (that is, that they be constituted as fighting formations—but that was precisely what the British were against). "I am prepared to enter a discussion on what the borders are. But we must not budge from the position that the defense of the Yishuv and the country are our A to Z [or rather] A to W; you have X, Y, and Z left."[28]

The Hagana itself understood well the necessity of conserving the strength of the Yishuv. This was obvious (as we have seen above) both in the negotiations for units inside the country as well as in the negotiations for the creation of the division. But in this argument of Hashomer Hatzair was concealed a basic tendency which was not the possession of that party alone. Even in Mapai circles (in the Kibbutz Meuhad in particular) the view had taken root that the center of gravity in the military effort must be the defense of the country and, first and foremost, *self*-defense. "Our chief front is not in Libya or with units of trench diggers, but in the protection of our own settlements." One must not draft troops for the army at the expense of the Hagana; hence the opposition to "sending Jewish youths out of Palestine."[29] In discussions in the Executive Committee of Histadrut, Golomb and Jakob Riftin (Hashomer Hatzair) expressed fears that an overenthusiastic enlistment of Hagana members might weaken it seriously. Here, for the first time, there appeared the problem that was to deepen in gravity during the next few years: the Hagana versus enlistment in the army.

In 1940 the static Hagana, with the grass growing under its feet, could not serve as banner and symbol for those who were fervently striving under the slogan of mobilization for war against Hitler. But the fundamental concept of the opposite approach stood out in Tabenkin's statement:

If we reach the point where we have no value here without the English, then, even in the eyes of the English, we shall have no value. [The framework of Jewish power], the political and factual center for us, is the independent Hagana. That must serve as our springboard. . . . I say straight out, our independent army is more important than any under British authority.

In summation he said that the Jews must mobilize for the British Army, "but let us do it with common sense."[30]

The essence of the debate was not whether Jewish soldiers should or should not be sent to foreign soil. On this point the leadership and the opposition were not so divided—as becomes clear from the stand of many Mapai people in the central institutions during their negotiations with British elements. In these negotiations they frequently advance the opinion that as few Jewish soldiers as possible must be sent out of the country. The focus of the controversy lay rather in the fact that Sharett and his associates looked upon the Hebrew units in the British Army as a potential Jewish army, not accepting Tabenkin's argument that as long as the command was British this was not a Jewish army. The difference of approach flowed from unlike evaluations of the tie to Britain. Ya'ari and Tabenkin saw that tie as a passing tactical phase or a painful fact; Sharett and Ben-Gurion viewed it favorably and hoped for its permanent continuation, on the condition that England back down from the White Paper policy.

◢ The Hagana and the Fight against the White Paper, 1939–1940

In the first two years of the war, the Hagana found itself in the throes of a crisis. At the beginning of the war, attempts had been made to organize the Hagana on lines set down by Ben-Gurion during the period of the Special Squads. A General Staff was formed, and attempts were made to wrench the active units away from the National Command and transfer them to the direct control of the Agency Executive chairman.

The Field Force, which was supposed to include 12,000 men according to plan, reached eleven battalions (at most), with a complement of 450 men each. The level of training was not high. It was stated that "this force is designed and trained for

active defense and definite military assignments in areas beyond
the bounds of local defense. The Field Force is detached from
any other formation and absolutely freed of local security demands." But in reality it was entirely otherwise. Ultimately,
the Hagana chief of staff put out a directive that stated that the
Field Force would have a commander who would serve as an
active liaison between the chief and the district commanders
(to whose command the Field Force was, in fact, subject). The
Field Squads episode was now to be repeated. In theory there
was to be a national formation; in practice, a localized one.
Nevertheless, the Field Force won over, and served as a refuge
for all those bold-spirited men of initiative who had been dis-
charged from the Field Squads and believed in active defense.

At the same time, the creation of a popular force (which
was also supposed to be broken away from the National Command) was being spoken of. This was to be a body of broad
compass, working in the open, with the goal of preparing young
Jews for military service. This plan was a complete failure,
both because of lack of funds and because the English, as we
already know, showed no desire to enlist the people of the
Yishuv in the British Army.

The National Command itself passed through a period of
severe crisis. Rattner left his position as its head at the beginning of the fall. Another "neutral" chairman was sought.
In November Ben-Gurion appointed the engineer Jacob Reizer,
who had worked until then on problems of settlement and was
far removed from security matters.

Reizer worked with the National Command to the best of his
ability. He did not succeed in overcoming the constant spats and
quarrels, but he set improved working arrangements. Directives
were sent out settling organizational problems, the division of
authority in the General Staff, and issues concerning the Field
Force. The entire Hagana was divided into eight districts; thus
its structure was improved. Later (September 5, 1940), three
regions were established—north, central, and south—to take

in seven of the eight districts (only the isolated Jerusalem district remained independent). These steps and the reorganization of the budget constituted a sizable achievement that has to be chalked up to Reizer and his team.

In June 1940 disagreements within the National Command reached their peak. Sitkov, a right-wing representative who stood for local autonomy and decentralization, was the focus of controversy. Fundamental differences between him and the Histadrut representatives brought the latter to a notice of resignation. Their goal was to bring about Sitkov's departure. This came before the Committee of Eight. Rokakh presented far-reaching political and organizational demands to the committee, including a call for the resignation of Reizer. Rokakh, being in the minority against all the rest of the committee members, withdrew from the committee and from his position as chairman of the Kofer Hayishuv as well. Thus in the summer and fall of 1940, three years after the Hagana had become reunited, a crisis was created that once again threatened to split the Hagana on the same lines as in the thirties. Rokakh's demand was that authority over the Hagana be delivered to the Kofer Hayishuv, which was supplying the financial means.

Meanwhile, four new members were appointed to the National Command: two people (one of them Levi Eshkol) representing the Left, Dr. Moshe Sneh for the "A" General Zionists, and one man for the orthodox. For the time being, Reizer continued to function as head of the National Command. There was a plan to add one or two representatives of the Left, and a discussion was conducted with the Hashomer Hatzair, which was demanding such position for itself.

The people of the Right did not look upon Sneh as their representative and insisted that all their representatives be appointed by the Middle-Class Union—a body that had been created by various economic organizations of the private enterprise sector, mainly to represent the middle class in negotiations over the composition of the security agencies. Mapai was ready to come to an agreement with the progressive General Zionists and the orthodox, so as not to find itself all alone with the Middle-Class Union in the National Command. And indeed, if the command was to articulate the principle of community control over the Yishuv security apparatus, the composition of its membership could not be confined solely to Mapai and the Middle-Class Union.[31]

In this situation, the Right opened a public attack on the Hagana. At the end of 1940 articles against the Left in the Hagana were published in right-wing newspapers (*Haaretz, Hamashkif,* and *Haboker*). They opposed the concept of national defense and attacked the Hagana in general. The most extreme position was taken by Moshe Smilanski of Rehovot in two articles in *Haaretz* (November 5 and November 19, 1940). He took issue with the Histadrut concept, which looked upon the Hagana as the security arm of the Yishuv—and he stressed the independent character of the organization:

> The weapon is only for time of need, for difficult periods, few and passing, and not, heaven forbid, as a permanently standing phenomenon. For any weapon, if standing permanently, even if created for pure purposes, will be converted by its very permanency into a sword of the Devil. . . . Seventy-five percent of the money for security is now wasted.

On November 15 *Haaretz* printed an article in which the particulars of the quarrel were set before the public—and the C.I.D. This was a unique event in the history of the Yishuv and its press, an event that could have lead to the gravest consequences for the Hagana, its chiefs, and commanders. Of course, the Hagana responded sharply to this development and published illegal leaflets criticizing this method of propaganda. But the damage was done. In spite of it all, negotiations between the parties did not halt, but continued until the spring of 1941.

Just at this nadir in the Hagana's fortunes, the agency was confronted with one of the gravest security crises in its history, an attempt by the authorities to break the Hagana once and for all. The Mandatory government had known of the existence of the Hagana all along. Time and again, the government had carried on negotiations with the official Jewish institutions to put an end to the Hagana (most recently in 1935). However, national instinct and wisdom prevented the abandonment of the nucleus of an independent Jewish armed force. At the time of the Arab riots, the government did not openly oppose the Jewish self-defense organization, which was lending a hand against the rebels. This condition changed radically after the outbreak of World War II. The government viewed this as the right moment for the liquidation of the Hagana. From a formal point of view, the government's stand was superficially logical. In no country can there normally exist an armed force which is not an instrument of the government and subject to its discipline. In the past, riots and unrest justified, to a substantial degree, the existence of the Jewish force. But now that justification was removed. The Arab rebellion was over, and a large British Army occupied the country. Jewish settlers had no need to fear for their own safety. Such were the regime's arguments. Furthermore, British suspicion had been aroused (as we have already perceived in the dealings carried on in London over the division) that the force, which had been moderate and pro-British, might take a different position under White Paper rule, and the weapons in its hands could be used in actions against the British.[32]

At the end of September of 1939, the Hagana set up an officers' training course. Ninety of the best leaders in Palestine participated in it. They were veterans of the Field Squads and the Special Night Squads. The purpose was to prepare a cadre of commanders for the Field Force. For security reasons, the course was transferred from Kefar-Vitkin to Yavniel. Several police officers made a surprise visit and were, apparently, unimpressed by the explanation that this was purely an athletic training program. It was therefore decided to move the course to the vicinity of Ein-Hashofet. Some of the participants (with

Yigal Allon at their head) took a side road and reached their objective safely. But the forty-three others (including Moshe Carmel and Moshe Dayan) were captured by a patrol of the Transjordan frontier force near Sharona and arrested. Their imprisonment—and the trial that followed—came as a hard blow to the leaders of the Yishuv who had not succeeded in coordinating their thinking with the new course of British policy. Ben-Gurion requested a meeting with General Barker (November 1). Barker refused to forgo either the trial or the punishment of the prisoners. Furthermore, he demanded that the Hagana be disbanded and even threatened its destruction by force.

The same regime, the same commander, and the very same army that knew how to close their eyes, encouraging the Hagana and even working with it when that was expedient, did not hesitate for a moment to be amazed at the Hagana's existence and enraged to the "depths of their being" that the Jews could justify it. Barker was the first—but not the last—who set forth the argument that the arms of the Hagana might serve enemy agents, a fifth column, or Revisionists. The intent of the authorities to deny the Yishuv the practical potential of opposing government policy was rather obvious.

Yet even at the summit of the British Army, opinions were divided on the matter. Ironside—and during a certain period even Wavell—opposed arms searches and confiscations in the Jewish community. Ironside made an effort to lighten the sentences pronounced on the forty-three prisoners ("the Forty-three") and even promised to free them "after a short while." The concept of a short while appears to have been relative, in that the Forty-three went free only in February 1941, after sixteen months' imprisonment. The Hagana had now learned a vital lesson. From now on, it conducted its affairs by the rules of conspiracy.[33]

After the imprisonment of the Forty-three came additional arrests and searches. On November 17 thirty-four Etzel people and four Supernumerary Policemen (who were also Betar members) were arrested while in a training exercise near Mishmar-Hayarden; the agency made efforts to free them. Ten men from Kibbutz Ginossar were arrested; they had defended their fields against an Arab raid, killing one of the marauders. On January 14, 1940, a search was carried out at Mishmar-Hashelosha and arms were found. On January 22 there was a search at the youth village of Ben-Shemen, where a magazine was uncovered. (We may safely assume that an informer was involved, because the police went straight to the secret caches in which the arms were concealed. Despite great efforts, no trace of the informer has been found, and the matter remains a mystery.)

At Ben-Shemen several local people were arrested, including the institution's director, Dr. Ernst Lehmann, a close friend of Martin Buber and a known proponent of pacifist and internationalist ideas. At the trial, which was held April 15–23, 1940, counsel did not defend the Hagana but only the accused themselves. This approach caused great resentment in both the Agency Executive and Histadrut circles. It was remarked at the time that one must publicly defend the Hagana's right to exist. Accordingly, the press subsequently stood by the Ben-Shemen people. In the community actions (strikes and petitions) taken as a result of the sentence, some expression was given to the feeling of identification of the Yishuv with its security arm.

But the foregoing episodes were nothing more than skirmishes before a far vaster battle. Lieut. Gen. Giffard, Barker's successor, demanded that the Hagana turn over its arms to the British. A clear reference to British intentions had already been contained in MacDonald's remarks to Ben-Gurion in their meeting of November 15, 1939. Since rebellious acts by the Arabs had ceased, there was a large British Army in the country, and great quantities of ammunition had also been confiscated from the Arabs, he asked "How can His Majesty's government tolerate the presence of secret arms and underground military organizations among the Jews?" He said that he knew that the overwhelming majority of the Yishuv took an attitude of boundless friendship to the British; perhaps they opposed the White Paper, but they remained good friends of Britain. Nevertheless, it was possible that there were some Jews who aspired to acquire arms in order to dominate Palestine, not out of enmity toward Britain, but rather because they wanted a country of their own. The British government could not permit this. It did not wish a repetition of the Arab rebellion. It would be a very grave thing for the Allies. The British had to conduct themselves in the same manner toward both parties.

The new commander, Giffard, apparently decided to use kid gloves to achieve his ends. However, the high commissioner (according to Sharett's appraisal in the Agency Executive) preferred the mailed fist. The first explicit information regarding the regime's intentions was given to Pinchas Rutenberg, head of the Vaad Leumi (National Council), by the first secretary of the government (Macpherson) in the second half of April. Rutenberg, apparently, stated that he would advise the Jews not to surrender their arms. To that Macpherson replied that "the government had decided to take the arms away from the Jews." At the end of April Sharett had a talk with Giffard himself, and, once again, there were allusions to the commander's intention of pressing more vigorously in the search for weapons. On May 10, 1940, a talk between Sharett and MacMichael took place. Sharett forcefully stood by the Jewish refusal, while trying to assuage British fears of Jewish rebelliousness. "To our despair, there is an opinion in government circles that the Jews may use their arms in revolt. We were shocked to hear this from the commander. . . . If they take arms from the Jews by force, who knows whether they might not push the Yishuv too far."

But Sharett's threats were to no avail. On May 15 the commander invited the representatives of the Yishuv to talk with him. The two chief rabbis took part along with Sharett for the

Agency Executive, Yitzhak Ben-Tzvi for the National Council, representatives of Hapoel Hamizrahi, the Agudath Israel, the Revisionists, and Dr. Judah Magnes. The very invitation itself testified to a desire to bypass the elected institutions of the Yishuv and the Zionist movement and to deal with representatives appointed for this purpose by the authorities, with malice aforethought, to crumble the Jews' opposition to governmental steps. The commander demanded that the Jews hand over their weapons to the authorities, and he set a further clarification meeting for May 30.

That meeting was attended by Sharett, Ben-Tzvi, and Rabbis Maimon and Porush. The commander gave notice that he could not rest easy as long as he knew that in the country there were arms over which he had no control. In passing he suggested that the Jews at least inform him of the numbers of weapons in their possession. (Here it must be recalled that those were the days of the fall of France and of Italy's entrance into the war. It was not easy to take a stand against the reasoning that, in time of war, one must not withhold information from the supreme military commander on the quantities of armament to be found in the country.)

Giffard's suggestion gave rise to heated discussions within the Jewish community. Sharett believed that if it were possible to reach an agreement with him they should tell him that "we are prepared to canvass the settlements and inquire after the quantity of weapons—on condition that he give assurance that the arms will not be taken away—that might be the way out." Other members of the Agency Executive sought to avoid a definite answer until the hoped-for division was confirmed in London. And there were some who said that there was no choice but to specify the number of weapons in the possession of the Hagana. The majority in the executive saw it as an inviolable condition that the general not take the arms but should only be informed of their existence.

On this issue a sharp debate also spread through Histadrut

circles. Ben-Gurion was then staying in London, and his position regarding the surrender of arms was decidedly negative. Berl Katznelson took an even more extreme position. He started young Hagana officers thinking of revolt against the Agency Executive and the Hagana command if surrender of arms were discussed. Considering Katznelson's deep influence over Hagana leaders, it must be assumed that if the agency had come out for reporting quantities of weapons, a major rift would have appeared between the Yishuv and the Hagana. Golomb, in contrast, argued that the numbers must be made available. Otherwise, the legalization of the Hagana by the British (a goal to which he looked forward) would never come. And without legalization, Hagana arms would never become effective arms.[34]

On June 14, 1940, a decisive meeting was held with the commander. It became speedily apparent that when quantities of armaments were made known to the general, he would not leave them in Jewish hands. He explained to the Jewish representative that he would have to take offensive weapons (like hand grenades and machine guns); of the rest, he would leave only a part. These arms would be reapportioned according to his preferences. At the same time, he undertook, as a concession on his part, not to decrease the number of Jews in the Supernumerary Police Force. Naturally, the Jews refused to deal with him on this basis. The general burst out in rage, accusing the Jews of not wanting to cooperate against the Nazis and looking only for narrow political advantages. When he finished speaking, he permitted no reply. With this, the meeting ended. The general never knew how close he had come to "making a substantial gain" by undermining the independence of the Hagana. Only his crude behavior had prevented it.[35]

Of course, any professional soldier would find it difficult to understand how civilians could defend their right to possess illegal arms in time of war. But Giffard's arguments contained an overdose of hypocrisy. For if the issue was mutual cooperation in the war against the Nazis and Jewish willingness to enlist in the army, it was well known that the Jews were most willing to take part as a nation at war but not as "hewers of wood and drawers of water." It was none other than the Palestine administration that, in Marlowe's words, "with almost unbelievable persistence devoted a large part of its fortunately inconsiderable energy and ability to preventing Palestinian Jews from fighting Hitler."[36]

At any rate, the grave fear was created (and further reinforced by Giffard's explicit warning on June 24) that, as a result of the bitter exchange of words, large-scale arms searches would begin.

At the crucial moment fate, apparently along with the high commissioner, intervened—this time in favor of the Jews. Giffard was transferred out of Palestine at the end of June. His successor, Godfrey-Austin, came at the beginning of July. He had been an officer in the Galilee during the Arab rebellion and was a friend of the Jews. Godfrey-Austin explicitly informed Sharett and Joseph that he had no intention of searching for Jewish arms or plotting against the Hagana—on condition that the agency, for its part, take care to halt training exercises that might lead to incidents such as that of the Forty-three. If there were no maneuvers, the army would not have to arrest the maneuverers; and the country would be quiet.

The entire episode took place in an unreal atmosphere, and not only on the English side. Sharett's position was that the agency knew nothing of an entity by the name of the Hagana. But it was vaguely aware that in Jewish settlement areas there were unlicensed defensive arms. Those responsible for the arms and numbers of weapons were unknown to the agency; to clarify these details, it would have to inquire in every settlement separately. Sharett specified to Giffard that the agency, as a legal body, could not know more and would even be consciously restrained from knowing more. This position was taken also by the Jewish Agency toward personalities who looked upon themselves as moderate intermediaries between the authorities and the Yishuv—people like Dr. Magnes, who was president of the Hebrew University. Magnes spoke to Giffard with such candor that this entire political fiction was almost wrecked. Sharett, therefore, wrote him a sharp letter on July 26, 1940, a letter in which the complexity of the agency position stands out.

It is correct to say that any other stand would have endangered both the agency and the Hagana. And if the agency had simply and truly surrendered its control over the Hagana, the wheels of progress would have been reversed and the national force would have been turned into a military clique working on its own initiative.

Despite the voiding of the ruling on arms searches, relations between the Yishuv and the government steadily deteriorated. The cancellation of the immigration quota at the end of 1939, the case of the Forty-three, the land law and its consequences, the Ben-Shemen trial, the demand for the arms—they were all links in the chain of relationship.

By chance, a tiny peephole has been opened on the government's (or at least the police's) position with the uncovering of C.I.D. reports on the Yishuv from 1939–1942. We can learn a great deal from these reports about the attitude of governmental officialdom toward the Jews, about the government's concept of security, and about other matters. We shall confine ourselves here to some general conclusions.[37]

It is clear that C.I.D. connections with the Revisionists and Etzel were very close. The whole terminology of the reports is decidedly Revisionist. Etzel and the New Zionists are called the "national movement," while the Hagana and the agency (including their rightist branches) are entitled "the Left." In the eyes of the secret police, Hashomer Hatzair and the Left Poale Zion were transformed into dangerous terrorist organizations, while Etzel and the Revisionists were favored with C.I.D. sympathy. C.I.D. looked on the Histadrut as a fascist organization under the domination of dictators, such as Ben-Gurion or the very moderate David Remez. The Histadrut sergeants-at-arms group was a gestapo (just so!); enlistment efforts were nothing but camouflage behind which lurked nefarious intentions to achieve "political advantages." However, this hardly reflected the opinions and the views of Ironside, Churchill, and even Lloyd or Halifax. John Bull was not made of one skin, and many were the spirits struggling inside him.

The worsening relationship between the authorities and the Yishuv deteriorated drastically with the *Patria* and Mauritius cases.

During 1940, small ships carrying unofficial immigrants tried to reach the shores of Palestine. In the summer of 1940 the condition of the Jews in Europe grew a hundredfold worse. Columns of refugees organized themselves in the ports of Rumania and Bulgaria in order to set sail for Palestine. One ship, the *Pencho,* ran aground off Rhodes; but three others (*Milos, Pacific,* and *Atlantic*) ploughed their way toward Palestine. In the beginning of November the *Milos* and the *Pacific* arrived at the port of Haifa. The agency was informed that these "illegals" were about to be expelled to the island of Mauritius, since their entry into Palestine would enrage the Arabs. On November 20 the expulsion order was issued. But meanwhile the Hagana—and Etzel as well—prepared an act of sabotage against the French ship *Patria,* to which the newcomers had been transferred for explusion. Munia (Meir) Mardor, a Hagana man, succeeded in smuggling explosives aboard the ship. But in the explosion that occurred on November 25, the ship swamped and sank because of an error in calculating its scantlings and the amount of effective explosives. More than 250 immigrants drowned in this chilling tragedy.

Meanwhile, the *Atlantic* had arrived in Palestine on November 24. The high commissioner later informed Sharett that the people saved from the *Patria* were about to be expelled with the "illegals" who had just come. The expulsion of the *Patria* survivors was prevented by the intervention of the authorities in London. But the *Atlantic* immigrants were expelled, on December 9, to Mauritius, after being very badly mistreated in the camp at Atlit. MacMichael, without receiving confirmation from his government, then published a government announcement proclaiming that the exiles would never be permitted to return to Palestine. It seemed that the torment had reached its peak. A chasm yawned between the Yishuv and the Mandatory regime.

3 ◢ The Beginnings of an Independent Jewish Force

◢ A Period of Cooperation—1940

The fact of mutual cooperation between the Hagana and the English in executing underground operations is no longer a classified secret. It is worth dwelling on this chapter, since it possesses an acknowledged importance that goes far beyond the few actions that were carried out under that policy. Those operations not only bespoke the possibility of a continuation of friendship and cooperation with the English, they also unlocked the door to aid and rescue missions in the Diaspora. Furthermore, they created a most vital thrust for the reestablishment—and this time on a firmer basis—of the nucleus of an independent Jewish force.

Before the war, amiable connections had been established between various Jewish personages (David Hacohen, director of the Histadrut Construction Company, Solel Boneh, among others) and British military leaders. One of the latter, Vice Admiral Godefroy, was appointed chief of British naval intelligence at the beginning of the war. By his initiative and that of Lord Melchett (head of I.C.I., the chemical monopoly), a friend of Weizmann's, connections were established between the agency in London and British departments engaged in all sorts of clandestine operations. At the beginning of 1940 these contacts reached the point, under the direction of Moshe Sharett, of David Hacohen's being invited to London to speak with the British about actual plans. However, he fell sick on the way and returned to Palestine.

Several weeks later, in March and April of 1940, he received instructions to go to Rumania. There he was to meet with George Taylor, an Englishman who was chief of operations for section M.O.4.* That department was engaged in the preparation of acts of sabotage and other anti-German activities in neutral countries where Nazi conquest seemed imminent. After consultations in Rumania and exploration of possibilities for action, they both went to London. A detailed discussion began there toward joint programs of M.O.4 and the agency.

Conditions at the front during the London talks gave aid to this mutual effort. The start of negotiations fell during the last days of Chamberlain's regime. They continued through the period of the great German victories in the west and Churchill's ascent to power in England. With Italy's entry into the war (June 10, 1940) several of the officers of the department were transferred to Cairo, and the talks went on there. One can almost formulate a law of British behavior toward the Jewish Agency and of the Yishuv toward the British war effort. During periods of relative quiet, the British avoided any step likely to be interpreted as helpful to the Jews and their cause, but in periods of crisis their attitude changed, and the Yishuv won gains (for which it had to do fierce battle when the immediate danger was past).

In the summer of 1940 the Jewish units in the Buffs were first confirmed, and the era of cooperation was opened. The British tried as hard as they could to get along without Jewish help, so as not to incur even moral-political obligations. But

* In 1942 the name was changed to Special Operations Executive (S.O.E.).

when the water reached their chins, they turned to the Jews. The same scene was to be reenacted in the summer of 1941 and once again in the summer of 1942. In the Jewish community, too, response to the agency's calls to volunteer for the British Army depended largely on the state of the war. For example, out of 6,534 enrolled up to the end of 1940, 3,108 had enlisted during the months of July, August, and September of 1940. In sum, cooperation tended to occur in times of danger of invasion in the Middle East. The same was true of the Yishuv's response. Community responsibility and the willingness to act appeared only in times of crisis. Cooperation was connected with the deterioration of general conditions at the fronts.

Cooperation with intelligence agencies was fostered, also, by the kind of men who represented the British. They were civilians recruited for their positions for the duration of the war only. They hoped for a quick victory, and the tortuous ways of British policy in the Middle East disgusted them. Taylor was typical of these men. He had an independent character and sharp mind, and he became a friend of the Zionist project. M.O.4 recognized the agency as an ally, something that was very desirable for the Jews as a precedent at the time because of the negotiations for the division that were then going on. No wonder the M.O.4 people sometimes tangled with the Middle East staff people because of the department's routinely straightforward approach to the Jews of Palestine. It is natural, from the Jewish point of view, that M.O.4 men were welcome partners in the negotiations.

At a certain stage of the dealings taking place in London, Lord Melchett (then chief of the world Maccabi—a Jewish sports organization) sought to transfer this entire secret work to the auspices of his organization. M.O.4, fearing the political complications involved with agency contacts, welcomed his suggestion enthusiastically. However, David Hacohen explained to Melchett that there was danger in involving a popular club, purely devoted to sports, in underground activities. This would be especially true since the Maccabi had no training or tradition in such matters. Nor did its organizational pattern conform in the slightest to that type of work. Melchett was convinced by these arguments and withdrew the proposal.

Mutual cooperation along general lines was agreed upon in London. Matters were confirmed in an exchange of letters following further negotiations in Cairo, participated in by Sharett and Reuven Shiloah. Testimonies by Jews indicate that the following conditions were included in the agreement: The agency was to be the sole Jewish body with which M.O.4 would have contact; all instructions to activists in the underground were to be given by the agency; the agency reserved for itself the right to refrain from actions it found unsuitable. It was agreed that types of training and a plan of activities would be determined after consultation between the two bodies. Assistance to Diaspora Jews, their organization, and other Jewish operations were all recognized as inseparable parts of any mission in foreign countries under the department's direction. Even more, M.O.4 undertook not to interfere with "Jewish" operations of which the Palestine government did not approve. The underground activists received no bonus for their activity, only a wage to cover living costs. Expenditures incurred in operations and training were met by the department.[1]

Meanwhile, Wingate languished in Britain, dejected by the lack of activity that had been imposed on him (he was responsible for antiaircraft batteries in one region of England). He offered himself as commander of the special operations. At his urging, Sharett put in a request to the British chief of staff to free Wingate for this purpose. Ironside was agreeable. But first he invited Wingate in and explained that with the assumption of the requested duty, Wingate's military career would be finished. Once connected with secret operations of this type, one could never again command regular troops. He further told Wingate that if he did not take this command, other use would be found for his talents. Wingate gave in, and with the consent of Weizmann and Sharett, at whose disposal he placed himself, he passed up the "Jewish" program.[2]

On May 10 Hacohen returned to Rumania. Yehuda Arazi and two other men had, meanwhile, arrived there and begun preparing acts of sabotage and the creation of an information net. M.O.4 had established contact with Gypsies and also, naturally, with Rumanians. One of the latter was a Rumanian prince whose personality made a deep impression on the Hagana people. With this outside help and the guidance of several Englishmen, an information net was set up and explosive material collected. The British ambassador suspected these Jewish agents of being connected with the clandestine immigration organization against which he was fighting with all his might. But according to Hacohen, despite the ambassador, the relationship with M.O.4 came to a paradoxical pass—the Hagana Immigration Bureau received, from the head of a British shipping company (free of charge!) a vessel in which the bureau was most interested, for transporting illegal immigrants from Yugoslavia to Sulina at the mouth of the Danube.

The plan to activate Palestinian saboteurs and agents in Rumania failed, and one gets the impression that the major factor in this was the inexperience of the British department. The three Hagana men were forced to leave Rumania in the fall, after the sabotage plans were canceled. Only the information network remained; but we can describe three plans for carrying out acts of sabotage and infiltration which, for various reasons, were never executed.

The first plan was to send a ship loaded with scrap iron and some explosives into the Iron Gate gorge of the Danube. There the ship was to be sunk, thus blocking the passage of German tankers for a long while. The difficulties involved in carrying out the plan were many. A license to export scrap iron to nations of doubtful neutrality had to be obtained. A suitable purchaser had to be found. The ship and its cargo had to be camouflaged so as not to arouse the suspicions of the German espionage service.

Yitzhak Hos was the responsible party from the Jewish side. He arrived with his ship in Piraeus on July 16, 1940. The vessel, with its dangerous cargo, was ready to sail. However, the matter became known to a British merchant in Rumania, and he sent a warning to London; from there the order was given not to send the ship. Perhaps that order was issued because at that very moment a British ship laden with explosives was being held on the Danube, and the British feared a diplomatic complication that might force Rumania into the arms of the Germans. The opinion has also been expressed that the Palestinian authorities had a hand in washing out the plan. After protracted expectation and feverish negotiation in Constantinople, London, Bucharest, and Cairo, Hos received instructions to disperse the cargo in Greece, which he did on September 18, 1940.

At that time another still bolder action was being planned. At Sulina, at the mouth of the Danube, there was anchored an "illegal" immigrant ship which had little chance of sailing. The plan was to send a ship (in another version, two ships) from Palestine with a Jewish detachment. The ship from Palestine was to meet the immigrant ship at sea and exchange passengers. The immigrants would reach safe shores, while the men from Palestine would go back to Sulina in the immigrants' ship, claiming that the sailing had not gone well. When the Germans conquered Rumania, the men were to break out in the harbor area, destroying everything possible, then disperse among the Jewish communities of Rumania and organize cells of resistance against the Nazis. In the Hagana Command, Golomb tied this plan to the "intention that many of them [the Hagana personnel] would try to filter from Rumania into Poland" and give leadership to the resistance movement there.

Hacohen flew to London to check the details, but the plan was rejected—apparently under pressure from the authorities in Palestine who viewed it as an aid to unofficial immigration. Of course, the army's excuse for the rejection of it was weighty when considered on its own merits, since this was a suicide mission—there was no possibility of getting away. In 1940 the British still recoiled from such desperate acts.[3]

Parallel to these programs were the guidance and training actions undertaken at various places in Palestine. Within the context of defense industry, a workshop for making small time bombs was established, and chemicals were developed for the use of the Allies. Hagana men participated in exercises and activities such as radio signaling, naval drills, and demolition practice.

This period of activity in the Balkans terminated with an episode that undermined, in no small measure, the cooperative connections between the agency and the British. It also caused a great deal of internal complication. This was the affair of the ship *Darien,* which was involved in a plan to infiltrate Palestinian youths into Rumania.

The *Darien* was the property of the British D Branch,* which had bought her from the agency (in fact, from Mosad) for a price much higher than her true value. The object of the purchase was to avail the department of a vessel under a neutral flag, so that she could be used in actions in the Balkans. However, at the same time it sold the ship, Mosad sent it to Sulina in Rumania to pick up immigrants who were waiting there for their journey to Palestine; it also sent its emissaries to Istanbul to organize the immigration of a Jewish convoy that was stuck in Kladovo, Yugoslavia. The *Darien* then waited in Sulina to pick up these immigrants and bring them to Palestine.

Neither the fact of the sale of the ship nor the plans of the British department were known to the emissaries, and certainly not to the intended immigrants. In the end, Mosad did not succeed in bringing the Kladovo immigrants to Rumania. But 180

* The Jews' name for M.O.4 (later S.O.E.)

Jewish refugees who had been waiting in Sulina were taken aboard the ship. Meanwhile, instructions arrived in Istanbul, along with more emissaries. The immigrants were to be disembarked and the ship turned over to the British. The responsible party in Istanbul, Yehuda Braginsky, refused to disembark the refugees. But the matter was decided against him. After the decision was made, however, no one would carry it out. It meant the abandoning of 180 refugees to the very real danger of murder at the hands of the Rumanians or the Germans, when the latter invaded Rumania.

When it became plain that no one would carry out the disembarkation order, the emissaries saw no way out except to continue the loading of the ship with immigrants and then to take it to Istanbul. Despite explicit instructions from the chiefs of the Hagana in Palestine (orders brought by Arazi and Hacohen) the men of Mosad continued their activity (December 1940). Later (January 3, 1941) Weizmann himself intervened, expressing agreement with the position of the agency (Sharett) that the ship should be returned to its British owners. But neither coaxing nor commanding could overcome the sight of the suffering of the refugees for whom the *Darien* was the sole chance of survival. The ship was taken to Istanbul.

In Istanbul the cooperation people, particularly Hacohen, tried to find another ship to transport the immigrants and thus free the *Darien*. But such a vessel was not to be found, despite the fact that according to Hacohen the British offered £100,000 for one. An alternative plan—to transport the immigrants to a Greek island until the storm had passed—was also rejected because of the threat of an imminent German invasion of Greece. Finally, even David Hacohen agreed, certainly with a very heavy heart, to the departure of the *Darien*. It arrived in Palestine in March of 1941.[4]

A lively debate between the cooperation people and the Mosad people developed about the *Darien* incident. The former argued that it was a gross breach of faith on the part of the Jews, in work which was categorically built on mutual trust. True, a few hundred refugees had been rescued. But the chance to save masses by means of cooperation with the British secret service had been lost. Arazi, involved in daily negotiation with the British, looked upon the entire affair as a break in national discipline by a body (Mosad) which was not subject to community-at-large or nonpartisan control. In fierce bitterness, he abandoned his cooperation activity. And indeed the mutual effort with the British had been damaged.

Still, the coin had another side. The chances of rescuing refugees by means of the British department were quite doubtful, while the Mosad was under the terrible pressure of those refugees who could actually be saved. Furthermore, the cooperation continued, though not without suspicion and the breeding of suspicion, and not in that somewhat innocent atmosphere that preceded the *Darien* case. The final score was eight hundred lives saved from the Nazi hell.

All these activities were carried out under the authority of D Branch (M.O.4, S.O.E.) which engaged not so much in intelligence work as in sabotage. The central British intelligence department (M. I. 1) was under the influence of British government elements that were unfriendly to Zionism. That section, therefore, was in no hurry to form ties with the agency, though the latter was most eager for such contact. The only contact made with that section up to 1943 was by means of the intelligence section of the Royal Air Force in the Middle East. Along with the S.O.E. (Special Operations Executive) department, the R. A. F. initiated the establishment of the Haifa Investigation Bureau with the engineer Immanuel Yalan at its head. At a later period, Gideon Raphael joined him. At first, escaped British prisoners who had reached the Middle East were interrogated, as were people of other nationalities who had happened to come to Palestine; later, it was mostly Jews. By methodical examination the interviewers sought to obtain maximum information on military objectives and industrial and economic secrets, as well as to discover the state of mind of the populations in the countries under enemy domination.

The work of the Haifa Bureau won high praise in British Army circles. From its founding on July 15, 1940, until its closing in November 1944, 4,400 persons were interrogated, 1,786 reports were prepared, and 530 papers on special problems were submitted. After April 1943, the Haifa Bureau worked on questions of the European Jews; in March 1944 this section (under Raphael) was detached and transferred to the authority of the Political Department of the agency. In July 1944 the British cut the connection between the Haifa Bureau and the central intelligence department. In November 1944 the work was halted altogether; many commendations of the twelve bureau operatives were distributed.

From the Jewish point of view, this bureau was to have a twofold importance. It represented a vital participation—and an autonomous one—in the war effort; and the material collected by the bureau served later as a principal guide for the agents who would be parachuted into Nazi-occupied Europe during 1943 and 1944. We shall see that some of those parachutists were sent by that same central intelligence department.

All the actions so far discussed were, directly or indirectly, connected with the war in the Balkans. But with the beginning of the Italian invasion of Greece in the fall of 1940—and particularly after the entry of German armies into Rumania in the spring of 1941—all contact with those countries was cut off. D Branch began to operate in the Middle East (to be exact, insofar as the agency people knew, the field of action was shifted to that area).

As early as the summer of 1940, cooperation was shaped (with D Branch) in the area of staff work. With the fall of France, the whole array of British forces in the region started to totter. The Allies' main land force had been the large French Army in Syria. Now it was removed from action, and in the course of time it even became a hostile element. With the German victories, it became necessary to plan demolition operations in the possible paths of advance of the German Army toward the Middle East and to match such plans to the modern war methods the Germans were employing. Operations of that type had so far been planned only by the French staff in Syria, since the English lacked experts to carry them out in Palestine.

The English eagerly accepted the agency suggestion of drafting Professor Rattner for this work. Rattner's professional knowledge and military experience in World War I (as a staff officer in a Russian corps) made him seem a desirable co-worker to the British. With the help of young British officers (including Hammond, son of a member of the Peel Commission and a lecturer at Cambridge) and by dint of studies in the literature of engineering, geology, geography, and economics, Rattner delineated the weak points on the supposed German route. It led, according to the British assumptions, through Turkey (the U.S.S.R. was still neutral) and the Taurus Mountains to Iraq and Syria. The weak points were the railroad tunnels through the Taurus Mountains, and plans were made to blow them up—along with other strategic points in Turkey, Iraq, Syria, and Iran. The objectives included "factories, bridges, railroad bridges, tunnels, harbors, dams, and anything of value, especially in the field of transportation." The plans were completed in about a year—in the summer of 1941—and with that, Rattner finished his job.

An outstanding operation, also within the aforementioned structure, was executed by a unit of "Arabists" (Jews disguised as Arabs) in Syria before the Allied invasion there in June 1941. At the end of July 1940, Sharett had reached an agreement with a branch of S.O.E. in Cairo and with the Political Warfare Executive, which was under the chief of information services in the Middle East, Brigadier Clayton. The original plan was broad—to spread a net of agents throughout the

countries of the Middle East—but only the Syrian portion of
the program reached fruition.

In August and September of 1940, a few Arabic-speaking
men, mostly natives of Arab countries, were sent into Syria
and Lebanon. Their task was to observe public moods,
foreign propaganda, visits by German agents, arms smuggling,
military movements, the condition of arsenals, and fortifications.
Tuvia Arazi commanded the unit (about twelve men). Contacts
were made with sympathetic Frenchmen and with Arabs who
worked for hire. Anti-German and anti-Vichy handbills in
Arabic and French were smuggled into Syria.

The British, apparently, were satisfied with the way these
activities were conducted. But in Hagana circles there was no
ignoring the setbacks, which were traceable to inexperience and
lack of preparation. At times "it seemed as if the exaggeration
in the tall stories matched the people they were dressed up
for."[5] Thus, for example, on the eve of the action against the
refineries in Tripoli (see below), when the men of the unit were
required to render documented information on the objective,
their report was disallowed; they were forced to recheck the
area and report again.

The propaganda operations were assisted by the Free French
radio broadcasts that emanated from David Hacohen's house,
where the station had been established (August 16, 1940).
The broadcasts were in Arabic and French, and later in
Bulgarian and Hungarian for the Balkans. They continued
until the conquest of Syria; but even after that, the partnership
went on. Contact with the Free French was with the knowledge
of the British command. But the agency was warned not to
interfere in the quarrels that started up anew with every sunrise
between the British and de Gaulle.

A serious problem was created by the British because of their
desire to work with resoluteness against Arab enemy agents.
"The problem of direct liquidation or the use of assassins was
discussed relative to several Arab leaders who were known to be

German agents and were receiving money from German sources. We refused to take a hand in these operations."[6]

At the time of the invasion of Syria (June 1941), two saboteurs were sent to Aleppo. They succeeded in demolishing the railroad station and an enemy camp in the city. This operation was also carried out by the Arabists.

The end of the Arabist chapter in Syria was marked by suffering and torture. Toward the close of 1940, twelve men of the unit were captured by the Vichy secret police. Except for the commander, Arazi, they were all local agents. After months of imprisonment and torture, the result of which was that the authorities became aware of some details of the espionage operations, Arazi was sentenced to fifteen years at hard labor. During an attempted escape from prison he was wounded in the leg. While in the hospital he succeeded (with the help of the Lebanese chief of police, an Allied sympathizer) in getting free and reaching Palestine. For his proud posture in the affair, Arazi won high commendations from his English superiors.

In this first phase of cooperation activities, the phase that ended with the invasion of Syria, only a small number of people took part. The "many companies" of which some have written are, unfortunately, only a figment of the imagination. Except for the Arabists in Syria, who also worked on unofficial immigration (a matter still needing investigation), the cooperation people never operated in specifically Jewish matters. The self-criticism was later to be heard that "perhaps, even then, we should have been working on our own."[7] This does not mean that the agency failed to preserve its independence from the English. On the contrary, it did so most emphatically. For example, Hacohen and Shiloah refused to accept courtesy ranks in the British Army so as not to be forced to obey higher officers.

It is not improbable that, during the war's first period, there were still possibilities (later to disappear altogether) of organizing the Jews of the Diaspora. But no one could possibly have guessed the enormity of the Holocaust that was to fall upon European Jewry—though many sensed perceptively the road of misery and pain that lay before them. Inexperience and lack of time, when it was still possible by means of the cooperation apparatus to make some approach to the Diaspora countries, are what prevented the organization of underground work among the Jews. At any rate, it is a fact that the cooperation bequeathed a decidedly positive heritage to the development of the Hagana in Palestine, though its effect was not felt in the Diaspora until the parachutists period in 1943 and 1944.

Who was actually responsible on the inside for these operations? Not the Hagana with its community apparatus. The Political Department of the agency conducted the operations, yet we find not the slightest mention of them in its reports to the Agency Executive—a circumstance to be explained by the secrecy of the operations. The apparatus of the department that took care of these questions was most compact. It was made up of a few men with identical views. A mood crystallized in which, "at times one cannot bring such matters before the Hagana Command. There are things that should be brought to certain persons for consultation; to Berl [Katznelson], Ben-Gurion, Tabenkin; to get their advice on how to handle things."[8]

It is easy to guess that community circles, particularly the bourgeois Right, were not pleased with this approach. The main acts were being carried out without community control. The ideological problem necessarily born out of all such activity was clear. Do those who head the political structure of a democracy have the right to engage in military actions—whose significance is clearly political—without prior discussion in a public forum? If matters were carried out under such restraint, the speed required for the execution of an activity vital to the public interest would probably be lost. But without the intervention of a controlling arm, a situation might be created in which the military sector would be making *de facto* decisions on political issues—and not always in a spirit congenial to the majority of the community.

It cannot, of course, be argued that the 1940 operations (or indeed later ones) were broad enough in compass or significance to confront the Zionist movement with this dilemma in all its force. But the problem was there. It has faced most of the democratic nations of our times, including the political movement of the people of Israel. There was no great probability that such operations would win the support of all sections of the National Command in 1940. The job was done under the auspices of the Histadrut (practically, under Mapai) and even without the knowledge of the Hagana Command. Even Hashomer Hatzair, which agreed in general with the policy of operations in the Diaspora and cooperation activity but was not represented in the command, was not involved in these operations.

🔖 *The Political-Military Crisis in the Middle East in 1941*

At the end of 1940 and the beginning of 1941, Nazi Germany reached the peak of its power and dominion. The conquest of Western Europe and domination of Hungary, Rumania, and Bulgaria early in 1941 put the keys to a major assault on the Middle East into German hands. The small British force in that region could expect a severe test against the mighty German war machine. This was a decisive hour, not only for the Jews of Palestine, but for the entire world. At that moment the German command was faced with a choice. It could wipe out the British forces in the Middle East and advance toward India. Or it could liquidate the Soviet Army and reach the rich food-producing areas of the Ukraine and the oil fields of the Caucasus.

As early as the end of 1940, "Operation Barbarossa" was

being worked out, making the Soviet Union the next intended victim of Nazi aggression. The whole powerful German Army was turned east toward the U.S.S.R., thus saving the Middle East from invasion. The Balkan fighting in the spring of 1941 was, from the German point of view, nothing but a mere side battle, preliminary to the invasion of Russia.

On December 9, 1940, Britain's General Wavell opened an offensive in the western desert against Italian forces that were three times larger than his own; he completely routed them. On February 6, 1941, Benghazi, Cyrenaica, fell to the British. At the same time, other Royal forces assaulted Eritrea, Ethiopia, and Somaliland from north and south. Wingate, who had been placed under Wavell in the fall of 1940, also took part in the attack on the Ethiopian front, heading a guerrilla unit that reaped amazing successes. Hagana member Avraham Akavia took part in the Ethiopian campaign as a close aide of Wingate.[9] In February of 1941, the main Italian positions of Keren in Eritrea were captured. In this engagement, the Fifty-first Commandos shone. It was a unit made up mostly of Palestinians, veterans of the Pioneers. Addis Ababa, the capital of Ethiopia, fell in May, and the main Italian force surrendered at Amba Alagi.

Meanwhile, the situation in the Balkans reached a crisis. The Italian invasion of Greece began on October 28, 1940. But the war became a stalemate, with the Italians defending their positions in the Balkans with difficulty. Therefore the Germans decided to extricate their ally and conquer the Balkans, so as to secure the German flank in the assault on the Soviet Union. In February and March of 1941, German armies entered Hungary, Rumania, and Bulgaria without opposition. Yugoslavia signed a surrender to the Germans. But on March 27, an anti-German revolt broke out there. The Germans replied with an invasion of the country and, at the same time, went into battle against the Allied forces in Greece.

Now Churchill and his advisors decided, against Wavell's

judgment, to send most of the British forces from Egypt to the aid of Greece. This act laid the British flank in Cyrenaica open to an Italian-German attack under General Rommel (who had arrived in Tripolitania in February). The attack began on March 31 and pulverized the tiny British force. By April 4 Rommel's troops stood at the Egyptian border. They had left behind them the port of Tobruk, cut off and defended by Allied units.

Britain's aid to Greece was a vain sacrifice. The small, exhausted Greek Army quickly surrendered to the Germans. The English withdrew to Crete on May 1, leaving all their equipment behind for the foe. They also left 15,000 prisoners, among them 1,600 Palestinians. The British command never denied that these people were discriminated against and refused admission to the ships leaving for Crete. On May 20, before the stricken British could clear their heads of their defeat in Greece, the island of Crete was attacked by an elite detachment of German paratroops. Though the Germans sustained heavy losses, there was insufficient strength to prevent the island's fall and another bitter British defeat.

If that were not enough, England also became entangled in a number of Middle Eastern difficulties. Since the resignation of the pro-British ministers from the government (September 1940), a group of neutralist politicians took power in Egypt. Their leader was Hassan Sabry and, after his death on November 14, 1940, Husein Sirri. The pro-Fascist wing, inspired by King Farouk, was growing continually stronger. On May 16, 1941, the British arrested Ali al-Masri, a former Egyptian chief of staff, as he was attempting to flee by air to Vichyite Beirut. The situation in Egypt also deteriorated because of the economic depression and the drop in living standards during the first two years of the war.

Conditions especially worsened at the beginning of 1941 in Iraq. The strong man, Nuri Said, a supposed friend of the British, brought Rashid Ali al-Qailani to power in March 1940.

Rashid Ali was an extreme nationalist and a Nazi sympathizer. He instituted a "neutralist" policy, with Nuri serving as foreign minister in his government. Iraq did not break relations with Italy when Rome declared war on England. Instead, Nuri offered the British (through the pro-Arab Colonel Newcombe) an Iraqi declaration of war on Italy in exchange for the immediate activation of those White Paper provisions that promised independence to the Arabs of Palestine (July 1940). England, however, refused to accept that condition (August 29, 1940). It appears that the pro-Zionist members of the government prevented a capitulation to such coercion on Palestinian matters.[10]

Iraqi policy became more and more pro-Nazi, until even Nuri turned his back on Rashid Ali and succeeded in bringing him down at the end of January, after strenuous efforts. The new pro-British government under Taher al-Hashimi was unable to hold power. It was deposed on April 2 by an army revolt staged by Rashid Ali, who headed a nationalistic and pro-Nazi military clique known as "the Golden Square." Churchill immediately grasped the size of the imminent peril for the British forces. With a correct evaluation of the quality of the Iraqi Army, he ordered the British Army (contrary to Wavell's view) to make a landing, from India, in Basra (April 17). The Iraqis—who had not in the least expected such a speedy British reaction—gave their approval to the landing, but, naturally, without much joy. However, when additional British troops landed in Basra on April 29, Rashid Ali protested violently and placed the British air base in Habbaniya and the British Embassy in Baghdad under siege.

British forces of only about 2,000 men, mostly from non-combatant services, attacked at Habbaniya on May 2. Although the Iraqis had 9,000 men with artillery and an air force, the British victory was complete. The Iraqi air force, though assisted by German planes, was put totally out of action. Other small units arrived from Palestine. A detachment of the Transjordanian Frontier Force rebelled when given an order to leave for Iraq. They were disarmed, and replaced by a small unit from the Arab Legion. After a brilliant campaign, the British troops (1,500 men) reached and captured Baghdad (May 30).[11] The entire Iraqi Army surrendered. But before the English entered the city, terrible pogroms were conducted against the Jews on June 1 and 2, 1941.

It turned out that all the White Paper concessions made by the English to Arab chauvinism were of no avail the moment it appeared that Germany would be victorious and that England's days were numbered. Only the courage of a handful of Englishmen saved the line of communication through Iraq.

Events in Iraq put the Syrian problem back on the agenda. Since July 29, 1940, Vichy had controlled Syria and Lebanon. A few anti-Nazi French and Polish units had been able to cross the border into Palestine (and on the eve of the British invasion in 1941, a Circassian unit also came in). In August, Italian officers of the French armistice commission arrived in Beirut. In the beginning of 1941 they were joined by German representatives.

General Dentz had been appointed governor of Syria and Lebanon in November 1940. With the beginning of the rebellion in Iraq, Dentz received orders from Vichy not to interfere with German airplanes landing in Syria on their way to Iraq. On May 12 the first German planes arrived, and 120 of them landed there through June 4. On May 14 and 15 the airfields in Syria were bombed by the R.A.F., causing a further worsening of English-French relations. The British government, under growing pressure from de Gaulle and his representative, Georges Catroux, who were demanding the conquest of Syria, passed the buck to Wavell, who was pressed to carry out the conquest.

Wavell opposed the venture—a fight against enemy forces in large measure superior—but finally gave in and prepared an invasion plan (May 25). The chief military consideration justifying the action was the existence of the German air bases in Syria. Dentz sensed the gathering storm and pressed his government to work for the removal of the German planes; and, indeed, the aircraft were taken out on June 4. But that step came too late. The British plan was arranged and prepared, and they put it into action. On June 8, Allied armies invaded Syria.

How was the military situation around Palestine pictured by Zionist leaders on the eve of the Syrian action? Naturally, they knew nothing of the German intention to invade the Soviet Union. On the contrary, they expressed fears regarding Russia's intentions toward Britain in the Middle East. The Germans were in Crete and on the Egyptian border, having demonstrated air and land superiority in both places. Turkey's ambiguous attitude also caused anxieties. There were some who doubted her willingness to oppose the Germans should they decide to cross Turkish territory on their way to Iraq and Syria. The rebellion in Iraq showed how shaky Britain's position in the Arab East was. Syria was in the hands of Vichy, and German planes were operating from her territory. In Palestine itself there were signs of renewed activity by Arab gangs. All the facts made it seem that an invasion of Axis forces into Palestine, accompanied by supporting uprisings, was a very real danger. Consternation broke out in the Yishuv.

Such was the situation in Palestine and its surroundings when the decision was made to create the Palmakh.

✄ The New National Command and the Separatist Organizations

It will be remembered that in the summer of 1940 a crisis had broken out in the National Command, owing to a division of opinion between Left and Right on the functions of the Hagana. In 1941, with the external threat growing, the injury done by the absence of unity was sharply felt. Steps were taken toward an agreement on rounding out the command and re-organizing the rest of the security bodies (the General Staff and the Committee of Eight). The Middle-Class Union threatened that, if the negotiations failed, it would create, together with Etzel, a sort of reorganized breakaway formation. Nor was the loyalty of the orthodox to the Hagana assured.[12] As it happened, during that very spring, the Irgun Tsva Leumi (Etzel) was engaged in extorting money by force from none other than the middle-class elements, who were thus put in a state of panic from this inside intimidation.

The history of Etzel and Lehi (Stern group) do not belong directly to the subject at hand. But since it is impossible to discuss the negotiations within the Yishuv during that period without referring to Etzel and its policy, we shall sketch out its history during the first two years of the war.

With the outbreak of the war, Etzel announced an inter-mission in its struggle against the British. Etzel's commander, David Raziel, accepted Jabotinsky's instructions in this respect without reservation. The Revisionist line was extremely pro-British. In New Zionist circles, the assumption was widely held that

the [New Zionist] political program embodies footholds for the political interests of most of the Allies. England, whose between-the-wars Arab policy has ended in definite failure, desires the creation of a "Hebrew Australia" in the Middle East, containing at least six million inhabitants; that is to say, a modern Hebrew state dependent on the British Empire to the exact same degree as are South Africa and Australia, and which will be the faithful guardian of the principal connecting arteries of that empire.[13]

This stand also influenced the attitude of a portion of the Revisionist movement to issues of mobilization. Within the movement, opinions on the problem were divided. The Etzel

Command opposed enlistment in the British Army as long as no Hebrew military force was created into which the ruling bodies of Betar could introduce loyal "nationalist" elements. However, another branch of the Revisionist movement waved the flag for mobilization. In September 1940 the enlistment office of the New Zionist Organization was opened. In the first two years of the war, more than one thousand pro-New Zionist recruits passed through it.[14]

In May 1939, Raziel and some other Etzel men were arrested, but they were released from the prison camp at Mizra after the outbreak of the war. Avraham Stern and several of his comrades, however, were not set free. That was un-explained. Why did the British have divided feelings about Etzel? How did they know that Stern represented the activist anti-British opposition? Stern's view, like that of his fellows in Poland—Dr. Israel Scheib, Menachem Begin, and Nathan Yellin (Mor)—was that the political orientation focused on Britain should not be continued. Over against Jabotinsky's pro-British line, he posited enmity for Britain as the basis of his policy. But in contrast to Begin, he concluded that allies must be sought in the camp hostile to Britain, that is to say, in Berlin and Rome.

In June 1940, Stern and four comrades were let out of prison, and a bitter quarrel broke out between him and Raziel against this ideological background. Stern forced Raziel to resign. Jabotinsky intervened and put Raziel back in his post. Stern, however, did not obey the instructions, and Etzel was split. At first, most of the members of Etzel joined Stern's group ("Etzel in Israel"). But when Stern tried to translate his programs into reality, many left him; and his organization shrank drastically in contrast to the Revisionist "Etzel in the Land of Israel."

Stern tried to get in touch with the Axis powers, first of all with Italy, (perhaps only as a ruse to achieve contact with the Germans). In Italy Etzel (as well as he, personally) had had contacts even before the war. The Italians maintained a pitiful information network among the Jews of Palestine. Their agent was an Etzel member who was working for the C.I.D. Stern attempted to win this man over, perhaps with the idea that he might betray the British and really work for the Italians. However, the man seems to have remained loyal to Raziel and the British. Then Stern conceived the idea of sending one or two men to Lebanon to make contact with the Germans. It is clear that at least one emissary, Naphtali Lubinczik, arrived in Beirut and established contact with the Germans: Roser (a local German intelligence agent) and Otto von Hentig, a Foreign Office man who was paying a visit.

Early in January 1941, a proposed agreement of Stern's people with the German Reich was transmitted to the German consulate in Ankara. According to that proposal, the Stern group would assist in the conquest of Palestine and its delivery from the British to the Germans, in exchange for a Hebrew state and the transfer of the Jews of Europe to that state. Understandably, the mission ended unsuccessfully; Lubinczik returned from Lebanon to be incarcerated at Acre. Probably the Stern people suspected the Etzel intelligence service of delivering Lubinczik to the English.[15]

At the same time, the pro-British stand of Raziel's people brought Etzel to doubtful, even dangerous, acts. The head of Etzel intelligence was Israel Pritzker. First Raziel and then Aryeh Possak and Jacob Meridor were the commanders of Etzel; but for practical purposes much of the real power had quickly passed into the hands of Pritzker. Etzel intelligence obtained information, astounding in its detail, on all Jewish elements in Palestine, thus having its revenge on the Stern people and the Hagana. There is no doubt about Pritzker's firm connections with the C.I.D. We have already seen that information from Etzel sources served in making up C.I.D. reports on the Jews of Palestine. These contacts with the secret police gave birth, at the time, to deep hatred between Etzel and Stern's "Etzel in Israel." According to one source, Stern passed a death sentence on Pritzker and, if we may depend on a report from Hagana sources, several Etzel men threatened to kill Stern if anything untoward happened to Pritzker.

The command of Etzel remained in Raziel's hands until November 1940. After internal disputes and allegations against his conduct of office, Raziel resigned at a meeting of commanders, early in December. At a second meeting, the position was offered to Aron Heichman, one of the Tel Aviv commanders, but he declined (according to his own statement) because the type of command he suggested was not confirmed. No new commander was chosen. The Etzel members received their "freedom until notice of change," and Raziel went to study at the Hebrew University in Jerusalem. In actuality, Etzel ceased to exist as an organization.

Against the background of internal crumbling, negotiations began between the New Zionist people and central members of Mapai. Such talks—with the purpose of patching up the split created by Jabotinsky's withdrawal from the Zionist Organization—were held from time to time: at the time of the 1939 London Conference and again throughout 1940. In December 1940, Katznelson and Dr. Aryeh Altman of the Revisionists signed a draft agreement (which they were obliged to bring before their parties and the Zionist Actions Committee) that featured the close rapprochement in political positions between Mapai and the Revisionists.

The agreement spoke of the establishment of a Jewish state in the historical boundaries of Palestine; the creation of a Jewish army as an Ally, with rights equal to those of the other Allied armies; mass *aliyah* of Jews immediately after the war; solicitation of an international loan; and a renewed "Faisal arrangement" with the Arabs (a Jewish state in exchange for support of Arab aspirations for independence). The principal obstacles to the signing of the agreement were problems of economy and labor (that is, mainly class problems), although the Revisionists were prepared to reach an agreement with the labor organizations.[16]

Section three, article three of the agreement is of particular interest. It speaks of the unification of the two security organizations (one of which had, practically, ceased to exist by that time). At present, there is no free access to the archival material pertaining to these questions. There is, therefore, no possibility of tracing the involutions of the negotiations conducted between Mapai and the New Zionists preceding the signing of the draft agreement and thereafter. It is clear, however, that the opposition to the agreement arose within the ranks of Mapai itself. There the echoes of the murder of Chaim Arlosoroff* still reverberated, and earlier unsuccessful attempts to bring the Revisionists back to the Zionist Organization and reunite the underground groups were not forgotten.

At any rate, the agreement was never ratified, or even brought up for discussion before the bodies of Histadrut or the Zionist Actions Committee. Thus, the chance to put an end to organized schism, with all the dangers it involved, was missed.

Etzel's opponents in the Hagana were seized by an error that was both practical and logical. In light of Etzel's past, there were some who looked upon it as a fascistic, adventurist organization, likely to bring staggering disaster down on constructive Zionism. Insofar as it accepted this view, the Hagana had only two alternatives: either dominate this supposedly destructive force by means of agreement and merger or fight it determinedly—with all the grave conclusions flowing from such a course. But those responsible for Zionist policy and for Hagana constantly blundered in bewilderment between these two extremes, never making the ultimate unequivocal decision. The result was the survival, expansion, and flowering of the

---

* Arlosoroff was murdered in 1933 on the Tel Aviv seashore. Some members of the Revisionist movement were suspected but were acquitted in court.

Etzel group during the period of the Holocaust and the government's anti-Zionist policy. Etzel became an influential factor in the life of the Yishuv.

After a brief recess, Raziel returned to activity in Etzel. The tie between Etzel and Army Intelligence grew faster during the months of severe British defeats at the beginning of 1941. During that period the Stern people were informed on, and some Etzel members received C.I.D. documents as anti-fifth-column fighters. The British then proposed to Raziel that he go to Iraq and engage in activity against the men of the mufti. This pro-British and anti-mufti wartime mission decidedly suited Raziel's philosophy. He arrived, with an escort, at Habbaniya at the time of the Iraqi siege of the airfield; but he was killed in an aerial bombing immediately after his arrival. The mission remained unfulfilled. And Etzel had lost the only commander who had possessed a high reputation throughout its own organization.

Raziel's death gave Etzel the myth indispensable for any underground group and especially for Etzel, which was undermined by schism. Raziel, the observant Jew, the commander—honest, sincere, disciplined—became symbol, saint, and hero, even to his successors, whose political views were diametrically opposed to the philosophy of their idol.

Relations were also rather difficult between the Hagana and Etzel, with its two factions. In August 1940 a fight developed in the village of Herzliya when Etzel men took arms from the local Hagana arsenal. Hagana people discovered those responsible for the operation and obtained confessions in writing from them. Three arms caches of the Etzel were also confiscated (including a large arsenal in Kefar-Saba). This happened at the start of the Etzel split, and it was not clear as to which of the two Etzel groups the arms belonged, as the confiscation occurred before the division of arms stores among the factions.

Plans were also uncovered for attacks on various Hagana

persons and other objectives, for example, on a bus station. Hagana counterespionage was therefore strengthened. And in April 1941 the intelligence service, until then independent (under Histadrut and the agency) passed to the jurisdiction of the Hagana.

Such was the situation at the time of the negotiations conducted in the spring of 1941 between the Middle-Class Union and the Histadrut. The union claimed the sole right to determine the nonlabor representatives on the National Command—they were fully one-half of that command—just as the Histadrut determined the labor representation. They also demanded that one of their representatives be appointed to a responsible post on the General Staff. Rokakh further demanded that the authority for day-to-day control be vested in the Kofer Hayishuv (in which the Middle-Class people had a powerful influence), while the Committee of Eight should fulfill arbitrational functions only.

The proposal would have meant an additional intermediate step (in the form of the Kofer Hayishuv, where controlling posts with the power of decision would be located) between the Committee of Eight and the National Command. This further padding out of the already ungainly administrative machinery had been proposed purely to increase right-wing influence. It was rejected by the Agency Executive. The Middle-Class Union did not include the "A" General Zionists (Gruenbaum's people and Weizmann's supporters) or the religious community, and even the membership of the "B" General Zionists in this "union" hung by a hair. By contrast, the Mapai people spoke in the name of the Histadrut, which tied together all the secularist (and even some of the orthodox) workers, members of the Zionist Organization.

However, the chief problem was that the active men of high initiative—those who were candidates for responsible positions of command in the General Staff or the National Command—for the most part came from the labor groups, while the middle-class people prepared for such posts were few in number. There was nothing new about this condition. It had existed since the start of the Hagana and explains the strong feeling of deprivation that always prevailed in right-wing circles. Of course, Mapai's party interests, too, made it want to obtain control over the Hagana. This led Mapai to oppose increasing the influence of any other political element, be it middle-class, religious, or left-wing Histadrut. Nevertheless, insofar as there was a Mapai monopoly in the Hagana, that condition originated in the plain fact that a large number of dedicated and talented Mapai people worked night and day in this service to the nation.

The "A" General Zionists, the orthodox, and the Hashomer Hatzair also demanded the right to have a part in the administration of security matters. In the temporary National Command that was appointed in July 1940, Reizer (the chief) was joined by Levi Eshkol, Aaron Zisling (labor), Shimon Wassermann (religious), and Moshe Sneh (representing the "A" General Zionists). Then in 1941 the "A" General Zionists demanded a "regular" member on the command in addition to Sneh, who had been nominated as new chief by Ben-Gurion, the Agency Executive chairman. Sneh was looked upon as a neutral even though he was very close to Mapai circles, participating in meetings of the Histadrut Security Committee and in the Histadrut group of officers (the "Young Turks," of whom more later).

When the Middle-Class Union realized that its demand for the right to appoint the bourgeois segment of the National Command would not be fulfilled, it delivered an ultimatum to the Agency Executive (May 25, 1941). This stated that negotiations would be halted if the agency did not accept the following demands: (1) appointment of the National Command with three specifically named Middle-Class Union men, three Histadrut people, and Sneh as chief; (2) appointment of a right-wing officer to a responsible post on the General Staff; (3) broadening of the Security Committee to include representatives of various economic groups, while keeping the power of political decision in the Agency Executive; and (4) appointment of a financial body (the Kofer Hayishuv) by the Security Committee to control Hagana appropriations.

The agency, of course, formally rejected the ultimatum. But the pact that was signed later, and ratified on June 19 by the Middle-Class Union, actually included all the right wing's demands. On July 1, 1941, a National Command comprising the following was appointed: Dr. Moshe Sneh (commander), Shimon Wassermann (religious), Yitzhak Sitkov, Rosetzki, Rosenthal (Right), Zisling, Eshkol, and Golomb (Left). Galili later replaced Zisling. The "A" General Zionists gave in on the matter of an additional representative on the command. The Middle-Class Union appointed all three of their representatives, including Sitkov, over whom the crisis of June 1940 had broken out.

The loser in this new arrangement was Hashomer Hatzair. It was promised that within three months of the date of signing . the agreement, one of the three Mapai representatives would resign to make way for a Hashomer Hatzair representative. The promise was broken, and instead a Hashomer Hatzair representative was appointed secretary of the Histadrut Security Committee and one representative included on the Security Committee. A right-wing officer received a responsible post on the General Staff. The Security Committee (formerly the Committee of Eight) was broadened to a membership of eighteen. Most of the time it actually contained a smaller number of members, because its complement was not filled over a long period of time and because its members were frequently being replaced. The Security Committee also had a financial subcommittee.

The only body that vigorously opposed the new pact was Hashomer Hatzair. It looked upon the agreement as a surrender to all the bourgeois demands, especially to those for the appointment of Middle-Class Union representatives in the command. Even in the Middle-Class camp there were some who could not reconcile themselves to the pact. One of them was Rokakh. And on the eve of the agreement's signing, a Middle-Class Union defense committee was put together with Tehomi, the former commander of the breakaway Hagana, as chairman. There is substance to the supposition that Tehomi was among those who did not favor the new agreement.

When the Middle-Class Union people arrived to take their places in the National Command, it became clear to them that some innovations had been introduced during their absence from the security institutions. For one thing, a national force had been formed in the middle of May—the Assault Companies, the Palmakh.

🦋 The Danger of Invasion and the Founding of the Palmakh

Since the discontinuation of the activities of the Special Squads in September 1939, no independent national force of the Hagana had existed. The Field Force, which had originally been intended for this purpose, was subject to local Hagana control. Its countrywide character was only theoretical. However, the Special Squads had not been disbanded; only their activities had been discontinued with the outbreak of the war. It is doubtful whether any organizational structure whatsoever survived, but small units continued to exist here and there as the need dictated. For the most part, they engaged in action against informers and the Stern group. There was possibly a roster of names somewhere, from which men were mobilized for activities. During that whole period, there existed a group of men, veterans of the Field Squads and the Special Squads. The Palmakh myth labelled these men retroactively as "Yitzhak Sadeh's boys." They thronged around the "Old Man's campfire" and were ready to go into action when called.

Who were these men? There were men from the Field Force and its officers. There were also men who had taken part in the "cooperation" actions with the British, since Sadeh had also been engaged there; for example, the Arabists and the seamen from whom the Twenty-three were taken (see below). Many of them were men from the agricultural settlements, particularly members of the Kibbutz Meuhad. In 1940 all these men were organized in the Field Force, in the cooperation structure, in arms acquisition, or in the Supernumerary Police Force. Others remained at home, for the most part in the villages, unemployed by the Hagana. Even so, the Hagana resisted their enlistment in the army so as not to expend completely the reserves of trained Hagana officers and men.

The inactivity that marked this period of depression brought some of the men, especially city people with extreme activist opinions, to the threshold of schism. Thus, for example, one group was organized (though tenuously) in Jerusalem among the local battalions of the Field Force. Its leader was Israel Livartovsky. This group operated, according to one witness, with Sneh's knowledge. Many of its participants later entered the Palmakh, some of them even joining the Am Lohem, the "Fighting Nation" group, in 1943 (see Chapter 8). Their actions included distributing anti-British leaflets, the bombing of two printing houses in June 1942 because of the pro-British position of their German refugee owners, and other similar activities. The group apparently survived from the winter of 1940 and 1941 until the summer of 1942. Livartovsky and Meir Batz, two of the group's leaders, left it in the summer of 1942 because of Etzel-like political tendencies which began to emerge, and the group was disbanded. The value of this group should not be exaggerated, but it can serve as an example for the moods that reigned among the young people whose hunger for real action was not satisfied by regular Hagana activities.

The concept of a national defense force was not completely

shelved during the period between the Special Squads and the Palmakh. It was given expression in the circle of "Young Turks" created by Israel Galili as early as 1939 and

> motivated by a search for organized contact with the stratum of young officers of outstanding promise with whom connections were established outside the regular hierarchical channels. There was a wide-ranging critique of the routine concepts in which the General Staff was caught up. Within the official structures, it would have been nearly impossible to carry on an examination on a basis of equality. Therefore, this noncommittal framework of friendly discussion was created. Our assumption was that one should not differentiate among professional, social, and political factors. But we were warned not to enter on a clarification of "politics" because that might blast the circle altogether. Tendencies, structures, and (up to a certain point) professional questions were discussed. The group had a Histadrut makeup, because we wanted to consolidate the Histadrut section of the officer corps. Many decisions which were prevented by the right-wing veto required explanation which would have been impossible to render in an official way. There were also some who wanted the voice of the young people to be heard. Especially when the debate about the pros and cons of recruitment for the the British Army began, they were interested in a recognition of the value of the Hagana being expressed and its having an influence.[17]

This circle survived until the War of Independence. Hagana commanders and men of other ranks, officers in the British Army (Eliyahu Cohen, Israel Carmi), and one man who was not from the Histadrut—Moshe Sneh—participated. The group's members came mostly from the "B" Faction and those who sympathized with it. The circle discussed development plans and tendencies, and it was to have a vast influence on everything that was done in the Hagana. In a word, officers and men of the Hagana were dreaming of the creation of a national force, a continuation of the tradition of the Field Squads and the Special Squads. The dangers of an Arab uprising or a

German invasion, the fear of an anti-Zionist solution after the war against which the Yishuv would be forced to resist, and the chance of a Zionist solution which the Yishuv would have to defend—all these reasons dictated the establishment of an immediately effective national force.

When Rommel's troops reached the Egyptian border early in April 1941, followed immediately by the great defeat in Greece, the agency and the National Command roused themselves to increased defense activity.

The British government was called upon to expand Jewish enlistment in the army and to cancel the binding parity of Jewish and Arab units that had been decreed at the beginning of the mobilization for the Buffs in September 1940. The desperate situation had its effect, and the British agreed that Jews could be enlisted for the army beyond the quota of Arab recruits (May 1941).[18]

A second demand touched upon the problem of the defense of the Jewish community of Palestine by legal forces. It seemed clear to most of the representatives of the Yishuv that, under existing conditions, only a regular army could stand up against a German invasion, and even the British Army's chances were not promising. However, even earlier, the agency had sought defenses against the dangers of paratroop landings, harassment actions, and Arab uprisings. This had been done through recruitment for the legal Supernumerary Police Force, almost the only bright spot in the development of the Hagana during those first years of the war.

A wide difference prevailed between the mobilized strength (3,595 men at the beginning of June, including 1,073 Jewish Settlement Police) and the authorized force (about 5,500), and the agency called for a narrowing of the gap through rapid mobilization. It also demanded military training for these units, so that they could be given actual battle assignments. Under the press of events, the British authorities also responded positively to these points. In fact, though, recruitment had proceeded at a snail's pace, and the fault was not all British. Up to August, 1,161 additional Supernumeraries were enlisted in the Jewish Settlement Police, some of them kibbutz members; by the end of August, the number of Supernumeraries reached 5,300. But all the promises given as to their training and assignments were speedily broken. On July 7, McConnell, the then commanding general of the army in Palestine, informed Sharett by letter that the government had no intention of employing the Jewish Settlement Police for tasks other than the local defense of Jewish colonies. With that, the plan for broadened training necessarily collapsed.

The agency put no credence whatsoever in the claim—frequently heard from government spokesmen— that the British did not have sufficient equipment, not even simple rifles, to arm the Supernumeraries or any other Jewish force; yet it is a fact that the armament, equipment, and logistic situation of British armies in 1941 were very poor. Things reached the point where Lord Moyne (on whom the suspicion of particular amity for the Jews ought not fall) stated that the Jews would have to use their illegal arms for the defense of Palestine.[19] Of course, the intent was to liquidate the whole question of Jewish arms by legalization, registration, and control. However, it appears that the situation in the Middle East had become so grave that the addition of some thousands of rifles was most desirable for the Allied forces from a military point of view. The new Supernumeraries were equipped with Italian arms of dreadful quality—the weapons of the Hagana were, after all, better than that.

The official Jewish bodies not only increased enlistment for the army and the Supernumeraries but also strengthened the self-defense force—once more against the danger of invasion and all it involved. To improve the defensive position, an overall defense plan (Plan A) was worked out and systematized on the basis of experience during the years of the Arab riots. The static elements were the main factors in this plan. The Field

Force became a local battle reserve for reconnaissance or attack activities within the local command structure. The number of operating Field Force battalions was set at seventeen in January 1941. Despite the army enlistments, which came mainly from this force, those responsible tried to preserve it through an additional recruitment order for the Hagana. Thus we have seen already that in April the intelligence service, which had previously been under the protection of the Mosad and the Histadrut, became a Hagana body. Other branches of defense work were also reinforced and reorganized.[20]

In Plan A, with the Field Force being placed under the orders of district and regional commanders, signs of the autonomous approach were already discernible. However, because of the perils facing the country, the opposite approach—the centristic—was also bolstered. In the middle of May several instructions of focal importance for the history of the Hagana were published. Their function was to strengthen the organization, centralize it around the command, and establish new bodies in it that would be suitable for the new tasks.

We must remember that those orders were issued about one month before the Middle-Class Union members came back to the National Command. Sneh's statement that the creation of the Palmakh was made possible partially by the absence of the middle class from the command is thus applicable to the whole set of the May orders.

On May 15, 1941, the National Command published its Principles of the Hagana, which had gone through various transformations and reformulations. They state that "the Hagana is subject to the authority of the World Zionist Organization together with the people of Israel in the Eretz Israel [Palestine]. It stands under their jurisdiction and responds to their command." Its duty was to protect the Yishuv from any attempt on the Yishuv's life, property, or honor; and the Hagana was the sole agent permitted to operate in defense matters. Taking the actual situation at the fronts into consideration, it was noted that one role of the Hagana was to defend Palestine from any hostile operation from outside; the Hagana's character as a unified and national detachment with a military chain of command, centralized and ordered by rank, was emphasized. The national unity embodied in the Hagana was stressed, and expression was given to this fact in the selection of the flag and anthem. "Hagana discipline is based on the member's inner recognition, on the prevalence of amicable relationships, freedom of opinion, and human equality." The Hagana, free of non-Jewish rules and regulations, trained for "loyalty to People and Land, love of freedom, Jewish sovereignty, courage, perseverance in the face of suffering and oppression, willingness for sacrifice, respect for human life, honesty, simplicity of life, and for Jewish and all human culture."

Yitzhak Sadeh's influence on the wording of these principles was great. If we compare the articles and training methods of the future Palmakh with the guidelines the Hagana set out for itself in 1941, we see that one hand and one heart guided them both. The spirit of the Palmakh, myth as well as reality, grew at the bosom of those Hagana values that found expression, among other places, in the Principles.[21]

The focal point in the group of orders of May 1941 was Order of the Day No. 8 (see Appendix VII), which discussed the policy and organization of the Hagana in the existing political and military situation. After an introduction, which contained a great deal of embellishment of the reality, it was stated that in view of the dangerous situation in the area, new action was contemplated by the Hagana.

The action was specified in eight paragraphs, with "enlistment and training of units for special duties which may be needed" appearing in fifth place (after training, acquisition of tools, preparation and execution of defense plans, and improvement of communications). This order shows the real position the Palmakh and its creation occupied in the eyes of the molders of security policy in 1941.

Within the larger framework of preparations for a possible invasion or Arab uprising, the structure for which so many Hagana officers had long been hoping was finally established. On May 19, 1941, by Emergency Order No. 2, the Assault Companies (Palmakh), for execution of any special or dangerous duty assigned to them by the High Command, were created.

Very little is known to us of the meeting and talks (May 14 to 16) that preceeded the National Command decision to create the Palmakh. The minutes of the command's meetings were destroyed on June 29, 1946 (Black Sabbath). It is possible that copies were preserved in various places or in the keeping of individuals, but so far such have not been found. The men who took part in the creation of the Palmakh and delivered testimony on it do not generally remember more than the bare decision to create the force. One of the witnesses deposes that

> these were intended to be special companies; and, since there had been an enlargement in regard to the Field Force, it was decided to take a more select force for the Assault Companies. We sought a way to concentrate elite units. This subject had been on our agenda for quite some time. . . . Therefore, it was decided to bring together distinguished officers for bold actions, to elevate the professional level of the personnel, and to maintain them in a state of readiness.

This deposition receives confirmation in the statement of Dr. Sneh who adds that "for budgetary reasons, we could not raise a standing battalion; and we were forced to construct this force, too, by regions, though it was detached from local command."[22] According to Sneh and Reizer (the latter was still chief of staff officially), Eshkol objected to the new unit for budgetary reasons. And Reizer claims that the first money was given the Palmakh on his own responsibility, without the knowledge of the Hagana treasury.

Such testimonies contain nothing to answer the question of the Assault Companies' role. From an analysis of the decisions of the National Command, this picture emerges: In the face of the expected danger, it was decided to create a defensive force, on the model of the Field Force in its beginning, which would function as a Hagana battle reserve. If the possibility arose of cooperating with the British in definite actions of importance, the reserve would also serve that goal. And if illegal actions became necessary, the new reserve could be mustered for that also. But it would be most desirable if, at a time of danger of invasion, this could become a legal force.

> We are proceeding on the assumption [Golomb stated] that some isolated settlements may not be able to stand by themselves now, without some more widely oriented force, a force based more on the idea of mutual help among the localities, based more on activism. . . . A centralized legal force is likely to arise as an outside force which, despite its subordination to all kinds of British inspectors, will be subject also to our own jurisdiction. The defense will have to base itself on a legal force.[23]

One must not conclude from the above that all the elements that participated in the creation of the Palmakh shared Golomb's opinion. It may be supposed that Sadeh did not subscribe to those words. And we know that Tabenkin and Riftin did not agree with them either. However, it is clear that there were central personalities among the founders of the Palmakh who, like Golomb, expressed such "legalistic" opinions aggressively and emphatically.

The new force was a battle reserve created, at a time when very grave danger was anticipated for the Jews of Palestine, by a security staff responsible for the Yishuv's welfare. This force was intended—and this is a matter of first importance—for "any duty assigned it, at any place or time decided by the High Command" (from Emergency Order No. 2).

Thus, not only was the idea of a national force crowned with victory, but also a second concept that had been nurtured within

Histadrut circles: the Hagana as a security arm of Zionist policy.

This also answers the question of whether the Palmakh was formed as an outgrowth of the cooperation with the British or as a result of internal Hagana developments. David Ben-Gurion writes (in a Hebrew article in 1949) that

> with the help of the British Command, special Assault Companies (Palmakh) were established within the framework of the Hagana—though the Hagana, theoretically, had not been removed from its illegal status. The new units received intensive training in sabotage and were designed to fight any enemy who might succeed in invading Palestine.[24]

Obviously, he confused the establishment of the Palmakh in 1941 with the training of the Palmakh by the British at the time of the danger of the invasion of Palestine in 1942. But Moshe Sharett, who distinguishes clearly between 1941 and 1942, does not have a much different idea. He states that the creation of the Palmakh was planned a long time before May 1941. "But such is the fate of many necessities in human society. Just recognizing them is not enough to bring them to fulfillment, until some external emergency arises."[25]

Continual contact and cooperation with the British in all the battles of the war, in his opinion, brought about "the formation of the first nucleus of a standing, independent Hebrew army." (Actually, the Palmakh was put on a "standing" basis only in June 1942.) On another occasion, Sharett expressed a somewhat different view. He stressed rather the evolutionary growth of the Palmakh as an imperative of defense. Even so, however, he set forth that another aspect of the problem was how this force had been made possible from the point of view of enlistment and that of training. The potentiality arose during a world war. Such a unit was necessary for participation in that war. The Palmakh depended on recruitment for the army and profited from it. If that had not been the case, the Palmakh would have encountered many diffi ulties from right-wing circles in the Yishuv. Emergency conditions alone persuaded them to support it, even though only to a slight extent. David Hacohen and others also tend toward the view that the Palmakh was actually formed through the "cooperation." In contrast, Israel Galili believes that the cooperation was nothing more than a convenient cover for it and offered some budgetary aid, but nothing else.[26]

The documents themselves speak a different language. The very question about the origins of the Palmakh and its genesis is not properly phrased. Clandestine cooperation with the British did not stand in contradiction or conflict with the internal development of the Hagana. Cooperation, as distinct from the recruitment for the British Army, was the demonstrative activation of an independent Hebrew force, appearing as an *ally* of certain British military sections.

But the answer to the question, Was the Palmakh created as a result of the establishment of the cooperation network, in order to serve it and render it assistance? would be in the negative. The founding of the Palmakh was, first and foremost, a result of the inner development of the Hagana which demanded the creation of an independent Jewish force. Its establishment was determined by the danger that threatened Palestine and by the internal need for a battle reserve for self-supported tasks of all types, including aid to operations in cooperation with the British. The matter of Palmakh participation in British operations came up only after its creation and was not a factor in the deliberations of the National Command in its sessions in the middle of May.

This view also receives confirmation from the analysis of a second document of May 15, 1941 (apparently not published until June 30). That document was entitled "Roles and Composition of the Assault Companies." According to it, the Assault Companies were intended for two principle tasks: action against gangs and Arab riots, and support operations for the British forces in the event of an invasion of Palestine. There is no proof that this second role was designed for the companies on the basis of coordination with the British. Quite the contrary, this point was never seriously discussed until after the Syrian operation, as we shall see.

The Palmakh was founded for the defense of the Yishuv. The question of its cooperation or noncooperation with British activities was only of secondary importance. The cooperation network with the British was—from the Zionist standpoint—a vital part of the efforts to participate in a war which was a Jewish war no less (and in fact much more) than it was a British war. But the influence of the cooperation was not direct; it was not for its sake that the Palmakh was set up.

We can learn about what is unique in the attempts to establish the Palmakh from a comparison of the order on its creation with the articles of organization of the Hagana Field Squads in November 1938. Several points stand out in this regard:

The Field Squads' centralized character found expression in the fact of its being separated from local Hagana programs, in its countrywide training program, and in its being subject to the direct orders of the National Command (reference here is to the regulations and not the reality, which was somewhat different). The Palmakh, too, was proclaimed from the start as a "national and regional battle detachment," "absolutely separated" from the local Hagana organization. Together with the emphasis here on centralization, there is also a concession to local organization ("regional battle detachment"). This is repeated in the directive that a company commander of the Palmakh is subordinate to the instructions of a Hagana regional commander as long as the company is located in the area of the latter's command (article four). The point is further stressed by putting responsibility for the training, preparation, and readiness of the Assault Companies on the regional officer (article seven). Article six of the Field Squads directive paralleled these points. It stated that the chief of the National Command was to exercise his command of the Field Squads through district commanders. Dr. Sneh explained that the Palmakh was left under local command for financial reasons. But it is reasonable that there was also the desire not to quarrel with the local command, and especially not with the Tel Aviv people, for whom the creation of a national force was not a pleasant matter (as Dr. Sneh asserts).

The Field Squads were a mobilized force. In contrast, the Palmakh was first planned—apparently out of budgetary considerations—as a reserve force in constant readiness, but not on a mobilized basis. The only mobilized component of the Palmakh were the company commanders. In article nine of the later document, it is further stated that regular training should be given on weekends.

The Field Squads were a popular force, open to anyone. This was not true of the Palmakh, which was established as a commando force. Sadeh and his co-workers were certainly influenced by German and Russian military literature and British attempts to create a commando unit in the Middle East. Hence the directive (article six) that no personnel changes were to be introduced into the Palmakh without the confirmation of the High Command.

In 1938 the question of the command of the Field Squads had been left open. In the regulations, a vice-chief of the National Command, who would take care of the Field Squads, was mentioned. But his powers were never defined, and in fact no such officer was ever appointed. Instead, Eliyahu Cohen and Yitzhak Sadeh made their appearance as the actual commanders of the Field Squads. We may suppose that this time Sadeh stood up for the necessity of setting up a somewhat more formal chain of command. According to the order setting up the Palmakh (article eight), a General Staff officer was appointed with command authority in Palmakh matters. And in an abbreviated version of that order, it was stated that this officer should be Sadeh—not *Palmakh Commander*, but *Officer for Palmakh Affairs* with command authority (again a reference to unwillingness to quarrel with local commanders). It was further specified that this officer's power should be exercised by means of the local Hagana chain of command.

The Palmakh that was established in 1941 was different in

composition, duties, and character from its successor, the later Palmakh. That later Palmakh was popular, was wrenched loose from all local ties, and had its own staff; also it was a standing force. The "first Palmakh" was planned as an elite corps of commandos with a partial tie to the local Hagana commanders. It had no autonomous command body, it was not a standing force, and its training was not continuous.

4 ☙ *Difficulties of the First Year*

☙ *The Twenty-three and the Syrian Operation*

The beginnings of the Palmakh are inextricably connected with two events: the sailing of the Twenty-three, who comprised the complement of the boat *Sea Lion,* to Tripoli (Lebanon) in order to blow up the refineries there and their disappearance on May 18, 1941; and the participation of the Palmakh in the invasion of Syria on June 8, 1941.

We know that the center of gravity of cooperation activity shifted to Palestine in 1941 because of the German conquest of the Balkans. British sabotage and espionage services were seeking allies and agents among the population of the Middle East for purposes of sabotage and guerrilla warfare, in case the region should be conquered by the Germans, something which appeared very possible at the beginning of 1941. The ties that were formed as early as 1940 between the M.O.4 and the Hagana, plus the fact that the Jews were obviously anti-German, overshadowed the anti-Zionist considerations of the top echelons of military and political authority in the Middle East. Cooperation, therefore, continued.

The British D Branch was mostly interested in training men

for naval operations, sabotage, and communications, insofar as these activities contributed to its plans in the Middle East. A course had been set up in the Carmel forests during the summer of 1940; in it seven young men learned sabotage operations from British instructors. After that other courses were conducted. In February 1941 a course in seamanship was opened in Tel Aviv, under Katriel Yaffe. The course contained about twenty-five participants.

At the same time, three graduates of earlier courses—Ben-Shaprut, Agiov, and Leszczinsky—went to Egypt to take part in special operations of the Department of Naval Intelligence and D Branch. The three were placed on the *Dolphin,* a small diesel-powered ship, and sailed for Crete and Greece. The men of the *Dolphin* took part in a British-Spanish (Republican) commando operation on the island of Castellorodos. They then moved to Greece, where they were joined by three men (Kostika, Y. Spector, and Yoel Golomb) who had completed the Tel Aviv course on March 26, 1941. The youths helped with the removal of soldiers and materiel from Greece, and later from Crete, and also performed other tasks. Two days before the island's fall, all six were rescued. They reached Egypt safely, and on June 6 they all returned to Palestine.

These six young Jews were sent out on dangerous and responsible quasi-military assignments—and fulfilled them faithfully. They were structured in the same framework as the Twenty-three and the participants in the invasion of Syria. But the fact that their activities had no direct connection with Palestine prevented the six from becoming Palmakh heroes. They were not made part of its collective consciousness. Legend escaped them, despite the fact that they were worthy of the crown of heroism no less than the Twenty-three.

In April and May of 1941 the British command began to plan an operation against Vichy Syria, though the decision to invade was only taken on May 25, 1941. Because it was known that German planes were stopping over in Syrian airfields, it was determined to bomb and sabotage them. In conjunction with that, D Branch was assigned the task of sabotaging the refineries in Tripoli. After two earlier reconnaissances by a squad of Arabists in Syria, an amphibious sabotage operation plan was set up. The ship *Sea Lion,* the property of the Palestinian government (which intended to use it to hunt for Jewish immigrants!), was turned over to a group of twenty-three Jewish men under the command of Tsvi Spector and accompanied by an observer (Sir Anthony Palmer) from D Branch. The men of the ship were to approach the refineries and (except for three who were to remain with the vessel) come in on three small landing craft. They were to divide into three groups on shore: a guard group with the landing craft, a holding group along the road leading to the refineries, and a point group to break through and demolish.

Notice of the operation apparently did not reach the agency until the beginning of May. There was insufficient time to check the plan and make preparations. And the Jews' suggestion—to approach the objective by land and sea simultaneously—was rejected by the English. On May 18 the boat went its way with twenty-four passengers; not one came back.

A myth was created around their disappearance. Yitzhak Sadeh's statements in *Magen Beseter* are typical. He concludes: "To this day it is not known how the Twenty-three fell or met their end" (p. 93).

The Jewish Agency made great efforts to shed light on the fate of the Twenty-three. Immediately following the conquest of Syria, two Hagana men were sent there. They organized a searching investigation and turned in detailed reports on their findings. From the reports, it seems likely that the boat lost its way and came near shore to get its bearings (which may explain its sudden discovery). Examination of four bodies which were buried in Tripoli shows that the ship, which was loaded with explosives, was apparently broken up as the result of an explosion. According to the statement of a French judge, the prisoners were taken to Aleppo. There all trace of them is lost, and it must be supposed that they were executed.

A doubt arises as to Palmer's fate. In a letter to Sharett, on September 16, 1941, Shiloah states that Perkins, an intelligence officer, claimed that "several new threads have been uncovered in the Palmer case: according to information in his possession, a British officer by the name of Palmer was shot by Junier (a French police officer) after being captured, imprisoned on the Island of Arwad, taken to Latakia," and from there to another place, the name of which is not known. A single man is being spoken of here. Shiloah thought that Palmer had perhaps saved himself in one of the small boats tied to the *Sea Lion* and had then been captured. After the conquest of Syria, when the Vichy general Dentz was moved to Jerusalem before being sent back to France, Sharett requested the British Army command to detain the officer until the fate of the Twenty-three was made known (there was no doubt that Dentz was familiar with the case). But the army apparently attached no importance to the matter—or perhaps details were known to them and not turned over to the Jews—so Dentz and his people were sent back to France without the agency's being informed of any further particulars of the affair.

The episode of the Twenty-three brought rather regretful thoughts to those responsible for it. The view was expressed that it had been a mistake to involve the best of the trained men in one daring mission. But it was plain that despite the inadequate preparation and the slight chance for success, the agency could not have refused to execute the operation, nor could it have been delayed. There was a risk—as in any like military action—but the risk had seemed acceptable.

What historical value did the deed of the Twenty-three have? There is no doubt that its chief importance lies in its becoming a sort of epic of sacrificial courage. Under the conditions of World War II, in which the Jews were generally the persecuted sacrificial lamb, the mythos of courage in battle had a major value for those who were trying to rear a young generation of fighters in the Land of Israel. If we compare the action of twenty-three boys and their fate with large-scale commando operations (whether successful or not) in France and elsewhere, then this was an act of very minor proportions. But it was a signpost at the start of the Palmakh's way. Through the Palmakh, it became an educational symbol of great significance.

It is very doubtful if the Twenty-three knew of the decision that had been taken in the National Command of the Hagana to create Assault Companies. And if they knew about it, they probably did not consider it important. The date of the pertinent order is May 19—one day after they went out on the operation. Nonetheless, it makes sense to tie in the episode of the Twenty-three with the establishment of the Palmakh. The two events were the children of the same circumstances: fear of a German invasion and anxiety over the direction of events in Syria and Iraq. Yitzhak Sadeh, the man appointed officer for Palmakh matters, was also responsible for the "special operations" in which the six who went to Greece and the Twenty-three who went to Tripoli took part. The Twenty-three were "Yitzhak Sadeh's boys." They would have been natural candidates for enlistment in the Palmakh. The tradition that looks upon the Twenty-three as the first men of the Palmakh has, therefore, well-based historical roots.

For a long period of time the agency had been pressing the British to take Syria, but the British gave no consideration whatsoever to the agency's opinions or advice. The situation changed with the landing of German planes in Syria. After strong pressure on Churchill's part, Wavell consented to attempt the conquest of the two Levantine protectorates. The operation was assigned to General "Jumbo" (Sir Henry Maitland) Wilson. An Australian division (the Seventh, less one regiment), a regiment of Indian infantry, two Free French regiments, and several other smaller units were placed under him. Altogether, they comprised about fifteen full battle battalions, with a few tanks. Thirty Vichy regiments would oppose them, with ninety tanks.

A whisper of the invasion plans crept into Sharett's ear, and he sought to confirm the rumors. But at the beginning of June, Wilson was still denying that there was a decision to invade. It is difficult to determine the exact date on which the Jews were requested to supply guides and demolition men to the Allied forces for the needs of the expedition. From the available notes, it is likely that it was only a few days before the invasion. In the eyes of the British Army, these volunteers were nothing more than guides who belonged to a local "subversive organization."[1] But the Jews viewed matters in an utterly different light.

Yitzhak Sadeh was assigned to assemble the volunteers. He decided to turn the nucleus of the Palmakh, the creation of which had been begun only a few days previously, to this purpose. Two companies of people from the Jordan and Jezreel valley settlements were then about to be made up, under Moshe Dayan and Yigal Allon respectively. The order to the two commanders—to assemble units as rapidly as possible for action in Syria—was received in the very midst of the enlistment of these clandestine units. The necessity to work quickly was stressed; therefore they both stopped routine recruitment procedures.

Within a day or two, thirty young men had been gathered in each formation. The British Army supplied neither arms nor equipment. (It was agreed upon with the army that if weapons were lost, they would be replaced.) Only with difficulty were the men given military papers. In the June 22 session of the Agency Executive, one member complained that they had sent Jewish lads to war without uniforms; if captured, they would have been condemned as spies. The feeling prevailed among the recruits that even the Hagana did not care enough about them. Dayan wrote that

it is superfluous to state that the new recruits had not had time to train, nor even to organize. They had not yet been divided into platoons and squads. We had no leaders. . . . I gave my superior [Sadeh] a detailed list that included first aid kits, mattresses, shoes, canteens, flashlight batteries, maps, and Arab dress. . . . Down to the last day, we got nothing. . . . I don't blame anybody for it—I only wish to complain of our form of organization by which the commander had to see to every single thing, from the smallest to the greatest.[2]

The "pathfinders" did not know the path on which the army would have to move. They were forced to turn to local Arabs and learn about the surroundings and the right roads from them. Dayan has pointed out that the boys' training was quite uneven. It was necessary to complete their basic training with maximum speed and to impart auxiliary skills (like map reading) so that the recruits would not fail on the day of the invasion. Advance reconnaissance actions were also taken. These were to have great importance from the Jewish point of view, beyond their value for the operations on the invasion date, because practical field skills were learned through them, and a knowledge of the northern frontier was acquired. The invasion began at dawn on June 8, 1941. The previous night, the various Palmakh squads were active.

Several facts must be pointed out here. The number of participants was small. There were thirty-three members of the Assault Companies, plus a member of Kibbutz Dan who was not a Palmakh man. They operated in squads of two or three, or even alone. Of the twelve squads, two guided the army, seven cut telephone lines, and only three had combat or demolition duties: those of Dayan at Iskenderun (Escandelion, Lebanon) and Allon at the bridges over the Litani, as well as Meir Davidson's squad, which was guiding an Australian battalion and participated in the capture of the villages of Aitaroun, Bent Jbail, and Ain Ebel. The casualties were one seriously wounded (Dayan, who lost his eye), and three slightly wounded.

At the same time a small detachment of Arabists, under the command of Yisrael Ben-Yehuda (Abdu), crossed the border to Beirut and Damascus. The unit was, apparently, unable to organize and operate until the capture of those cities by the Allied forces. However, with their capture, two men of the unit crossed the front lines and carried out sabotage operations in Aleppo.

How the invasion of Syria looked to the Australians with whom the men of the Palmakh were working is very interesting. An Australian military historian, Lang, for example, gives us an interesting description of the Iskenderun operation (well known to Hebrew readers from Dayan's report—see Appendix VI).[3] The Australian states that Australian and Palestinian scouts guided the men to the rural Jewish settlement of Hanita, where they were well fed in the communal dining hall. From there they went across the border at an unguarded place, over hills covered with thorn bushes. The night was rather dark and cloudy. One group, under the command of Captain Henry Gowling, turned toward the road north of Ras En-Naqoura. The rest—Lieutenants Kiffin, Allen, and Cowdery with fifteen men, including three Jewish scouts and an Arab—continued on their way for about fifteen miles.

At approximately 3:30 they reached the road north of the point where they had been told explosives were kept, near Ras el-Abyad. Kiffin left Sergeant Wardley there with three men to stop vehicles coming from the north, and led the rest of his men south. Various bridges and passes were quietly checked and found to be unmined. At one of the bridges, Allen was left with three men to block the road while Kiffin advanced southward with the rest to search out the mined location. At approximately five o'clock, as they were north of Iskenderun, someone opened fire upon them from a stone emplacement. The Australians stormed the position and took it. Allen heard the shooting and joined them.

A long fight began, Lang continues, with French reinforcements coming to the aid of the men of the position. A group of Kiffin's men attacked French units on an adjacent farm, and a machine gun was put out of action there by Private Henderson, who attacked it with hand grenades. A mortar was taken. Two of the Jewish scouts were wounded. Kiffin's men, while still under fire from the field, set up the mortar as well as a Hotchkiss gun which had been captured on the roof of the fortified stone building. They exchanged fire with a French column advancing from the north to meet the invaders. A few trucks of the column were stopped and their occupants taken prisoner. A shell from the captured mortar stopped two armored cars that had appeared, and their crews surrendered. A dozen cyclists who appeared were also dispersed. Wardley and three of his men (two of them Palestinians) were summoned from their northern position and joined the defense of the stone building, while others were fighting with the French in the planted field.

The Australian notes that at about seven o'clock an explosion was heard from the south. The demolition they had wanted to prevent had been carried out.

The summation of the action is positive in the view of this Australian historian. Most of the details agree with Dayan's statements, except for the number of Palestinians (five, without the Arab scout) and the casualties. It is interesting that the Australian report delineates the capture of the stone building as a combined action of the group, while according to Dayan he took it himself.

We learn from this incident how limited this action actually was, though it too was to become a part of Palmakh tradition. Legends were woven about it, and the song of "How through Syria Marched the Palmakh" was sung.

We have already remarked that the importance of this episode did not lie in the dimensions of the operations, but in the historical development that began there. Thereafter, the Palmakh looked upon this as its beginning. It is no accident that in 1944, when the Palmakh had become a mass body, they came back to this and elevated it to a symbol and model for Palmakh members. Of course, Moshe Dayan was not convinced of the usefulness of the action:

If there is any reason to come now and tell the Syrian story (our Syrian story), it would only be, in my opinion, for members who could learn a lesson from it. I am not sure of the political gains or the indirect value that accrued to us from the operation.[4]

And indeed, there was one who did "learn a lesson," in keeping with Dayan's desire. When Allon encountered a stubborn refusal from the Australians on his plan to seize two bridges over the Litani with a large force, he understood and "learned his lesson" from that. The men of the Palmakh saw the cumbersome and tradition-bound British military machinery in action without being part of it, and from that they learned much. But the main thing about the Syrian operation was that a small Jewish force had acted as an independent Ally—though on a minute scale—on an actual battle front, and had acted with success.

True, the Palmakh did not "march through Syria" as in the words of the song. In fact, it hardly existed. But the foundation laid in the Syria operations was sufficiently firm not to become a mere fleeting episode but the beginning of a long and fruitful road.[5]

⚑ *The Palmakh on the Threshold of Disbandment— June 1941–March 1942*

At the end of the Syrian campaign, the efforts to translate the order regarding the establishment of the Palmakh into the language of reality were renewed. Skeleton commands were set up for nine companies. The idea of creating permanent encampments for the first two companies was conceived. They were to be in the wooded area of Ginossar for A Company, and in Beit Oren for B Company (of which Meir Davidson was appointed commander after Dayan's injury and reassignment to a new post on recovery). There is no doubt that Yitzhak

Sadeh and his associates were striving for the creation of such camps. One may guess that they realized, after the Palmakh's success in Syria, that the time was right to demand the realization of their concepts.

The General Staff, however, rejected their program and went back to the original proposal, according to which the companies were not to be standing ones, and training was to be confined to a few days a month. The encampments were dispersed from both locations, apparently in the beginning of August 1941.

The development of the Palmakh was slowed by a lack of funds. There is no doubt that the sums were very meager. Out of the Hagana's overall budget for September 1941 to September 1942, which was £229,484 (that was the gross budget—but without cost and sales exchanges, the net budget totaled £176,549), the Palmakh got a total of £23,240, most of which was received between July and September of 1942. Until July it was given only £7,388. It is difficult to suppose that, up to March, an average of more than £500–600 was received per month; that is, about £2500–3000 through the end of February 1942. Under such conditions it would be hard to create a national military structure, properly trained and mobile.

The Palmakh staff (Sadeh and his deputy Giora Shinan) were on the brink of despair. There were days when their treasury was absolutely empty, and they lacked the most trifling amounts needed to continue their work. On September 17 Shinan noted: "Got the August payroll."[6] On September 29 Shinan and Sadeh were expecting a budget of £1,200 for October. But on October 3 the amount was reduced to £800 (apparently per month) for the next three months. And even so, budget was one thing, appropriation was something else. On October 14, Shinan noted: "Budgetary situation is hopeless"; on October 20, "Despair. The chief [Sneh] promised £400." The following day he wrote: "Waited till 15:00 for a reply on the matter of the £400—nothing. Yitzhak told me that if things do not clear up he will turn in his resignation."

In November, the situation improved somewhat. "The budget allowed bivouacs" and company maneuvers. At the beginning of December, once again: "No money. E Company march canceled." On December 4, a meeting of the commanders of A, B, and C Companies took place, with all of them in a mood of "money or resign." Under these conditions, all sorts of proposed solutions flowered. It was none other than a city man, Israel Livartovsky, commander of F Company in Jerusalem, who brought up the idea of sending twenty men of his company to work in a kibbutz, where their earnings would cover their training (December 8). But only isolated individuals were brought into this work, and the result was nil.

On December 8 a meeting of the National Command was held with the Palmakh staff on the matter of "the operatives' demand to decide on the continuation or liquidation of the Palmakh." The command's response was typical of the difficulties involved in questions of the Hagana Assault Companies: "(1) Final answer in the course of one month; (2) fulfillment of budget promised for immediate work in December." From this it is discernible that the National Command was still not clear on what the future of the Palmakh would be. Its very existence was again in doubt. However, by December and January, a turning point became apparent. We no longer hear the strong tone of bitterness of earlier months. At that time, new programs of cooperation were entering the operational phase (see next chapter), and the Palmakh was being placed on a fresh basis.

What was the background of this development? It is possible to differentiate between two aspects of the budget problem. On the one hand, the national funds had difficulty collecting money during the war period. Their income sank while needs were mounting. In October 1941 the Jewish Agency treasurer, Eliezer Kaplan, faced the probability of an income of £400,000–425,000, over against expenses of £700,000 for the agency during the year 1941/2. The attempt at surmounting the difficulties by taking bank loans (in exchange for a lien on future income) proved that this way was generally valid only in time of emergency, when the bankers did not tighten their fists. Thus, for example, it was stated in the Agency Executive session of August 10, 1941, that the Anglo-Palestine Bank had refused to issue a loan of £50,000 intended mainly for security needs (£10,000 were loaned). Nor were the English in any hurry to organize courses or encampments within the cooperation framework, unless the matter was very important for themselves. We have already pointed out that such courses ceased in the summer of 1941.

The other aspect of the budget problem was the question of internal relations within the Yishuv. A considerable portion of the Hagana budget came from the Kofer Hayishuv and other community funds (the Fund-Raising Service of the Hagana, the Emergency Tax, Histadrut support, and so on). Middle-class circles played a large part in these collections. There was also definite "bourgeois" influence in the Agency Executive (which contributed £60,000 of the £176,500 Hagana budget for the year 1941/2). The very creation of the Palmakh was aided by the absence of the Middle-Class Union people from the National Command. When they came back, they continued their opposition. They looked upon the Palmakh as a Histadrut army, "playing soldier," and asserted that in a time of invasion a few hundred boys—untrained and unarmed—would be unable to stand up against the mighty German war machine, that the money used for their maintenance could be used for recruitment for the British Army.

There is certainly a basis for spelling out the fact that Etzel, along with rightist elements in the Hagana, was trying to split the Hagana during the summer and fall of 1941. It follows that middle-class opposition to the Palmakh in 1941 was especially grave because it posed a constant threat of schism. In very large measure, this explains the Palmakh's budgetary difficulties.

Under these conditions, the nuclei of the first companies of the Palmakh were formed and their training set up. Except for A Company—which was located in the Jordan Valley and the eastern Emek (Jezreel), where the tradition of the Field Squads and the Field Force was quite strong—not one of the companies established reached the full complement of 120 men.

On November 9, 1941, it was finally determined that only six companies, instead of the original nine, would be established. Four were based in agricultural areas—A Company under Allon, B Company under Meir Davidson, C Company under Uri Yoffe, and E Company under Avraham Negev. Two companies were based in Jerusalem and Tel Aviv respectively: D Company under Binyamin Tsur in Tel Aviv, and in Jerusalem F Company, which included the people of the settlements in the mountains around Jerusalem and in the Dead Sea area, with Israel Livartovsky as commander. Three of the commanders (Allon, Davidson, and Yoffe) were kibbutz members.

These companies were mainly composed of people from the agricultural collectives and settlements, as well as "Yitzhak Sadeh's boys" from all parts of the country. In Jerusalem, people from the agricultural settlements were recruited for the company, as well as people from the Field Force, especially students. The question came up as to whether girls should be recruited for the Palmakh. The Hagana chief of staff had issued explicit instructions that they should not, but during the winter of 1941/2 Livartovsky disobeyed the order and assembled a small group of Jerusalem girls, the first women's formation in the Palmakh.[7] The Tel Aviv company was, even more than the Jerusalem company, an exception in regard to the rural character of the units. It was composed of working-class youth, which meant that the prevailing spirit in the Tel Aviv company was different from that in the rest of the Palmakh units.

These small units would meet on weekends and go out once or twice a month on hike-marches that included a few field exercises. In all, from June until the middle of November 1941, 205 training days were held for the companies in the entire

Palmakh. It is easy to imagine the low professional level of the units (compared to the later Palmakh). By November 15, the Palmakh numbered 462 men; about 100 of those were in A Company, while B Company included about 80. The number of members of Kibbutz Meuhad in Palmakh reached approximately 100 at the beginning of October. We have no details as to the organizational affiliation of the rest of the Palmakh's members. But it is known to us that Hashomer Hatzair required every kibbutz to send 2 or 3 of its members to the Palmakh, which would mean about 60 to 70 men. The rest of the people came from the cooperative settlements, the villages, and the cities.

Such was the shape of the Palmakh at the beginning: a shaky unit, impermanent, and with an insufficient budget. Only the hope and iron resolve of its officers and men carried the Palmakh past all obstacles. It may be said that the Palmakh, as a national force and battle reserve, hardly existed in 1941.

In the spring of 1942 its reestablishment was undertaken, and this time on far firmer foundations.

⚑ *The "Palestine Scheme": The "Private Network" of Moshe Dayan*

With the German invasion of the Soviet Union on June 22, 1941, the imminent direct danger to Britain's position in the Middle East during 1941 passed. Indeed, in August 1941 the British, in cooperation with the Soviets, took Iran. Thus, a further front was created (the British Ninth Army front), which stretched from the Indian border to Syria. The British forces were drawn thin throughout this entire expanse.

Very soon the fear arose that the Germans would come through the Ukraine to the Caucasus, attack Turkey (or pass through its territory without encountering resistance), and capture the oil fields of Iraq. From there, they would likely turn south toward Suez, and east toward the Persian Gulf. In 1941 this peril seemed more real than the possibility of the Suez Canal's being taken from the direction of Libya. After all, the Germans could employ their entire powerful army in Russia and Turkey, while on the Libyan front they would meet the obstacles of fortified Malta and the British Mediterranean Fleet. The British, therefore, planned to withdraw from Iraq and the Turkish border (if forced to do so) and concentrate their forces in Lebanon and the Jebel ed Druz region. Then, if they were unable to defend even that line, they would try to hold the Lebanon Mountains as an enclave within the territory captured by the Germans.

In the summer of 1941, the British began to prepare suitable defensive positions in this region. As we have previously noted, Professor Rattner was already taking part in working up these plans in the spring of 1941. In the summer of 1941, the British began taking measures to ready Palestine and Syria for the possibility of German conquest.

From available material, it seems likely that British intelligence proposed (at the end of July or the beginning of August) that the Jewish Agency establish several small radio stations to serve as centers for spy groups, should Palestine be taken by the Germans. The assignment was delegated to Moshe Dayan, who had just been released from the military hospital after losing an eye in the Syrian campaign. Dayan proposed (August 15) the establishment of broadcasting stations in the south, in Samaria, Haifa, and the Beit Shean district. Each station would be tied in with three or four men (including a group head) who would supply it with information. The English approved the plan on general lines.

On September 2, 1941, the Jews suggested that the British D Branch set up a course for twenty men. The course was opened on September 26 and ran until December 27, 1941. Twenty-three men took part, learning receiving and transmitting as well as electricity and radio theory. Sixteen of those enrolled (eight from the city or village, two from cooperatives, and six from kibbutzim) passed the course, and seven failed. D Branch, represented in Palestine by Squadron Leader G. S. Reed, agreed to carry out the original program, but it opposed various enlargement proposals that came with frequency from Moshe Dayan and Shaul Avigur, Dayan's superior.

One of the interesting expansion proposals was an idea offered by Dayan on October 20, 1941, to create units of Arabists and Germanists (Jews masquerading as Germans) that would operate within the framework of the "Palestine Scheme" (P. S. —as the radio network was called by the British). Moshe Dayan asserted that

> in light of the harsh persecution to which the Jews have been subjected in the conquered countries, there is a strong basis on which to assume that, after the enemy conquest of Palestine, the Jews will have severe difficulty visiting or working in various areas. Even if the most optimistic guess proves correct, life will be possible only for those Jews who can be exploited for the needs of the war and its economy; and such people will, certainly, be under the pressure of backbreaking labor and strict control. Should there be acts of sabotage, the number of free work areas will be reduced to a minimum (in contradistinction to working concentration camps). A drastically limited number of Jews will be permitted to work in such free areas. Without going into detail, one can assume that information collecting would be adversely affected and, over large areas, completely impossible, unless a number of people who appear to be Arabs are not employed in the job.

Similar statements were made on the need to prepare a group of Germanists. The English did not accept these suggestions until July 1942, by which time circumstances were very different (a subject to which we shall return later). At any rate, it was Moshe Dayan, apparently, who first suggested the creation of a group of Germanists.

In a letter of February 3, 1942, the agency proposed expanded fundamental military training, an increase in the number of stations included in the network, better equipment, and other improvements. From the British reply it is clear that the British feared any expansion program and confined the Palestine Scheme to the few stations that had been established: Jerusalem, Tel Aviv, Hadera, Haifa-Yagur, Geva-Ein Harod, Maoz Hayim-Ginossar. This network, known in Hagana circles as "Moshe Dayan's private network," operated until March 17, 1943, when the danger of a German invasion had already passed. It was then abolished by the British along with the routine citations about "nice work," and so on.

The Palestine Scheme was important from several points of view. Through it, contact was created between the agency and the Central British Intelligence department. This tie was not subsequently broken off. It bore fruit in 1943–1944, when the project to drop parachutists into Europe was organized, in part by the same department. The Palestine Scheme was also connected organically with other plans (to be discussed later) which undertook to prepare the Yishuv in case of a German takeover in Palestine. The Palestine Scheme also gave the Hagana's own communications system a push forward. The Jewish boys knew how to turn the training and the radio sets they had acquired to good use, other than for cooperation with the British.

Since Palestine remained unconquered by the Germans, Dayan had a hard time holding the people of the network in the state of preparedness required of them. That, possibly, is the reason for his resignation on August 5, 1942 (which the agency, of course, rejected).

The Palestine Scheme was only one of the steps—the first—taken against the growing German threat, some in partnership with the British and some outside that partnership.[1]

❦ *In the Shadow of German Invasion—The "Debate on Preferences"*

In the middle of November 1941, the British Eighth Army attacked the Germans and Italians in the western desert, defeating them and seizing all of Cyrenaica. However, by the end of 1941 and the start of 1942, the situation had begun to alter. In a series of naval engagements, the power of the British fleet was badly reduced. Malta was subjected to such heavy bombardments that it was no longer capable of serving as an effective base for operations against enemy convoys making their way from Italy to Libya.

The Germans were successful in reinforcing their army in the western desert. On January 31, 1942, General Rommel's forces—with superiority of quantity and, for the most part, of quality in equipment over their opponents—attacked the British Army. They speedily conquered Cyrenaica as far as the line of Bir Hacheim–Bir Ghazala–Tobruk. Both sides prepared for another battle, feverishly replenishing their equipment, especially tanks and tracked vehicles. The Germans attacked first on May 26, 1942, and inflicted a severe defeat on the British armored force. On June 21, Tobruk fell in a surprise attack, and 33,000 men, mostly South Africans, were taken prisoner.

Auchinleck, the British general, felt that the sole chance to stop the Germans short of Alexandria lay in defense of the El Alamein line, which had been fortified back in 1941. Its fortifications had been strengthened in 1942, with engineering units from Palestine taking part in that work. Auchinleck took over direct command of the remnants of the Eighth Army and conducted the battle at El Alamein (July 1–4, 1942) with real talent. Logistic difficulties as well as stubborn British opposition forced Rommel to halt his advance toward Alexandria and reorganize his forces.

German progress was impeded at the beginning of July. But authorities expected it to resume, and there was no confidence that it could be stopped again. Against the worst that might happen, Auchinleck began to prepare a further British retreat, apparently even from Palestine. The military-administrative steps the army took to prepare a possible retreat caused panic in Egypt and Palestine. That feeling went on until faith in the British ability to stand fast was restored. The appointment of Sir Harold Alexander as supreme commander in the Middle East and Lieutenant General Montgomery as commander of the Eighth Army did more than a little to raise morale. But the threat that loomed over Egypt and Palestine was not removed until the British victory at El Alamein (October 23 to November 4, 1942).

For the purpose of our discussion, we are interested chiefly in the fact that in the spring and summer months of 1942, thanks to Rommel, a German army stood on the outskirts of Alexandria. The immediate danger of a German invasion of Palestine was quite real, especially in light of the intense summer campaign of the Germans in the Ukraine, which brought them to Stalingrad at the end of August and to the Caucasus oil fields in September and October 1942. The peril of a two-pronged attack, from the Caucasus and the western desert, hung over the British armies in the Middle East. The German Afrika Korps, relatively the weaker prong, was brought to a stop at El Alamein (however, disaster was only averted by the Russian stand at Stalingrad). To all these threats must be added the constant danger of an Arab rebellion in the style of Rashid Ali in Egypt, Iraq, Syria, and Palestine.

Such was the background of the internal developments that took place within the Jewish community of Palestine. The possibility of invasion brought about an increase in the political-military activity of the Zionist defense machinery. This flowed in three main streams: recruitment for the British Army, accompanied by pressure for Jewish units under Jewish control; pressure on the British to expand the Supernumerary Police Force and make it into an important military auxiliary force for the defense of the country, not just a protective guard for Jewish settlements against Arab raids; and the strengthening of the independent Hagana in its various branches.

Along with this activity, a debate resumed in the Yishuv, a debate that had waxed and waned ever since the outbreak of war, called the "Debate on Preferences." To understand its nature in light of the 1942 invasion threat, let us go back over its history in the earlier phases of the war.

The argument revolved about the policy of mobilization and its manifold ramifications.

One view could be stated this way: The Jews cannot rely on a foreign command, to which the Jewish force assembled for the British Army has been made subordinate. A Jewish force which does not *directly* serve Jewish ends cannot be looked upon as an independent Jewish force.

The advocates of this view did not in the least deny the need for recruitment for the British Army in the war against Hitler. They even asserted that the number of recruits for the army should be larger than that for other formations. But at the same time they reemphasized that Jewish and Zionist interests must come before all else, that the defense of Eretz Israel, the Land of Israel, the ultimate hope of the nation, was of primary importance. This stand led to the qualitative stress placed on concern for the Hagana, which stood at the behest of Zionist policy for any required task. From a practical point of view, this approach meant the development of active Hagana units and the subordination of the Jewish force in the British Army to Hagana command, despite outward obedience to the British. Thus Galili spoke of

> a very important concept, that of the priority adhering to the independent force of the Hagana over and above the legal Hagana; the superior value that is bound to come from this branch's service, over and above all other tasks and assignments placed upon our members.[2]

Another view stated: When the fate of the Jewish people hangs in the balance, one should not be making calculations. The front is wherever the battle against the Nazi enemy is taking place. If the Germans invade Palestine, the independent Hagana will not be worth much. It has been devised to fight only against irregular forces, Arabs; therefore for defense, mobilization for the army is the only alternative. Army enlistments must be increased. (And there was an aside here that hinted that anyone of draft age who had not signed up was obviously a slacker. Against this background, conflicts were created between the

"soldiers without uniforms" of the Hagana and the army volunteers.)

The third opinion sought a compromise between these two
positions. Its distinguished spokesmen—Sharett, Golomb, and
Ben-Gurion—stated that the debate over emphases was superfluous. Both the security arms were vital, the Jewish force in
the army and the independent Hagana. However, based on an
evaluation of the course of the war, they were inclined to look
upon mobilization for the army as the imperative of the moment.
They acknowledged the importance of the Hagana in principle
and took a position in favor of the protection of "clandestine"
arms. But they viewed mobilization for the army as a supreme
moral and Zionist imperative, since it was out of the question
to hold back from a war against Hitler on a front close to Eretz
Israel. They saw the Jewish units in the army as a step in the
creation of a Jewish army—within a British framework—a
step that would lead to political gains after the war. "Every recruit is a note, and it is to our interest to pile up these notes,"
according to the words of Golomb.[3] Nonmobilization would
gravely endanger the Jewish position, even if mobilization
brought no political advantage.

In February 1941, there were 2,558 Palestinian Jewish soldiers
stationed in Palestine, and 4,829 serving abroad. Criticism was
leveled at the Agency Executive by both those demanding an
exclusive and total draft for the army and those who looked
upon the army as merely one arm of the Jewish defensive force
(the major role of which was, even so, to protect Eretz Israel
and not Egypt).

The extremist proarmy opinion had found expression back
in 1939–1940, when there were Mapai members who demanded
a fuller mobilization for the army—for example, for the Pioneer units, for which the agency refused to recruit. This mood
grew in 1941. It was expressed in the Mapai ranks, among
others, by members of the Hever Hakvutsot settlements. They
were demanding full mobilization for the army on two grounds:

that the war against Hitler took precedence over all else, and that the Hagana alone could not, they felt, stand against the Axis forces.

The same view—in a far more extremist form—was expressed by various center and right-wing circles. Pinhas Rosen wrote a letter, in the name of the Union of German Immigrants, in which he stated that "our opinion is that cooperation with England in the war must be unconditional," though one should also work for the creation of Jewish units. "Like it or not, we must limit certain operations and try to achieve the fulfillment of our goal through petitions to the authorities," even in matters of immigration and land. Rosen opposed strikes and acts like "the *Patria* which cost the empire a ship and us 200 precious lives."

Such was also the view of industrialist Erich Moller: "All the arguments about the urgency of remaining in the country to guard farms, women, and children are superfluous. As long as the British Army is in the country, there is no danger of [Arab] riots; and if, God forbid, an enemy invasion should come, the unarmed and untrained men will not be able to protect the farms, women, and children anyway. The only defense is— join the army!"[4]

Similar views were voiced by Dr. Shmorak and Dr. Senator in the Agency Executive and among various middle-class circles.

However, the most penetrating and earnest debate was conducted with the people who stood for the primacy of an independent defensive force. It was no accident that none other than the men of the Mapai "B" Faction and the members of Hashomer Hatzair voiced these slogans. Their attitude toward England was quite untrusting, though they were sure that England would continue to rule Palestine for a long time. They looked upon the Yishuv as the last hope of the Jewish people and sought to preserve the forces necessary for its defense.

It is true that the positions of the "B" Faction and Hashomer Hatzair were not identical at the beginning of the war. Ha-

shomer Hatzair, placing primary emphasis on the defense of
the country, opposed a draft for service abroad (except in the
form of an expeditionary force after most of the Yishuv's enlistees were stationed in defense of Palestine). In a period when,
for Jewish volunteers, there was no alternative to army enlistment because there were no effective Hagana units except
for the Supernumeraries (who also were not under Jewish command), Hashomer Hatzair perforce stressed the necessity for
units within the framework of the British Army—as long as
their sole task was the protection of Palestine. For that reason,
Hashomer Hatzair accepted the mobilization for the Buffs,
despite the fact that the unit was not beloved by its members
because of the inactivity characteristic of a second-class force.
No wonder, therefore, that Hashomer Hatzair (though it was
not made a part of the Hagana Command) gladly favored
every opportunity for the strengthening of the Hagana or the
creation of Hagana fighting units. Such units could serve as internal Jewish alternatives to enlistment in the British Army.

In the "B" Faction, the crucial nature of the defense of
Palestine was also stressed along with the acceptance of the
Buffs. The "B" Faction's representatives ("unofficial," because
they were all still members of Mapai) demanded a reasonable
allotment of troops for the defense of the country and mobilization for overseas service. They never opposed recruitment for
service abroad on principle, but they favored—as did Hashomer
Hatzair—the primacy of the independent Hagana. The "B"
Faction people looked upon all forms of mobilization as Hagana
missions, and they demanded Hagana command over them.

The Hagana, and especially a segment of it close to the "B"
Faction, asserted the priority of the illegal arm even within
the Jewish units of the British Army. The commander representing the Hagana in such a unit would have to be the ultimate
decision maker, even in matters between officer and private in
the army. Behind this approach was the premise that the Jewish
units in the army were not "independent," because the com-

mand over them was in the hands of foreigners and their operations were shaped to British strategic considerations.

Golomb, opposing this view, felt that troops in the army were, in fact, a Jewish army. He asked, "A battalion with Jewish noncommissioned officers, a Jewish commanding officer, the Hebrew language—is that a battalion of the Jewish army or not?"[5] The Left gave a negative answer to that question. Hazan (Hashomer Hatzair) stated,

> We approve recruitment for all defense units—army, Supernumeraries, and our own independent Hagana. . . . [But] we must make our own calculation within this recruitment, because no one else will do so. And that calculation states that we may not neglect, because of our mobilization for the army, any other form of defense, and especially not our independent Hagana. Why the debate? We have been afraid, and we are still so today, that those into whose hands we are placing the major part of our defensive force—the army—will not involve it in planning the defense of our land. . . . In regard to our units, they will make only their own abstract strategic reckoning, in which Palestine is only one point on a gigantic front. But, for us, that point is the center of the war. . . . Who will assure us that, when trouble comes, our armed brothers will not be far away? . . . I am certain that a Jewish army located in Eretz Israel would have an utterly different strategy. It would not be busy analyzing the value of long and short lines of supply to the battle area. It would be engaged in defending the country.[6]

As long as the independent Hagana was confined to the Field Force, the Guard Force, and a few groups for "cooperation" with the British, it was impossible to place enlistment for the inner security service on a plane with enlistment in the army. Until 1941 the Hagana was set up only to hold against local Arab rebellion.

> It must be remembered that a force *inside* the country is good only for defense against the Arabs, but not against Hitler. If the enemy reaches the portals of Palestine, every Jew who

can put on a uniform will be obliged to do so. We will continue the war against Hitler even if, God forbid, the country is in his hands; though, of course, we will be able to continue then only outside the country.[7]

It was impossible to refute these words of Ben-Gurion from a technical-military point of view as long as the Hagana itself did not have a mobilized force standing at the disposal of Zionist policy for any purposes whatsoever—including resistance to a German invader—and serving in the first rank as a reinforcement to the regular army in Palestine. However, in light of Nazi policy in Europe (the full significance of which, in 1941, was still not known) there was, perhaps, some sense to the approach of those who were prepared to attempt a fierce total opposition even without a considerable locally mobilized force. Such a force was first formed in 1941 at the time of the danger of an invasion of Palestine. It was reorganized and enlarged at the time of the battle of El Alamein.

The battle over "preferences" in enlistment and response in time of invasion began again in 1942 along the same lines as in 1941; however, its tone was altogether different. In 1941 the Palmakh was still in its beginnings, with a few dozen unequipped, raw boys. They did not provide even a shred of probability for the survival of the Yishuv in a time of trouble. One could only demand that this defensive arm be strengthened, that it be made into a weighty factor for the future. Even those who favored the Hagana as an element of first-rate importance in the defense of the country were forced to look upon enlistment in the army—in the Buffs or other units stationed in Palestine or its immediate vicinity—as the major war effort. The Hagana was only a form of popular militia for a final, desperate resistance.

The questions of defense are the questions of our future. They are, first of all, questions of our conceptions about ourselves and about the world that surrounds us. . . . Therefore, our thoughts must be concentrated on the amassing of strength, on the creation of an independent force standing at our own behest, serving the defense needs of the Yishuv. . . . [This force] will have to serve us not only by protecting our settlements. Very important political functions are locked away in it. It contains a great worth in regard to the troops in uniform. And, one of these days, it is likely to comprise a very serious element—together with our colonization, our collectives, our cities, and our settlements—in determining the shape of this country, in deciding its political fate. This force—big, loyal, Jewish—may someday serve as a vastly worthwhile factor in preventing a non-Zionist solution of the destiny of Palestine.[8]

We can see that the Left was emphasizing the possibility of action against the British after the war, as well as the defense of the country. It was in this that the policy of creating an independent force, subject to the command of the Zionist bodies, found its continuation.

Various leaders in Hagana and political institutions were frequently close to such opinions. Golomb sat on the fence, in some instances supporting Galili's outlook, though he always rejected any statement about the "superiority" or "priority" of the independent Hagana. At the same time, Golomb never stopped longing to turn the defense force into a legal formation, that is, one subject to the control of British "inspectors"—including even the Palmakh at its inception. Nevertheless he defended recruitment for Hagana purposes, against those who sought to enlist the bulk of the men in Hagana for the British Army.

The problem became quite clear and present when a German invasion appeared to be very near. At a session of the Histadrut Executive Committee on April 29, 1941, the Histadrut Executive demanded the enlistment of a maximum number of Jews for the army. The Jewish units would withdraw with the British from Palestine and later take part in its reconquest with the Allied forces. Golomb sought to draft twenty thousand men, who would "open the door for a larger Jewish army that would be able to do much to aid our return to the country." The Hagana would be assigned only tasks of protection against Arab riots that would most likely break out during the day or two between the British withdrawal and the German entry. The representatives of the political executive said nothing of partisan warfare or mass self-defense.

An awareness of the meaning of a German invasion caused the representatives of the Left factions to favor exactly such a line of action, despite the actual hopelessness of a desperate mass war. Memories of Masada and the Bar-Kokhba rebellion, and their lessons, rose to the surface. Tabenkin asserted that

> the greatest danger is that Hitler will come and annihilate us. But, first of all, there is not a thing that will help us against that. . . . Let us stop informing ourselves and our members that there is a Polish army fighting outside Poland. In order for Jews to fight for Palestine from outside, there must be Jews in Palestine, living here and dying here. . . . I hope we will not get out, not leave [the land] while we are still alive.

In these words opposition was being expressed to Golomb's plans to focus chiefly on an army that would retreat—and then return to retake the country. In case of invasion, Tabenkin demanded, when the time came,

> other methods of defense: a knife, a stick, partisan warfare. . . . I do not support the idea that there are places from which one may evacuate the children, because the place with children will stand all the stronger. . . . Every spot, every man in every spot, with every kind of weapon, must be ready for self-defense; because the Arabs will also attack us. And I say, even in a time of invasion, [there must be] preparedness for partisan warfare. . . . The German Army, if it comes, will be stronger than we are. But it will not annihilate the Yishuv with one blow. If it wants to annihilate the Yishuv— then, even if we do not resist, it will annihilate us. But if it does not annihilate us—then train our people for partisan warfare.

The center of the battle, Tabenkin went on to say, was the Hagana. It must be enlarged and strengthened; and that would not conflict with recruitment for the army. Riftin expressed a similar thought in the name of Hashomer Hatzair.

Of course, one should not gather from the above that the Histadrut Executive shunned war by the Yishuv against an invader or that only the "B" Faction people and Hashomer Hatzair favored it. Golomb and other Mapai leaders also viewed such a stand as imperative. However, Golomb felt that *after* an honorable stand had been taken against the Nazi invader, most of the men of the Hagana would retreat from Palestine with the British Army. He did not believe in the practical possibility of further struggle after the invasion; in this he differed with the Left factions. In his view, a proud communal stand during the time of invasion could open the door to political opportunities in the future. If the Yishuv held

> with a spirit of self-sacrifice beyond that of regular armies, if such happens, our worth as a factor may rise to such an extent that, at the end of the war, we shall assure ourselves of things which, under normal conditions, we would be unable to attain. There is no way out for us, anyway. We shall have to fight, for otherwise we shall not save ourselves; and we should only bring more shame on ourselves.[9]

Sharett, too, voiced a similar view, in opposition to the position of some persons who held that the main thing was to fight Hitler within the framework of the British Army, and all the rest was nothing but baseless theorizing.

This debate was renewed at the time of the danger of a German invasion in the spring of 1942. This time it took on a new tone, since the chances that the Yishuv would be able to stand by its own strength (of course, together with British forces), in the face of the peril, had increased. The fact that the Palmakh—which in the fall and winter of 1941 was still on the brink of disbandment—was in early 1942 being reestablished contributed more than a little to the change.

⚑ *Mishmar Haemek*

There is no more typically astonishing example of tradition-shackled methods of operation or bureaucratic red tape than the planning by the British political apparatus and the army command for the defense of Palestine. It was those plans which, among other things, made possible the rebirth of the Palmakh.

In the beginning, the peril of German invasion from the north was foreseen, for the British had won a victory in the western desert at the end of 1941. The situation at the fronts changed rapidly, however, and after February 1942 the situation at the front in Cyrenaica, by elementary logic, should have compelled the commander of British forces to make at least a preliminary plan for the defense of Palestine from a German invasion from the *south*. But that is not what the British did. As far as they were concerned, invasion would only be from the *north*.

They did not cease grand preparatory activities in that direction, even when Rommel opened his campaign in the western desert in May. Tobruk fell, Auchinleck's armies retreated from Mersa Matruh—but with tremendous energy the command in Palestine, with General Wilson at its head, continued to fortify northern Palestine and the eastern slopes of the mountains of Judah on the approach to Jericho—fortifications intended to prevent a German invasion from Syria and Transjordan.

Really ridiculous actions were taken in anticipation of invasion from the north. In May and June, military stores were transferred from Palestine to El Qantara, Egypt—so they should not fall into the hands of an enemy who would be advancing on Palestine from the direction of Damascus! The Jewish Agency, where not generals but mere civilians with clear minds sat, tried to find an explanation for these odd moves. But since the steps being taken were completely devoid of logic, the clever Jews said to themselves that it must be assumed that the English were no less sagacious, that the British purpose was none other than to raise the sense of security and feeling of confidence of the inhabitants of Palestine in the strength of the British Army. To prove it, at the height of the battle for Egypt, the English were not only not retreating from that country but were also transferring military stores to it!

The truth was exactly the opposite. Only on July 4 (that is, at the end of the first battle of El Alamein), with the transfer of the Ninth Australian Division from Wilson's area to Egypt, did Wilson receive an order to make preparations for the possibility of invasion from the south. In his book, Wilson goes into a rage over this sudden change in plans. He writes that this about-face was unforeseen (!) but that he immediately began sending out scouting parties. It apparently never occurred to this highly placed commander that an officer responsible for an entire army (the Ninth) had an obligation to draw up contingency defense plans, even without specific orders to that effect from his superiors. It is a fact that the Palmakh—before El Alamein and at the beginning of the battle for El Alamein —was included in defense plans for Palestine, but with its *back* toward the real front.[10]

It is obvious that the British gave some weight to the Yishuv in their plans for the defense of northern Palestine or southern Lebanon and Syria, in order to deny the enemy an approach to the Suez. It will be recalled that Professor Rattner began working on plans (even in 1941) for demolition, sabotage, and other partisan action in the mountainous region of northern Palestine. Then it became clear to him that Yitzhak Sadeh had similar plans. The two of them coordinated their plans and presented them to Section S.O.E., which had its seat in Cairo and was represented in Palestine by Lt. Gen. B. T. Wilson.

Today it is difficult to determine exactly when Rattner, Sadeh, and Wilson met. At any rate, it could not have been before December 1941 or after the middle of February 1942, because in February the negotiations had already entered the practical stage, and the English had accepted the Jewish plan on general lines. According to the plan, the British were to train a number of units of saboteurs and scouts, whose task it would be to carry out acts of sabotage in the northern part of Palestine, in case of a British retreat and a German conquest of Palestine. This plan was named the "Palestine Post-occupational Scheme," but people began calling it the P. S. Thus, it was sometimes confused with the radio station plan. These were two separate plans, with two different British sections working on them. Many claim—perhaps with some hyperbole—that one section was not aware of what the other was doing.

The body that was capable, by nature, of carrying out such a plan was the Palmakh, especially since its commander, Yitzhak Sadeh, was one of the plan's initiators. Final confirmation of the plan was received in March. And on March 8, 1942, the National Command assigned the Palmakh to execute it.

If we recall the low state into which the Palmakh had sunk during the winter months of 1941, we can understand how much it profited from this plan. This cooperation rescued the Palmakh from a crumbling decline, the result of the Yishuv's miserliness. The Palmakh was not born as a result of cooperation with the British, but thanks to British aid, it was saved from disintegration.

The reawakening of the Palmakh, which had started back in January, now continued apace. The first courses for platoon leaders were set up in January and completed in March. Company meetings and marches were held. On March 17 an exercise of one of the Palmakh units was demonstrated for the British, to their satisfaction.

On March 27, at a joint meeting of the Palmakh company commanders with the National Command and the Hagana chief of staff, a large-scale training program was decided upon. During April, the feverish preparations continued, and even the necessary money was forthcoming. British agreement to these exercises seems to have brought a change in attitude toward the Palmakh on the part of Sitkov and his right-wing associates, at least for as long as cooperation with the army continued.

In Haifa a semiofficial staff was established, the members of which were known to the British partners. It included Rattner, Sadeh, Shinan, and David Nameri (the last-named was, as far as the partners were concerned, the vice-commander of the Palmakh).

The English officers with whom they worked were interesting personalities. First and foremost, there was Captain Abba Eban, who had previously worked in the Political Department of the Jewish Agency in London and was of great help when there were quarrels with the British. The British instructors included Major Grant Taylor, a veteran expert in sniping and pointing (firing a weapon without aiming), who reputedly had at one time been an instructor for the Chicago Police Force in its war on gangsters. Then there was Captain Hammond, the son of one of the members of the Peel Commission and a friend of the Jews, a lecturer in Greek at Cambridge. There was Lieutenant Hawksworth (nicknamed "Hawk"), a careerist and an English patriot, who worked with the Jews as long as that was in British interests, but after the war aided the C.I.D. against the Jews. The immediate superior over the execution of the plan was Major Ringrose, a friend of Palestinian officialdom. The English promised financial aid, which apparently totaled £4,000. In addition, they supplied part of the equipment and food of the trainees. Kibbutz Mishmar Haemek was selected as the training area.

On April 20, 1942, the "great encampment" opened at Mishmar Haemek for a staff course which began with 125 men from all the companies. They learned sabotage and reconnaissance. The graduates were intended to serve as the principal nucleus in cooperative operations, with the remainder of the people of the Palmakh designated as a reserve. On April 30, 147 men completed the course (instead of the 100 approved by the British). With that, the first phase of the Mishmar Haemek encampments ended.

The second phase began with mass training for all the members of the Palmakh. The British, of course, had approved only a 500-man "reserve." However, the entire Palmakh was introduced to the course; and the 600-man figure (100 nucleus and 500 reserve) underwent some stretching as the need arose. On May 14 company encampments were opened at various places in the country for 214 men. These camps met with difficulties because of the open use of arms. Against this background, there occurred (apparently in May) an encounter between the men of D Company, encamped at Ben-Shemen, and the Palestine police. Though the British military department saved the Jews from detainment (to the heartfelt sorrow of the local police commander), the episode caused the first grave crisis between the partners.

We can guess that the Palestine authorities did not display an excess of enthusiasm over the partnership between the Hagana and the army; the problems, according to several witnesses, occupied the attention of the high commissioner. On the other hand, the agency exploited every opportunity to expand the training.

It soon became apparent that the operations were going beyond the bounds agreed upon with Wilson. First, exercises were being held in a number of camps, so of course control over them was more difficult than over one centralized encampment. Second, although the English supplied demolition materials and some few arms, this did not include rifles. It was therefore agreed upon with some junior officers that David Hacohen would "buy" one hundred rifles in "Syria" at the expense of the British partner. Obviously, the "purchase" was not consummated in Syria, but in the depots of the Hagana; but formally the weapons were the property of the British S.O.E.

Wilson dispatched two very sharp letters (May 22) to Avigur. He consented neither to the dispersal of the camps nor to the arms "purchase"—he apparently wished the arms to come from British sources. He also expressed the fear that those who had warned him about any cooperation with Jews had been right. "I was warned when I came to Palestine that if you give the agency an inch, they take an ell. It seems unfortunately to be true, and I won't have it."[11] In his second letter, Wilson expressed his opposition to the Zionist flag-raising ceremony in the Mishmar Haemek camp; he looked upon this as an expression of nationalism. He suspected the Jews of intending to drive the Arabs out of Palestine and to conquer Syria. His attitude—he had generally shown friendship toward the Jews—sheds light on the moods prevailing in Middle East army circles.[12]

The agency argued against Wilson that the various camps had been set up with the knowledge of his officers; nor had the arms "purchase" been concealed from them. Nevertheless, the order was given to concentrate all the camps at Mishmar Haemek. The order was carried out. The training camps were closed on June 4, 1942, after a solemn muster of the Palmakh in the fields of Mishmar Haemek on May 30. At that moment, the number of Palmakh members on the fields of Mishmar Haemek was 443.

The proximity of the enemy to the gates of Palestine and the increasing cooperation made possible further recruitment for the Palmakh. We do not know much about the discussions that preceded this decision. But within the structure of general mobilization—which was declared in the Yishuv, in general, and in the Histadrut, in particular (at its Fifth Convention, April 19–23, 1942)—the decision was taken to double the number of Palmakh members. At the same time, a motion of great importance was passed which provided for the mobilization of the Assault Companies in the encampments into *permanent* bases, with their living expenses to be covered by their work on the farms. (We shall return later to this matter, which determined the future character of the Palmakh.) For the first time in the history of the Yishuv, a standing Hebrew force came into existence, an actual army—though on a minute scale—stationed in training bases and living under a military regime. "The great enlistment," as it is called, was carried out on June 14 without incident and brought 399 new members into Palmakh. The over-all number of Palmakh members was now 842.

What was the composition of the Palmakh in June of 1942? By our estimate, there were, at that time, about 350 members of Kibbutz Meuhad, about 200 members of Hashomer Hatzair, and about 70 members of Hever Hakvutzot in the Palmakh. In all, about 600 to 620 were members of kibbutzim and kvutzot. (This count apparently included members of youth movements who were later to join kibbutzim.) We have already spoken of the two city companies, D and F. A small unit of Technion students had enlisted in B Company; one section of people from collectives in the south had joined E Company (which also contained a small orthodox religious unit). There were in the Palmakh about 200–250 people from rural nonkibbutz settlements and cities. In the summer of 1942, therefore, less than one-third of the members of the Palmakh came from the nonkibbutz sector; about 41 percent came from the Kibbutz Meuhad and about 24 percent from the Kibbutz Artzi of Hash-omer Hatzair. Fifteen women were enlisted in each company, 90 in all, as against 750 men.

With the approach of the front toward Palestine and the large enlistment, bases were set up for scouting and demolition units which had received their special training at Mishmar Haemek. The permanent bases for the various companies were also determined: A, B, and C Companies in the north of the country and the others in the neighborhood of Tel Aviv.

In the meantime, maneuvers continued at Mishmar Haemek —within the cooperation framework—even after the official closing of the "great encampment." Special courses were given for Arabists and Germanists (see below), as well as for demoli-tion men. In the middle of June, the number of trainees reached 105.

The order given to General "Jumbo" Wilson—to make plans for a German invasion from the south—reversed the entire P. P. S. program. Though in conflict with the British commander,

Rattner and Sadeh, as we have said, had begun in good time to plan a defense of Palestine from the south. However, they were not in charge of the army. S.O.E. also set up its plans with attention to the "new" peril and asked that the Jews concentrate forces in the southern areas. The National Command passed on this request, in the form of an order, to the Palmakh staff. On July 4 and 5, two companies (A and B) were transferred from north to south in an underground operation. Within twenty-four hours, each company was stationed at its new location. A Company bivouacked at Negba, Gat, and Dorot, south of Tel Aviv. B Company was moved to the center of the country from the Galilee.

With the posting of the two companies southward, the original P. P. S. plan was vitiated in practice. The English, who had previously taken pains to insure that no more than the agreed-upon number of men should receive training, now sought on their own to call up "reserves" (which in theory were not even supposed to exist) for emergency use.

The arms problem also became more serious. It was apparently impossible to obtain arms for the Assault Companies from Hagana magazines, which were tied in to local defense units. In the first days of the two companies' transfer south, an absolutely absurd situation was created. The primary Assault Companies of the Yishuv faced the danger of a German invasion with nothing but sticks in their hands. Only after several days had passed did weapons arrive, apparently from the Rekhesh (Hagana arms "acquisition" unit) in Haifa.

The emergency condition did not last very long. During the first two weeks of July, the Palmakh companies were engaged exclusively in training exercises. When it became clear that the German advance was halted—even temporarily—the regime of physical labor by which the trainees made their living was resumed (July 12–15).

In August a course for platoon leaders was held in Mishmar Haemek; it was a Palmakh first. The course commander was Meir Batz, who served for a short time as chief instructor for the Palmakh. A brief snipers course was also conducted there. With this, the Mishmar Haemek period ended. Only the Germanist section continued to train in that camp.

With the passing of the invasion peril, the British stopped their support of the guerrilla units they had been training in Palestine. The Palmakh went back underground. No longer an ally, it resumed the status of a "subversive organization." People who looked upon uniforms and legal arms as the *sine qua non* could not persevere in the Palmakh, especially when its underground character was combined with a program of labor and training.

The Mishmar Haemek chapter had ended rapidly, but its achievements were lasting. For the first time, an independent Jewish force was created. It was to become an appreciable factor in the defense of the country

🎗 *The Haifa Program—Plan North*

With the German incursion into Egypt—in April 1942 at the latest—Rattner and Sadeh had begun to draw up not only plans for sabotage actions along the presumed route of German advance, but also programs for a stand by the Yishuv en masse, in defense against the invader. Their plan, in Galili's words, was that

> if the worst happened, the possibility of fortifying a portion of the country would present itself. All arms-bearing men and women—our comrades in the army, our comrades in the Supernumerary Police Force, and those in the independent Hagana—can all be concentrated in a joint plan with the British command with help from the air and sea and support from their artillery, by which they will stand until the end with the purpose of holding on or being destroyed.

Professor Rattner himself, though at some distance in time, described the plan in scope. It would be quite difficult to stop a powerful mobile force like the German Army in southern Palestine—but that would not be true in the north. The threat from the south

> presented us with the peril of extermination. Meanwhile, it was important to keep in mind that people were taking a sceptical attitude to accounts of extermination of Jews by the Nazis. But, just about that time, we began to take such reports more seriously and they began to believe there could be a wholesale slaughter in case of invasion.

In the event of an English retreat from Palestine, various possibilities came under consideration. One of them provided

> a stimulus, to an appreciable degree, for a scheme of self-defense that would go far beyond the structure of the P. S. [P. P. S.] itself. There was a possibility that the Germans, in a flanking movement, would pursue the English from the eastern side of the Jordan, in order to beat the retreating British Army to Iraq. In that case, the thought occurred that the conquest of western Palestine would be carried out, to a large extent, not by top-grade troops, German troops, which would then be busy pursuing the British Army, but, for example, by units of the Italian Army. Against that background, we began thinking of means of self-defense.[13]

Yizhak Sadeh and Professor Rattner crystallized a proposal, "Plan North." The plan included not only Haifa, though that city was its crucial area, but also Mount Carmel, the Valley of Zebulon, and the Emek with a section of the mountains of Gilboa. A force quantitatively equal to thirty-six British regiments would be necessary to defend that region, not counting demolition teams, technical units, and auxiliary formations. Solel Boneh and other companies were to construct fortifications at weak points and positions powerful enough to stand under artillery fire. For the plan, Hagana people who had received any training at all, the Supernumerary Police Force, and the men of the Jewish units in the British Army were taken into consideration. The planners sought to influence the English to allot British naval and air forces for this self-defense action.

"We had worked the plan up in rather explicit form and suggested handing it to British officers, the High Command and staff, as we had done with the P. P. S. But in this case we met with a very sceptical attitude among the Jewish community leaders. They considered the plan fantastic in our circumstances."

The two planners involved other experts and officers in the work. One of them relates that he visited a number of locations with Rattner and Sadeh over a period of ten days. "We planned fortifications, weaponry, positioning of arms, interior routes, and all the logistical problems connected with the maintenance and care of such a large number of people."[14]

The Upper Galilee Command was also brought into the planning. It especially dealt with the possibility that the British would refuse to cooperate.

> The possibility of taking over arms depots by force, at the time of a British withdrawal, was planned for—including guns, antiaircraft guns, ammunition, stores of mines that could help in the creation of impediments around the fortified, defended area. . . . Tobruk, of course, served as the example. . . . There was anxiety over the small antitank capability, and we therefore laid stress on mining and irregular antitank warfare, like Molotov cocktails and such things, in addition to a plan of trenches. . . .[15]

The groups engaged in planning were limited, and the plans did not filter down to lower ranks.

The Yishuv and Histadrut leaders, as we have remarked, took quite a doubting attitude toward these plans. Golomb himself felt that it was feasible to fight against Germans only at the time of the invasion and immediately before liberation, but not during an occupation. Rattner states that some of the Kibbutz Meuhad people were talking about a village-by-village defense, something completely lacking in military value in the face of overwhelming German might. That would have been nothing more than a waste of heroism, in his opinion.

Hashomer Hatzair supported Plan North. Others (apparently Sharett and Golomb) asserted that the main part of the Jewish force should withdraw with the British. But in spite of everything, they continued to persevere with the planning. Fortunately, the question itself never came up for decision, since the Germans were halted at El Alamein.

It must be kept in mind that the planners had no intention of fostering mass suicide, though the current historic symbol was that of the courage of Masada. A stand with some chance of success was being spoken of. Therefore, it would be interesting to know whether the entire Jewish civilian population was to be concentrated in the defensive zone. The depositions contradict one another, and the firm truth is not to be had.

It is also difficult to find out, at this date, whether the English had drawn up a similar plan (as Professor Rattner relates). One gets the impression that they did, indeed, consider such a possibility. But they did not reach a decision. And it is certain that the idea of taking part in the program of the chiefs of the Palmakh was never discussed among them.

Today it is entirely impossible to determine what the military chances of the Yishuv would have been (in the context of Plan North) in the face of a Nazi invasion. In light of what is now known to us about Nazi plans for the Jewish population in conquered countries (to say nothing of the Jews of Palestine!) there could not, perforce, have been any "practical" program other than resistance. But that does not evaluate the plan, because nothing can compare with its psychological effect on the people of the Palmakh.

Later on (the plan became known to members in the ranks only after the danger was past) a few hundred Hebrew youths saw themselves retrospectively as the pioneer army of a grand host fighting for its life against a demonic foe. The youth, nurtured on legends of Plan North (as well as on stories of the

Twenty-three, the invasion of Syria, and the deeds of Jewish soldiers in the British Army), did not ask about the chances of a stand against Rommel. For the first time in our age, independent Jewish troops were about to defend the country—that fact became interwoven into a web of similar facts, creating an aura of radiance made up of the legends of courage that are so vital for a people at war.

It was the Yishuv's good fortune that Plan North was never tested in the fires of reality.

✌ Special Sections of the Palmakh, 1942–1943

With the invasion of Syria and immediately thereafter, the Arabist unit in Syria experienced a grave crisis. Its numbers were meager (about fifteen men) and the commander had been relieved. The first commanding officer after the conquest of Syria was Abdu (Ben-Yehuda); he was replaced by Aharon Leshem. The Palmakh staff opposed the group's continued existence unless it received fundamental training.

> To send them now is risking failure, it will endanger the members of the group and lower the value of the matter in the eyes of our ally, and that could bring about the breaking off of the partnership. The Palmakh staff has decided that the members are not ready. But now diplomatic politics have prevailed, the English have set a date. And instead of explaining to them that the preparation of the men is a difficult business requiring a lot of time, the considerations are otherwise.[16]

Those are the words employed by Allon in evaluating the Arabist operation as a failure during its first months in the autumn and winter of 1941.

In January 1942, after Leshem's enlistment in the British Army, Yigal Allon, commander of Palmakh A Company, was appointed as head of the Syrian unit. He set one condition, which was accepted: that the unit become a part of the Palmakh. Five members were separated from the group; ten remained, eight of Syrian-Jewish origin and two Palestinian Jews. Captain Hammond, an English friend of the Jews, was appointed commanding officer of the unit. Allon worked with him on a basis of full mutual agreement.

The unit's first task was to infiltrate a number of people into Syria and Lebanon. There they would live as inhabitants in every way. At the same time, however, they would maintain military discipline and would set up a radio network to keep in touch with the British command. Should Syria be conquered by the Germans, the group would (parallel to the execution of plans pertaining to Palestine) sabotage military objectives of importance, supply information to Allied intelligence, and carry on favorable propaganda.

They entered Syria as Palestinian Arabs or as soldiers (with the Buffs) or by stealing across the border. The last-named route was employed by the unit's people "when we wished to operate conspiratorially apart from our ally"[17] (when it was necessary, for example, to give the men leave without English approval, or when the men were helping immigrants who had clandestinely crossed the northern border). It was very difficult to obtain identity papers.

Even while the Arabists were trying to settle in as citizens, they were tried by hard experiences. In one case there was even danger of death. The British were also operating in Syria at the time against de Gaulle's agents, and two Jews were taken prisoner under suspicion of being agents of the Axis or of de Gaulle. They were rescued thanks only to the intervention of the responsible British officer from S.O.E.

Arabist cells were established in Damascus, Aleppo, Beirut, Tripoli (Lebanon), Riyak (Lebanon), and, for a time, in Deir ez-Zor as well. The men worked in a variety of trades. They set up a garage, a carpentry shop, a workshop for scales; they worked as electricians, army camp laborers, and engineers.

Several of them received proposals of marriage with local girls, and squirmed out of them only with some effort. Along with all the civilian occupations, they set up four radio stations which operated to the satisfaction of the English. After a time, about thirty to forty people were involved in the activity. But the "field workers" remained few; there were only nineteen at the end of 1942.

In this operation the Palmakh sought not only to aid the general war effort, but also

> to exploit these points [the cells] for our own purposes. Syria served as a base for the Arab gangs, and it was of top importance that our members enter the Arab centers and be able to pass information to us on what was being done. . . . We looked upon this as a big school with the tuition being paid by "Uncle." This would make it possible for us to establish something similar if it were broken up by the English or disintegrated by itself.[18]

In the meantime, others were undergoing a more thorough training in courses at Beit Oren and Ramat-Hadar, apparently within the cooperation framework. Allon estimates that about fifty people received training within the structure of the Arabists' unit.

When the camp was founded at Mishmar Haemek, the question of the "Arab Section" (as they started calling the Arabists) and its expansion came on the agenda. The P. S. framework (the radio stations) facilitated the preparation of several Arabists in July 1942. A unit was combined with this, whose task was to serve the needs of the Palmakh in Palestine. This unit was trained at Mishmar Haemek. But apparently it did not make much progress. Its people conducted themselves in an irregular fashion, to the annoyance of their officers.

At the end of the cooperation period in the summer of 1942, relations with the British sharpened in the Syrian program. Less amiable officers replaced Hammond. A struggle over control of the unit began. The English looked upon it as only a net-work of British agents, while Yigal Allon regarded their inde-pendence as a decisive point. In order not to be overly dependent on the Jews, the English established a similar unit (or units) using inhabitants of Syria of Armenian and Circassian extraction. At the beginning of March 1943, they presented Yigal Allon with a demand that he resign from his post. And indeed, Allon left this work during that period, either as a result of British pressure or because of the impossibility of independent ac-tivity in the position.

The Jewish Agency was interested in the continued existence of the Arabist unit, even on a reduced scale of the order of ten people. Abdu was reappointed commanding officer, but the arrangement did not continue very long. On August 31, 1943, Shiloah wrote to Gardner, the Englishman in charge of the unit, suggesting that, since a German invasion of Syria was now only a vague possibility and the people were sitting around in Syria with nothing to do, the unit be liquidated altogether.

The conditions of life and work in Syria were, in fact, very hard for the Arabists. Remoteness from Palestine, lack of con-tact with it and with the underground, and the need constantly to observe the intricate forms of Arab courtesy—all these had their effect. The Palmakh did put out leaflets—"A Word to the Name-less"—intended for the Syrian unit. But they were not a satisfactory substitute for contact with home. The Jewish com-mand, therefore, had to give the men leaves in Palestine (of course, without the knowledge of the English). When by chance this fact was revealed to the English, it caused a worsening of relations. As Allon stated, however, this was not what brought about the unit's breakup. That was caused rather by the problem of its control and questions of mutual confidence between the partners.

From the point of view of its "Arabic" as well as its military preparation, the Arab Section attained a rather high standard in 1942 and 1943. On the return of most of the men from Syria (there were also a few girls in the Arab Section, but they did not have time to get to Syria) the Shahar unit was established in Palestine, in the spring of 1943. It was composed of the returnees and a new group of Arabists who had been trained by Yitzhak Hankin at a camp on Mount Carmel. The task of the unit was to provide information about Arabs in Palestine, and this of course was done outside the framework of cooperation with the British.

The Arab Section, including both of its branches (the Syrian and Palestinian units) and later the Shahar section, was shrouded in secrecy and mystery, a deep underground within the Palmakh underground. However, the Palmakh contained a further unit, also top secret, about which much was made known only at a far later date, the German Section. It seems to have been founded in May 1942. It will be recalled that the idea of establishing a Germanist unit was not new; Moshe Dayan had thought of it back in October 1941. Only in the spring of 1942, however, did conditions make it possible to actualize the concept, with the full knowledge and consent of the English co-workers from S.O.E. (after M.I.1, with which Dayan was connected, proved hesitant about getting into such an adventure).

The task of assembling men for the Germanist Section was assigned to its commanding officer, Shimon Avidan. Within two or three months, about sixty men had been enlisted from the members of the Palmakh and from their acquaintances of German extraction in the settlements.

At the same time, a similar unit (S.O.S.) was being formed in the British Army in Egypt under the command of Beck, a German-speaking British captain. Its sergeant major was Israel Carmi, one of the veteran activists of Rekhesh, who had joined the British Army. The unit numbered thirty-eight men, and its people were assembled from Palestinian soldiers in the Buffs and the remnants of the Fifty-first Commando, which had previously operated in Eritrea. Its tasks included operating in the enemy's rear and carrying out acts of sabotage on his installations. It included in its ranks two Germans who had cooperated with the Allies. Beck's fundamental error was that he placed too much confidence in these two men.

After several small operations, carried out with the help of de Gaulle's soldiers, the unit swung into operation on June 12, 1942, against airfields behind the enemy's lines. One of the two Germans betrayed the mission, as a result of which the operation failed, and two Palestinian men, Peter Haas and Ernst Gottlieb, went to their deaths.

After this experience and the British retreat to El Alamein, Beck set out to create a still larger unit to be composed of Jews (two hundred men, according to the plan), which would work behind enemy lines. The command in Cairo gave its consent to this. So Beck, Carmi, and the remaining German were sent to Palestine to explore the possibility of combining with the people of the German Section of the Palmakh. They were quite impressed by its level of training, and it was agreed that three of the Palmakh people would go to Egypt to examine the operational potential. It was then proposed to the Palmakh that the entire unit be listed in the British Army. This was refused because the Palmakh wished to preserve its independent structure. But the Palmakh suggested that some of its people be coopted for operations undertaken on British initiative.

Avidan and two of the men went to Egypt for this purpose (in August or September), as well as to collect information and as much German equipment as possible. The three stayed in Egypt only three days, because the High Command in Cairo had meanwhile canceled its approval of the creation of a larger unit and was also opposed to keeping three civilians in a military camp. The attempted cooperation had failed. But the German Section had extracted some use from it. It had gained quite considerable booty of German arms, documents, and uniforms, as well as information.

A short while later most of the men in the military unit were sent on a combined commando operation with the British Army's

Long Range Desert Group (LRDG). Together, they were to take Tobruk and carry out acts of sabotage on Bengazi at the time when Montgomery was about to open his attack at El Alamein. The Jewish youths took part in this operation despite Carmi's objection. He had sought to make their volunteering contingent on the mobilization of a large unit, including the Palmakh section, according to the original plan. The commando operation failed, either because the Germans knew about it from the start or by reason of plain bad luck and faulty organization. The Palestinian participants were killed or captured, and their unit in Egypt was dispersed.

At the time that the commando operation was being prepared and immediately after its execution, another opportunity of proving its fitness for action was provided for the Germanist Section of the Palmakh, apparently by means of the S.O.E. Around the beginning of October, two members of the Germanist Section were sent off to Cairo. There they received further training and instruction in "Germanism." After passing their examinations, they returned to Palestine. But shortly they were recalled to Egypt and assigned to work in the prisoner-of-war camps. They were to turn over any information they succeeded in obtaining from the prisoners to British intelligence. They both worked for about a month in various camps and reached Tobruk. It is difficult to judge the importance of their activity, but their British superiors seem to have been satisfied. At the end of November, they were both returned to Palestine. The operation was not reactivated, apparently for political, not for military, reasons.

This, in fact, ended the military operations of the Germanist Section, on which such high hopes had been placed. During 1943, many plans were made for it—operations in Yugoslavia or Austria, even with Wingate in Burma—but because of British refusal, they were never carried out. The section attained a very high degree of training and efficiency. Nearly all its members reached the rank of platoon leader or better, and most of them acquired a multitude of military skills.

During 1942, the section remained under the direct order of the Palmakh staff. But in the beginning of 1943, Avidan was named commanding officer of F Company and the Germanist Section was combined with that unit. In the middle of 1943, a special unit was formed—also under Shimon Avidan—which the Palmakhniks nicknamed "the Foreign Legion." It included the special sections, plus those who were taking part in European parachute drop programs, both Palmakh members and others. This unit was finally approved in 1944 as a part of the Palmakh and became the Staff Company (G Company). Until February 1945, Yehuda Ben-Horin was commanding officer of the Germanist Section. In 1945 the unit was enrolled in the Jewish Brigade and succeeded, after three years of expectant preparation, in carrying out important escape and rescue operations with Jewish displaced persons in Germany and Austria. The costly training and the long years of anticipation were not wasted. However, these activities are beyond the scope of our present subject.

One unique chapter is difficult, at present, to understand fully. In February 1943, within the framework of contacts with the British, four men were sent to Egypt for a secret operation. They received special amphibious and demolition training. But the object of their preparations was not made known to them. They were simply told that their chances of coming back were rather slim. One of them got a leave in Palestine before the operation and went to say good-bye to his friend Yigal Allon, who was sick in the hospital at the time. When Allon heard the story, he took issue with this kind of "blind" dispatching of Jewish youths to their deaths, and he roused Galili and Golomb. At the latters' intervention, the agency demanded that the English reveal to it (or to some trusted party) the object of the four-man mission. The English refused, and the agency instructed the four not to return to Egypt. Some contemporaries thought that the British wished, by an act of provocation, to draw the Turks into war against Germany. Be that as it may, nothing more was heard of this particular project.

✌ *The Work and Training Camps*

The question of the Palmakh's survival, even in its original organizational form as a temporary body, was above all a problem of budget. After the enlargement of the structure at the start of the cooperation period, the Palmakh staff did not want to have to make do again with irregular units organically bound to limited localities, as during 1941; it sought instead to create actually mobilized units. But the means for this were insufficient; the English paid only for those units officially authorized by themselves (about one hundred men) and supplied their food and equipment. It was clear that mobilized encampments would cost large sums. It was calculated that the maintenance, clothing, and shelter of one man in training would cost £10 per month. That would mean that 840 members of the Palmakh (after "the great enlistment") would cost £8,400. And that would be without staff expenses, family allotments, equipment, arms, and so on. In actuality, the Palmakh received £10,396 for July, August, and September for maintenance and ongoing expenses, an average of £3,500 per month.

The nature of the situation compelled the Palmakh staff to strive for a compromise. On March 24, it handed the chief of staff a proposed budget of £4,300 per month to train four hundred men just ten days out of each month.

The expansion of the framework was still not considered here. The number of training days was only slightly more than those during the winter of 1941/1942 (six or seven). It was quickly made plain that even this budget would not be granted. And at the same time it was clear that there was a need to train more men, at a far greater cost. Thus, the Palmakh staff found itself facing a blank wall.

It will be recalled that the concept of training paid for by the labor of the trainees was not new—in the winter of 1941 it had occurred to Israel Livartovsky. Apparently Yitzhak Sadeh had also thought, on the founding of the Palmakh, of work and training camps. However, until the spring of 1942 no substantial steps were taken toward the realization of these programs.

In the middle of April, the Sixth General Council of Hashomer Hatzair was held at Mishmar Haemek. That convention met under the threat of the military dangers looming over the land. A large portion of its deliberations was devoted to security matters. Ya'ari, Hazan, and Riftin waved the flag for the Palmakh as a new form of community-wide defense organization. At the same conference, Tabenkin and Sadeh appeared and demanded increased defense preparedness. Sadeh's speech contained a note of despair, owing to the absence of opportunities for activity, and the overwhelming responsibility placed upon him and his comrades in the Assault Companies was stressed.

After the council, Galili and Tabenkin drove to Allonim. There a discussion was held, with several of the members of the secretariat of Kibbutz Meuhad participating. At Allonim, Tabenkin put forward a program whereby the Palmakh soldiers would work part of the time and thus earn enough to enable them to train the other part of the month. This would make possible the establishment of a mobilized force,

so that every settlement [will] be a base for a standing unit. That day or the next, we continued the discussion in the kitchen at Yagur with Sadeh, who was then a member of that kibbutz. Then a proposal for seventeen workdays [a month] was crystallized. Tabenkin then asserted that the Hagana had no right to exist if it could not raise standing units. In the event that it could not do so, it was fulfilling no function other than to interfere with enlistment in the British Army.

The present function of the workers' establishment* is to serve as a base for a standing army. If there is no budget, then the answer must be that it is every kibbutz member's obligation to bear the expense for the maintenance of one soldier. This was Tabenkin's original formulation, and only at Allonim did he say work and training. A small committee was appointed to make the necessary modifications of the raw idea. Tabenkin added that he was sure that all the kibbutz treasurers in the movement would be glad to bury him with the epitaph HERE LIES TABENKIN, THE MADMAN.[19]

On May 16, the council of Kibbutz Meuhad convened at Givat-Brenner. Tabenkin and Galili appeared with firm proposals for a solution of the Palmakh problem on the general lines we have set forth.

In order to comprehend the background of this proposal, we must remember that side by side with the iron resolve of the people of the agricultural settlements to be a base for the first independent Hebrew force were internal kibbutz problems, which were also playing a certain role.

After 1940 the kibbutzim had suffered greatly from a shortage of labor (in contrast to the previous years, when the kibbutzim were looking outside for sources of livelihood for their workers). With the establishment by the British of the Middle East Supply Center (M.E.S.C.) in Cairo, the army ordering system was regularized, and the economic situation in Palestine improved. Unemployment completely disappeared, and at the same time a very large number of kibbutz members enlisted in the army and the Supernumerary Police Force. Up to July 1, 1942, 1,093 kibbutz members joined the British Army. They comprised 9 percent of enlistees, although the kibbutz movement represented only 5–6 percent of the Yishuv. And the proportion of kibbutz people in the Supernumerary Police Force and the Palmakh

---

* What is meant here is the whole variety of economic institutions, co-operatives, factories, and so on set up by the Histadrut, including the smallholders' agricultural settlements (moshav) and the kibbutz movement.

was much greater still. Kibbutz Meuhad enlisted 1,580 members for the various formations by October 1, 1942—that is, 13.2 percent of its membership—while the entire Yishuv enlisted only about 5 percent. As a result, the kibbutz community suffered a severe labor shortage. At the Givat-Brenner Council, the shortage for Kibbutz Meuhad alone was set at 4,000 hands. The work-training program could serve as a partial solution for these problems.

Of course, from a purely financial point of view, these camps usually brought a loss. Damages caused by those Palmakh members who were inexperienced in farm work, pilferage, and the many famous "get-togethers" which ate up (in two senses) large sums, the lack of regularity of work because of the military character of the camp—all these factors caused the kibbutzim to hesitate over acceptance of the Palmakh camps. But there were also many sections of the Palmakh on which rural people had placed their stamp. The relationship of these sections to the kibbutzim on which they worked was usually serious and responsible; not a few of them really "saved" various branches of agriculture in the collectives, not only by mass labor, but by skilled labor as well.

We must by no means draw the conclusion that Kibbutz Meuhad suggested the creation of work-training camps for the Palmakh in order to relieve the labor shortage in their own establishments. Tabenkin and his comrades were striving, first of all, to lay a basis for the survival of the Palmakh. But the labor pinch made the acceptance of his idea easier.

At the Givat-Brenner Council, the suggestion was also made to draft youths seventeen to nineteen years old for one year of service in the work and training camps. Kibbutz Meuhad was prepared to absorb 1,700 to 2,000 of them, as well as Palmakh members and workers who would come from the city. In Tabenkin's words:

> Two people for labor and one for training. The worker will support the recruit. Our economy will drink them in as

parched ground does the first rain. A standing army for the Hagana will also be able to work. But, in principle, it must be mobilized, subordinate to its own military command and not subject to the work regime; not like members in their kibbutz, but like Cossacks who work at home on a temporary basis. We need an army of Jewish Cossacks now.

The point of Tabenkin's concept was the *permanence* of the life of these "Cossacks"; it was not a one-time mobilization, even for a long period, that he was contemplating, but watching and working as a permanent way of life. It was not by chance that he turned to the example of the Cossacks.

"We need a Hebrew army, and not just for a year or two. How shall we construct it? On the basis of labor. . . . Trumpeldor always dreamed of military and labor battalions. This is the only way for the Jews."[20]

This idea of working fighters was not new. Tabenkin consciously based his concept here on the traditions of the Hebrew labor movement. Along with factors such as the need to create new forms of organization and the shortage of manpower, an ideological factor, not to be dismissed, was at work here: a continuation of the dream of the men of Hashomer* (Tabenkin had been one of them in his youth). They had conceived of a powerful chain of pioneer settlements engaged, at one and the same time, in work and guard duty. Now the time had come to give this dream shape in keeping with the highly temperamental, ideologically visionary thrust which characterized Kibbutz Meuhad.

At Givat-Brenner, three proposals were set forth: absorption of the Palmakh into the settlements, mass draft of youth under conditions of work and training, and enlistment of masses of workers who would join the kibbutzim. Of the three, only the first won through to complete fulfillment. Attempts to enroll masses of youth ended in a complete failure, and the few young people who joined the kibbutzim went to the Palmakh.

At the council, the proposal for a loan from Kibbutz Meuhad

---

* An organization of Jewish watchmen set up before World War I.

to the Palmakh of around £15,000 was also discussed. That was an enormous sum for those days, especially for a kibbutz movement. Tabenkin was hoping that other movements would follow Kibbutz Meuhad.

In the first phase Hashomer Hatzair advanced its own mobilization plans together with those of Kibbutz Meuhad. It had also recruited more than its proportional share for the various military formations. Kibbutz Meuhad, which numbered 9,000 members, announced a mobilization of 600 more volunteers from its establishments. So Kibbutz Artzi of Hashomer Hatzair, numbering 5,500 persons, decided on the same recruitment ratio: 350 volunteers (40 percent for the Palmakh, 30 percent for the army, and 30 percent for the Supernumerary Police Force).

But the differences in approach of these two kibbutz movements must not be ignored. Hashomer Hatzair had an anti-militarist tradition. It did not see defense as an ideal per se, but as an inescapable necessity caused by the times. In this it was like a great many members of the Mapai majority faction. The concept of "fighting workers" was alien to its spirit. It rejected the "Cossack" romanticism which marked Tabenkin's stand. But from a different starting point, it reached conclusions identical with those of Kibbutz Meuhad. Hashomer Hatzair realized that under existing circumstances it was imperative to have full (though temporary) mobilization for the defense of the land, especially in the ranks of the Hagana and the Palmakh. It rejected the labor camps because it believed that if the time had really come for training, then *all* the required time should be devoted to that. It therefore at first repudiated work and training camps, though the basic principle of combining work and training was congenial to it. It also feared that the suggested loans would provide a moral shield for the Yishuv middle class in its attempts to evade payment of a portion of the community's defense expenditures. The burden must not be placed on the shoulders of the Histadrut, and suitable means would have to be taken to prevent the middle class from shirking responsibility. Very reluctantly it finally agreed to labor camps.

Yitzhak Sadeh was one of the few who held up the combination of labor and training as the ideal for a working army in principle. In the order of the day that was written on the eve of "the great enlistment," Sadeh stated that this combination, "although dictated to us by the external conditions under which we work, gives us a guarantee that a balance will be preserved in the lives of our comrades, most of whom have been called up from an agricultural or labor way of life."

Hashomer Hatzair, therefore, participated in the mobilization effort and gave its consent for the creation of the camps. In contrast, the Hever Hakvutzot did not enter the discussion on these problems at all. When it, too, began to recruit some of its people for the Palmakh, they were informed that this represented no deviation from the principle of preferment for enlistment in the army—Hever Hakvutzot had been the chief advocate in Mapai of definite priority for army enlistment.

In the councils of Kibbutz Meuhad at Givat-Brenner, Ein-Harod (July 15), and Naan (August 23), the problems of combining work and training were considered. One gets the impression that a clear proposal had still not crystallized. At Naan, Tabenkin spoke of 90 days of training (7.5 days per month), as against 176 days of labor per year. At the session of the Center for Mobilization of the Yishuv on June 29, 180 days of labor were discussed, along with 102 days of training; and this was the proposal which was finally accepted. In the summer of 1942, set patterns were still lacking, and the settlements were guided only by the general principle of two weeks' work per month.

To what extent did the labor in the camps cover the expenses of training? A conservative estimate would be that it paid for two-thirds of the Palmakh's overall expenditures—a remarkable accomplishment in the budgetary circumstances of 1942.

The concept of work and training camps encountered opposition on the part of the middle-class representatives. They viewed the program as aid granted to the class enemy and as the exploitation of labor without pay. Galili claims that their opposition flowed from several sources. In their opinion, labor and military service were two different things; and, in an emergency, the kibbutz would interfere with the mobilization of "the formation," as the Palmakh began to be called. They had no interest in providing work forces for the collectives. And to them, the Palmakh seemed to take the shape of a Histadrut "Red Army," toward which they therefore conducted themselves according to the principle of "honor it and suspect it." The middle class also feared encounters with the English and the creation of a "Cossack" elite, to which the rest of the Hagana members would have to yield rank. Furthermore, they asserted that recruitment for the Palmakh detracted from that for the army, and they pointed to the disproportion between the huge budget for the maintenance of the Palmakh and the visible results in terms of members. In a word, the right-wingers gave their grudging consent to the establishment of the Palmakh; but they looked as if they had seen a ghost.

In 1942, twenty-eight collective establishments served as bases for Palmakh encampments (seventeen Kibbutz Meuhad settlements, six of Kibbutz Artzi, and five of Hever Hakvutzot). Kibbutz Artzi, which suffered less from a shortage of working hands (it still had preparatory groups in its colonies) and in which certain antimilitarist feelings were marked, accommodated fewer camps. At times Kibbutz Artzi collectives were forced by the movement's ruling bodies to accept Palmakh encampments, even when the kibbutz was not anxious to do so. There were isolated instances of a similar nature in Kibbutz Meuhad as well. On the other hand, settlements which accepted Palmakh establishments and then saw them removed, complained quite bitterly. In September 1942, for instance, Negba (a Hashomer Hatzair kibbutz) made a sharp protest to the Histadrut Actions Committee because a Palmakh unit had been withdrawn from the collective.

After the severing of relations with the British and the

battle of El Alamein (November 1942), the circumstances of the encampments also changed. Budgets were cut off. Chances for immediate action diminished. The Palmakh, which had been during the summer a pioneer army designed for the defense of the Yishuv against an imminent invasion, once again became a national reserve. For a fleeting moment, the floodlights of public interest had been turned upon it; then suddenly it receded into a dreary day-to-day existence.

Another crisis in the annals of the Palmakh had broken out.

☙ The Danger of Invasion, and the "Debate on Preferences"

Zionist self-defense faced two focal problems in regard to the danger of a Nazi invasion: how to apportion the Yishuv's forces most rationally among the various branches of recruitment; and what the security policy at the actual time of an invasion would be. The two problems were naturally interconnected, and the answers to them were bound up with a third question: how the strength of the Hagana should be evaluated. In other words, in the event of an invasion, would the Hagana be able just to *assist* the British Army, or could it be a substantial *independent* factor? In Plan North, there emerged the belief—mainly on the part of Histadrut members, especially the leftist factions and the Palmakh staff—that in a time of danger for Palestine, it would be possible to assemble an independent force of considerable worth from the ranks of the Hagana. The response of individuals and groups to these questions determined, more than a little, their position on problems of budget and manpower.

On April 6, 1942, the Mandatory government published an order by which there were included in the framework of fighting forces the Supernumerary Police Force and the Jewish Settlement Police, but not the Temporary Auxiliary Policemen, who furnished a potential structure for Hagana operations. There was, therefore, a fear that the men of Hagana would be forced to fight the Germans without either uniforms or any official standing. Those who did not favor partisan warfare did not wish to endanger the lives of men out of uniform, and this fact determined their answer to the problem of the Yishuv's conduct during an invasion. Delusions were still widespread in the Jewish community regarding European Jewry before the indubitable fact of the mass annihilation was known. Information or rumors that trickled through to individuals were looked upon as exaggerations, if not figments of the imagination. It must be kept in mind that only in the spring of 1942 did the Nazi extermination machine begin to work at full force in Poland. And that fact was not known in Palestine until several months later.

The bitter questions of the Yishuv's security policy were considered in two sessions of the Agency Executive. The most moderate position, replete with delusions about Nazi intentions, stated:

> If there is danger for the Yishuv from the invaders, there is danger double and treble lying in wait for us in the event of guerrilla warfare against the invaders, and that with illegal weapons. We can fight against commandos with illegal arms, but the enemy will say that we are doing so as partisans, because we do not constitute a part of the British Army. We have to remember the fate of the Jews of Kishinev* and other places and the behavior of the Germans toward partisans in all countries. . . . We must defend Palestine by all means, but in a legal manner; and we must demand that the government constitute us as a legal segment of the army. Only in case the British leave the country—and let us hope that it never comes to that—while there is no authority in Palestine during the interim period, will we have to protect ourselves against the Arabs by our own strength . . . but it is

---

* Rumors had been spread in 1941 that the Germans and Rumanians had murdered the Jews of Kishinev in Bessarabia because of alleged Jewish irregular warfare. In actual fact, of course, this had been merely a groundless pretext for a large-scale pogrom and expulsion.

not desirable that the Diaspora should suspect that the Agency Executive, with its own hands, caused the destruction of the Yishuv.

A similar view stated that a war by the Yishuv against the invader had no chance. In contrast, another participant said that "our position in Poland would have been no worse had we met the Germans with weapons in our hands." The tragedy was that there were those who preferred the life of a whipped dog to death, and there were those who "seem to favor the life of a whipped dog even here, in order to save the Yishuv." The speaker demanded that people not be seduced by delusions as to the Nazis' plans and averred that it was not right to wax enthusiastic over the operations of Russian partisans and, at the same time, reject that path for Eretz Israel. Naturally, one must try to get the British to put the young Jews into uniform, but that was not an indispensable condition for their fighting. In or out of uniform, they must defend the land and the honor of the Jewish people.

A different opinion again expressed the hope that the Nazis would permit the Yishuv to exist under ghetto conditions. Of course, if the Jews became convinced that the Germans were seeking to exterminate them, then, the speaker added, "Let me die with the Philistines." But there was no proof that this was the case. In regard to German intentions, "Some see the glory of the Jew in the morality of Judaism and in the fact that we do not belong to the race of murderers. . . ." On the basis of this approach, the speaker opposed giving "the Vandals an excuse to exterminate the Yishuv. . . . [The Jews must reject] all guerrilla action, for it may bring with it the destruction of the Yishuv. There is no disagreement among us that all the forces of the Yishuv have to be mobilized for the defense of the country, but that must be done in uniform. . . . Our whole concern must be—come what may in Palestine—to leave a saving remnant in the land under any possible circumstances."

The people of the Center and Right on the Agency Executive differed in their views. Mapai representatives appeared in the executive with a unified stand, expressed by Sharett:

> He that says that "If we are 'good boys,' the invaders will leave us alone" has no basis on which to stand. The opposite is a more likely outlook—we are no different from the rest of the Jewish people. We must also realize that the destruction of the Yishuv means the destruction of Zionism. The invaders, if they come, will try to introduce their "New Order" here. They will tell the Arabs that, once and for all, they are freeing them of the plague whose name is Zionism. They also know well that, if they do not destroy us, the Yishuv is sure to be very dangerous in a time of crisis. . . . Better death with honor than with shame.

Sharett promised to do everything to enable the Jewish youth to fight in uniform. But he did not look upon that as the *sine qua non* and was prepared to take the responsibility upon himself for warfare in all its forms, even without uniforms, including partisan fighting. But at the same time he went back to his concept of 1941 that, "in case of invasion, it were well that a portion of our young people should go with the British Army," that is, retreat with the Allies so as to return and participate in the reconquest of the land.[21]

Parallel to the debate in the Agency Executive and the National Council, a debate was conducted in the Histadrut in which three views came to the fore. Zev Shefer* and Ben-Zion Israeli did not believe that it was possible to fight an invader with the forces of the Hagana and the Supernumerary Police Force. They headed the group that looked upon recruitment for the army as the all-important thing. And indeed it was difficult to imagine a guerrilla war by Jewish partisan units at that time. Shefer and Israeli were not opposed to recruitment for independent Hagana units. But they placed the stress on the army,

* A leader of Hever Hakvutzot.

claiming that army enlistment was also the key to satisfying
other, less important, needs.

Sharett and his associates in the party leadership (Ben-
Gurion was staying in the United States at the time) took the
field against this view, which was winning broad support in
Mapai circles. Sharett saw a need for a rational apportionment
of the forces available to the Yishuv; he sought to unify the
machinery, simplify organizational forms, and reduce divisive-
ness. Recognizing that the Yishuv must do "two things at once,"
he agreed that the emphasis must be put on army and Supernumerary enlistments, without downgrading the independent
Hagana.

> When we speak of the volunteering of the community, we
> must realize that mobilization in uniform is, first, the thing
> of special political value we are doing during this period and,
> second, also the most difficult thing from several points of
> view. Therefore, donning the uniform demands special stress.
> . . . As the direct danger to Palestine increases, we say that
> military interest requires [the British] to give us maximum
> potential to fight in Palestine. For a consolidated Jewish
> force, properly trained in the broadest possible framework,
> without or in different kinds of uniforms, military effective-
> ness will reach a peak if it fights on the soil of Palestine.

Sharett's attitude found expression in a remark made about
"comrades without uniforms" when he stated, "There has been
no period in the course of this war when their service was not
necessary." Thus, he viewed it as imperative to support the
Palmakh and the rest of the formations of the independent
Hagana. This, however, was a secondary necessity compared
to army enlistment, which for him embodied the Yishuv's participation in the war against Hitler and the Zionist battle for
independence. The more Jewish units in the British Army, the
stronger the Zionist pressure on Britain and the greater the
political possibilities that were opened. Along with Shefer, he
looked upon mobilization for the army as the way to assure the

independent Hagana its part. At the Forty-seventh Convention of Histadrut (in September 1942) Sharett emphasized the numerical limitations placed on recruitment for the Hagana, as against the relatively mass mobilization for the army. "We would be politically insensitive if we did not all agree that the major stress must be on enlistment for the [Jewish] battalions. That is the imperative of the moment."[22]

There was a certain difference of shading in the statements of Eliyahu Golomb. He was entirely wrapped up in Hagana matters and could not, therefore, agree to Sharett's emphasis. In the September council, Golomb defended the equality of worth of the various defensive branches. To the Hagana he assigned not only tasks of a protective nature against Arab attacks, but also defensive roles in Palestine in case the Jewish battalions were not permitted (or able) to perform them. He stated that "we must create a mobilized internal force, capable of serving as a cadre, around which the entire fighting Yishuv can consolidate in time of trouble." At the Histadrut Convention in April 1942, he had demanded an equal apportionment for the Hagana, Supernumerary Police Force, and army. However, in September, he consented to Sharett's stipulation that two-thirds of the enlistees be diverted to the army. But he still demanded, in principle, equality of worth for the Hagana.

As the Germans approached the borders of Egypt, the left wing of Histadrut emphasized its outlook all the more strongly. Galili expressed the opinion that even the Jewish units in the army were a branch of the independent Jewish force—except that that force was not subject to the Yishuv leadership. He threw down the gauntlet on behalf of the "comrades without uniforms" who were going about with a feeling of inferiority vis-à-vis those enrolled in the army. He pointed out the great value of

that original way which was conceived within the bosom of the workers' movement, because the labor community is the

embodiment of both the goal and the means to the goal—
within it lives and beats the instinct for self-rule; it looks
upon itself as the base of Jewish strength and it plots the
course for that, to design mobilized units dependent upon
Hebrew settlements and founded upon labor and training.

The *qualitative* emphasis was once again placed upon the
Hagana. Insecurity over the possibility of activating the Jewish
battalions, in an emergency, while they were under British
command served as a fundamental justification for the left-
wing people. The leftist position was absolutely clear. During
a German invasion, the Jewish community was obligated to
battle the Germans in a "fight to the finish" in every form.
Retreat was unthinkable. "These half-million Jews do not have
to retreat. Not one of us has to be saved," said Tabenkin.[23]

At the same time, a different tone was heard, one that seems
to have turned mute for a brief while. That was the demand for
military self-reliance in case of the need to battle, at a later
stage, against the White Paper ("as if there were no war," to use
Ben-Gurion's words). The demand was not openly voiced—the
times were not right for that. In closed meetings, however, the
words were explicitly uttered. Speaking against the priority of
army enlistment, Natan Peled stated, at a session of the Actions
Committee of Kibbutz Artzi, that

> this tendency is likely to present the Hagana once again
> with the necessity of separating an important segment for
> army enlistment. In no way can we surrender that fundamen-
> tal defense dictated by Zionist and labor policy. An indepen-
> dent defense force must be created in the country. It must
> be directly subject to Jewish authority. It must be a force
> operating on the basis of independent Zionist goals, though
> it may find itself in a situation of cooperation with the
> government.[24]

In summary, within Histadrut circles no one took exception
to the need for defending against invasion by every means; but
there were those who cast doubt on the Hagana's ability to fulfill

the assignment. The majority of Mapai looked upon army recruitment as the main thing, but it was ready to designate a portion of the manpower for the independent units. Another section argued for equality of worth for the various security arms. But the Histadrut left wing demanded special attention for the independent units, though it affirmed army enlistment on broad dimensions (and so conducted itself).

The Zionist executive bodies in Palestine and London acted in accordance with the considerations and views expressed in the discussions going on in Palestine. But we must emphasize that for the purposes of our subject matter, we have conspicuously stressed one side of the overall picture; to the public in Palestine and the heads of Zionism, however, other factors were more important. Hagana matters were not the main news of the day, but the *front*, enlistment in the army, and the Supernumerary Police Force were. And those were also the main arenas of Zionist activity in the summer of 1942.

During the winter of 1941/1942, Weizmann resumed his efforts to advance the cause of the Jewish fighting force by Churchill's personal affirmative intervention. On February 18 Weizmann received a friendly, though noncommittal, reply from the prime minister. As the German peril neared the portals of Palestine, the Yishuv redoubled its efforts to mobilize a maximum number of people for the army's Jewish units. On March 26 the agency issued Recruitment Order Two, in which it called upon bachelors, married men without children, and unmarried women between the ages of twenty and thirty to volunteer.

The approaching front quickened the official bodies' activity. The danger of invasion seemed imminent. On April 17, Sharett addressed the British general Auchinleck in a lengthy and detailed memorandum. In it, he proposed the following: creation of a Jewish fighting force in Palestine, turning the Jewish companies in the Buffs into combat battalions capable of fighting like any British battle unit; raising the number of auxiliary policemen to fifty thousand and training them under the instruction of army personnel; preparing noncommissioned officers in numbers appropriate to the training of this large force; and concentrating arms to equip this force.[25]

The agency's entire activity during the spring and summer of 1942 was conducted according to the principles of that memorandum, and any attempt to study or examine Zionist security policy during that period must take that document as a starting point. The memorandum was sent at a time when Britain was being compelled to mobilize all its strength against the mounting German torrent, and the instrument appears to have made its impression. At the same time, Weizmann was also continuing his activities in the United States. In June, after the fall of Tobruk, he sent Churchill a letter demanding once again the establishment of a large fighting force in Palestine (June 21). Sharett's plan spoke of massing ten thousand more men in the army and fifty thousand in permanent or temporary units connected with the Supernumerary Police Force.

But carrying out such large-scale changes was too difficult for the British military machine. The British were short of arms. As fast as weapons arrived, they were channeled to the front at El Alamein. Nevertheless, a slight shift in the attitude of the high British officers occurred; and when Tobruk fell, a course for thirty-six police sergeants was started in Palestine, in order to raise the effectiveness of the Supernumerary Police Force as an army auxiliary force.

Army enlistment was a grave problem from the Jewish standpoint. The Buffs were not popular in the Jewish community. They were given inferior training, and the tasks assigned them were confined to guarding depots and other military points, roles that could not inspire men who had turned out for war against Hitler. As we have said, the agency tried to change this situation, and its pressure did bring some results. After several months of hesitation, with the British stating that there was room for an increase in Jewish enlistment even under existing conditions, the British war secretary announced to Parliament on August 6 that Jewish and Arab battalions would be established within the framework of a special Palestinian regiment. The enlargement of the Supernumerary Police Force by 1,500 men was also promised. It was further said that the new battalions would offer the Jews and Arabs the opportunity of "uniting in defense of their common homeland."

At first the Jewish leadership accepted the announcement joyfully, but the deceptive intention quickly became apparent. The battalions received neither new arms nor substantial new training, and their assignments also remained as they had been: monotonous service, boring and degrading, calculated to embitter the soldier. There was progress only in the fact that the individual companies had been formed into battalions and the battalions removed from the British Buffs regiment. In sum, the success of the agency's efforts in the area of recruitment was rather modest.

The same was true of the Supernumerary Police Force. The 1,500 new men were not put into the standing force but into the framework of the temporary village police (Temporary Auxiliary Policemen), which lacked proper training and equipment. The "further training" to be given amounted to another course for thirty-six more police sergeants in Sarafand. The course was, indeed, conducted at a rather high level; and now, with the graduates of the first course, there were seventy-two trained men. That was the total progress in the area of the Supernumerary Police Force.

In the summer of 1942, 2,572 men were serving in the Jewish Settlement Police. There was a rifle for every man, plus 291 rifles in reserve. The 3,845 Supernumeraries who were outside the structure of the Jewish Settlement Police possessed 2,500 rifles. The 14,318 Temporary Auxiliary Policemen in the villages had 2,053 rifles, and there were several hundred rifles for the 2,600 Auxiliaries in towns. Forty-eight machine guns and forty mortars completed the Supernumeraries' battle gear. All of this taken together was hardly enough equipment with which to face the German Army.

The agency devoted great efforts to increasing the enlistments and trying to persuade the British command to supply training and equipment. Sharett soon realized that the command would never agree to such an expanded program. On July 8 he suggested to McConnell, the general in charge in Palestine, that as a first step ten thousand men be trained as a "home guard." The Jews prepared to form such an organization and even started training, openly and without authorization, on their own. Brief rotating encampments were set up which took in, in the first (and last) month of operation (August 1942), five thousand men. The British, however, despite their promises, rendered no assistance to the operation. In September the agency was forced to cease training for lack of funds.

What were the results of these efforts?

The most significant positive result was the enlistment of 4,619 men and women in the army, from June through the end of September 1942. They strengthened the existing Jewish units, materially expressed the Yishuv's participation in the Allied war effort, and later blazed a trail for the creation of the Jewish Brigade. With the aid of this enlistment the Jewish battalions, which represented some progress along the way toward a Jewish fighting unit, were established.

Organizationally and financially, not inconsiderable attainments must be noted. On May 28 the Yishuv Security Committee—at Sharett's inspiration—decided to appoint a new presidium for the Kofer Hayishuv, with Dr. Barth of the Anglo-Palestine Bank as chairman. At the beginning of June this presidium was asked to head a new Yishuv financial apparatus, the Mobilization Campaign, which was to unite the functions of the Kofer Hayishuv, the Emergency Tax, and care for soldiers' families. In the first half of its first year (June to November), the campaign collected approximately £180,000, making possible the budgetary appropriation, meager as it was, for the Palmakh. From this point of view, Sharett was right when he said that army enlistment facilitated the creation of the Palmakh.

During the same month (June), the Yishuv Security Committee took general control of all forms of enlistment and troop apportionment. This was a sharp deviation from the line taken by Ben-Gurion during 1939. He had tried to fragmentize the powers of the National Command and concentrate all authority (by bypassing the other community institutions) in the hands of the Agency Executive. The Security Committee appointed an enlistment center (with Dr. Joseph as chairman) to take care of manpower apportionment and the routine operations of recruitment. During the summer of 1942, the committee decided to recruit high school seniors for a year of service in the agricultural establishment or the Palmakh and set in motion increased publicity for army enlistment.

The general line of Zionist security policy was to get the English to call on the Jews to participate in the defense of Palestine and to bring about the enlistment of masses by means of a renewal, if only for a short time, of the spirit of partnership with the British. This line failed in its main objective, for the British did not respond to Jewish demands. Army and government bureaus proclaimed the mobilization and carried it out, but without enthusiasm. Only by superhuman exertions did Sharett and his associates succeed in surmounting the obstacles heaped up in their path. One fact became clear. Even in time of imminent peril to the very existence of the British position in the Middle East, the British hesitated to warm up their relationship with the Jews, the only trustworthy element in the entire region. Thus while the achievements attained by the Jewish Agency were no doubt important, they matched neither the efforts put forth nor the needs.

There is no doubt that army enlistment represented the broad stream of Yishuv participation in the war, and only by virtue of that did the Yishuv acquire the operational machine which later facilitated the existence, insecure as it was, of the Palmakh. A sort of paradox operated between the two lines of development. On the one hand, army recruitment was stiff competition for Palmakh enlistment; and on the other hand, it was, in the context of those days, a supportive factor. There were many who felt that the lesson to be drawn from the Rommel episode in Palestine was to doubt the possibility of arriving at military-political achievements by way of mobilization for the army, that one must stress the Yishuv's own Hagana, demand the establishment of independent instruments, and allocate men and means for them. Nor could the Supernumerary Police Force stand in the breach. What would the English do if the Germans invaded Palestine, and where would the Jewish battalions be stationed then? There was room for the opinion that, in the circumstances of 1942, only the Hagana could serve as the nucleus for a fight to the end by the Jewish community in Eretz Israel.

The Birth of a Zionist Political Platform, 1940–1942

At the beginning of the war (1939–1940), the Zionist leadership had still not crystallized its postwar program. Weizmann had been demanding, since the fall of 1939, that all of western Palestine become a Jewish state. This was a mere slogan. Its actual political content varied according to the situation at the front and in keeping with the considerations of the moment. Weizmann gives the impression of having been pondering an all-inclusive solution of the problems of the region, not simply the Palestine problem. More precisely, he favored a broad Arab federation, or any other arrangement that would satisfy Arab demands for national unity—as long as the Jews were assured their state in all of western Palestine or the larger part of that territory.[1] Sharett, too, expressed a similar view and attached his agreement with the program for a state to Weizmann's concept of an Arab federation.

It is very possible that Weizmann's position was influenced by the imaginative program of the Anglo-Arab diplomat-romantic, St. John Abdullah Philby, the friend of Ibn Saud. Philby had two conversations with Weizmann and Namier. The first took place on September 28, 1939, and the second, in which Sharett took part, on October 6, 1939. Philby felt that Ibn Saud held the key. If they would help the desert monarch unite the Arab lands under his scepter, the Jews could demand Palestine as their price—all of western Palestine. It would be possible to work out population transfers. "The main thing is to get England and France to give the Arabs complete independence and to get the French out of Syria."

What would force France to quit Syria? For that question, Philby had no answer. But Namier found the answer: As a result of the war, the problem of Jewish refugees would worsen and powerful pressure could be brought to bear on the Western powers to find a solution for the problem; that solution could mean only Palestine. Palestine could be given to the Jews only on condition of union of Syria with the Arab countries—"The way to implement the program has been found, and the Zionists hold the key."

Ibn Saud possessed a very good chance of uniting the Arabs, but he lacked money. There, said Philby, was the chance for an agreement with the Jews in which Ibn Saud would no doubt be interested—if a large sum were to be guaranteed, one could suggest that he concede Palestine. Sharett replied that if the Jews gave money, it would be to finance the resettlement of Arabs transferred from Palestine; of course, those investments would be a blessing to the neighboring lands. But Philby was not satisfied. Ibn Saud needed cash for himself.

A second thing was required of the Jews for the actualization of the program—to influence the English to fulfill Sir Henry McMahon's promises *in toto* to the Arabs (1915–1916), in accordance with England's interpretation of their territorial scope. Sharett inquired what that meant. Philby responded: Absolute independence. Philby was convinced that complete independence, without any tie to Britain, was the most desirable solution.

Philby's answers amazed Sharett, who felt that this was the

way a charlatan or political tyro, not a serious diplomat, would talk. In Sharett's view, the man's concepts of independence were vague and devoid of realism—for example, his statements that independence was imperative and possible, that England had no rightful interest in the Arab countries, that the Arabs would willingly acknowledge Ibn Saud's domination; and that it was within the power of the Arabs to raise a mighty armed force and hold out against anyone who took arms against them —"especially if you help," as Philby added.

When Sharett questioned the source of such confidence in the Jewish influence over British and French policy, Philby answered: "You have a great influence!"—as if an Arab were speaking, not an Englishman who should have realized that the Jews had not even been able to prevent the promulgation of the White Paper. Sharett ceased questioning. The entire program seemed to him unrealistic in the extreme, though it contained one important political point: St. John Abdullah Philby's appearance before Ibn Saud with the proposal to deliver all of western Palestine to the Zionists, and to evacuate the Arabs from it. Sharett felt that Philby should be allowed to proceed on the strength of his belief (or his deception) without burdening him or putting obstacles in his way. Sharett informed him that if he reached an agreement with Ibn Saud which assured Jewish interests, everything of course would be done on the part of the Zionists in order to obtain Britain's approval of that agreement.

The most interesting part of these negotiations was the sum of money that was to be paid Ibn Saud. Here it became apparent that Weizmann's attitude to the Philby proposal was different from Sharett's. Weizmann expressed the opinion that if the Jews were to get all of western Palestine, one could talk in terms of ten to twenty million pounds sterling. At the mention of such numbers, Sharett became nervous. Naturally Philby, on the other hand, rose to the bait. Weizmann explained that if he received notice during his stay in the United States that Ibn Saud was prepared to negotiate an agreement, he would propose to the U.S.

president that the American government should assist in financing a plan which would open broad opportunities for a solution of the Jewish refugee problem, through the creation of a Jewish state and the transfer of Arab populations.[2]

The proposal was clear—and fanciful; but Weizmann seemed to take an absolutely serious attitude to it. At that early stage of the discussions, the plans were ended with no results whatsoever. Philby was received in an audience by Ibn Saud on January 8, 1940, and presented the program. Ibn Saud did not reject it—but he made Philby swear not to breathe a word of it to any Arabs. It was plain that His Majesty had no objection to adding territory to his provinces and silver to his coffers at the expense of the Arabs of Palestine, especially since Palestine was not in the least within his sphere of influence. In order to stand honorably by his obligations to his fellow Arabs, however, Ibn Saud requested that the program be put before him in forceful terms by the two Anglo-Saxon powers. He was willing to agree if he could appear in the role of a man compelled.

The importance of this episode ought not to be exaggerated. At this stage (and there were, it seems, further stages), Philby's plan can serve us only as an example of the type of agreement for which Weizmann was striving, and that is the light in which one should also view his statements in regard to the Arab federation. He appears to have looked upon the program of a Jewish state in all of western Palestine as practical—because he believed in the possibility of creating an Arab federation, in exchange for which the Arabs would consent to the establishment of a Jewish state.

Nevertheless, Weizmann's approach is marked by a good number of vague points. Did the Zionist leader seriously believe that arrangements could be made between feudal princes of Ibn Saud's type and the Western powers—and on a very dubious financial basis, at that—without asking the opinion of the Arabs of Palestine or the national movement in the rest of the Arab countries? We know that Ben-Gurion and Sharett hoped to achieve a pro-Zionist solution by way of strong Western pressure on the Arabs. This was an illusion, as became obvious in the course of time. Weizmann, however, went much further than they with his feeling—on the lines of nineteenth-century diplomacy—that the fate of lands and peoples was determined by the word of the world's powerful men. Insufficient attention was paid to the fact that Arab nationalism was an ascendant force which Western statesmen would have to weigh and to which they would have to make concessions. Weizmann's mental process was approximately this: The White Paper is the result of appeasement; it is a failure; the Arabs have been a disappointment in the war, but the Jews have played a part in it; the refugee problem will get worse. All this presents an opportunity for Zionist strategy. In exchange for a solution to the troublesome refugee problem, the Western powers will agree to a Jewish state within the borders of an Arab federation.

The British did indeed give their consent to the establishment of an Arab federation—but their reasons were diametrically opposed to those of Weizmann. As practical politicians they were afraid of more uprisings on the order of the rebellion in Iraq. In the search for immunity from that plague, they gave their blessing to the desire of the Arab nation for political unity within the framework of a pro-British Arab federation, under the leadership of men loyal to Britain. An announcement in this spirit was made by Anthony Eden in his Mansion House address of May 29, 1941. Palestine was not mentioned, but it was clear that widely influential circles in Britain were hoping for a continuation of the White Paper policy and the inclusion of Palestine within this sort of federation.

So as not to present Weizmann's programs in a distorting mirror, we must add that he was always ready to retreat toward an agreement on the more modest solutions of a "good" partition, if only they would assure the continuation of the Zionist work and its development. One should also bear in mind that even his most grandiose plans, which today sound like fantasies, had a certain political basis, though a very weak one. The information passed on by the Polish government in exile in London, concerning Nazi terror and the concentration of Polish Jews into ghettos during 1940 to 1942, made a deep impression on pro-Jewish figures in Parliament and the cabinet. The government could not completely abandon the Jews.[3] Precisely on this point, the dread significance of the White Paper was sensed.

Members of the British government were of divided opinion on questions of Palestine (as on many other questions), and a deadlock within the government developed on this. Unable to decide the Palestine question, the government became unwilling even to discuss it. The upshot was that they concluded they should do nothing about the matter until the end of the war. This meant the preservation of the status quo for the time being; the British government would clear things up and choose its path when the battles had abated. But that frozen condition, the status quo, was the White Paper policy. Do-nothing, in this instance, meant anti-Jewish and anti-Zionist action: cessation of immigration and reduction of settlement.

The Arabs tried to get Britain to fulfill the political part of the White Paper, that is, to turn Palestine into an Arab state, and they won the support of the Palestine administration for their cause.[4] The Jews, on the other hand, sought to nullify those provisions of the White Paper that had already been put into practice and, at the same time, to achieve *de facto* recognition as a nation by the creation of a Jewish fighting formation (which would constitute one more stage in turning Palestine, or a part of it, into a Jewish state).

When all is said and done, the assurance of immediate British interests—the protection of positions in the Middle East—hand in hand with the inability to arrive at a clear decision, comprised the axis for all considerations on the Palestine problem. It would seem that the White Paper was considered by the British to be the best guarantee for these interests and thus was regarded as at least a temporary, immediate answer in this thicket of problems. The White Paper policy was good enough to serve Britain until the end of hostilities—and then it could be reexamined.

The Jewish labor movement in Palestine, with its numerous branches, was optimistic about Zionism's prospects in Britain and the United States after the war. Everyone expected that Britain would reverse itself on the White Paper and facilitate the realization of Zionist aims, if only in part. However, while the Histadrut minority, Hashomer Hatzair, was working for a solution of the political problems through *direct* agreement with the Arabs, Ben-Gurion, Sharett, and the rest of the Mapai leadership saw an agreement that would be *forced* by the Anglo-American powers as the sole possibility. In this regard, Ben-Gurion had undergone a certain mental development.

As late as the middle of May 1940, on the eve of his departure for the United States, Ben-Gurion felt that *various* solutions should be taken into consideration: Jewish independence in Palestine (the word "partition" was never uttered, but it was implied); a commonwealth within the structure of the British Empire; a state that would be part of a Middle East federation. Ben-Gurion pinned on the British government his hopes for enactment of one of the alternatives. He stated that "the new colonial secretary and Britain's ambassadors in the Arab countries must try to arrive at an agreement with the Arab states in regard to such a solution."[5]

Ben-Gurion had not yet breathed the air of America's massive wave of war preparations, had not yet felt the pulse of her great Jewry, with its five millions. Prior to this, he had not accepted Weizmann's program. But during his visit America made a powerful impression on him. He discovered the New World, though this was not his first visit to the United States. The mammoth scale of America's projects and programs cast a spell over him. He returned to Palestine in February 1941 with his own version of the Weizmann program.

Just one week before Ben-Gurion's return, Sharett explained

to an American visitor that "our goal is to have a higher British authority, with which we would reach an agreement, remain here." He remarked that the ultimate aim of Zionism was a Jewish population of three million in Palestine on both sides of the Jordan, with an Arab population of two million.[6] In contrast, Ben-Gurion was reaching for the stars: the transfer of five million Jewish refugees at the end of the war, and Jewish independence. Ben-Gurion knew that a transfer of such immense proportions could not be carried out by any foreign government, no matter how friendly, but only by the Jews themselves. So in order to effect the transfer, "Palestine must be turned into a Jewish state, not as a final goal, but as a means of moving millions of Jews to Palestine after the war, at the fastest possible rate."

A more polished, and yet intentionally vaguer, formulation, which could serve as the starting point for various philosophies, was presented in "Lines of Zionist Policy." This document was circulated by Ben-Gurion among the members of the Agency Executive in the middle of March 1941:

> The political direction of Zionism during this period is to bring about a condition whereby, at the end of the war, a regime will rise in Palestine with the intention of facilitating immigration and settlement of the Jewish masses on a grand scale. Governmental authority and financial capability must be granted the representatives of the Jewish nation [the agency or the Jewish government] to execute the rapid transfer of millions of Jews and their settlement as a self-governing people.

In regard to the Arabs, the program proposed a voluntary exchange of populations. Should the Arabs not consent to be interchanged, however, "not only will full civil, political, and national equality be assured them, but the Jews [will aspire] also to equalization of the Arabs' standard of living economically, culturally, and socially with that of the Jews."

If Palestine were to be accepted as a dominion in the "British (or British-American) Commonwealth of Nations, a regime will be set up in the country on the order of that prevailing between the English and French in Canada." It was also stated that, if an Arab federation should rise and recognize Jewish Palestine, the latter would affiliate with that federation in exchange for adequate guarantees. Here, once more, the relations among the dominions and the British Commonwealth of Nations served as a model for the desired relationship between Eretz Israel and the Arab federation.[7]

The drift of Ben-Gurion's thinking was, therefore, that the most desirable solution was a tie to Britain, and perhaps one to the United States at the same time. However, Ben-Gurion was also ready to join an Arab federation which would, likewise, be connected with the Western powers. We can see that the plan was clearly constructed around the possibilities of propaganda and persuasion in the United States, with attention to the refugee problem that would worsen at the end of the war.

The rest of the members of the Agency Executive were not enthusiastic about the idea of publicizing this program, though most of them agreed with it. In the plan as finally submitted (March 23), the original formulation of a "Jewish state" was kept under wraps and traded for "Jewish authority" in Palestine —in order to avoid debate with those who were afraid of demanding a state from England. In the discussion, Dr. Senator resumed his compromise position in relation to Arab demands. Menachem Ussishkin, precisely because of his anti-British maximalist stand, arrived at the demand for immigration and settlement and a "mere" nullification of the White Paper, so as to leave the door open for as many alternatives as possible. Other members, especially Sharett and Eliezer Kaplan, agreed to the proposed program as a goal to strive for—but they expressed fears that the time was not ripe for its publication. And indeed the program was not publicized or even discussed within a broader forum. It was tabled.

In spite of that, Ben-Gurion had achieved his purpose. The

discussions had taught him that most of the members of the Agency Executive would not oppose the line of diplomacy he was proposing. The obscure close of the debate left him more maneuvering room than he would have had under an affirmative public resolution.

We have given emphasis here to Ben-Gurion's attitude toward Britain and the United States. However, we shall miss the whole truth if we ignore the other side of the coin—the choice that would remain, in his view, if negotiation, argumentation, and the like should fail to get British agreement:

> To be ready, also, for another way, the way of armed struggle. . . . Our youth must be prepared to do everything possible when the right moment comes. I cannot force the executive to do this. But the executive that prevents this act will not survive, it would not deserve to exist.[8]

Those words were absolutely plain. The program of struggle had been temporarily tabled when alternatives were created. But it had neither been canceled nor forgotten.

In July 1941, Ben-Gurion again left Palestine. He stayed in London for a time and reached America in the winter. During this period, relations between himself and Weizmann continually deteriorated. Those relations had reached the point of crisis back in the summer of 1940, while Ben-Gurion was visiting in London. We have already learned that in Weizmann he saw the embodiment and personification of the extreme pro-British Zionist line. For that reason, Ben-Gurion denied Weizmann's fitness to negotiate with the British, and accused him of foot-dragging on the issue of creating the Jewish division and of making concessions on the problem of mobilizing Jewish power for the defense of Palestine.

There is no escaping the conclusion that, in no small measure, a personal quarrel was involved here. More correctly, a battle for top leadership in the Zionist movement was finding expression. Ben-Gurion made a suggestion that would inevitably shock a leader of Weizmann's stature. He proposed that Chaim Weizmann conduct political negotiations only in the presence of David Ben-Gurion! Weizmann, of course, refused. And, with that, the matter ended for the time being.

🖋 The Biltmore Program

In the free world, particularly in the United States, the foundations had meanwhile been laid for large-scale political work by the Zionist movement. During his 1940/1941 American visit, Ben-Gurion lectured the national convention of the Zionist Organization of America on "turning Palestine into a Jewish commonwealth," so as to assure "the moving of millions of Jews to the land after the war."[9] This proposal was accepted by the United Palestine Appeal Convention in January 1941, in which more than two thousand representatives of American Jewry took part. Later, the term "commonwealth" (instead of "state") became an accepted political fixture ratified by various Jewish organizations.[10] Its manner of formulation allowed its use later, when the recognition of the fact that partition must be the goal grew stronger and stronger.

Most of the Zionist forces in the United States were concentrated in the American Zionist Emergency Council, where vital roles were played by people close to Weizmann in approach—Rabbi Stephen Wise, Nahum Goldmann, Louis Lipsky, and others. During 1941 Weizmann worked to convince American Jewry to support the demand for the establishment of a Jewish state. In January 1942 an article by Weizmann was printed in *Foreign Affairs,* arguing for Jewish independence in Palestine and mass immigration as the solution to the refugee problem. He spoke of two million refugees who would have to be transported to Palestine at the end of the war. (On another occasion, in a letter to Leo Simon on November 11, 1941, he had talked in terms of five million.) In his article Weizmann came out, for the first time publicly, in favor of the establishment of a Jewish commonwealth. Typically, he based this on the Peel Commission report, which had concluded that the principle of Jewish independence was to be realized within the framework of a partition of Palestine.

The responsibility for establishing the commonwealth, Weizmann stated, rested on the Western powers; and it was also necessary to try to persuade the Arabs to consent, "of their own free will and accord," to an exchange of populations. On the political future of the Jewish commonwealth, he suggested two possibilities: its inclusion in the British Commonwealth of Nations (the most desirable solution) or its affiliation with an Arab federation. The article placed the commonwealth question on the stage of international diplomacy, and sketched out Zionism's political line for that fateful year, 1942.[11]

At the beginning of the year Meyer Weisgal, one of Weizmann's closest aides, agreed to supervise arranging an American Zionist conference to define the goals of Zionism and mobilize the Zionists of the United States for broad political and fundraising activity. In March the date of the conference was decided upon, as was a formal dinner in honor of Dr. Weizmann.

Weizmann arrived in the United States in April, after preparations for creating the conference had been completed through the efforts of the Emergency Council. Its program was worked out and draft resolutions were formulated before the convening of the conference. Most of that labor was done by Weisgal. However, sometime before the meeting of the conference, quarrels erupted between Ben-Gurion and the members of the Emergency Council, for the most part over the question of authority to conduct negotiations with Jewish and non-Jewish parties. For example, there were differences of opinion about Dr. Neumann's right, as head of the publicity committee of the Emergency Council, to carry on such business in Washington (in this case, Ben-Gurion finally dropped his objection). Then a dispute broke out on the problem of relations with the Committee for a Jewish army, an Etzel-sponsored group with a Revisionist sympathizer, the famous Dutch-American author Pierre van Paassen, at its head. The committee's purpose was to win the minds of American political leaders and the American public to the idea of a Hebrew army. Weisgal and his collaborators claimed that the army committee was ready to surrender its right to conduct political negotiations in favor of the Emergency Council, but Ben-Gurion refused on principle to sit down and talk with the Etzel people. To Ben-Gurion's way of thinking, they had removed themselves from the ranks of the Jewish people, and until they rejoined the Zionist Organization, all contact with them was precluded. Ben-Gurion's opponents asserted that, because of his stand, the extremist Etzel elements had been strengthened within the army committee, which now continued to survive in opposition to the Emergency Council.

Such misunderstandings troubled the atmosphere among Zionist leaders even before Weizmann's arrival in the United States in April 1942. With his coming, relations with Ben-Gurion deteriorated badly. We have seen how this situation budded in connection with the division programs during 1941; now it reappeared, worse than ever. Ben-Gurion made trouble over Weizmann's "uncooperative" methods of operation. The veteran leader was subject to moodiness. Periods of near inactivity alternated with days of feverish industry. Weizmann, like all leaders of his stature, was proud and self-confident. He brooked neither criticism nor competition.

In London, the political work was carried on by an office in which Professor Selig Brodetsky was the only Agency Executive member, other than Weizmann. Brodetsky's part in political activity was quite small, because of his many other responsibilities. Others taking part in the political work were Sir Louis Namier, the celebrated historian and veteran Zionist who devoted all his time to Zionist activity during the war period; Berl Locker, the Mapai representative (Poale Zion) in London and chief liaison with the Labour party; Joseph Linton;

and Lady Blanche E. T. Dugdale, a Scot of the Balfour family who tied her life to the Zionist enterprise because of her personal friendship with the Weizmann family. The people of this office were numbered among Weizmann's admirers and identified with his main diplomatic policies. Weizmann consulted them, of course, and gave their views a hearing. But in the last analysis, *he* made the binding decisions.

To Ben-Gurion, this method of operation was fundamentally unacceptable. He did not agree with Weizmann's view that the president of the Zionist Organization was responsible only to the congress for the execution of policy (though Weizmann, of course, recognized the Agency Executive's right of veto over his operations). Ben-Gurion sought to subordinate Weizmann to a system of political activity conducted according to the instructions of the Agency Executive in Jerusalem (of which Ben-Gurion was the authorized representative). Outwardly this was a procedural debate. But when Weizmann also monopolized the political activity in the United States—though he consulted both with the members of the Emergency Council and his associates in London, and submitted reports in every instance—Ben-Gurion sought, as in 1940, to set the limitation for Weizmann that all negotiations be conducted in the presence of additional representatives.

In truth, the debate was not in the least procedural. One gets the impression that Ben-Gurion's main objective, at that stage, was to avail the Agency Executive, of which he himself was the head, of status equal to that of the president of the World Zionist Organization. The controversy between the two men took on several simultaneous colorations; it was a personal, political power struggle.

In Ben-Gurion's view, Weizmann's line seemed pro-British in the extreme; and that made it antiquated and purposeless. Ben-Gurion's orientation was now Anglo-American, and certainly not purely English. By 1942 Ben-Gurion had, in contrast to his position of 1940, a deep sense of the hopelessness of a unilateral approach to Britain alone. He also had an awareness of the "right time," a last opportunity for a once-and-for-all determinative solution to the problems of Zionism, now that the United States was in the war.

In an Agency Executive session (October 4, 1942) Ben-Gurion stated: "My assumption was that, under conditions prevailing in the government in London, there is no hope. . . . Not that nothing can be done in England, but that it is impossible to change the existing situation; if it can be changed, it will only be through the power of America; thus a further assumption: the position and appearance of American Zionism have a crucial importance."

The center of the conflict of 1942, however, was the basis which Ben-Gurion laid for the Jewish commonwealth program. Although Weizmann was also talking about a rapid transfer of millions of Jewish refugees to Palestine within a period of a few years, there seemed to be a qualitative difference between the statements of the two leaders. Ben-Gurion was speaking of an *immediate* transfer

> of millions of Jews, at least two million, to Palestine, should political conditions be right. . . . We are not the ones who have created this reality, but we must adjust to it. . . . We must move a maximum of those Jews who have been uprooted in a fundamental sense—to Palestine, or Palestine will descend from the political stage.

The realization of this concept—which had its roots in the vision of the catastrophe that would be created at the end of the war—depended on the Western powers, and especially on the United States. Ben-Gurion hoped that there would be American soldiers in Palestine by the close of the war. Above all, he placed a very high estimation on America's postwar strength. He believed that Zionism would succeed in convincing American political leaders of the justice of the movement's demands, by virtue of the sweeping vision of its program.

To bring another ten thousand Jews into Palestine over dozens of years, for that they are not going to get into a quarrel with anybody. They *would* quarrel with the Arabs if there were a solution that would alleviate the condition of the millions of Jews who will remain, if Hitler does not kill them.[12]

To Weizmann, the plan to transfer two million Jews *immediately* seemed like a fantasy. Even Ben-Gurion did not so much as mention his transfer plans until the end of his stay in the United States, when he presented them before a small, select group of Zionist leaders. Weizmann complained to Wise, the president of the Emergency Council, that Ben-Gurion had discussed this plan of his neither with him nor anyone else. Instead, just hours before leaving America, "he blurted it out in a few hysterical sentences." Sharett had spoken of 100,000 newcomers a year, a slogan which Weizmann was willing to accept, but not the one-time transfer of two million that Ben-Gurion was discussing at present. All these "mock heroics" were disquieting, most harmful and demoralizing.[13]

Here was the conflict of 1942 converging with that of 1941. The differences of opinion between the two leaders now centered on two main points: first, the stress on the value of a Jewish army. Weizmann looked upon it as an expression of Jewish participation in the war and a means of exerting pressure on Britain. Ben-Gurion, on the other hand, saw all of that, plus a political weapon which could be used—if there were no choice—against Britain. Second, rebirth of the Nordau Plan.* Weizmann rejected it, while Ben-Gurion spoke of active American aid in moving two million Jews to Palestine in a single operation.

But there was a difference, too, in their two versions of the same commonwealth program. For Weizmann the program was,

* A plan conceived by Max Nordau after World War I to transfer large numbers of Jews to Palestine in a very short time.

first and foremost, a tactical propaganda step, a *political* demand on which negotiations must be carried on—leading, perhaps (under pressure of the refugee problem) to diplomatic achievements, to a territorial compromise. We are aware that Weizmann, at the time, was speaking of Palestine except for the mountainous Samaria region, where the bulk of the Arab population was located, as the area for a Jewish state, and of the entry of millions of Jews over a period of a number of years. He put the stress on the political *slogan* and valued it as a device of Zionist diplomacy. Ben-Gurion, however, turned the Biltmore Program (see below) into an ensign and standard that would lead the Jewish people to direct victory—or to destruction. His approach was marked by a messianic reach.

The program itself, expressed in Weisgal's wording with certain changes, was adopted by a very impressive assemblage convened from May 9 to May 11, 1942, in the Biltmore Hotel in New York. The resolution stated that with the coming of victory, the reordering of the world on the bases of peace, justice, and equality would be impossible unless the problem of Jewish homelessness were definitely solved.

The proposed solution (which followed long lists of other resolutions concerning questions of the Diaspora and the Zionist movement) contained three provisions: (a) opening the gates of Palestine for Jewish immigration; (b) availing the Jewish Agency of the power over entry into Palestine and granting it all necessary authority to develop the country and build it up, including the development of all uninhabited, uncultivated lands; and (c) constituting Palestine as a Jewish commonwealth, integrated in the new democratic structure of the world.

A goodly number of question marks inhere in the Biltmore Program. What was the difference between points one and two? If Palestine was to be constituted as a Jewish commonwealth, did it make sense to specify that the Jewish Agency was to have control over immigration and settlement? Was this not likely to be interpreted as a presumption that in practice Palestine was not to become a Jewish commonwealth? If only a political *proclamation* on the part of the Western powers was intended, an announcement of intention to constitute the Jewish commonwealth, how could a non-Jewish regime—which would turn over to the Jews such decisive areas of operations as immigration, settlement, and development, but not customs, taxes, defense, or internal administration—be continued in Palestine?

The two Zionist leaders settled these perplexities in various ways. Weizmann stated in his opening and concluding speeches in the assembly that at the end of the war there would be three million refugees in Europe (he feared then, in May 1942, that about one-quarter of the Jews of Europe would perish during the war). He viewed their suffering as the lever that would move the West to constructive action. Weizmann did not consider the Arab factor a serious obstacle. He asserted that evasive politicians were regularly exploiting it as a pretext for their machinations, that only a minority of the Arabs of Palestine were opposed to Zionism. Until the establishment of the commonwealth, or until the achievement of a Jewish majority in Palestine, a friendly regime would be set up in Palestine that would turn over control of immigration and settlement to the Jewish Agency. The vague wording of the convention's resolutions suited Weizmann's aims. He was interested in entering into negotiations toward any feasible solution, including a "good" partition or federation—any solution offering chances for mass immigration and settlement.

Ben-Gurion saw no difficulties. The single-action transfer of two million Jews would solve the problem of the majority in the country. The agency would be invited to cooperate in the execution of the transfer. The ambition for an "immediate" solution was here being voiced.[14]

The basic difference between the two approaches lay in this: Weizmann and his aides in the United States did not in the least intend to formulate a new line of Zionist policy at the Biltmore. They were formulating a political *demand* suitable for conditions in the United States, worded in language comprehensible to its Jews and non-Jews and not calculated to stir up sharp objections in Palestine. Ben-Gurion, on the other hand, turned a local resolution of American Zionists into a new political formula—affirmative, a standard for the nation.

Immediately after the Biltmore Convention, relations between the two leaders reached the breaking point. Ben-Gurion sought to bring about Dr. Weizmann's resignation. Weizmann, however, not only did not resign but rallied the leaders of American Zionism against his opponent. And they, in overwhelming majority, proved to be definite supporters of Weizmann.

At the end of July, Ben-Gurion called a meeting at Wise's home and in Weizmann's presence repeated his accusations that the older man was pro-British, unreliable, and weak. After hearing Weizmann's frank reply, the group expressed the opinion that the charges were baseless. In the fall Ben-Gurion left the United States, transferring the political, and the personal, battle against Weizmann to Palestine.

🗡 Biltmore in Palestine

What Ben-Gurion could not do in the United States was accomplished with his return to Palestine. The Biltmore Program was turned into a banner, a consummately important political slogan.

Back in Palestine, Ben-Gurion submitted a comprehensive report to the Agency Executive on his activities and the Biltmore Program, as he understood it. A majority of the Agency Executive approved his position and brought the Biltmore resolutions before the Smaller Zionist Actions Committee on October 15 and November 10, 1942. In those sessions Ben-Gurion, as a matter of course, was the sole authoritative interpreter of the program, and his statements naturally stressed the transfer of two million Jews (and the transformation, thereby, of the Arab majority into a minority), as well as the decisive help of the United States in the operation. The chairman of the executive made abundantly clear the fundamental assumptions on which, to his thinking, the program was based: the problem of millions of Jewish refugees at the close of the war and the pressure on the West to solve that problem.

His major political premise, however, was being shattered during the very period that the discussion was going on within the bodies of the Zionist Organization. On November 25, 1942, Eliyahu Dobkin of the agency's Immigration Department, turned in the first authoritative report on the Holocaust in Europe. This was based on information from a group of Palestinian citizens, mostly women (including two members of Degania B), who were permitted to leave Poland and other European countries on October 28, 1942, and arrived in Palestine in the middle of November 1942. Information about the annihilation of Jews had appeared in *Davar* as early as July 18. But no one wanted to believe it then, and no one added up the bits of facts into the total picture of all-encompassing destruction. After November, it was clear that there would be no millions of Jewish refugees— they were rotting in mass graves. They could no longer exercise any pressure to find them a land of refuge.

But at the same time, the emotional underpinning to the plan grew all the stronger. It was out of the question that justice should not be done the Jewish people, that it should lack a home, a state. In other words, just at the moment when the politico-diplomatic value of the Biltmore Program crumbled, the heart-touching summons, on which the program rested, grew stronger. This was thoroughly felt in the ensuing debate. People closed their eyes to reality and conducted themselves as if the Holocaust had not altered the political assumptions of Zionism.

As far as the second premise was concerned—willingness on the part of the Americans to render aid—it must be kept in mind that during the 1941–1942 period, things seemed possible which two or three years later were in the realm of fantasy; for example, the moving of millions of people from one country to another by the American Army. The policy of the United States appeared more pro-Zionist in Jerusalem than it did in Washington. And the dream of the United States Army's assistance in the transformation of Palestine into a Jewish state seemed not too far from the world of reality.

England, as we have pointed out a number of times, was sitting on the fence. On the one hand, the Palestine administration and the London government actually intensified their struggle against Zionism. On the other, Zionism also had friends in the British government who were prepared to lend an ear to the Jewish claims. But their friendship would not stretch to the point of a serious political battle.

Indeed, it is a historical paradox that it was precisely the deterioration of relations between Zionism and Britain during 1942 which contributed to the acceptance of the Biltmore Program, one of the basic assumptions of which was the friendship of the Western powers toward Zionism. Those relations worsened after a period of relative tranquillity that lasted for about a year after the *Patria* experience and the exiling of the immigrants of the *Atlantic* to Mauritius (at the end of 1940 and beginning of 1941). Then once again the question of "illegals" took a position at the center of the controversy.

At the end of 1941, a convoy of 769 unofficial immigrants was organized in Rumania. It reached Istanbul in an unsound Bulgarian craft, the *Struma*. The Jewish Agency immediately began determined activity to send the immigrants to Palestine. The colonial secretary, Lord Moyne, rejected the demand, and the agency then petitioned that at least the children be landed on the coast. The British agreed, but the Turks refused to make the necessary arrangements. The ship was expelled from Istanbul into the Black Sea and on February 24, 1942, sank there with all hands except one.

At the news of this tragedy, a mighty wave of resentment and rage gushed through the Yishuv. At the same time, the inner need to give a political reply to this disappointment was born.

The community was helpless from a military point of view and its responses to British policies were also limited. It therefore gladly received a political program that would raise the horizons. Only few people noted that this program was based on assumptions that were obsolete even before the program was cast in its final form.

But there was something more. The Biltmore Program was not just an emotional response to the need for Jewish liberation and independence. It could also be viewed as the solution for the confusion that had reigned among the leaders of Zionism since the promulgation of the White Paper. Ben-Gurion cleverly united men and parties of varying colorations around his program. Each of them saw in the Biltmore Program, not just the announced contents, but his own aspirations as well. Thus, for example, Ben-Gurion was supported by Yitzhak Gruenbaum and Yitzhak Ben-Tzvi, both of whom favored partition and saw nothing in the program to contradict their position; if Zionism should win all of western Palestine—very good; and if not, the program would meanwhile unite all those striving for Jewish self-rule.

Sharett and Kaplan expressed, with or without intention, explicitly "Weizmannistic" views in these deliberations. Sharett's statements contain not a word about the concept of a transfer. Moreover, he speaks of the problem of transition from the mandate to the Jewish state. But that problem takes on meaning only if Ben-Gurion's postulated transfer of two million Jews is removed from the calculations. For this transition period there was needed, in Sharett's understanding, at least partial Jewish control over matters of immigration and settlement. In the November 11 session of the Agency Executive, Eliezer Kaplan spelled out the fact that the Biltmore Program made sense to him as a political slogan. With that, he confessed the fact that he did not see it as a genuine political platform. On the same occasion, Sharett also remarked that the program "was, perhaps, somewhat utopian."

However, Sharett, Kaplan, and other Yishuv leaders felt that at a time when many nations were formulating their plans and requirements for the arrangements to be made after the war, the Jewish people should not be condemned to silence. The chief question was: What does the Jewish people want? and not What can be obtained at this moment?

The Jewish people, they said, demands all of western Palestine as its state. That is the demand, and it must be voiced unequivocally. Even a political slogan, they said, was a powerful weapon.

A majority of Mapai united on this basis. The nonsocialist circles—"A" and "B" General Zionists, organizations of the Sephardim, and others—also supported the Biltmore Program, although their support was not lacking in a baker's dozen of reservations. Thus, for example, Dr. Shmorak, representative of the "B" General Zionists in the Agency Executive, as early as 1941 expressed doubts as to the realism of the demand for a commonwealth. The Mizrahi looked upon Biltmore as a minimal program, since the ultimate goal was Eretz Israel in its historical boundaries, as promised in the days of the patriarchs.

Severe objection in principle to the Biltmore Program was voiced only by Hashomer Hatzair, to which Dr. Saly Hirsch (of Ihud circles) and Kaplansky, an independent left-winger, adhered in the Smaller Zionist Actions Committee. Hashomer Hatzair did not dispute this one basic assumption of the Histadrut majority: that the British would remain in Palestine after the war. But the party saw British power as a fundamentally negative factor. Of course, Hashomer Hatzair also spoke of a temporary coincidence of interests between the British Empire and Zionism, but the party looked upon that as merely transient, a momentary contrast with the party's fundamentally antiimperialistic commitment.

This fact found expression in its approach to the Arab question. In May 1942, Sharett stated that "one must by no means conclude that the royal road for Zionist diplomacy runs toward

the Arab nation. Ours is not a problem of the Arab East. . . .
The principal ground of our diplomacy and our political adherence remains in the sector of the great democracies,"[15] to
which the Arab world was also bound. Hashomer Hatzair differed with that vital point, feeling that direct contact must be
sought with Arab elements precisely by circumventing "the
great democracies."

The attempt to enter political negotiations with the Arabs
did not involve, according to the thinking of Hashomer Hatzair
—despite the claims of the party's opponents—any concessions
on the principles of Zionism or its aspirations for a Jewish
majority, which would be achieved through mass immigration
into Palestine. Hashomer Hatzair favored such an immigration
as a gradual, orderly process. Over against the mass transfer
program, it proposed a plan by which a number of Jews, 200,-
000–400,000 of them, would arrive each year (these, too, were
astronomical figures in 1942) but only after everything had
first been done in Europe to return the property of these refugees
and to reconstruct their cultural and political lives. Hashomer
Hatzair opposed a flight in panic out of Europe, but exactly
what would constitute such flight was not defined at the time.
However, it was clear that this was in opposition to Ben-Gurion's
plan. In the program Hashomer Hatzair was trying to preserve
an order of gradual progress in mass immigration, out of real
fear of a catastrophe that might occur if too many people came
at once and no sufficient preparations were made to receive
them; while Ben-Gurion envisioned that the right moment had
come for the single, dramatic, revolutionary, national solution.

Above all, let it be noted that Hashomer Hatzair's understanding of this immigration did not include the condition of Arab
consent. Said one member:

If we can arrive at an agreement with the Palestinian Arabs,
we shall do so. If not—we shall go our own way. On immigration, we shall make no concessions; that is unconditional.

If we can concentrate the democratic world about us for a solution by agreement, if we can win over Arab forces, if we can do that—we shall have greater security.[16]

Another commented:

In order to gain allies in the awesome process of changing the Arabs of Palestine, by means of our immigration, from a majority to a minority status—we must propose to them a political framework constructed on nondomination over them in the country.[17]

From this stand, the proposal of "binationality" sprang forth. It was nothing new; as a general tendency, it had long been widespread in Hashomer Hatzair circles. Until the Biltmore Convention, however, Hashomer Hatzair was of one mind with the majority opinion in the Zionist movement that one should not deal in pronouncements about the *Endziel,* that is, Zionism's ultimate goals. But when the commonwealth was decided on at the Biltmore, Hashomer Hatzair found it necessary to announce the political alternative that appealed to it: a federation of peoples (not of territories) on the basis of parity in government, along with a recognition of unlimited Jewish immigration into Palestine. At one time the majority of the Zionist Organization had favored this concept, and the idea had not been removed from consideration by Ben-Gurion and Sharett until their plans of 1940–1941. It was invalidated for the majority in the World Zionist Organization only after a different program had been accepted, that of the commonwealth.

Even among the Hashomer Hatzair people, there were various shades of opinion. Mordechai Bentov, for example, one of the authors of the binational program of the League for Jewish-Arab Cooperation in 1941, looked upon that program as a practical political alternative to the Biltmore Program or the partition plan. Others saw binationality as an ideal toward which one might strive, but not as an immediately achievable program. This led them to propose a transition period under an international mandate which would facilitate mass immigration and settlement. The transition period was also to be a time of preparation for conditions leading to an Arab-Jewish dialogue on the basis of nondomination.

During the first stage of the political debate over the Biltmore Program, the Mapai "B" Faction had still not fixed its position with complete clarity. It sharply opposed a partition plan. And the anti-British moods prevailing among the "B" Faction people caused them, too, to seek a way out through an international mandate. In contrast to Hashomer Hatzair, however, they had no real alternative to Biltmore. Thus in practice there were only two programs—Ben-Gurion's and that of Hashomer Hatzair—for the continuation of Zionist policy.

One may, of course, assert that as a real political program binationality was as much a fantasy as the Biltmore Program was. But Hashomer Hatzair never deceived itself that an Arab-Jewish agreement was just around the corner. It sought to explore the path leading to such an agreement, while observing Zionist principles under all circumstances. The party's emphasis on the international mandate that would assure a large immigration (though a planned and selective one) demonstrates the general trend of the policy proposed by the Hashomer Hatzair people.

Among the opponents of the Biltmore Program, Kaplansky stood out in the Smaller Zionist Actions Committee. He claimed that the aim of the demand for a commonwealth was justified only if Zionism's political circumstances were favorably altered. Since the opposite was the case, this was not the time to publicize new formulations. Furthermore, in his judgment, the demand for a state led logically to partition. At that time both the Jews and the Arabs were demanding *all* of Palestine. England would not want to quarrel seriously with both of them and would, therefore, render judgment by dividing the claim equally. Kaplansky also pointed out the basic weakness of the Biltmore Program. It was not reasonable to expect Britain to establish a Jewish commonwealth on her own initiative, when she had not even been willing to fulfill the mandate. And the mandate was universally regarded as less pro-Zionist than the planned Jewish commonwealth. Aside from everything else, the demand for control over the entire country was absurd; such control would not be established even if the Jews comprised two-thirds of the population, judging from the reluctance of the Allied powers to disagree with the Arabs for the sake of Zionism.

On November 10, 1942, the Zionist Actions Committee voted on the Biltmore Program (its name, by then, having been changed to the Jerusalem Program). Twenty-one members of the committee voted in favor; three (Ya'ari, Bentov, and Hirsch) were opposed. Yaakov Zerubavel of the Left Poale Zion voted for a plan of his own. Kaplansky and Shprinzak of Mapai abstained. Zisling and Tabenkin of the "B" Faction were not voting.

We cannot close a description of the events leading to the crystallization of the Biltmore Program without pausing at one accompanying episode which strode anew to the center of Zionist diplomacy's stage: the Philby-Ibn Saud affair.

Philby's plan was naturally known to the British government, and it was discussed by British representatives with Dr. Weizmann in July 1941. We may suppose that the British politicians looked upon the plan as one possibility among many for a solution to the problems of the Middle East after the war. However, a breathtaking surprise was in store for Weizmann. In a fleeting, chance meeting between Weizmann and Churchill on March 11, 1942, Churchill brought up the Philby plan as a solution for which to aim. He even suggested that Weizmann speak about the plan with Roosevelt.

In 1942 Weizmann held two talks with the president of the United States. The Philby plan was not discussed, but Roosevelt affirmed his positive stand on Zionism. Only at the beginning of 1943 did the plan come up for reconsideration during a conference between Weizmann and the president, this time in the presence of Sumner Welles, a friend of Zionism. Welles suggested that Roosevelt send a personal representative to Saudi Arabia to clarify the possibilities of negotiation with Ibn Saud on the issue of Palestine. He proposed Colonel Hoskins as the proper man for the task. Weizmann opposed his nomination, but nevertheless the man went on this mission, arriving in Riyadh in August 1943. According to Hoskins's statements, he brought with him only an offer to serve as intermediary in negotiations with Weizmann, not substantive proposals; the Philby plan had never been mentioned to him; he was now hearing of it for the first time from Ibn Saud. As a result, Ibn Saud gathered that the United States had no intention of pressing or forcing him to accept the Philby plan. Under these conditions, he himself spoke of it to his visitor and harshly deprecated it.

Both Weizmann and Philby blamed the United States government for ruining the negotiations by not bringing any position or political decision of its own before Ibn Saud. They both felt that if the American government had made known its support of the plan to the king, his response would have been completely different. Weizmann supported the Philby program even after the failure of Hoskins's mission, probably because he looked upon it as a chance—perhaps the only chance—for the full realization of the Biltmore Program.

It is difficult to assess the influence exercised by the Philby plan on Zionist diplomacy. But it is plain, beyond the shadow of a doubt, that after the fall of 1942 it was, at least for Weizmann, one of the last resorts for the rescue of the program to turn Palestine into a Jewish state. It served a purpose at a time when it was plain that the chances of the Biltmore Program's being realized were reduced almost to the vanishing point.

We have seen that Britain assumed, for the period of the war, a policy of watch and wait regarding all the problems of the region. That applied not only to Zionist plans, but also to those of Nuri Said, who was seeking to exploit the war in order to construct an Arab "federation of the Fertile Crescent" under Iraqi leadership. His plan favored the liquidation of Zionism and the granting of local autonomy to areas populated by Jews. This was proposed by Nuri Said at the end of 1942, in a memorandum and letter to Richard Casey, secretary of state for Middle Eastern Affairs, who replied in short order. (Nuri Said's letter was published by the Iraqi government in a "blue book" at the beginning of 1943, but the document was not distributed.) Casey's answer was utterly negative. It prominently displayed the British government's resolve to do nothing in Palestine until the end of the war.[18]

From a practical political point of view, the Biltmore Program was an unrealistic plan from the moment of its inception. Its value was emotional-symbolic, an expression of the will and yearning of a people crushed by suffering but longing for life.

⧏ *Political Problems during 1943 and 1944*

The victories of the Allied armies at Stalingrad and in North
Africa during the winter of 1942/1943 brought about changes
in the world political climate. Their effect was felt in the Middle
East. Now, with the peace already appearing on the distant
horizon, complex political problems that had been shunted
aside in favor of more urgent war needs were again beginning
to demand solution. Such was the situation all over the world
(for example, with the problems of Poland and France), and
thus it was in the Middle East. In that area, the farther the front
was, the worse the problem grew. The pressure of various
elements and interests on Britain (and, to a certain extent, on
Free France as well) to make final determinations about the
future of peoples and countries also exacerbated the situation.

It will be remembered that on May 29, 1941, Anthony Eden
had already voiced the British government's desire to assist the
movement that was striving for the unity (or coordination) of
the Arab countries. Britain hoped to secure her vital economic
and military interests by means of an Arab league that would
be subject to her influence. Meanwhile, Syria and Lebanon were

conquered by the Allied forces and turned over to de Gaulle's government; on July 25, 1941, the de Gaulle-Lyttelton agreement was signed, leaving those countries within the French sphere of influence. With that, the plan for Arab federation or union was—temporarily—tabled. Its enactment might have continued to complicate the already tangled relations between Britain and the French general, for it was surely obvious that France would oppose any pro-British union of the Arab states, especially if Syria and Lebanon were to be included.

The changing situation at the front in 1943, and the need to define the future of the Middle East more clearly, led the British again to turn a listening ear (or was it perhaps they who whispered it into the proper auricle?) to the words of Arab political leaders seeking to speed up the process of coordination and liberation of the Arab peoples, even under Britain's protection.

Meanwhile, Anglo-French relations deteriorated in the Middle East because of French entanglement with the nationalists in Syria and Lebanon. The situation reached a dangerous stage in the summer of 1943, when an anti-French Arab uprising became imminent. Britain feared the loss of her influence among her Arab friends if she did not lend support to their stand against France. Crisis followed crisis in the two Levantine countries. England finally intervened with armed force in 1945, bringing victory to the Arab nationalists.[1] The French were pushed into sullen hostility, while English policy on the Arabs more and more ignored the French factor. Within that context, Arab unity plans flourished again.

At the end of 1942 and the beginning of 1943, Nahas Pasha and Nuri Said, the leaders respectively of Egypt and Iraq, took up the question of Arab unity. It would not have been comfortable for Britain to take an active part in this intra-Arab negotiation, so she only reemphasized her sympathy with any unity plan that would win general Arab approval. Throughout the summer and autumn of 1943 and into the winter of 1943/

1944, consultations between Nahas Pasha and the representatives of the rest of the Arab states continued. Finally, an organizing session was decided on. It convened in Alexandria in September 1944. The statement published at its conclusion (October 7, 1944) spoke of the founding of an Arab league, the chief concern of which was to be the Palestine problem. To represent the Arabs of Palestine, Musa al-Alami took part in this and subsequent meetings.

On March 22, 1945, the League Convention was signed in Cairo at the end of an assembly of the Arab states. The signatories were Egypt, Syria, Lebanon, Iraq, Transjordan, and Saudi Arabia. Yemen joined them on May 11, 1945. The degree of unity here achieved was much more limited than that set by the statement of October 1944. The League Convention reflected the conflict of interests among the various Arab states and rulers. Nevertheless, this was an important stage on the road to the achievement of the announced aspirations of Arab nationalism. And, we have said, the league enjoyed Britain's support.

This development, of course, had a definite effect on Zionism. Sharett voiced his opinion (in the Zionist Executive, November 7, 1943) that the proposed federation of the Arab peoples would logically lead Britain to suggest the partition of Palestine. Such a federation, which would not include the Jews, would automatically exclude them from the future political structure and leave them those areas in which they were already the majority population. And indeed, since the summer of 1943 there had been ever-increasing British pressure for the reexamination of Palestine partition plans.

The partition proposal arose again when a special cabinet committee for consideration of the Palestine question was set up. It was composed of the colonial secretary, Oliver Stanley; Lord Cranbourne; and Leo S. Amery, with Herbert Morrison as chairman. The committee was constituted on July 12, 1943, and submitted its conclusions to the government on December

20, 1943. It proposed two alternative solutions—partition or cantonization (division of the country into semi-autonomous zones)—but it preferred a partition plan. The advantage of this proposal from the British standpoint was that it seemed to offer a compromise between the supporters and opponents of Zionism in the cabinet and in British public life. This was particularly important in view of the fact that the cabinet, a coalition of England's three major parties (Conservative, Labour, and Liberal), was internally divided on a large number of issues. And Churchill generally avoided bringing up problems of that type for consideration until some compromise had been worked out.[2]

The committee seems to have offered a "good" partition; that is, it apparently proposed to turn over to the Jews the territories within the frontiers of the State of Israel after 1948 plus the Gaza Strip, but without the cities of Ramla and Lydda —and without Jerusalem (which the British were to rule). Frontier corrections of a serious nature were suggested for the northern part of the country, in favor of "Syria" (Lebanon seems really to have been meant), according to Smuts's statements. Churchill himself was also willing to annex the regions of Transjordan's southern desert to the Jewish state. But details of the plan were still quite obscure, and the agency had no reliable, official information.

Increasing pressure was brought to bear on the agency, not only in London, but in Cairo as well, to accept the partition plan. In August 1943 Sharett met with Lord Moyne, at that time assistant secretary of state in the Middle East, and his deputy, Arthur Rucker. They both sought to convince him to accept the partition plan as a basis for negotiations. But Sharett —no less adamant in Cairo than Weizmann in London—rejected the offer, maintaining his faith in the Biltmore Program.

British pressure reached its peak in the Weizmann-Churchill meeting of October 1943 at which Attlee, Randolph Churchill, and Lord Portal were present. Churchill hinted at the possibility that the Jews would be permitted to use up the remainder of the immigration certificates owed them under the White Paper, even after the date fixed for ending immigration (March 31, 1944). However, he explicitly stated that a solution for the Palestine problem would be found only after Hitler's defeat. When he spoke of a partition by which the Jews would receive the Negev and parts of Transjordan—among other areas— Weizmann objected to the very concept of partition. But it appears that Churchill was not very much impressed by his opposition. The important element was that the talk clarified the prime minister's position. Though no written obligation was involved here, the presence of the opposition leader lent the conversation a binding, if unofficial, character. It may be said that until the murder of Lord Moyne by members of the Stern group, the position of the British government remained unchanged.[3]

This political development provided a certain satisfaction for the helmsmen of Zionist diplomacy. There, in the year 1943, which was replete with bitter disputes with the authorities in Palestine and Egypt over matters of mobilization and armaments (see below), a certain political shift occurred. The principal achievement was that every plan for a solution to the Palestine question had to be based on an assumption that the White Paper must be abandoned as an underpinning. This fact strengthened the opinion that it was clearly possible to bring the English to renewed support of Zionism. "Neither England's power nor England's conscience nor England's historic needs and vital interests stand behind the White Paper," Ben-Gurion stated at the session of the Smaller Zionist Actions Committee of July 5, 1943. At the same time, he reemphasized the other possibility also—that the Yishuv would be forced to use pressure to get England to fulfill Zionism's requirements, whether by means of mass immigration or by what was covered in the loose phrase "nonacceptance of this government." Zionist fulfillment would be reached, in Ben-Gurion's view, by way of

London and Washington; he therefore rejected again any attempt at a mutual compromise with the Arabs.

> The crucial time for Zionism is the period when the Yishuv is turned from a minority into a majority, not after that. For that period, not the Arabs but the English and the Americans are essential. The Arabs are not the ultimately decisive factor in the world, not even here. Let us not accept a status of going to the Arabs and bargaining out a compromise as equals. Taking that position would be plunging a knife in Zionism's back. We must address ourselves directly to England. . . . If you need a decision, you must go to the decider. I point to the breakdown of agreement with the Arabs not with any malevolent joy, but with deep sorrow. I was among those who preached agreement. I believed, and I still do, that our work in Palestine and the Zionist endeavor, which will be realized in full, will be a great blessing for the Arab world.

In general, the Zionist Executive took a negative view of partition, and a unified stand was displayed for public consumption. In truth, however, there was more than a little conflict in this area. The Biltmore Program bridged the differing philosophies and made a unified façade possible. On partition, it was unanimously agreed that, if it was to be carried out, it would be better if it was forced upon Palestine by the British. Some members of the Zionist Executive did not believe that partition could be avoided in one form or another. But they, too, preferred that outside elements thrust the plan upon them.[4]

Sharett was not among the outright advocates of partition. Like Weizmann, Sharett realized that partition would diminish the potentialities for absorbing newcomers en masse. He therefore sought to avoid that solution. However, it appears that his sober political judgment more and more convinced him that there would be no escaping partition.

Thus those who favored partition, its opponents, and the fence sitters united in agreeing to a maximalist demand, a slogan by which they all hoped to obtain a state in all of Palestine—

or at least gain a comfortable position in negotiations over partition (should it be offered). For this reason, the representatives of the Agency Executive repeatedly rejected partition plans that were brought up before them during 1943/1944. They even tried to convince the government, by strategic, economic, and political arguments, that Britain's interest made imperative the literal execution of the Biltmore Program.[5] At the same time, however, the Zionist representatives were careful—Sharett was particularly so—not to close the door to further negotiation on a partition plan. The agency memorandum that was sent to the government on October 10, 1944, was worded with this position in mind. In it, the English were petitioned to enact the Biltmore Program, and opposition to partition was explained—but no categorical rejection of partition was included.

Because of internal difficulties, a serious political problem arose with the renewed proposal of partition. A large section of Jewish communal opinion opposed partition. This included parts of Mapai (with Katznelson at the head), the "B" Faction, Hashomer Hatzair, the Mizrahi, and a segment of the General Zionists. A representative of the "B" Faction even announced that if he had to choose between partition and a continuation of the White Paper, he would choose the latter, which at least gave him the opportunity to fight for the realization of Zionism in the whole of the country.[6] Those who opposed partition feared not only the choking off of the Zionist enterprise in a dwarf state, but also the ceaseless war with the Arabs that would come as the automatic result of the country's partition.

An independent Jewish state in Eretz Israel can be only a democratic state. It will exist only in that area where democratic elections can be held. At present, that means a state in a small part of the land. From the first moment, that state will confront boundaries which it must break through. It will have to invest its strength in military factors, pseudopower, and deny itself the possibility of investing its strength in the exercise of genuine power through immigration and settlement.[7]

This was the feeling of the entire left wing of Histadrut ("B" Faction, Hashomer Hatzair, and Left Poale Zion). Since the Left looked upon the Biltmore Program as the road to partition, it opposed Biltmore all the harder.

Thus discussion of the Biltmore Program was resumed in the debate over partition during 1943/1944. One receives the distinct impression that, except for Ben-Gurion and Rabbi Maimon, there were no longer any Zionist leaders who believed that the Biltmore Program was realizable. In sessions and meetings, Ben-Gurion never expressed any doubts. On the contrary, in the sessions of the Agency Executive on May 21, 1944, and June 20, 1944, he reemphasized that "in practice, a decision on a Jewish state means the immediate transferral of a sufficient number of Jews to Palestine to establish the state and assure its functions." Without such a transfer, Jewish demands would be baseless, with the transfer of a million Jews would come the guarantee that "the misunderstanding with the Arabs is ended." Ben-Gurion assumed that the transfer would be acceptable to the West. "We assume—otherwise there is no sense to all our activity—that it is reasonable." First, because the policy of Britain and her allies was no longer that of appeasement, as in 1938. Second, because the Arabs had given the democratic camp no aid during the war, while the Jews had rendered assistance. Third, because of the Holocaust and its effect.

Events proved all these assumptions to be untenable from the start. The White Paper, as we have seen, was never the outgrowth of appeasement. Britain ignored the aid she had received. Only the Holocaust was a real factor.

But even this was not enough to make Britain accept a transfer program of even the most modest proportions. The very opposite was apparently true. The political power of world

Jewry, real or imaginary (and it was mostly imaginary), had been a very important factor in crystallizing British leadership's positive attitude toward Zionism during World War I; but that power was utterly absent during World War II. The Holocaust threatened to turn the remnants of European Jewry into a group of refugees stripped of political influence, in contrast to the Arab factor rising in the Middle East. Postwar developments were to bring about a partial change in this situation when those survivors of the Holocaust concentrated in Germany, Austria, and Italy once more became, in an unprecedented form, a vital political factor. But during the period of 1943 to 1945, this was not yet the case.

Biltmore may have helped the British to suggest partition as a solution—that the Biltmore Program became more and more a slogan which in practice led to partition should be emphasized. As against it, the opposition to the Zionist leadership proposed the continuation of the mandate under international control, or an international mandate, which would guarantee a large immigration. This was supported during the later war years by the Left factions in Histadrut and by the Aliyah Hadasha, a party of German-Jewish newcomers. Even Sharett raised a similar possibility, at least as a transitional plan. Obviously, the difficulties—internal and external—in realizing such a policy were multitudinous. At any rate, its advocates were in the minority, and it was never tried in the crucible of reality.

In the meantime, anti-Zionist elements in London and Washington were suggesting plans that the Jewish leadership had to fight. The United States government was making preparations during the summer of 1943 for the Anglo-American conference that was to convene in Quebec in August 1943. Colonel Hoskins, Roosevelt's adviser (who had previously been sent to Ibn Saud) suggested that the United States and Great Britain announce their intention of maintaining the status quo in the Middle East for the present, until the end of the war.

The British sought to turn Hoskins's suggestions into a

political pronouncement of vast importance. They gave it a distinctly anti-Zionist configuration. In article four of the pronouncement, it was stated that any decision made by force of arms could not win the approval of the Allied powers. In light of the anti-Jewish arms sentences then being pronounced in Palestine and the English fear (real or pretended) of a Jewish uprising, the announcement was looked upon as a confirmation of the White Paper, with its point aimed directly against Zionism. In a conversation with Roosevelt on July 23, Rabbi Stephen Wise protested the anti-Zionist character of the proposed statement. American Jewish pressure caused the United States representative to back down, and the declaration was never promulgated. (The exact wording of the proposed statement is not available.) At any rate, the Agency Executive people achieved a significant victory in averting this unfriendly act.

The pressure exerted on the agency by the two English-speaking powers to conduct direct negotiations with the Arabs was also looked upon by the Jewish leaders as a trap or diversion from the main point. And that main point was the obligations of the powers themselves. During Weizmann's audience with Roosevelt on June 13, 1943, and Sharett's conversations in Cairo, as well as on other occasions, the Zionist leadership was pressed on the issue of direct Arab-Jewish negotiations. So, even though the agency people set no special value on such talks, they nevertheless maintained contact with Arab political figures.

It is proper to mention the attempt by Amir Abdullah, after the partition intentions of the British became clear to him, to reach an understanding with the Zionist movement. Abdullah felt—as did so many Jews—that Jewish pressure for the realization of the Biltmore Program would bring about "the partition of Palestine and the protracted separation of the Jews from the Arab peoples, and that would be of no value." He therefore suggested that Britain and the United States press the Arab countries to agree to the continuation of a Jewish immigration "of reasonable size and in keeping with the economic absorptive capacity of the country," and that the agency's efforts be turned in that direction. Control over immigration would be given to an international commission with a Jewish and an Arab member (but he did not explain whether there would be additional members on the commission, or who they might be). A local government would be created in Palestine, with Arabs and Jews participating in proportion to their numbers. But this authority would have no influence over the immigration commission. All of Palestine would be included in a four-sided federation with Transjordan, Syria, and Lebanon. It is superfluous to add that Abdullah reserved the role of ruler of such a federation for himself. Both he and Nuri Said proceeded on the assumption, identical with that of the Agency Executive, that Britain and the United States would determine the fate of Palestine by reason of their power.[8]

Against this political background, a serious split occurred among the Zionist leadership—just at that moment when it seemed that substantial opportunities for a solution were opening as a result of British partition proposals. We know of the grave differences of opinion between Dr. Weizmann and David Ben-Gurion in the Biltmore period. Now the quarrel was resumed, more bitterly than ever.

Weizmann favored partition; Ben-Gurion feared that Weizmann would abandon the Biltmore Program. In June 1943, Ben-Gurion announced his intention to resign as chairman of the Agency Executive if Dr. Weizmann continued his activities in London. Ben-Gurion again accused Weizmann of being uncooperative, unbending to the will of the majority, and prone to act on a personal basis—even of being unfit for the conduct of Zionist work. Relations also deteriorated because of disagreements about the carrying on of Zionist activity in the United States, where Weizmann had recruited a loyal colleague-aide to work in his spirit among American Zionists. The lack of orderly communication between Jerusalem and London further increased mutual suspicion.

Nor did the accusations come from only one side. Both Weizmann[9] and Professor Brodetzky (who was also a member of the Zionist Executive) charged Ben-Gurion with neglect of collective responsibility and uncooperativeness. They pictured Ben-Gurion as a man of extremist tendencies who could lead the movement into a labyrinth of dangers—they had reference, especially, to the activitistic part of his program, the population transfer involved in the Biltmore Program and his emphasis on the issue of a Jewish army and of a future independent Jewish force (unconnected with Britain).

During the summer of 1943, the crisis was put off through a promise given to Ben-Gurion by his associates in Jerusalem that a Zionist meeting would soon be convened in Palestine in which everything would be ironed out, clarified, and put right. However, due to transportation difficulties (and also to Weizmann's refusal to come to Palestine) the meeting was not held. Weizmann dodged an appearance in Jerusalem as the accused by order of the Zionist Executive. He sensed quite accurately that his contacts with Palestine were weakening and that this was not the way to repair his fences. The crisis burst out. On October 26, 1943, suddenly and without informing his colleagues, Ben-Gurion submitted his resignation. This happened at a regular meeting of the Smaller Zionist Actions Committee, after Berl Locker had delivered an optimistic report on contacts with the government in London. The session was adjourned, and the Agency Executive convened to dissuade Ben-Gurion from resigning. Its efforts bore no fruit. On November 3, 1943, Ben-Gurion sent a formal letter of resignation to the executive.

This crisis (like its 1942 forerunner in the United States) was a personal and political one, the roots of which lay in lack of mutual trust. It was a struggle for the crown of leadership in Zionist affairs. Ben-Gurion sought by his resignation to bring about the resignation of Weizmann. But it quickly became apparent to Ben-Gurion that his own support in Palestine was not broad enough and that his best friends were trying to effect a compromise between Weizmann and himself.[10] Also, Weizmann refused to give in, defending himself and his position with energetic forcefulness. Apparently Ben-Gurion finally became convinced that there was no point in continuing the struggle. With his consent, a delegation of three (Sharett, Rabbi Maimon, and Dr. Shmorak) went to London to reach a compromise with Weizmann that would permit Ben-Gurion to return to the executive.

Ben-Gurion did so on February 27, 1944. He had achieved exactly nothing by his dramatic resignation.

The affair had its epilogue in the winter of 1944, when Weizmann arrived in Palestine to find that important things which had been done there, particularly in the area of security and underground activity, had been totally kept from him during his stay in London. He attacked his fellow members of the executive, above all Ben-Gurion, for leaving him without information in London and working on their own initiative in Jerusalem. But by then the roles had been reversed; Weizmann learned how helpless he was in the absence of any organized public support.

✍ The Crisis in Relations with the Authorities in Palestine

As the front receded from the borders of Palestine, relations with the British authorities grew worse and worse. During 1942 the relationship with the army had been markedly better than that with the civilian authorities; but things changed during 1943. Of course, the Jews still had some friends in the army who had not changed, even though the general atmosphere was very different. Nevertheless, an alteration of attitude was detectable.

As in the spring of 1940, the focal point of British moves was the arms problem. One or more attempts were made to weaken the Hagana, confiscate its weapons, silence the independent recruitment activity of the major Jewish bodies, and give Zionism a bad name in world—and especially American—public opinion. But the primary target was arms and their acquisition.

On January 9, 1943, a truck from Kibbutz Ayelet Hashahar was searched, and ten thousand bullets were found. This was Palmakh ammunition, and two Palmakh members were arrested.

In the British view, one episode was particularly serious. Though it received no publicity in the Hebrew press, it caused consternation among the British military. It will be remembered that one hundred rifles were "bought" for the Palmakh being trained by the Hagana in Mishmar Haemek. This "purchase" was supposedly consummated by David Hacohen in "Syria," that is to say, the rifles came from Hagana magazines. The British insisted on paying for them out of a desire not to use illegal arms. When the exercises at Mishmar Haemek were over, because of tension created between General Wilson (who was in command of the S. O. E. in Palestine) and Hagana people, the English took these weapons (which in a formal sense belonged to them) and moved them to a camp on Mount Carmel.

> This was a violation of a Hagana principle, one on which the men of the Palmakh were most sensitive—the protection of Hagana arms [wrote Allon]. The British made a formal claim that the weapons were theirs since they had paid the Hagana cash for them. The Hagana, on the other hand, claimed that this represented a breach of agreement on the part of the British who had suddenly broken the partnership; and the money that had been paid could be considered as rental for the use of the rifles. At the most, the British Army could demand its money back. . . . There was no choice but to recover the rifles by force.[11]

Yigal Allon's argument is not very convincing from a legal standpoint. But the motives at work here were those of the feeling of ownership and of prestige. Also it is likely that the

Palmakh leaders had no idea of the details in the letters exchanged with the British on this issue. Those documents left no doubt about the British right of ownership over the arms. At any rate, the issue was settled with the execution of a Rekhesh (arms acquisition) action by a unit of C Company of Palmakh, under the direct command of Yehuda Arazi, on the night of March 6, 1943. The arms were "recovered," with interest.

It is easy to picture the anger which this act caused among the British. For S. O. E. this was the perfect excuse for finally halting that close cooperation which had already become repugnant. It is still not clear whether the action was used as a pretext for the rash of operations launched by the British against the Yishuv in the following months. Likewise, there are hints that the matter may have caused B. T. Wilson himself to be brought before a court-martial in Cairo.

Relations with the government on the issue of recruitment began to worsen as early as January. The agency exerted economic and moral pressure on those "subject to mobilization" in order to give the operation greater status (there were some who interpreted this as official sanction for the use of physical force). Suitable machinery was established, directives were issued, badges and certificates were distributed as a sign that their owners had fulfilled their duty, and so forth. The government decided to put an end to these actions with the statement that no compulsory draft existed in Palestine, that the citizen must be protected against pressure and terror. In directives published on January 23, 1943, the authorities prohibited anything that might "cause annoyance" in the matter of recruitment. They forbade the wearing of badges and emphasized that enlistment in the army in Palestine was solely on a voluntary basis. It was implied that the Jewish Agency was dictatorial and terroristic, which explained the measures to be taken against it. We may guess at the government's motives. It sought to arrest the development of the agency into a "state within the state" that would even be capable of conducting an independent mobilization. Some British officials may even have decided that the British were no longer interested in Jewish enlistment in the army. At any rate, to the agency this step indicated an obvious determination by the government to prevent the recruitment of Jews for the British Army.

Immediately after this, a company from one of the Jewish infantry battalions was detached and sent abroad. This was contrary to the assurance by General Neame in 1940 that these battalions would be used solely in Palestine. In an exchange of notes during February and March, the agency stated that it regarded this act as motivated politically with the clear intent of weakening the Yishuv and removing trained soldiers from it.

On April 29 a serious blow was delivered to Anglo-Jewish relations. A search was carried out in the recruiting office of the Jewish Agency in Tel Aviv. Equipment and furnishings were scattered, and a Jewish soldier who had fought with the commandos in Ethiopia was badly beaten. A Jewish liaison was removed from Sarafand training camp, though till then there had never been any objection to his presence there. In reply, the agency closed its recruiting offices and announced that they would not be reopened until the government changed its attitude toward Jewish enlistment. By this step, the agency was trying to demonstrate to the military authorities that without its help they would not be able to recruit Jews for the army. The Jewish leaders felt that, despite continually worsening relations, the army still needed Jewish volunteers.[12]

The fact is there was no unified opinion in the Jewish community on the issue of closing the recruiting offices. The German-Jewish newcomers' organizations opposed this action out of a desire to support the war effort. Hashomer Hatzair recommended demonstrations and opposition to searches instead of closing the offices. Sharett himself, though he had at first consented to the measure, later made determined efforts to wind up the matter.

It was, indeed, proved to the British that without the agency Jews could not be recruited for the army. Even after the reopening of the recruitment centers, however, the decline in enlistments continued. In the three months preceding the closing, there were 1,149 volunteers. During the three months in which the offices were closed (May–July), 379 Jewish men and women enlisted; in the period of August through September (after the reopening), 493; and during November–December, 243. Much of the change must be chalked up to the fact that the fighting front had meanwhile receded from the borders of Palestine.

The Jewish Agency, recognizing the weakness of its stand, prepared to retreat; after penetrating discussions, the centers were reopened on June 24. The British informed the agency that there had been no intent on the authorities' part to hinder Jewish recruitment. There was not the slightest British retreat, nor any apology for the beatings and acts of provocation. The entire episode was marked down as a political defeat for the agency. The "B" Faction, Hashomer Hatzair, and sections of both Mizrahi and Mapai opposed the reopening of the offices. However, the majority in the agency felt that a continuation of the closing of the centers would cause a full-scale British campaign of mud-slinging. Yisrael Bar-Yehuda, a member of the "B" Faction, noted that the minutes should include the statement: "Reb Cossack, shem zakh!" (Shame, Mr. Cossack!).

Public opinion on the recruiting office affair had hardly begun to quiet when the issue of shipping out the second Palestinian battalion was raised. The Jews viewed this not only as a violation of the principle that part of those recruited would be turned to the defense of the country, but also as a sign of British suspicion and fear of a Jewish revolt. It was obvious that the British were trying to weaken the Jewish force in Palestine. A heated exchange of notes with the British Army again ensued —without results. The Jewish view, based on the 1940 promises of General Neame, demanded that the battalion be assigned combat duty (only on that condition was the agency prepared to agree to its being posted abroad). But the British had not asked for Jewish consent, and the battalion left the country on July 6. Opinions among the Histadrut leadership were divided as to whether the soldiers of the battalion should resist the transfer. The final consensus—contrary to the view of Hashomer Hatzair and the "B" Faction—was that they should confine themselves solely to verbal protest.

On March 29 the government had offered a postwar reconstruction program which had as its basic postulate the continuation of the White Paper regime. Ben-Gurion flatly rejected this plan the day after its publication. He thus avoided a confrontation with nonsocialist circles, which were inclined to compromise with the government in matters relating to the economic future of the country.

Public chagrin reached its peak on the issue of arms sentences. The English, of course, knew that arms were being smuggled from their stores into Jewish hands. During 1943 British fears of a Jewish revolt grew, and the government became determined to liquidate this contraband network. They succeeded in catching two British deserters who were selling stolen material, arms, and ammunition to Arabs and Jews alike. Unwarned, the Rekhesh activists with Yehuda Arazi at their head came into direct contact with the deserters.

Although the C.I.D. did not succeed in arresting Arazi, Eliyahu Reichlin and Lev Sirkin (who was not in the least connected with Rekhesh) were detained. They were tried in a public trial that was set up with great fanfare. American reporters were invited and everything was done to blacken the name of Zionism and the Jewish Agency in the world at large and in the United States in particular. The ground was being prepared for anti-Jewish action on a large scale. Relations between the military authorities and the agency grew especially tense when Major Vardin, the defense attorney for the two accused deserters, made a personal attack on Ben-Gurion. In a letter which he sent to the army's commanding officer in Palestine, Ben-Gurion called his antagonist a liar. The trials ended on September 27. Reichlin was sentenced to seven years' imprisonment and Sirkin to ten.[13]

On July 10 Avraham Saharov received a long sentence for the crime of possessing two rifle bullets without a permit. Saharov was known as "Weizmann's bodyguard," and that fact gave his trial an even graver significance. It was obvious that the authorities were making great efforts to demonstrate the inevitability of White Paper rule and, by continually repeated provocations, to test the Jews' response to imprisonments.

Tension reached a new peak with the searches at Hulda (October 3, 1943) and Ramat-Hakovesh (November 16, 1943), where a kibbutz member was fatally wounded by a well-known police officer by the name of Caffaratta.[14] The search at Ramat-Hakovesh ended in complete failure. The British were supposedly searching for deserters from the Polish Army, using that thin cover to camouflage the thorough arms search conducted there. As we have said, however, no arms were discovered (though a Palmakh unit was stationed there, and there were weapons aplenty!). After the search, Sharett had a meeting with the high commissioner on November 17 and warned him, diplomatically but frankly, of the consequences of further searches.

"Not every search has to end like the one at Ramat-Hakovesh" [the meeting occurred in the morning, before the death of the kibbutz member was made known]. "It can lead to bloodshed and vast sacrifices on both sides" [Sharett told the high commissioner]. "Does anyone really desire that Palestine should begin to appear in the news as a land of clashes and killings? . . . We do not want our people killed by British policemen, we do not want our people killing British policemen. . . ." He responded: "You are really delivering a very serious warning here, in a decidedly official manner. I understand. I admit that you have worded your statement quite moderately."

The government was faced with the fact that its very acts against the Hagana were likely to bring the result which it was trying to avoid through the searches, namely, a Jewish revolt.

Parallel to this, a stormy debate was going on in the Histadrut over the issue of the searches and the response to them. The Hashomer Hatzair people and some of the veterans of Mapai* opposed the use of arms as a means of resisting searches— which had been proposed by the "B" Faction as well as by Golomb in case the British should discover weapons or open fire on unarmed civilians. Hashomer Hatzair stated that it did not reject on principle the use of weapons during searches, but that should only be done when all resources in the political sector had been exhausted. Some people asked where one would get weapons with which to resist if the arms had already been found, or unarmed bystanders had already been fired upon; what sense was there to armed defense under such conditions? In practice, a directive was given to the men of Hagana not to employ arms except by special and explicit orders.

Sharett's warning, and similar ones in London, bore fruit[15] —the government cautioned the army about further provocations or searches. It is an unassailable fact that the Hagana was not broken, nor were its stores uncovered, by the searches. At the start of 1944, a distinct lull in Jewish-British relations occurred. But the Yishuv, particularly its internal security forces, had learned the lesson of 1943. From that moment on, a decidely anti-British spirit began to spread throughout the community, and especially through the Palmakh. Preparations for battle began.

---

* In 1930 Hapoel Hatzair ("Young Worker") and Ahdut Avodah had joined to form Mapai. Hapoel Hatzair had been a moderate, non-Marxist, and antimilitarist labor group. Its leaders, like Shprinzak, Kaplan, Eshkol, and others, usually took a moderate line in interparty discussions.

🏵 *The Holocaust and the Hagana*

The response of the Yishuv and of world Jewry to information on the annihilation of the Jews of Europe is, perhaps, one of the most awesome and grave problems facing modern Jewish historiography. This is not the place to consider it in any detail, but the bare skeleton of facts must at least be mentioned.

The Germans achieved mass annihilation in the whole of Poland during the spring and summer of 1942. Information reaching the Polish government in exile in London was partially or totally transmitted to Palestine. But people would not believe the reports and declined to accept them. The press, though it published isolated atrocity accounts, never wove them into a single fabric. It may be said that the community and its leaders put no credence in the possibility of total, planned extermination. Only in November 1942 (see Chapter 6, "Biltmore in Palestine"), with the return of several Palestinians who had been detained in Poland, were the reports verified. The knowledge of the extermination spread throughout Palestine. The first reactions were stupefaction and helpless rage. In the beginning of January, a large meeting of young people was held in Tel Aviv, at which Tabenkin and others spoke. A strong desire to come to the aid of the Diaspora was voiced. But the awareness that, because of the indifference of the enlightened world, Jewish youth had no practical way of reaching European Jewry was also expressed.

This awareness was reinforced in April 1943, when the facts about the Bermuda Conference—which discussed aid to refugees from Nazi countries—became known. The British government approved the condition laid down by the Americans for these talks, that United States immigration laws should not come under discussion; and the United States government agreed to the British condition, not to consider the entry of additional Jews into Palestine. The conference had no practical results, though it was a step toward the establishment of UNRRA. For the Yishuv, the conference represented a terrible blow to the prestige of the democracies because it showed their powerlessness and lack of will to render tangible assistance in the face of the extermination of the Jews.

Conscientious segments of the Jewish population—most of the enlistees, people who had settled on the land, and the organized community in general—raised demands for response in action: to help, to rescue, to fight with any means possible. But for the young Jew the path to the Diaspora was blocked by the British Army, which was battling the Nazis. The generals had a military and political logic of their own. The British Army had no interest in large-scale operations to rescue the Jews of Europe.

To these two factors—the desire to break through speedily to the aid of the Diaspora, and the inability to accomplish that—a third factor was added in the spring of 1943: the effect of the news of the Warsaw Ghetto revolt. Young people now wished not only to save persecuted brothers, but also to come to the aid of the proud resistance fighters. The Holocaust and the resistance were to have a powerful influence over the operations of the entire Jewish underground—Hagana, Etzel, and the Stern group—during the closing years of the war and the first years of peace. Both the parachutist operation in Europe and the Self-Defense Plan of 1944 (see below) must be chalked up to that influence.

The record of Hebrew parachutists is fairly well known, and we shall not repeat it in detail. But there are questions in the problematics of the affair which have still not received proper attention, particularly in its political aspect.

The parachutist project grew directly out of the "private network of Moshe Dayan," the P.S. (see Chapter 5). At the beginning of 1943, the agency was asked by its British Intelligence partners in I.S.L.D.[16] to send four radio instructors to Egypt.

Thus the parachutist program saw the light of day as a projection of the cooperative projects engaged in with the British back in 1941/1942. None other than Inter-Service Liaison Department (I.S.L.D.), with which the ties were very complex and fraught with difficulties, ran the program.

Toward the end of 1942, the British had made proposals for parachute drops on a somewhat larger scale—principally, the sending of a number of operatives into the Balkans. The agency, which had repeatedly made offers of this type throughout the war, naturally gave a willing reply. This proposal, too, came from the I.S.L.D. In January and February of 1943, Dr. Dov Joseph and Sharett made proposals of a far-reaching nature in Cairo and London—the creation of commando units to go to the Balkan countries—but the British rejected these suggestions.

Several British officers arrived in Palestine and examined thirty-three prospective parachutists. The majority of the candidates were Palmakh members, most of whom came from a farming background. Finally, fourteen of them were selected and sent to Cairo for training.

Meanwhile, the agency had also made contact with Allied intelligence services in Turkey (through Eliezer Kaplan and Eliyahu Elat, who paid a visit there, March 6–23, 1943). Ties were established with the I.S.L.D. branch in Turkey, which tended to be more cooperative with the agency than was the one in Cairo. Contact was also achieved with another British agency, the A Force, whose task it was to aid Allied prisoners of war to escape from the Nazis. Communications with the American intelligence service, the O.S.S., were opened as well.

An agreement was achieved with all these bodies (and in regard to the I.S.L.D., which made it a practice to work with paid operatives only, this agreement represented a very large gain) by which the operatives were to be permitted to work in behalf of their Jewish interests in addition to their limited military assignments. It was decided that for the group that had been trained in Cairo, military duty would be primary; for the rest of the operatives, the Jewish task would have equal weight. In partnership with the I.S.L.D., a local interrogation office was set up in Istanbul, similar to the one under the control of Immanuel Yalan in Haifa. The new office engaged in the examination of refugees coming from the Balkans and collected military information. The office chief was Zev Shind in the beginning; later, Teddy Kollek; and by the end of 1943, Ehud Avriel.

Meanwhile, serious problems had emerged in regard to the fourteen trainees in Cairo. They took a deeply suspicious attitude toward their British instructors and were trying to give the Jewish aspect of their mission top priority. Two Hashomer Hatzair men refused their assignment, on general principles. They had been slated to parachute into Germany. They stated that since there were no longer any Jews in Germany, there was no reason for them to go to that country. Others, from various political movements, dropped out for different reasons. Relations between the recruits and the British were tense, and the trainees did not even obey the orders of the agency's Political Department at all times. For example, they were unwilling to enlist formally in the British Army. Such enlistment was indispensable, for otherwise their lives would be endangered should they become prisoners of war. And they did not wish to receive pay from the army because of their desire to be completely independent of the British.

In May of 1943, its training completed, the group was sent back to Palestine—where it remained a whole year without being employed for the designated kind of action. There was obviously some significance to the fact that the I.S.L.D. operatives were kept in Palestine a full year at a time when not only were decisive changes taking place in their target countries, but the position of the Jews was becoming desperate. It seems that the British drew back from the plan which they themselves had proposed. The difficulties started in Cairo in the spring of 1943, precisely when the abrasive conflicts over the recruitment centers occurred and the illegal searches for secret arms caches began. There is no doubt that these events had their effect. We can further suppose that as long as the operatives were retained in Palestine, the British could "feel out" the moods and sense what was going on in the Hagana. A veteran institution like British intelligence would hardly miss an opportunity to do just that.

But it appears that the Jewish side, also, did not do everything to speed the operatives' departure and avoid unnecessary conflict. We have reference not to the directors of the operation (Shiloah, Avigur, and their colleagues)—they were the ones who were pushing for the progress of the work. We mean rather the parachutists themselves, who stirred up numerous difficulties, not all of which appeared justified at the time to Shiloah, the representative of the Political Department. It would be hard to suppose that this foot dragging on the part of the Jews did not have its effect upon the British.

Within the camp, too, there was a certain amount of misunderstanding. The parachutist project was originally a purely Histadrut matter. The Security Committee of Histadrut was responsible for assembling the men. Natan Peled centralized the operation and selected the first candidates. Later, differences of opinion between him and the people of the Political Department came to light. Peled claimed that the British were not taking the Jewish aspect of the mission seriously enough. At this stage —apparently in the summer of 1943—the Palmakh staff suggested that it take responsibility for enlisting the personnel. A general coordinating committee, composed of Avigur, Galili, Golomb, Shind, Shiloah, and others, was set up. Enzo Sereni (the liaison man with the British) was a member and was directly responsible for the entire project. In 1944, when Sereni went into action in Italy, Tzvi Yehieli inherited his place. We have mentioned that the parachutist candidates came chiefly from the ranks of the Palmakh and from agricultural pioneering backgrounds; most of the soldiers of the Jewish units in the army who were taken for this work also came from the farming sector of the population.

The Palmakh was responsible for the military training of most of the recruits. In the summer of 1943 those returning from Cairo and a few other men—about twenty in all—were assembled at Kibbutz Hazorea and put under the charge of Yehuda Ben-Horin, commander of the Germanist detachment. The men were given a lengthy course of ideological studies, with lectures by Zionist leaders and experts of all kinds. They also received military training by the Palmakh. The English again took the men for occasional courses in radio and parachute jumping. Thus the year 1943 passed for them.

At the same time, the emissaries of the agency were able to make contact with both the A Force and the American O.S.S. (see above), as well as the parallel Czech, Yugoslavian, and Polish services. These ties proved that the only way to the European Jewish communities led through the British Army, to which the rest of the Allies had entrusted the sole responsibility for the Middle East. Even the contact with the Americans, despite fine beginnings, brought no results. The one operative who went accomplished nothing until after the fighting was over (although that was mainly because of his ill health).

The tie with the A Force was the most fruitful. It was a young service, unbound by tradition, which gave the parachutists substantial freedom of action. These parachutists first went into action on October 1, 1943, when two of them were dropped into Rumania.

During the winter months there was also a certain amount of progress in relations with the I.S.L.D., and members of the two services trained and received preparation for action. Parachute drops were slowly carried out all through 1944, until the conquest of the Balkan lands by the Red Army. Altogether, thirty-one operatives were dropped or otherwise moved into the Balkans—ten of them by the I.S.L.D., and twenty-one by the A Force.

The first of these was Peretz Rosenberg, a young radio operator, who was parachuted into Montenegro in May 1943, with the first British mission to Tito's headquarters. He served there as the only link with the outside world, traveling and fighting through a large-scale German encirclement operation, until he arrived with the headquarters in Bosnia. In October 1943, he was called back to Italy.

Rehaveam Amir was another radio operator who was taken to the island of Vis in January 1944, to serve with Tito's headquarters there. His tour of duty ended in April of that year, but he also managed to help a few hundred Jewish refugees who were concentrated on the island. In May 1944 he was dropped into partisan-controlled territory in Slovenia, in order to organize radio contact between the Yugoslavs and the British in Italy. In early August he returned to Bari, collected quantities of much-needed equipment and was dropped with it again in Slovenia; there he taught transmitting techniques to a group of Yugoslav fighters and returned to Italy in late September 1944.

In March 1944 a group of four Palestinian parachutists were dropped into Slovenia. Two of them were destined for Hungary, but only one of them, the girl-poet Hanna Sennesz, crossed the Hungarian border, only to be arrested immediately by Hungarian security men, to whom she had been betrayed. After suffering torture at the hands of her captors, she was given a mock trial and executed by the fascist Szalasi regime on November 7, 1944.

In May 1944 two more men destined for Hungary arrived in Slovenia and crossed the Hungarian border soon after Hanna Sennesz, in June. They arrived in Budapest but became involved in the complicated negotiations between the Jewish Rescue Committee there and the Nazis. As a result, they were forced to give themselves up to the Gestapo. One of them, Peretz Goldstein, was ultimately murdered by the Germans; the other, Yoel Palgi, managed to escape from the deportation train, returned to Budapest, and survived.

Ten parachutists were destined for Rumania. One, Sara Braverman, was supposed to arrive there via the partisan-held territory in Yugoslavia, but the partisans refused to help her and she had to return. Of the others, two were accidentally dropped straight into the hands of Rumanian security police, and two were caught before they found their immediate destination. Four others managed to reach their destination, but they came late—in late July and early August 1944, just before the Rumanian king swung his country around to fight Germany and support the Allies. Together with local members of Zionist youth movements, they prepared for a possible German attempt to attack the Jews of Bucharest; a rebellion on the Warsaw Ghetto model was prepared. Fortunately, the need to test these preparations never arose. They also managed to organize the escape from German hands of a whole camp of American and British pilots in the days immediately following the Rumanian about-face.

In September 1944 five parachutists—four men and one woman (Haviva Reik)—were dropped into the territory liberated by the Slovak National Rising. They went to the town of Banska Bistrica and engaged there in various activities connected with the anti-German battle. When the town fell to the Germans on October 28, they organized a group of young Jews and left for the mountains to continue as partisans. On the 30th, they were discovered by a detachment of Russians who were collaborating with the Nazis ("Vlasovites"). Thinking them to be Soviet partisans—they did not see the uniforms properly because of heavy fog—they rushed toward them, and four of the five were captured. These, including Haviva Reik, were murdered in November at Kremnicka. The fifth parachutist, Haim Hermesh, survived, joined a Soviet partisan group, and fought with them until his area was liberated by the Red Army.

Two of the men were sent to Austria, though one arrived there too late to see any fighting. The other one, Dan Laner, of the Germanist detachment of the Palmakh, worked with some Austrian resistance groups in the southern part of the country.

In evaluating the parachutists' job, primary attention must be given the Jewish aspect. From that standpoint, the work had both a practical and symbolic value. The parachutists gave assistance in organizing immigration (especially from Rumania and Bulgaria). The moment fighting stopped, they organized Zionist and Jewish life in those countries. From their very presence, Jews and Zionists (especially pioneering elements) derived great encouragement. Their very appearance was symbolic, a sign and token that the Yishuv had not forsaken the Jews of the Diaspora. From a general military viewpoint, several important operations were carried out—in Austria, in Titoist Yugoslavia, in Rumania, and to some extent in Slovakia as well.

But anyone examining the history of the Jewish parachutists cannot escape the impression that, in general, the project did not win the hoped-for success. Most of the operatives were captured by the enemy. Seven fell. And many of them did not see any real action at all until the Russian takeover or later. The big plans—organization of an anti-Nazi Jewish underground, prevention of the extermination of Jews, active war against the German conqueror—were never carried out, mainly because of the tiny number of operatives and their late arrival—in other words, because of limitations imposed by the partnership with the British. One can take the view that success and failure had the same source. The tie to the intelligence bodies made the very project possible, but also caused it to fail. The chief positive results were, apparently, the consummate heroism of the individuals involved, Zionist activities in Rumania and Bulgaria after the Soviet conquest, the few military actions to which we have alluded—and that is all.

Is that really all?

The entire operation was elevated to the level of symbol. Tales were woven about the legendary few who risked their lives for the Jews of the Diaspora. The legend entered a generation's consciousness. It became a powerful national educational force. It was added to the stories of Hashomer, the Jewish Legion, the Field Squads, the Twenty-three, the invasion of

Syria, and similar episodes. It nourished the longing for Jewish independence.[17]

During the same period, the middle of 1944, hopes for broader action in the Diaspora were aroused, and the proposed action was given the title "Self-Defense Plan."[18]

At the beginning of 1944—with the parachutist program under way and because of the grave condition of Hungarian Jewry—the Agency Executive redoubled its efforts to get British consent for the Yishuv to lend military support to Diaspora Jewry. Those who promoted this concept were Eliyahu Golomb, Yitzhak Gruenbaum, and Yitzhak Sadeh. In early 1943 the agency had approached the British authorities with the proposal that Jewish commando units be parachuted into the ghetto areas of Poland, but the British rejected this plan, and repeated feelers throughout 1943 were of no use.

At the beginning of 1944, Jewish pressure was again renewed, this time with more vigor than ever. In January, Sharett suggested a program to Brigadier Clayton in Cairo which closely resembled that of 1943. Clayton "cut it down to size" so as to make it seem more sensible to the British staff. On February 7, 1944, the plan was submitted to Lord Moyne in the form of a memorandum. It proposed that operatives be sent to Hungary, Slovakia, Rumania, and Bulgaria (two to each country) as organizers and radio operators. Following them, five or ten additional people would be sent to each country as unit commanders and organizers. In a third stage, fifty selected fighters would go to each country and create an extensive underground movement to organize the Jewish communities for determined resistance against the Nazi extermination operations and also to build up the overall anti-Nazi sabotage activity. After the usual foot dragging, this plan, too, was rejected (though the American O.S.S. was willing to consent to such efforts).

In the meantime, the need for the greatest urgency in all these plans was made apparent through the mission of Joel

Brandt. Brandt and a Jew by the name of Bandi Grosz, who was a Hungarian Nazi agent, reached Istanbul in June 1944. They took with them a German proposal by which it was supposed to be possible to rescue a million Jews in exchange for the presentation of trucks and other equipment, as well as cash, to the Germans. Sharett tried to meet with Brandt, but the British prevented Sharett's leaving for Turkey. Then, when Brandt reached the Turkish-Syrian border, Sharett was kept from meeting with him except under British control. Brandt was arrested by the British and placed in detention in Cairo. The news which Brandt brought, about the imminent peril of annihilation for Hungarian Jewry and the Nazi offer, stirred the agency into forceful action.

During June 1944, Sharett flew to London on the Joel Brandt matter. During his stay in London, Sharett worked on the Self-Defense Plan as part of the general range of problems raised by Brandt's mission. He got in touch with Major Randolph Churchill, son of the prime minister, and presented the program to him in writing (July 2, 1944), so that he could show it to his father. The basic points of earlier plans were combined in this program. A force of one hundred men was proposed, to be raised from Jewish soldiers in the army or "Palestinian civilians." Some would be dropped by parachute in small groups in Transylvania and Sub-Carpathian Russia. Meanwhile, most of the force would be moved to Titoist Yugoslavia, to the province of Voyvodina, on the border with Rumania and Hungary. It appears that the elder Churchill welcomed this program and that made it possible for his son to travel to Italy and begin to work for its enactment among the political and military leaders there.

Reuven Shiloah reached Italy at the same time. Churchill's support for the program caused every door to open miraculously before him. Shiloah began consultations in Bari with the diplomats and military people responsible for Balkan operations (July 9–21, 1944). He met with General Stowell, who was in charge of underground and revolutionary movements in Central and Eastern Europe for the British; and with Phillip Broade and his aide, Deakin, political advisors for European matters on the staff in Italy. Most of the negotiations appear to have been conducted with Lord Harcourt, chief of the Balkan Section of Stowell's department. Shiloah also had talks with Vice-Marshal Elliot of the R.A.F. and with the commanding officer of M.O.4, Lord Caldecott. Broade was also connected with the S.O.E. So there was an air, here, of the continuation of contacts between partners who were acquainted with one another from earlier ventures.

Shiloah unrolled the entire plan before them once again. Soon the plan for the force in Voyvodina was rejected and only the dropping of small groups approved; Sharett's wire to that effect reached Shiloah in Bari. The bodies in Italy agreed to the reduced plan, but did not refuse to reexamine the larger program. Candidates for the drops were to be enlisted from among Jewish soldiers in Italy and "civilians" in Palestine. Before returning to Palestine, Shiloah received the promise that a British intelligence officer would go there immediately to pick the twenty to thirty "civilian" parachute candidates.

Meanwhile, the practical preparations had been started in Palestine. Four bodies were mentioned as a source for candidates. First, the Germanist Section of Palmakh, which had been waiting for some real action for a year and a half. Second, a Balkanist Section, a unit assembled by the Palmakh within the framework of the special units (G Company) at the end of 1943, to create reserves for parachute drops. The unit, containing twenty to thirty men, was stationed at Mishmar Haemek, with Yaacov Salomon as its commanding officer. The parachutist candidates, who had already passed through various stages of training, were the third group taken into consideration. They were assembled at Ramat-Hakovesh for a seminar organized by the Mosad. The fourth was the Palmakh itself, the commanders of which hoped for large-scale action that would enable them to drop a significant portion of their units into Europe.

The Palmakh was, as we have already seen, the party generally responsible for the primary recruitment and training of all paratroop candidates. The three Jewish bodies that had assumed concern for speeding help to the Diaspora—the Jewish soldiers in the army, the Palmakh, and the Immigration Bureau (Mosad) cooperated in the entire operation. The preparations were exhaustive, and talks were even conducted on whether or not Golomb and Sadeh should be permitted to participate personally in the operation.

But disappointment was not long in coming. Shiloah awaited the English intelligence officer, but that personage remained overdue. Instead, he telegraphed Shiloah on August 3 that the whole plan was still under discussion. That portended further delays. When no headway was made during August, Shiloah made another trip to Bari, with a very heavy heart. This time it was not so easy to get to Italy either; the British had piled up obstacles in his way. When he finally reached his objective, they put him off with weak excuses. Eventually, his ceaseless insistence aroused the ire of the high officer with whom he was dealing. The Englishman asked him if he didn't realize that the whole business had been cancelled. To make the point stronger, he showed Shiloah a directive telegram, the contents of which were in substance as follows: Pertaining to the plan presented to you by Mr. Shiloah, it has been decided that the expected military advantages of this plan are outweighed by the political considerations.

The wire made it plain to Reuven Shiloah that the authorities were afraid that the execution of the program might put the agency in the position of a claimant, by virtue of war services rendered. Political considerations of which we have already spoken, connected with Britain's attitude toward the Arabs in the Middle East, were also at work. But that was not all. It was made clear to Shiloah, by the same officer, that the telegram directed the officers in Italy not to give the Jews a negative answer, but to drag the matter out by formulating worthless counterproposals. Thus ended the chapter called the Self-Defense Plan.

It is proper to add that the Jewish Agency was not the only Jewish factor which tried to operate in the Diaspora. Both the Etzel and the Stern group attempted to prepare a similar operation, on a smaller scale. Two of their people worked within the A Force framework in Italy. Menachem Gepner, a Sternist, suggested to Eliyahu Golomb that the Jews operate on their own and reach the Diaspora by way of northern Italy. Gepner went to Palestine in the summer of 1944 and talked over his plan with Golomb, but after some consideration the latter rejected the proposal. The reason for that is rather understandable. They were pinning their hopes at that time on British agreement to a much larger program with much greater opportunities; thus there was no interest in Gepner's plan.

The question has been asked as to whether there were possibilities of penetrating the Diaspora by means that were not exploited. This tragic question must remain open until basic research into the matter of rescue in Europe provides an answer.

✍ *"Without Money You Don't Build an Army"*[1]

Kibbutz Meuhad's suggestion in the summer of 1942—to move the units of Palmakh into a regime of labor and training—was accepted as reasonable by the official Yishuv institutions. So after the fall of 1942, all the companies moved into permanent bases in the agricultural collectives. A contract was signed with the kibbutzim, taking effect November 1, 1942, under which the men of Palmakh would work fourteen days per month and train eight and one-half days per month. Problems of shelter, clothing, and board were also settled. In most of those areas, the kibbutzim took it upon themselves to care for the Palmakh people.

We have already noted that this system, the combination of work and military training, had its inception in the chronic lack of money in Hagana coffers. That lack had become more severe with the backing away of middle-class circles because of the centralized, independent, and "leftist" nature of the Hagana and its mobilized units. The budget of the Hagana for 1942/1943 was £281,470 in income and £310,740 in expenditures. The principal sources of the Hagana funds were the agency (£69,

336), Kofer Hayishuv (£40,000), and the Mobilization Campaign (£116,675). Palmakh expenditures amounted to £56, 918, that is, fifteen or sixteen piasters* (about fifty cents) a day per man. That sum, which of course did not suffice even for the most minimal needs, included allocations for armament, staff, administration, and such matters. It could cover only about one-third to two-fifths of the expenses.

The Mobilization Campaign, founded during the danger of the German invasion, had collected rather large sums. But after the retreat of Rommel's forces in Africa, the campaign's income declined. Right-wing groups pressed the campaign administration to allocate a minimum for actual security expenditures and a maximum for army recruitment and allotments for soldiers' families.

During the fall of 1942, increasing the army enlistment presented a problem, in light of a growing disinclination to enlist. In the Actions Committee of Histadrut, a levy of four hundred men was being spoken of. They were to be Hagana members, and the intent was that at least some of them would come from the Palmakh. Left-wing factions, zealous for the Palmakh, viewed that suggestion as a most serious blow at its very existence. And indeed, the enactment of this program would have spoiled Palmakh service for hundreds of its members, who definitely preferred the Palmakh to enlistment in the British Army. The very proposal pointed up very nicely the political background to the shortage of funds—money was forthcoming to invigorate the army recruitment drive, while one could ask: Why increase the allotments for the Palmakh, which is slated for reduction when some of its members are sent to the army?

Under these conditions, the labor-training system had not only an economic, but also a practical political justification. Tabenkin, among others, looked upon the new system not as an undesirable necessity, dictated by hard reality, but as a wel-

* There were 100 piasters to the Palestine pound, which was equivalent to the British pound.

come vision, a royal road to the building of a Hebrew army. Tabenkin, Hashomer Hatzair, and sections of Mapai viewed the Palmakh as the nucleus of concentrated Jewish power which was destined to decide the fate of Zionism at the end of the war. Moreover, in Tabenkin's view, life as lived in the Palmakh was not incidental, not a matter of a year or two, but a way of life for those who had realized Zionism's ideal and were fighting for it. Budgetary difficulties were a side issue—at the most, a push in just the right direction. If there were a sufficient number of enlistees, there would also be a budget; but since the Jews were a poor people, the budget would never be adequate. Thus the permanent necessity for labor-training camps.

So much for Tabenkin's view on the *economic* importance of labor in the camps. But, as we have said, for him this was but one side of the coin. The other side was a moral and socialist matter. A nonworking army would repel laboring people or destroy them, thrust on them an atmosphere of idleness and degeneracy. Tabenkin claimed that this working army must live in the very heart of the collective agricultural establishments, both for Zionistic and military reasons.

It was not the spirit which typifies Tabenkin's vision, however, that marked the Palmakh camps. October and November of 1942 witnessed bitter arguments in almost all the companies. One should distinguish carefully in this regard between the people in the ranks and those of the political leadership who opposed the labor-training system. The men in the ranks were largely from kibbutzim, and they were unanimous on this issue. They posed this difficult query: Why must we work someone else's kibbutz in unfamiliar branches of labor—just for eight and one-half days of training each month? Why aren't we allowed to work at home, in the circle of our own comrades, near our families, at our own regular skills—then every once in awhile leave for several days of training with the unit assembled? Why should it be impossible to get money to maintain the Yishuv's army—isn't there enough money in the country?

They made calculations which demonstrated that, with the proper collection of taxes, the Yishuv's income could afford to maintain more than one thousand Palmakh members in full training. It was but a step from such calculations to proposals of expropriations, and many were arguing for energetic—even very energetic—means to obtain the funds from those who were financially able.

Such views became current among the men in the ranks from all the political movements, and they won support from the leadership of Hashomer Hatzair. Peled, its representative on the Security Committee of Histadrut, opposed from the start the labor-training system as a means of solving the budgetary problem. He demanded pressure on the people of property (but explicitly opposed expropriation), asserting that there was enough money in the country for the maintenance of the Palmakh camps. Hashomer Hatzair's opinion was not accepted by the majority.

But the main point was still mutual responsibility for the fate of the Palmakh. And when the question of what to do about the rebellious men in the ranks came up, Peled, with a heavy heart, joined those who tried to persuade the Palmakh members to honor the agreement that had been signed and not to leave the Palmakh.

The discussions within the Palmakh were stormy and penetrating. The spirit of revolt was especially notable in B Company, where Hashomer Hatzair men had a marked influence. In a company meeting held at Ramat-Hakovesh on October 19, 1942 (with Peled, Galili, and Sneh participating), the debate reached a sharp pitch. The members of B Company argued that it was possible and imperative to obtain, by any means, the sums required to preserve the Palmakh on a full-time training basis. As an alternative, they could only see a return to the situation of 1941 (that is, the company gathering its scattered personnel for training on weekends). At the end of this debate and subsequent ones, the men accepted the discipline of obedience. And Natan Peled, though he agreed with them in principle, influenced the members of his movement to accept the decision.

Members of a company where most of the men came from farms could not be accused of wanting to escape work. But we know of controversies and difficulties over the work-and-training issue in almost all the companies. In A Company, there were acrimonious arguments not always becoming to men who had "placed themselves at the disposal of the Yishuv"; and on the heels of that came "numerous" resignations. A certain officer, for example, decided to join the army. A hearing was held, at which he made the claim that since there were no forests in Palestine, it was impossible to carry on partisan operations. Therefore the Palmakh was unable from the start to fulfill the role assigned it, and he left the unit. In C Company, "opposition of a majority of the members was voiced against this [work-train-ing] structure which limited the extent of the training." But even in that unit, there was heard the "clear resolution that the framework of the Palmakh must not be dispersed or reduced; on the contrary, it must be expanded and enlarged." In D Com-pany, though there were no discussions, there were many resig-nations. In F Company, there is also evidence of crises and resignations.

Signs of the crisis appeared not only among the men with pioneering farm backgrounds, who were usually the ones who got bitter complaints off their chests (although they remained within the ranks of the Palmakh). They appeared among the city people as well. These men did not argue much, but they also did not hesitate to leave their units when it became plain to them that thankless everyday work under severe conditions had replaced the national fervor and romanticism of the Rommel period. B Company lost about twenty members that way. In D and F companies the losses were still more serious. Total resignations from the Palmakh that winter reached the neighbor-hood of 100 to 150, a serious mortality rate for a unit which numbered 1,000 men in all and the recruiting sources of which were very scant. An official report, in the fall of 1942, spoke of thirty combat platoons without leaders and lacking proper training. The report posed the delving query: How long "will the departure of good platoon and squad leaders go on?"[2]

It is not easy to make a realistic estimate of the portion of the total Palmakh budget contributed by the work-training camps during the first period of crisis. In article 17 of the contract with the kibbutzim, one day's expenses are calculated at 22 piasters, or about £80,000 per year for a unit of 1,000 men. If we add clothing expenses of £4,652 for 1942/1943, plus shelter— both of which were provided at the expense of the kibbutzim in exchange for Palmakh labor—we reach a total of approximately £90,000 (over against the £57,000 budgeted for the Palmakh from Hagana funds). It therefore seems likely that in the first year of the Palmakh's existence as a mobilized unit, the work-training camps covered about 40 percent of the formation's maintenance expenditures.

During the first two months of 1943, tempers cooled, and companies got back in the routine of labor and military exercises. But this crisis, which had at least come out into the open so that it could be dealt with, was quickly exchanged for a still graver crisis that visited the young organization.

🖋 The Crisis of 1943

The Palmakh was created, mobilized, and trained primarily to carry out defensive roles during World War II. There were fears of an Arab rebellion or an enemy invasion of Palestine, or both simultaneously. From time to time, hopes were aroused for action within the Diaspora, to which parts of the Palmakh might be sent. Thus the Palmakh was born against the background of the emergency and tension of 1941/1942.

After the enemy retreat from El Alamein and the withdrawal of the front from the country's gates, the realities were no longer the same. Old concepts had been undermined, hopes for immediate action were shown up as delusions. Instead of invasion and Arab rebellion and mobilization for assistance to European Jewry, the new slogan was: Preparedness for the battles to come after the war! But in 1943 who could know how much longer the war would go on? Instead of bold programs, creating an aura of romance, there were work-training camps. Shortages of money, clothing, and shoes were part of the revoltingly prosaic trivialities. The few paltry days of training were followed by routine physical labor. Pervading everything was the feeling of purposelessness.

Like every organism, like every military unit, the Palmakh of 1943 had a primary need for the prospect of eventual action, clear purpose, and well-defined tasks. But the Palmakh men had no idea of what role they were now to play. Lack of perspective was, perhaps, the most outstanding factor in the crisis of 1943. A Palmakh member in B Company for example, wrote from the company encampment at Ein-Harod at the end of 1943:

It all seems old, everything is rolling down that same old slope of indifference. Everybody is affected by low morale and all the resignations. I got a cold shoulder from the gang. They all seemed surprised that I didn't use my illness to get myself out of the whole mess, because that's the heart's desire of a lot of the best of the gang here.[3]

In the *Palmakh Bulletin* (No. 14) this fragment of a diary appeared.

The emptiness of the passing days makes you forget the central purpose and goal for which we are living this way. Each person is alone with his problems and his thoughts, alone in his own corner with his spirit dragging. All the old thoughts reemerge and take shape: discharge, rotation, and the like. . . . Your feelings are choked by idleness so real you can touch it and by helplessness.

Natan Peled described the prevalent mood at the time in the following words:

> They thought they would be assigned real jobs, to be partisans, but that was not feasible. The men volunteered out of willingness to fulfill a dangerous and daring role. Instead, they find themselves working on farms. The training is not always enough to prevent a feeling of dissatisfaction. The expected danger to the country has gone away; and all of this, along with the absence of public sympathy, creates an oppressive feeling.[4]

To the lack of prospects for action, another factor was added, one that had its origins in everyday reality, in the streets of the cities of Palestine. In the community the main emphasis was laid on recruitment for the British Army, and the official enlistment orders enhanced that recruitment with obvious priority. There was surely substance to Sharett's statements that Palmakh enlistments were then possible only in connection with the overall war effort—at the center of which stood army recruitment. The Palmakh members, however, could not resign themselves with equanimity to priority for the army. The Palmakh, from its commanders to its most humble private, whatever their social backgrounds, felt itself to be "the Army of the Yishuv," a formation subject to Jewish command alone, the central pillar of the Yishuv's security system. The preference shown the army, the trifling favors given those wearing the uniform on various occasions (such as when standing in line for the bus or for amusements), the prestige that came their way—these were all thorns in the flesh for the anonymous lads who got to come to the city once every six weeks for four days' leave with ninety piasters in their pocket. They walked around the city in gray "civilian" farm dress, without uniforms, without badges.

And when there was an argument about their status, they were criticized as shirkers. Particularly grave expression in this regard was presented by the famous historian Professor Ben-Zion

Dinur in the (Hebrew) pamphlet *Milhamtenu* ("Our War") of November 1942. His article, called "Letters to a Soldier, from the Rear," included these words:

> The call to mobilization is issued only through a clear and definite order which demands one simple act: [*go*] *to the army. . . . That is your first duty, and you must fulfill it. No other duty can take its place.* Whoever comes to us with the command to mobilize for this and that and *also* for the army—let him not delude himself with empty deceptions. Nothing of any great significance can be achieved by force of *that* slogan. To build up the enlistments there is urgent need definitely to cancel out draft dodging . . . of all types and forms. Whoever is of draft age must go to the army. And only to the army. And not to any other job. . . . Whoever has eyes can spot, especially in the cities, a type of "important" youngster with an exemption notice in his pocket and a look of secret seriousness on his face. He is content at heart, and so are his relatives [italics in original].

This article—and expressions softer in language but similar in content—elicited a sharp response within the Palmakh, the echoes of which were audible at the Forty-eighth Convention of Histadrut and appeared in the Palmakh press. But only a minority within Histadrut had identified with Dinur's words. The vast majority supported the policy outlined by Golomb: preservation of a certain balance, so as not to damage the priority of recruitment for the army, and yet at the same time not curtail the independent force, the Palmakh. This article, however, brought forth the bitterness that was lodged in the men's breasts as a result of the generally low morale in Palmakh. The sense of depression that was now voiced slowly disappeared during 1944/1945, toward the end of the war, with the calling up for the Palmakh of the people in the Hakhsharot—groups preparing for settlement on kibbutzim—and the introduction of the rotation system.

We have already remarked that one of the outstanding reasons for the depression that ruled the Palmakh was its desperate material position. The agreement with the kibbutzim was not always carried out to the letter, because the settlements were in a difficult financial situation; and war prosperity had not yet had any effect. The Palmakh men suffered especially from poor clothing and shoes.[5] Leave allowances were also not always given on time, and it is understandable that there was great bitterness.

In a word, 1943 witnessed the Palmakh in deep crisis. The commanders fought the crisis by attempting to explain conditions and by taking disciplinary measures. Fifteen men, for example, were removed from the ranks of the Palmakh in the fall of 1943; and it was also decided to battle vigorously against desertion.

One of the difficult problems troubling the Palmakh was the question of its reserves, the expansion of its numerical framework. Enlistments in 1942 raised the number of members to about 1,000 (at the start of April 1943 there were 1,057 members). Beginning in the fall of 1942 and throughout 1943 the number of city people continually increased, while the percentage of kibbutz members fell. Kibbutz Meuhad's proportion for example, progressively declined to about one-third by the end of 1943 (378 out of 1,113). Overall, farming people comprised about one-half of the Palmakh membership; the rest were from cities or were members of youth movements.

Expansion was inextricably connected with the character of the individual companies. The members of A, B, C, and E Companies came mostly from pioneering agricultural backgrounds—though there were also people from Haifa in B Company; these were mostly students and numbered about twenty to twenty-five after the crisis of resignations in the winter of 1942/1943. D Company was from Tel Aviv. At first it was "loaned" by the Tel Aviv Command to the Palmakh, and even later the Tel Aviv Hagana tried to preserve the "autonomy" of this company. The men of D Company had a very hard time adjusting to the work-training regime. There was a small nucleus from the Mikveh-Israel Agricultural School, plus a few members of youth movements. But most of the D Company members were young people from the various neighborhoods of Tel Aviv and its suburbs. They adjusted to farm work only slowly, with suffering and some resignations. Binyamin Tsur, commander of D Company and a Tel Avivian, had no easy time of it. Quarrels arose between him and his charges because of the strictness he enforced in his camps, in contrast to the free and friendly atmosphere that marked the rest of the companies. Tsur claimed—and not without justification—that the pedagogic methods that worked well with men whose sociocultural origins were different would fail with "the human material" in his company. Tsur stuck to his guns and was replaced in 1943.

F Company from Jerusalem, stationed in kibbutzim in the Upper Galilee, experienced similar problems. The bulk of its members were students and members of the Jerusalem Field Force, and adjustment to work on the farms was also hard for them. In 1943 their founder and commander, Israel Livartovsky, joined the British Army and was replaced by Shimon Avidan of Kibbutz Ein-Hashofet. Not until the beginning of 1944—as a result of the entry of the first of the Hakhsharot —did the company recover from its crises.

In 1943, against the background of the crisis within the Palmakh camps, the debate over the duration of mobilization and the terms of service arose. In the beginning of 1943, the Palmakh tried to expand its ranks by sending special recruiters from its membership into the cities of Palestine. But the results were not particularly encouraging. Through the end of April, 120 men enlisted, an average of thirty per month. In May, 26 signed up; 51 in June; 31 in July; and a total of 510 men for all of 1943. At the end of 1943, the Palmakh had 1,113 members, indicating that at least 350 men had left during the year. The growth rate was, therefore, rather slow. How could 5,000 Palmakh members, in keeping with the September 1942 resolution of Forty-seventh Histadrut Convention, be mobilized? The Palmakh staff began to look for other solutions.

In this connection a most vital question came up: the problem of the character and quality of the Palmakh. Should it be a fighting elite which would halt an enemy's initial attack and thus facilitate the mobilization of the entire Hagana? Or should it perhaps be a cadre of junior officers and N.C.O.'s which would absorb the mass mobilization during an emergency and, in the course of time, itself become the mass army? Or ought it grow into a sort of reserve corps, the larger and expanding portion of which would pass into the reserves after a limited period of active service, and by this means become a well-trained popular mass militia, with a small regular army at its core?

All these concepts were at odds with one another within the Palmakh during its early years, and there were many discussions and debates about them. Generally speaking, it was Yitzhak Sadeh who first advocated the theory of the "fighting elite," and only very gradually abandoned it.

> In the beginning, he [Sadeh] felt that the Palmakh must be built on rigorous specific physical selectivity, applied to every individual. The standard was to be above average. He spoke of a small, select force. In the course of time, he changed his mind—under the influence of Tabenkin, Allon, and Galili— in the direction of a popular force, both as to numerical dimensions and personnel. He experienced the deep realization of how thorough training and proper esprit de corps can turn any healthy young man, and not just the select types, into a soldier.[6]

Members of B Company, which was marked by its "ideological" awareness, were inclined toward a mixture of the elitist doctrine with belief in a cadre of low-ranking leaders. However, the chief instructor of the Palmkah from the fall of 1942 on,

Yitzhak Dubno of Negba, wanted to see the Palmakh become a combination of a leadership pool and a militia. In an important article printed in the *Palmakh Bulletin* (No. 25) in the middle of 1944, Dubno asserted that the duties of the Palmakh were: (a) to serve as a reserve force for the execution of special operations during emergencies; for that purpose, men must be given special training suitable for such tasks; (b) to be the attack arm during any assault on the Yishuv; and (c) to serve as a force to block and weaken any anti-Zionist political solution of the Palestine problem. Dubno recommended a high degree of military perfection, individual fighting ability and control, and continuous numerical growth.

Both Sadeh and the people on the Palmakh staff came to the conclusion during 1943 and 1944 that it was possible to turn almost anyone into a superior soldier. The idea gradually crystallized that the Palmakh must be a broad-based militia with a permanent nucleus, and must encompass a large percentage of Hebrew youth. At the same time, its cadre must be able to halt an enemy advance during an emergency, so as to gain time for mass mobilization. And it must also be able to absorb such a mobilization, at least in part, into its own ranks.

The conflicts from which this image of the Palmakh were finally distilled left their mark on recruitment policy and term of service. The doctrine of a fighting elite—which was ultimately rejected by the Palmakh—inevitably necessitated maximalist standards, while the rotation concept was bound up with the view of the Palmakh as a popular militia.

Probing discussions on this subject were conducted during 1943. Yaakov Hazan's minutes of a joint session of the secretariats of Kibbutz Meuhad and Kibbutz Artzi of Hashomer Hatzair at Merhavya on July 19, 1943, have been preserved.[7] These minutes are unique, because care was taken during that period to commit virtually nothing to writing pertaining to the Palmakh.

At that session, Hashomer Hatzair made a number of suggestions (formulated by Hazan). (a) It demanded that a limited term of service be set for those enlisting in the Palmakh. Ya'ari felt that for such training approximately one year was required, but added that he would agree to a longer term if he were shown that it was necessary. (b) A rotation proposal was made, under which men of the kibbutzim would replace their comrades in the Palmakh at the end of each term. In regard to unaffiliated individuals from towns, Hashomer Hatzair had no clear suggestion. (c) It was proposed to reorganize the reserves on a territorial basis. The practical significance of these proposals was the transformation of the Palmakh into a popular militia.

Kibbutz Meuhad opposed all these suggestions, on grounds of both principle and practicality. Its representatives stated that it was not ethical to demand that soldiers serve in the army until the end of the war but return Palmakh members to their homes after a relatively brief term of service. They further declared that rotation was impossible for economic and organizational reasons, not only for the nonkibbutz elements of the Palmakh, but also for members of settlements. A territorial reorganization of the Palmakh was, for them, identical with a demobilization of the Palmakh, turning it into another Field Force; for the structure of the Palmakh was based on the idea of breaking down regional alignments and creating a nationwide organization, with no regard for the localities of origin of its members.

On the face of it, the positions of the two collectivist movements were far from one another. Hashomer Hatzair, with its basically antimilitarist leanings, was searching for a way out of the Palmakh's crisis by acknowledging the need to broaden and enlarge the force. In contrast, Kibbutz Meuhad opposed the idea of rotation on ideological grounds, ignoring the grave problems of idleness and decline in morale. Tabenkin and Dubno assumed stands of compromise at that meeting. Tabenkin did not absolutely reject the idea of rotation, but he ruled it out as long as the war continued. Dubno, like the rest of his comrades in Hashomer Hatzair, accepted the work-training camps as *faits*

accomplis and considered whether it might not be better to postpone rotation until the collective training, which the Palmakh had
just begun, was completed.

Toward the end of 1943, Sadeh submitted a plan for nine
hundred hours of training for each Palmakh soldier. The practical significance of the plan was a two-year term of service.
The replacement concept was finally accepted at the beginning
of 1944 when even the Hagana staff, which had apparently
opposed the idea at first, consented to the proposal. It meant
in practice that each Palmakh member was to serve about two
years and would then be sent home as a reservist.

Thus in fact Hashomer Hatzair's concept of the nature of
the Palmakh won out. For the replacement system and the
limited terms of service necessarily molded the organization's
character. It became a mass unit in the nature of a militia, possessed of superior combat capability, training a large cadre of
junior leaders within its ranks to serve not only the Palmakh
when the time came. The doctrine of a fighting elite, the "Cossacks" of Tabenkin, constructed around a more or less fixed
body of fighters and builders, was permanently tabled.

The execution of the replacement system was postponed
until September 1944. Meanwhile, the Palmakh was looking
forward to salvation in the form of new blood which would
rescue it from the depression into which it had sunk. Relief
and deliverance came to it from the calling up of the Hakhsharot.

These groups originated in towns and belonged to a number
of youth movements, mostly of a moderate to radical left-wing
line. The youth movements organized what were essentially
extracurricular activities for high school youngsters, based on
scouting, traditions of the German liberal youth movements,
and the general idea that a Jewish youngster in Palestine should
at least try to live the life of a pioneer in a kibbutz. National
motivations played an important part, and were combined with
socialist ideals of collective living and public service. At the
same time great emphasis was laid on the small, organic group

of individuals who would form mutual social attachments. High moral and cultural standards were implied.

The social origins of most of the youth movement members were lower middle class or middle class or else they came from well-established working-class families, mostly of Ashkenazi origin. Only a minority were working youth. At the end of their careers in high school, groups of seniors from these movements used to declare themselves as *gar'inim,* literally, "cores"—that is, solid social groups desiring to settle on a kibbutz or found a new kibbutz of their own. They then went to a kibbutz for a preparatory period and were there called Hakhsharot (plural of Hakshara, meaning preparatory group).

The initiative for signing up the Hakhsharot did not come from the Palmakh staff but from one youth leader who tried to organize a "revolt" of high school seniors and even juniors against the continuation of their studies at the end of 1942. The feeling was widespread, especially in student ranks, that one must respond to every national summons with a voluntary pioneering spirit.

It may be difficult for a later generation to imagine youth giving up accustomed comfort and all sorts of material blessings, as well as the building of their own futures, and instead bursting out into general social and national projects which were unthinkable without a measure of self-sacrifice. Indeed, the youth movements organized only a small percentage of the young generation, but the volunteers were the trend-setters among the young people. The feeling of self-confidence and the consciousness of social and national obligation resting on youth were very strong, while the atmosphere in the street—with the background of the war emergency and the news that had begun to arrive about the Holocaust—was sympathetic to the giving of self. This atmosphere is hard to describe in a convincing manner today. Perhaps the most outstanding thing was the will and passion of youth to know what was going on in the communal and political sphere and take part in it.

There were exceptions, of course. But instances of indifference to what was taking place, though not infrequent in themselves, were not characteristic of the youth as they pictured themselves. Those who did not conform to the idealistic pattern felt as if they had strayed from the path. They were aware of the need for rationalization and self-justification.

In that atmosphere it was difficult for the young to sit and continue their routine studies while their contemporaries, the working young people, were already being called to service. About thirty high school seniors went to Kibbutz Ashdot-Yaacov in 1942. After a rather short period, they were enlisted in the Palmakh. Others followed. At the beginning of 1943, a whole Hakhshara of Hamahanot Haolim went to Kibbutz Dafna.

In the meantime, Hanoar Haoved also decided on December 12, 1942, to enroll its preparatory groups in the Palmakh. In January 1943 that movement's representatives met with the Palmakh staff at Ein-Harod in order to specify the conditions under which the members of the preparatory groups would enlist. They wished to guarantee the survival of the group as a social entity even within the framework of the Palmakh. It was also necessary to surmount the political fears of some organizations—especially of Hashomer Hatzair—who looked upon Palmakh as a body subject to the discipline of the "B" Faction and were reluctant to place their young reserves in the hands of a different political element. Thus, Hashomer Hatzair was hesitant and decided to send only a certain percentage of the members of its Hakhsharot to the Palmakh, in the form of a quota.

The hesitations on the part of the youth movements were many, before enlisting their Hakhsharot in the Palmakh. There was fear that the group structures would disintegrate if only males were recruited. The Palmakh's attitude toward the autonomous life of the preparatory group was also quite uncertain. Both parties, the Palmakh and the youth movements, feared dual jurisdictions and the problems of maintaining social autonomy alongside military discipline.

After many struggles and after the first experiment at mobilizing Hakhsharot in the middle of 1943 indicated possibilities of a solution, the path ahead took shape. In 1944 an agreement was signed between the Palmakh and the youth movements. Communications between the preparatory group and the sponsoring movement were assured—a provision on which Hashomer Hatzair, especially, insisted—and the enlistment of all the girls into the Palmakh was also promised, along with preservation of the social autonomy of each group; the barriers between the Palmakh and the Hakhsharot fell. And it is proper to point out that, as a result of these arrangements, political frictions within the formation also decreased.

The Palmakh and the Hakhsharot saved each other. The Palmakh was up a dead-end street in its recruiting efforts. In the Hakhsharot it discovered a reserve, and became itself a symbol of labor and self-defense. In that spirit, it educated hundreds of youths who were trying to choose the kibbutz as their way of life. Throughout 1944 to 1948, the Palmakh became a home address for all the young Jewish men and women who were ready to fulfill what they themselves called "the duties of our generation."

On the other hand, the Palmakh saved the Hakhsharot by giving their members an alternative which was equal in military and national value to enlistment in the army—and without damaging the delicate social fabric of the group planning someday to establish its own kibbutz. The preparatory groups generally assembled in kibbutzim of their own organizations. They gained skills in both work and self-defense for their own future roles. They became an important part—both quantitatively and qualitatively—of the Palmakh. In their ranks, they concentrated some of the best of Palestine's Jewish youth and played a most important part in the Palmakh's stand in the test of the War of Independence.

9 ⫷ *At the Parting of the Ways*

⫸ *The Political Coloration of the Palmakh and Its Command*

Beginning in 1943, a penetrating debate spread throughout the political and defense summit of the Yishuv, over the tasks to be assigned the Hagana after World War II. Opinions on this issue, of course, corresponded to the overall political positions of the Zionist parties.

At the summit of the Histadrut and the agency, there developed the theory of the "bad partner." In the connotation given the term by the head of the National Command, Dr. Moshe Sneh, "the international factor" (for which, read Britain) "is not an enemy; it is a bad partner. We shall hit him to make him a good partner, but he is not an enemy."[1] The fundamental assumption was that Britain would continue to be the determining factor in the Middle East. Therefore, it was desirable to avoid a clash with the British "partner." But the deteriorating relationship between the Yishuv and Britain during 1943 necessitated a reappraisal of the situation. The direction of this reappraisal was stated by Eliyahu Golomb, who defined the Hagana's role as "the use of force—when the use of force is required and against whomever the use of force is required—for freedom of settlement, immigration, development, and autonomy."[2] Even Moshe Sharett was then speaking of the possibility of "the agency's being turned into a revolutionary body,"[3] during a clash with the government. All were agreed that such a clash should be avoided, if possible. One should try to extract concessions from the British through pressure, and, at the same time, defend the principles of Zionism—even if defense meant armed struggle against the English.

These reappraisals were naturally influenced by the actual strength of the Hagana during that period. At the end of 1944, it had 36,871 members—4,609 in the Field Force, 1,517 in Palmakh, and the rest (30,745) in the Guard Force. Only 4,372 of the Guard Force had a fair amount of training. The Hagana's weaponry situation was even worse: 10,338 rifles, 437 submachine guns, 132 machine guns, and 3,933 pistols. We know nothing about the condition of these arms. Against that "strength," at the end of the war the British maintained approximately 70,000 men in the army and police force, a fact that did nothing to strengthen the position of those who were demanding violent action against British authority.

On December 9, 1943, in an important discussion conducted in the secretariat of the Histadrut Actions Committee on the matter of protecting arms, Golomb recommended an aggressive line: to defend arms caches by force (in practice, his policy was identical with that of the "B" Faction on this point). Hashomer Hatzair looked upon this step as the beginning of an armed struggle with the government; they felt that such a fight should be avoided if at all possible, or at least postponed. In the secretariat session of December 9, 1943, Ya'ari made this clear:

When shall we have to do battle with the government? When it wishes to activate the third part of the White Paper, robbing us of our autonomy and turning us into a permanent minority. . . . However, until that happens, there is no reason to commit the Hagana against the "third factor" [the British]. . . . There are different views among us. Most of our members think that we do not have to answer with gunfire. . . . We do not assume the absolute position that one must not respond with gunfire . . . but only during a maximum emergency. . . . So far, things have not come to that.

Hashomer Hatzair supported the idea of an international mandate and sought to avoid a crisis in relations with a government whose position in the Middle East then seemed rather solid. Hashomer Hatzair did not regard Britain as a "bad partner," an anti-Zionist who, through pressure, could be turned into a "good partner"; nor did it accept the view that the British line might change in case the Labour party came to power. Any British government would be fundamentally unfavorable, and the Yishuv would have to struggle in the future to extract a maximum number of concessions from it. The fact that the war still raged was also a factor in Hashomer Hatzair's considerations, contributing toward the conclusion that relations with the British should not be actively worsened.[4]

In contrast, the position of the "B" Faction was very extreme. It was felt that

the Hagana, in its development and expansion, in its heightened importance in the life of every one of us and in the process of the realization of Zionism, contains in itself the seeds of the coming conflict with the regime that opposes us. . . . [It is even possible that] we shall be forced to conduct a zealots' war, and that war will be the foundation over which the political roof can be constructed.[5]

That these words were printed in the Palmakh press lent them extra gravity. The truth is that the "B" Faction did not believe the British would evacuate Palestine either, but in their opinion, there was no escaping a conflict with the British. Therefore, the "B" Faction was less cautious about the most desirable means of response. The Palmakh clearly oriented its training toward the probability—a probability that was close to certainty—of a clash with the British in one form or another.

The Palmakh staff was almost entirely dominated by the "B" Faction. There was only one member of the Mapai majority on the staff, despite the clear condition that there was to be no partisan "representation" on the staff. The only Hashomer Hatzair man on the staff was Yitzhak Dubno (Yoav), the officer in charge of instruction. We have seen that Kibbutz Meuhad was a primary factor in the founding of the Palmakh and in extricating it from several of its worst crises. Because of that, Kibbutz Meuhad looked upon the Palmakh as "its" body, and the political influence within the Palmakh was almost exclusively that of Yitzhak Tabenkin and his comrades. Such a situation naturally lead to fears and suspicions on the part of the other movements. Moreover, Tabenkin's military and political philosophy brought many young people from the ranks of Kibbutz Meuhad and its sympathizers in the cities to engage instinctively in defense matters.

There were also people of other political circles who were working in the Hagana and accepted that philosophy. The great amount of activity by "B" Faction members in the defense area increased their influence more than a little in the Palmakh. This must not be taken to mean that command assignments were apportioned by factional affiliation. We have no testimony that appointments of members with views other than those of the "B" Faction were hampered or delayed, if the candidates were truly men of proper professional qualifications.

How did the "B" Faction exploit its decisive influence within the Palmakh? It must be said that it conducted itself with great moderation. The firm tie between members and their own political movements was preserved. There was no attempt to influence youth movements or even individuals not committed to Kibbutz Meuhad. Most important of all, there was meticulous observation of the principle of the Palmakh's duty of obedience to the national institutions and the Hagana. This does not mean that the Palmakh staff refrained from expressing its views, whether on professional matters or recruitment problems and the like. In these areas, the men of the staff knew how to fight zealously. But on political issues, the people of the "B" Faction preferred to do battle for their views within the Histadrut bodies, the Zionist movement, and the community at large; they were careful not to plunge the Palmakh into such controversies. Golomb also expressed the view that the Palmakh was a disciplined body, and that there was no evidence of deviation from the principle of unity of the Hagana. To be sure, there were meetings of the members of various movements in the Palmakh from time to time. But from the disciplinary standpoint there was nothing wrong with this, since every party was allowed to convene those of its members who were fulfilling any task within the framework of the Hagana. In short, the Palmakh was not a private army of one or more groups, but a national body subject to national discipline.

The principle of nonintervention by the Palmakh in matters beyond its field of competence had three exceptions: the Palmakh opposed partition; it prepared its members for a very sharp response to the British when the war was over; and it opposed cooperation with the C.I.D. in activity against the separatists during the winter of 1944/1945 (see below).

The Palmakh's public battle against partition was justified from the point of view of formal discipline, because the Biltmore Program, which was also the official Zionist program, at least in theory, also rejected the partition concept. The Palmakh staff's propaganda was made easier because the "B" Faction, Hashomer Hatzair, and substantial segments of Mapai held identical views on this issue. At any rate, Yitzhak Sadeh specified that "from this issue we shall not retreat, we shall not betray it, and we shall not compromise on it."[6] But it was not clear *who* would not retreat, et cetera—the Palmakh, the Hagana, or Zionism.

Furthermore, the Palmakh staff sought to turn the Palmakh into a body fighting for a minimum political policy on which its entire membership could agree; thus the directive that the formation "must serve as a political idea for its members, out of the recognition that the tasks to be assigned it are a political imperative without which the rise of the nation is impossible."[7] On the other hand, the chief of the National Command (Dr. Sneh), in his greeting to the Palmakh, stressed the fact that the formation is

> an instrument of service of society and for society. . . . Freedom of thought does not impart freedom of action, but the contrary; it compels one to act in conformity with the will of society and the orders of that society's elected representatives. The sense of brotherhood toward the entire organization [Hagana], with all its formations, must be cultivated. Except for the organization's broad mass support, the mobilized formation [Palmakh] would have no worth.[8]

Sneh's words ring with concern for Palmakh obedience to the official institutions. They take on perfect clarity when viewed against the background of the Palmakh staff's opposition to any cooperation with the C.I.D. in the operation against Etzel— which was starting at that very time. Indeed, the National Command never opposed freedom of thought, especially on the partition issue, where there was conformity between the views published in the *Palmakh Bulletins* and the official program of the Zionist movement.

On the issue of possible operations against the British, too, nothing was ever published for which there was no "cover" in official pronouncements. Only the tone was a bit different, sharper.

Yet it must be admitted that ideologically the Palmakh was entirely subject to the influence of the Left. Yitzhak Tabenkin, at his meeting with the Hashomer Hatzair in Merhavya in 1943, indicated that while the Palmakh was not a Red Army, it reinforced the working class's domination over Zionism. This was also the position of the other segments of the Histadrut. They all looked upon the Palmakh as the creation of the Jewish worker and were proud of it, but they also stressed the "all-inclusiveness" of the Palmakh and looked to an increased recruitment of non-Left elements into it. Yet the Palmakh was actually composed of the organized groupings and strata in the Histadrut, and this, coupled with the fact that the units were stationed in kibbutzim, must have frightened off people of a different political and social outlook.

To sum up, we may say that the Palmakh was marked by the decisive influence of the "B" Faction. But that group was careful not to impinge on the principles of discipline relating to the Hagana. It only gave prominence within the accepted disciplinary structure, more or less, to those issues—such as its fundamentally anti-British attitude—which were especially close to its heart. The Palmakh's opposition to cooperating with the C.I.D. in the action against Etzel in the winter of 1944/1945 was a different matter altogether.

🖃 *The Operation against the Separatists*

This is not the place to review at length the problems bound up with the separatist organizations during the war years, nor even the very phenomenon of schism. We shall, therefore, confine ourselves to certain episodes in the history of Etzel and the Stern group (Lehi), episodes which touch directly on our subject.

Deep crisis visited the Stern group during 1941 and 1942. Its operations were mostly limited to acts of robbery that were carried out to get money. And the little money that was obtained, despite the frequent failure of operations, was employed to finance propaganda in the Yishuv and attempts on the lives of a few secret police officers—though most of the victims of the men of the Stern group were actually Jews. The police displayed great vigor in searching for Lehi activists, particularly the organization's leader, Avraham Stern. On February 12, 1942, British policemen discovered his hiding place and killed him on the spot in cold blood. In its operation against Lehi, the police force was assisted not only by the Jewish public in general, but also by its official bodies. The Stern people had tried to establish contact with the Axis powers, and they were demanding a war of annihilation on the British. In 1941/1942 such a position was tantamount to giving aid to the murderers of the Jewish people in Europe and waging war against those who were fighting nazism. The agency and the Hagana therefore carried out operations against Lehi to tear it out by the roots. Several Stern people were taken; some were handed over to the British police, and some released after interrogation and warning. Etzel, too, participated in this action and it seems that Pritzker, head of Etzel intelligence, was in contact with the British police and turned over to them the names of members of Lehi.

During the years 1942 through 1944, we hear nothing of clashes between the Hagana and the separatist organizations. At that time Etzel was mired in a grave crisis, and its commanders were being replaced (Aryeh Possak, Jacob Meridor). It continued to oppose enlistment in the army, unlike the Revisionist party, which joined in the recruitment propaganda after the front neared Palestine in the spring of 1942.[9] On August 21, 1942, an agreement was signed between the Revisionists and the agency on coordination of recruitment and apportionment of funds (the agreement remained in effect until the beginning of 1944).

The political position of Etzel was based on the pro-British doctrine of Jabotinsky. Its goal was to bring about, by various kinds of pressure, an alteration of British anti-Zionist policy. The main thrust of Etzel's fight until 1944 was on the home front, to win the Yishuv over to its slogans. Etzel was still a weak organization with few members. Its chief success was in the contacts created by Pritzker with the C.I.D. and the British police.

The political negotiations between the Revisionists and the agency, as well as the agreement on recruitment matters that resulted from those talks, stirred up a storm among the workers in Palestine. The Histadrut Actions Committee passed a resolution against the agreement (July 30, 1942), and the Mapai leadership was able to get approval of the agreement in the Forty-seventh Histadrut Convention (September 7, 1942) just by the skin of its teeth. Hashomer Hatzair delineated the Revisionist movement as fascistic, and Hazan, its spokesman, proclaimed that one does not sign agreements with Fascists. The "B" Faction was inclined in the same direction, while in Mapai opinions were divided. Some asserted that the Revisionists were not Fascists, because it was out of the question for Jews to be Fascists.

During 1942/1943, political moods in the Zionist camp underwent a fundamental change. The news of the Holocaust, the ghetto rebellions, the *Struma* incident, the continuation of the White Paper policy, and quarrels with the British during 1943—all these factors created a background conducive to a shifting of values within the separatist groups and afforded conditions favorable for the growth of new ones. In April 1942, Menachem Begin reached Palestine as a soldier in the Polish Army, and during the subsequent months his extreme anti-British opinions made deeper and deeper inroads within the Etzel leadership.

Late in 1943 Etzel attempted to sponsor an all-inclusive anti-British movement which would include members of all three Jewish military organizations. One of the initiators of this movement, called Am Lohem ("Fighting Nation"), was Dr. Binyamin Eliav (Revisionist). The chairman was Yosef Idelberg, a Hagana member from Haifa. Other Hagana people took part, some of whom subsequently moved over to Etzel. The Etzel people who participated belonged to a wing of their organization which saw a chance, through Am Lohem, of injecting their own ideas into the Hagana "from the bottom up." Even

Meridor was, apparently, one of them. The Stern group, on the other hand, did not consider it feasible to take part in the group.

The Hagana, of course, did not participate in Am Lohem as such. But among its membership were some, especially in the Jerusalemite F Company of Palmakh, who saw the embodiment of their aspirations in the new group. Am Lohem sought to establish a joint political body, composed of the activist parties and circles. It would struggle to put into effect Ben-Gurion's plan for the immediate transfer of masses of Jews to the country and the establishment of Palestine as a Jewish state. Am Lohem demanded a great political effort to turn the Jewish formations in the British Army into a Jewish army. This would be done by having every soldier wear Jewish symbols on his coat lapels, even if he was arrested for the violation. At the same time, ten thousand more young men would be mobilized in Palestine for these units. The sending of emissaries to the Diaspora was proposed, on an independent basis—without any connection with the British. Pressure was to be brought to bear on the English to do something to rescue the Jews of Europe. Rather vague talk was heard about operations against the White Paper.

The purpose of this whole "program" was to bring the British to the recognition of a Jewish state which would include at least Palestine on both banks of the Jordan, the entire Galilee, the Horan, and Sinai. The political alternatives in the Middle East, in Am Lohem's opinion, were either a continuation of the White Paper and Western domination by means of Arab friends in the region, or the domination of the Anglo-American powers by means of a large Jewish state. It was, of course, imperative to fight for the second possibility. The demand for vast territory for the state was explained by the assertion that the West would have no interest in the creation of a smaller state.

This transitory organization, Am Lohem, broke up after the Hagana General Staff warned the men on December 7, 1943, that they must cease their activity within seventy-two hours.

Yitzhak Sadeh, Shimon Avidan (commander of F Company of the Palmakh), and others conducted vigorous explanatory sessions among the men of the group; and the affair ended without a single dismissal from the ranks of the Palmakh.[10]

Immediately after the failure of Am Lohem, Etzel proclaimed a revolt against the British regime (January 1944). It is hard to believe that there was no connection between the two events. People were trying to win sympathy for Etzel ideology among other groups in a new way. When the way was found to be closed, Etzel went off in its own direction.

The political basis of Etzel's anti-British revolt, during 1944/1945, did not go beyond the limits of the Jabotinskyite "doctrine of pressure." They were still trying, by force of arms, to coerce England into supporting a Jewish state. One gets the impression (though it was never explicitly stated) that Etzel was not seeking to drive the British out of Palestine, but only to be rid of the components of British rule—the police, the administration, and perhaps also the army. It appears that there was to be no undermining of Britain's position of dominance in the Middle East in general or Palestine in particular—so long, of course, as the existence of the Jewish state was recognized.

To the Arab factor they ascribed little importance. In the eyes of Etzel, and Lehi as well, the Arabs were an element of no weight whatsoever; their strength had been artificially blown up by the English. The decision would be between the Jews and the British, and not between the Jews and Arabs. In this, Etzel took a position similar to that of the Agency Executive. The difference was chiefly a matter of method. Etzel sought to move the British toward a pro-Zionist policy by armed pressure and, in the first phase, by acts of sabotage on inanimate objectives (during 1944/1945 they tried to avoid injury to human beings). In contrast, the agency sought to arrive at the same goal by diplomatic negotiation, propaganda in the free world, and threat of pressure through unofficial immigration, mass settlement, and the like.

Etzel represented only a small segment of the Yishuv—in this period, only a very small segment. But it took it upon itself to speak for the community and to dictate the community's policy, although that community had freely chosen a leadership with a different policy. This attempt by a minority to dictate its views to the majority by violent means was at the root of the bitter polemics throughout that period over the question of national discipline. Etzel rejected the obligation of national discipline in regard to the agency; and Menachem Begin's arguments on the subject had, paradoxically, a distinct "revolutionary" ring. His line was that the Jewish people would learn the necessity for war through warfare and would come over to the side of the minority only if the minority acted in spite of the opposition of the majority. This dispute reached its zenith in the fall and winter of 1944.

The impact of the Holocaust, hostile British policy and its manifestations, and the brutality shown Jews rescued from Europe—all these were the basis for a military-political doctrine that preached the removal of the "foreign conqueror" from Palestine by means of a general revolt on the part of the Yishuv and the establishment of a large Jewish state. "Freedom or Death"—that was the slogan of Etzel in its battle. But that doctrine brought up several knotty problems:

First, there was the problem of the very idea of revolt. It was plain to all that, if she wanted to do so, Britain had the military strength to destroy the Yishuv. As long as most of the community opposed Etzel, the use of superior British force against the Jewish population was precluded; for that would make the British appear to the world as the brutal oppressors of a people which, for the most part, was friendly to England. If the entire population joined in open revolt, as Etzel wished, this restraint would be lost; the Yishuv could then expect utter ruin. The paradox was that only Etzel's inability to win over the majority of the community to its policy made Etzel's existence and activity possible. The agency's dominance of the Yishuv protected both the community and Etzel from serious harm. Begin claimed that if little Etzel could cause the English manifold problems, the Hagana, larger and better equipped, could cause many more. Should the Hagana join the revolt on the same basis as Etzel, British rule would come to an end. We know what the strength of the Hagana was, and there is no need to emphasize that an open revolt could have served the British as a convenient excuse to wipe out the organized Yishuv.

Begin also took into consideration the possibility that Etzel would fail in its fight. Should that happen, he saw himself and his movement in the image of the Irish Easter Rebellion of 1916, whose heroes had sacrificed themselves on the altar of the future. But it was never explained how one could draw an analogy between Ireland, populated by Irishmen, and the Palestine of 1944, which was two-thirds Arab and only one-third Jewish.

Second, there was the question of Arab nationalism. Etzel was of the opinion that if the British were removed from the country, the Jews could easily overcome the resistance of the Arabs of Palestine. The truth was otherwise. The British did support Arab nationalism, but it was definitely nourished also by independent sources. It was precisely the measured, cautious policy of the agency and the Hagana which made it ultimately possible to overcome the Arab invasion.

Third, Menachem Begin's position ignored the anti-Nazi struggle that was being carried on at the time. The war still raged. And in the period after the assassination of Lord Moyne in Cairo on November 5, 1944 (see below), the Germans were still able to make one more show of strength, initiating their final attack in the Battle of the Bulge (December 1944). The eyes of the entire free world were turned toward the fateful battlefield in Europe. Under those conditions, a general revolt of the Yishuv would have certainly stirred up potentially disastrous responses to the Jews of Palestine.

Fourth, the leaders of the community and wide circles within it suspected Etzel of seeking domination over the Yishuv. We have certainly found no evidence of this either in the writings of Etzel or in the statements of its leader. But one could, of course, claim that published material is not suitable for such purposes, that if there were widespread thoughts of this type in Etzel, they were expressed in any way but print. In a talk with Sneh (October 8, 1944), Begin stated that he would be ready to follow Ben-Gurion if the latter led the people in revolt against the British. This may have been just a rhetorical pronouncement, for it is difficult to imagine that the chairman of the Agency Executive would lead the nation in a revolt precisely as ordered by the head of Etzel. Or perhaps Begin was thinking of the other possibility hinted at in the same conversation: that the masses of the people would start a revolt out of which a *different* leadership would spring forth—that is to say, the leadership of the revolt would be in the hands of Etzel, while the political leadership would be new. The suspicion that Etzel intended, among other objectives, to dominate the Yishuv from within was still unrelieved.[11]

There was another side to the problem. With the relationship of forces then prevailing among the Jews, Arabs, and British, it appeared that an open military struggle by the Jews would, in case of a Jewish victory, lead to Jewish hegemony only over those parts of the country either already settled by Jews or altogether unpopulated. It is hard to believe that Jewish military power was then sufficient for capture-and-hold operations in Arab territory. And indeed, the view that the area of Jewish rule more or less corresponded to the area of Jewish settlement had broad adherence within the Jewish public and was one of the decisive reasons for the settlement policy of the national institutions. In other words, Etzel's armed struggle logically led to the partition of Palestine, the very result which Etzel sought to prevent. Etzel's actions paradoxically led to the same outcome (a "good" partition) which a part of the British war cabinet was prepared to grant Zionism as early as 1943 or 1944.

Etzel's reactivation began in February and March of 1944, with the blowing up of the government Immigration Offices (February 12), Income Tax Building (February 27), and the buildings of the C.I.D. in Jerusalem, Jaffa, and Haifa (March 23). These operations were accompanied by very lively propaganda which dwelt on three points: (1) expansion of hostile acts until there was general revolt by all the Jews of Palestine; (2) proclamation of a temporary coalition government, meaning the inclusion of Etzel as an element with equal rights within the existing coalition, once the latter had adopted Etzel's objectives; and (3) expulsion of the British from the land and creation of a large Jewish state.

On this basis, one of active warfare against the British, a certain rapprochement occurred between Etzel and Lehi. The Stern group had pulled out of the severe crisis which had plagued it, gathered strength, and expanded with the change of mood in the Yishuv during 1943. On November 1, 1943, twenty Lehi members escaped from the British prison at Latrun through a tunnel they had dug. A top leader, Nathan Yellin (Mor), was among them. He was a friend of Begin from their period of activity in the Revisionist movement and Betar in Poland. The central committee of Lehi was now composed of Yitzhak Shamir (*nom de guerre:* "Michael"), Dr. Israel Scheib ("Eldad"), and Nathan Mor ("Gera"). Negotiations to unite the two organizations were begun, but they failed (summer of 1944) because of ideological differences. The position of Lehi leadership was anti-British in principle. Lehi did not believe that political concessions could be squeezed out of the British by pressure. It aspired to definite independence, to Jewish rule over the land of Israel within very wide boundaries, and to ties with other powers. It is proper to note that the Stern group was at that time the only Jewish organization that went beyond "Anglocentrism." (The Communists also still supported the continuation of British rule in Palestine, together with a demand for the implementation of the White Paper. On the Arab side, only the mufti's supporters opposed a continuation of British dominance, and they wanted to substitute German rule for it.) In 1944 the Sternist position seemed utterly unrealistic, an excursion into pure political fantasy.

The agency looked upon Etzel's activities as a very grave danger to its own position in the community and to Zionism's political chances in the international arena. Etzel obtained necessary funds by collecting money from its sympathizers and, by threats and extortion, from its opponents. Thus it created a fringe group which, though opposed to its acts, heeded its instructions. From that to violent rule over the Jewish streets was a very short step.

The agency also feared Etzel's undesirable influence on the Hagana after it was found that many members in its ranks had tried to give vent to their feelings through acts similar to those of Etzel, even though they disagreed with Etzel's overall ideological system (Am Lohem provided evidence of this). Expression was given in the Agency Executive to the fear that if events were left to develop in that direction, the democratic organization of the Yishuv would crumble, that a "strong man" produced by some military group would determine the paths of Zionist policy.[12]

They tried, first, to reach Etzel by means of the Revisionist party, and thus to bring an end to its activities. But it quickly became clear that Etzel was not taking orders from the party which provided its political inspiration. The question of action against the separatist organizations was, therefore, put on the agenda.

The leaders of the Yishuv made a careful distinction between Etzel and Lehi. They saw Etzel as the principal political threat and the Stern group as a "classic" terrorist group on the Irish model (to which, by the way, the separatists continually referred in their literature). The people of the Political Department of the agency did not, therefore, hesitate to attack Lehi with all the means at their disposal; nor did they stop at cooperating with the British in this matter. After the killing of a Haifa policeman, the death of two Lehi members, Drucker and Luntz, who were surrounded by police and killed themselves at Yavniel when there was no hope of escape (April 1944), came as a direct result of Hagana Intelligence Service's cooperation with the British.

The Etzel problem was ten times more difficult, and opinions on it were divided among the people in the official community bodies. Most of the nonsocialist camp, from the radical Gruenbaum to the "B" General Zionists and the Mizrahi, opposed both cooperation with the British and strong independent action against Etzel. Most of them were willing to confine themselves solely to propaganda and verbal pronouncements. The representative of the "B" General Zionists even opposed the protection of people of means against extortion, perhaps out of fear of injuring the ties that several top people of his party had with circles close to the separatist organizations. In Histadrut bodies, too, there was widespread objection to cooperation with the police; and only Aliyah Hadasha (the party of German-Jewish newcomers) favored such cooperation as early as the beginning of 1944. In the Histadrut camp, the demand for independent Hagana action against Etzel was voiced. It was stated that if all other means failed, there would be no avoiding the use of force against force.[13]

One must also take into consideration the political reasons for the fierce enmity of the agency leaders toward the separatists. Daily political activity, with its problems and practical limitations, was the regular diet of men like Weizmann, Ben-Gurion, Sharett, and Kaplan. They knew that the problem of Transjordan, for example, was in no way a practical political question. They were carefully watching for a way to break through the White Paper wall—by political pressure on Winston Churchill and the helmsmen of the American ship of state—and make the largest possible political gain with the help of the prime minister's hesitant friendship and the pro-Zionist proclamations of the Labour party. The British cabinet was discussing partition at the time, and the hearts of the Zionist leadership were filled with simultaneous hopes and fears. The rise of a Jewish political-military power independent of the agency, working on its own and free from the responsibility of rendering reports to its electors or to any organized public whatsoever, represented a very grave danger to all potential diplomatic activity. There is no doubt that a number of Zionist leaders would have been willing to employ force against an anti-Zionist policy *after* the war; but in 1944 the time had still not come to resort to violent methods.

In light of these considerations, it was decided, after strenuous debate (April 2, 1944), that the following lines of action would be taken against the separatists: development of a broad program of enlightenment within the community; isolation of the separatists and their supporters—insofar as their identity was known—on both a public and personal basis; suppression of extortion and the use of terror; promotion of a more awakened and courageous response from the Jewish public to manifestations of terror; avoidance of actions likely to lead to mutual betrayal to the police; and activation of a Jewish force to put an end to the acts of the separatists. The question of whether cooperation with the British Army was permissible was not decided. But in practice no ties with the army in the fight against the separatists are known of.

The results of these resolutions were not great. The Hagana did not have a large enough force mobilized in the cities for action against an underground. Although means were taken to protect individuals and groups against extortion, and broad counterpropaganda was developed, the growth and operations of the schismatic organizations were not halted. The Sternists assassinated policemen. Etzel raided the radio station at Ramallah (May 17, 1944), carried out a second attack on the police station of the Tel Aviv-Jaffa district (August 22, 1944), attacked police buildings at Beit Dagon, Qalqilya, Haifa, and Katara (September 27, 1944), and looted textiles and linen goods from government warehouses (October 6, 1944). Members of the Stern group made an unsuccessful attempt on the life of High Commissioner MacMichael on August 8, 1944, as he was about to leave the country. On November 5, 1944, Eliahu Hakim and Eliahu Bet Zouri assassinated the English secretary of state for the Middle East, Lord Moyne, at the door of his house in Cairo.

In the fall of 1944 the question of the separatists reappeared on the agenda of the Zionist leadership. The British insisted that the agency respond to the separatists' acts. The police and the C.I.D., who, as has been pointed out, had not in the recent past shown any marked enmity for the troublemakers, now demanded[14] one of two measures: either the Jewish community must offer its help against the separatists, including informing on and delivering activists to the C.I.D.; or independent Hagana action must be taken against them. The representatives of the Political Department of the agency rejected both alternatives. They rejected the first for fear of reciprocal betrayal (because Etzel could also deliver Hagana men to the police) and because of unvarnished hostility and deep mistrust toward British overlordship. The second choice they rejected because they wanted to avoid civil war.

When all attempts by the official bodies failed, however, the Political Department decided to begin a more vigorous and aggressive operation against the separatists. The considerations that had until now prevented civil war were set aside, and it was decided to try to break up these groups by the use of Jewish force. For tactical reasons, it was decided to concentrate the operation solely against Etzel in the first stage. Otherwise, a united front of the two separatist groups against the Hagana might be created. And in passing we must note that the leadership estimated that the Stern group's power of resistance was greater than that of Etzel. But there were also political motivations. Some men were hoping that the tendency they then sensed in the Sternists to employ socialistic slogans and terms would lead to a rapprochement of the Stern group with the Hagana. Golomb was, apparently, in more or less continuous touch with Nathan Yellin (Mor), and during the fall a contact between them was made on the subject of a cessation of Sternist operations.

The motion on the program of action against Etzel was, apparently, passed early in October 1944. The execution was assigned to a body created solely for this purpose by the Hagana General Staff. In practice, Palmakh and Intelligence Service people participated in the operation. While every Palmakh member was permitted to decide whether to take part in the operation, city people from the Palmakh reserves were assembled for the task.

On October 20, 1944, special courses for those involved in the *Saison* (as the antiseparatist operation was called) were begun. Officers from the Palmakh and the Intelligence Service were appointed to lead the action. A total of 170 men from the Palmakh took part in the campaign, together with Intelligence Service operatives and those city Hagana people who were already working against the separatists with propaganda and as bodyguards prior to the *Saison*.

The object of the initial phase of the campaign was to put Etzel on the defensive, to cut it off from its financial resources, and to bring about the cessation of its operations. Someone suggested that this be a one-time action, but on a broad scale, since an organization like Etzel could be seriously damaged if three or four hundred of its men, including people from the top echelons, were imprisoned at once. The intent was to put the prisoners in Hagana jails and then release them under continual surveillance. However, the plan was rejected and replaced by action on a more modest scale.

Those taking part in the *Saison* had three tasks: shadowing and investigation, protection, and arrest. The men worked separately, according to the demands of the operation. The shadowing and investigation squads gathered material on Etzel.

In that way, the master list of its contributors was brought to light. There was quite a surprise when it became apparent that the list included institutions, organizations, and even newspapers and individuals very distant from Etzel—but these sources had been "solicited" by pressure and extortion. One such person was the owner of that very hotel in which the *Saison* staff was stationed, a loyal Hagana man. The "solicitation" was halted.

A similar operation took place in the diamond trade. Etzel had been carrying out "robberies" after getting the permission of its supporters among the gem dealers. The dealers then got their money back from the insurance companies. A smugglers' ring was broken up. According to the *Saison* operatives, it was composed of members of the underworld and dealt in the sale of merchandise from Egyptian sources (nylon stockings, eye-glasses, and the like) in Palestine. Protection squads were created to guard individuals against extortion-collection operations. Those on the fringes of Etzel were damaged in these actions, its sources of funds were demolished, and its potential for operation was reduced. But the most outstanding operation, and the one that has received the most publicity, was the arrests.

Many Etzel members, and one or two from the Stern group, were captured on the street or at home. They were taken to private guardhouses in both the city and country. There they were interrogated and, in certain cases, even punished. Those taken were, for the most part, from the upper echelons of Etzel. The Hagana sought to break their power of resistance by this affront to them. According to the statements of *Saison* operatives, the prisoners' holding strength against Jewish interrogators—in contrast to their resistance to the English—was not great. The vast majority of those questioned supplied the Hagana with the needed facts; in this way the Hagana reached as far as the local cells of Etzel and, for all practical purposes, silenced its operation.

At the same time, however, (October 18, 1944) the agency protested the exile by the British of 251 prisoners to Eritrea.

These were alleged "terrorists," some of whom had been arrested by the British on the basis of old lists but had long since ceased to be active. Though the agency supported the action against the Etzel as such, it was decidedly opposed to the removal of Palestinian Jews from the country into exile. At any rate, from October 6, 1944, the day when Etzel carried out the textiles theft, until May 12, 1945, the day on which the inhabitants of the country were warned not to come near British government buildings because Etzel would blow them up, there was an interruption of the schismatic group's activities.

The *Saison* underwent a transformation with the news of the assassination of Lord Moyne (November 5, 1944). This murder (the date of which, according to Stern group people, was not known to the Sternist Central Committee in Palestine in advance) substantially changed the political situation. Previous activities of the separatist organizations had jeopardized the diplomatic course of the Agency Executive. But the Moyne assassination, coming while the war against the Nazis was still raging, represented an explicit provocation that could frustrate all the diplomatic efforts of the agency and bring the military power of Great Britain in the Middle East down on the Yishuv. Moreover, under such conditions, a tiny coterie of fanatics might be able to seize the reins of power in the Yishuv and thus bring democratic public life to an end.

The agency, therefore, not only decided to redouble its activities against the separatists, but also to take a far-ranging step which stirred up stormy debates. It decided to cooperate with the British in wiping out the separatists.[15] The supporters of this plan claimed that it would be impossible to hold hundreds of Etzel people in private Jewish prisons. (And in truth, more than once prisoners had been freed because of the poor conditions prevailing in the confinement locations or because of the protests of local residents.) They argued that as long as there was not a Jewish government in Palestine, the Yishuv was compelled to work through the existing power structure, to the extent that mutuality of interests (even if temporary) existed between Jew and Britisher.[16] There were also those who rationalized their agreement to combined operations with the British by asserting that Etzel was a fascist outfit whose members were not entitled to the same consideration as the average Jew.

Cooperation with the C.I.D. stirred up a storm of controversy within the ranks of the Palmakh. Ahdut Avodah (the former "B" Faction) and Left Poale Zion opposed it, though the former did not object to the *Saison* and took the same stand on Etzel as did the rest of the Histadrut. But Ahdut Avodah looked upon the British as the primary foe and was not ready to cooperate with them. It feared, for moral reasons, to deliver Jews —even ones who had offended against their own people and violated national discipline—into the hands of the men of the White Paper. The party further warned that this cooperation might some day come back to haunt the Hagana during the struggle over immigration or settlement.

The debate over this question became public during the Sixth Histadrut Convention, the first session of which was held on November 20, 1944. The convention approved Ben-Gurion's motion, which contained four antiseparatist provisions: (1) expulsion of members of schismatic groups from teaching positions and places of employment; (2) denial to them of protection and shelter; (3) resistance to their threats and extortion; and (4) "to the extent that the British government and police are interested in wiping out the terror," cooperation with the British. Ahdut Avodah and Left Poale Zion dissociated themselves from the majority position on the fourth article of the motion. The two groups finally voted in favor of the majority resolutions, however, at the same time giving notice of their reservations. In the convention, as in the official community institutions, Ahdut Avodah found itself in the minority in its demand for continued independent action.

In the Agency Executive, opposition to cooperation with the regime came from Rabbi Maimon (Mizrahi) and Gruenbaum, who resigned over the issue. The remainder of the factions represented on the executive voiced no opposition to the new policy. The newspaper *Haboker*, the organ of the "B" General Zionists, objected to both independent action and cooperation with the government (in contrast to the stand of that party's representative on the executive).

The decision on cooperation with the British was abetted by Churchill's announcements and Weizmann's arrival in Palestine. Weizmann met with the prime minister on November 4, 1944, a day before the Moyne assassination, and received the promise that the Jewish cause would not be forgotten and that a disposition would be made after the war that would be agreeable to them. The immigration of one and one-half million Jews over ten years and the immigration of 100,000 to 150,000 orphans immediately after the cessation of hostilities were, according to Churchill, practical proposals which were within reason. Churchill stated that if all of Palestine could be turned over to the Jews, that would be fine; but if the choice was between the White Paper and partition, partition was preferable. He reemphasized his desire to involve the United States in the decision and also related that the British Cabinet Commission on Palestine was still in existence. Finally, he gave assurance that Weizmann's demands (for a large immigration and speedy explicit decisions) would be taken into consideration. And he hinted that the partition would be a "good" one from the Jewish point of view.

Churchill's words were interpreted in the Agency Executive as a renewed serious opportunity for ending the White Paper regime. The picture changed drastically, however, with Churchill's pronouncement in Parliament on November 17, after the Moyne assassination. Churchill took off in a most hostile manner against Zionism and the Zionists, expressing the "fear" that, after many years of support, he would have to rethink his position. There can be no doubt of the fact that up to that moment he had been a friend—though perhaps a critical one—of Zionism; and the key position was in his hands. It is obvious that Churchill's pressure and the fear of losing his friendship influenced the decision to build up the *Saison.*

In addition, Lord Gort, the new high commissioner, arrived in Palestine on November 1. There is no way of knowing whether he was a friend of the Jews, but there can be no doubt that he tried to win sympathy among the Jewish public and leadership (perhaps simply as a means to success in his job). By virtue of his judgment, patience, and practical understanding, his brief term of office was noteworthy for improved relations between the agency and the British. Gort pressed the agency to put an end to Etzel operations. The Moyne murder did not elicit a positive response from world public opinion, which was still attuned to the war against the Nazis; nor did Jewish public opinion in Palestine react favorably to the deed in Cairo. Dr. Weizmann returned to Palestine (after a five-year absence) a few days after the assassination. In the Agency Executive sessions, he voiced the feeling that the kidnappings must be stopped, and he approved cooperation with the British.

Logic required that the *Saison* operation now be expanded to include the Stern group (it was members of the latter, and not Etzel, who had assassinated Lord Moyne). But in practice the pressure was directed, as before, at Etzel. There were a number of reasons for that. One gets the impression that even some Sternist people were surprised at the power of the storm that swirled through the community at the news of the murder. Etzel explicitly dissociated itself from the act.

Though there is no direct evidence for it, it seems that the Stern group gave notice that they would interrupt their activities for a certain period. After the fact, Sternist leaders claimed that they wished to avoid any encounter with the Hagana—the logic of events would lead to an anti-British battle, and the *Saison* would, sooner or later, necessarily come to an end. Since Dr. Scheib, the most extreme member of the Sternist triumvirate, was in prison at the time, Mor and Shamir were responsible for their organization's operations.

Negotiations were begun between the Sternists and Hagana through the intermediacy of Joseph Liebstein, a relative of Avraham Stern's and one of the Stern group's top people. Liebstein was then residing in an agricultural establishment after having successfully escaped arrest by the British, and he was somewhat removed from current lines of Sternist thought. Liebstein tried to bring about a merger of the Stern group and Hagana. For that purpose, he initiated meetings between Mor and Golomb (the intermediary for Hagana was Moshe Dayan). The basis for the proposed union was apparently to be increased "activism" on the part of the Hagana and acceptance by the Stern group of national discipline. We do not know whether Golomb was seriously aiming for a merger of this type, and it is even more difficult to fathom Mor's intentions. An examination of Liebstein's letters brings one to the conclusion that the business was serious only to Liebstein. It is almost certain that Golomb hoped to effectuate an interruption of Stern group operations and to cause the organization to have second thoughts about itself, while Mor was trying to avoid a *Saison* against his group.

If such was the case, both sides got what they wanted. The Sternists refrained from activity throughout the spring of 1945; Hagana released one prisoner who was a Stern group member and confined itself to one large action against that organization: the seizure of Sternist archives on Arlosoroff Street in Haifa on December 8, 1944. Operations by the Stern group began again after the end of negotiations in June 1945.

To Hagana, Etzel was the more dangerous outfit, and the *Saison* was directed against it—this time, in cooperation with the British. The people on the Palmakh staff once again demanded that participation in the *Saison* be solely on a voluntary basis, so as not to force members of Ahdut Avodah to act contrary to their conscience. One of the top *Saison* operatives, an Ahdut Avodah member, resigned at that time. After there had been some words—more than a little due to Galili's influence—the Hagana staff finally decided to accede to the Palmakh staff's stipulation. The action, then, was carried out from the beginning on a voluntary basis; and in a formal sense there was no connection between the staffs of the Hagana and the *Saison*. The *Saison* staff answered to the chief of the General Staff personally.

It is likely that the number of Palmakh members participating in the *Saison* diminished markedly after the decision to cooperate with the British. The operation itself was very energetic. Within a short time, about one hundred Etzel people were turned over to the British. The addresses of others were supplied, and they were later arrested by the English.

The end of the *Saison* is wrapped in thick darkness, and we have been unable to clarify the facts completely. In March 1945 a meeting of *Saison* participants was held in Yagur. Sneh and Golomb there announced the cessation of activity against the separatists, who had supposedly sustained grave injury and had been put out of action. The statement is not very convincing, and we cannot assume that this was the sole or main reason for the change.

After the Yagur meeting, apparently only the Intelligence Service personnel continued the *Saison* (May and June 1945); during that period, cooperation with the British was expanded. In the middle of June, the entire *Saison* operation was halted. In May, Etzel carried out attacks on police stations and acts of sabotage on the telegraph network. In July a bridge and railroad tracks in the Yavne area were demolished in a joint Etzel-Sternist operation. The *Saison* faded away, and it is reasonable to suppose that the opposition of nonsocialist circles and of the Ahdut Avodah was the decisive factor in the cessation of operations, in addition to the complication of relations with the British that occurred in the spring of 1945. The *Saison*, its participants, the factors that called it into existence, and the responses to it are all very complex. The entire grave affair left a bitter residue in the hearts of all those who had taken part in it.

The *Saison* proved that Etzel was not during that period a strong, many-branched organization with popular roots. The Hagana demonstrated its own superiority and its power to halt Etzel operations and threaten the destruction of Etzel organizational structures. If we weigh the matter on the basis of practicality and efficiency alone, the ending of the *Saison* before the designated aims had been accomplished (that is, after the Yishuv leadership had decided to employ all means against the schismatic groups) was an error. Indeed, many of the Palmakh people who took part in the *Saison* were of this opinion. Theoretically, at least, there were two ways open to the Zionist leadership to be rid of Etzel: negotiations toward union, or vigorous political-military action. The agency had refused to travel the first road and stopped in the middle of the second.

Thus the results of the *Saison* were negative in the extreme. Etzel was not destroyed but instead dug itself in deeper as an underground, and benefited from spontaneous sympathy as a persecuted group betrayed to the hated government. Cessation of the operation also worsened the crisis with the British, who no longer believed in the sincerity of the agency's pronouncements on its battle against the separatists. Only the halting of Etzel operations for half a year can be chalked up to the *Saison*'s credit.

On the whole, therefore, the *Saison* could hardly be called a success. But there was more than the practical side to consider. The question was asked then, and has been asked since, what justification there was for handing over Jews to a regime which had watched passively while Jews fleeing for their lives were barred entry to what that regime itself still preferred to call their "national home." Even if Etzel was believed to comprise political criminals, handing them over to the British—and especially to the C.I.D., the most hated group of Britishers in Palestine—was and remains a moral blemish on the Hagana's name.

Yet Etzel could hardly be judged by criteria different from those used for judging underground movements of any other nation. Moral justification for action against the Mandatory administration was not difficult to find; the problem was rather one of juxtaposition of their actions against the background of a war that was still going on, and the additional question of the methods used and political aims pursued. In other words, the criteria for judging them had to be political in the main.

What was Etzel's position on the *Saison*? Under the influence of its leader, Begin, it decided not to respond in kind to the kidnappings. This was perhaps out of tactical considerations— so as not to be blamed for a civil war, but to cast the guilt on the other party. And indeed, it came out of the crisis of the *Saison* with an aura of national responsibility that glowed through Etzel publicity releases all during that period. But the decision not to respond in kind was taken only after stormy discussions within the Etzel command, for most of the leaders initially favored a violent response. This, perhaps, explains why the commander-in-chief of Etzel, just a short while before the *Saison*, threatened the Hagana with reprisals if any action was taken against his group. In the end, the other opinion won out.

🐦 *The Palmakh through 1945*

Despite the reawakening in its midst—in contrast to the lethargy of the preceding year—the Palmakh's growth rate was not very large during 1944. At the end of 1943, it numbered 1,113 members; in the winter of 1944, 1,517. In addition, approximately 400 members had entered the reserve after the rotations had been carried out (partially in May, but mostly in September of 1944). One or two hundred members were added through the spring of 1945. By the summer of 1945, after the current school graduates had joined up, there were about 1,900 people in the Palmakh. This growth was partially a result of the enlistment of the Hakhsharot. It was due also to the "year of service" that had been proclaimed by the Yishuv recruitment center under Dov Joseph. From 1943 on, high school graduates received their diplomas only after completing at least one year's service in one of the recognized branches of mobilization. This arrangement was arrived at after protracted negotiations with the highest pedagogical bodies in Palestine. As early as 1942, 97 high school graduates entered the ranks of the Palmakh; in 1943 there were 108; in 1944, 234; and in 1945, 213. It is proper to note that many of them were none other than members of the Hakhsharot (153 out of the 234 in 1944 and 142 out of the 213 in 1945). In most of these preparatory groups of the pioneering youth movements (with the exception of Hanoar Haoved, the young workers' group), the high school student component was the decisive element. The remainder of the Palmakh recruits of 1944/1945 came from the agricultural collectives, which replaced those of their members who were entering the reserve. A substantial number of new recruits also came from the ranks of young people from Jerusalem, Petah Tiqva, Tel Aviv, and their suburbs.

During the years of 1943 through 1945, the Palmakh included one other special formation, the Coastal Patrol Force, which had a composition very similar to that of the Palmakh. A coastal watch was set up during the period of the danger of a German invasion in the summer of 1942. The unit was assigned to create observation posts along the Palestine coast to guard against any attempt at invasion by sea. The British were responsible for this unit within the framework of the Supernumerary Police Force. But they did not set much store by the force, and it suffered from lack of equipment and training and from hard living conditions.

In January 1944 the Palmakh took over command of the unit; even prior to that, training exercises had been organized for it under Palmakh auspices. The number of men in the force was about five hundred. The unit lost its reason for existence when the front receded from the borders of Palestine, and it was disbanded in January 1945. Seventy-five percent of its members were enlisted in the Jewish Brigade, while the rest (especially the seamen and those with other skills) were transferred to the Palmakh.

Among the problems that came up in connection with recruitment and expansion was the issue of the Jewish Brigade in the British Army. When it became known in September 1944* that the brigade was to be established, great preparations to build up enlistments in its ranks were begun. In the Histadrut offices the midnight oil was burned over this problem. Moshe Sharett and Moshe Erem (the latter was responsible for Histadrut recruitment machinery) demanded the mobilization of men for the brigade. Sharett proposed the enlistment of 400 men from the agricultural establishments and 400 more from the ranks of the Hagana, the Coastal Patrol Force, and the Palmakh. From the latter he required simply a "symbolic" enlistment of 5 percent of the 1,600 Palmakh members. This proposal by Sharett later gave rise to all kinds of rumors. There were some people who accused him (in the press and in the Palmakh history) of having demanded the enlistment of the Palmakh, or a major part of it, in the brigade. The truth is that he asked for nothing more than the "symbolic" contribution referred to above; and in the secretariat of the Histadrut Actions Committee, Ben-Gurion and Lavon objected to the enlistment of a larger percentage of Palmakh men in the brigade, as demanded by Erem in the same session. Erem had suggested the enlistment of 300 to 500 Palmakh men in the brigade, but his plan was rejected.

Finally, a compromise was found. It was decided to enlist the Germanist Section of the Palmakh in the brigade. That unit had been anticipating action since 1942, and it was out of the question to hold its men in a state of inactive mobilization. In practice, only some of the section's members were enlisted and the gap was made up by recruiting men from the kibbutzim. A

---

* See below, the last section of this chapter.

total of forty-three men were enlisted, thirty of whom had previously been in the Germanist Section. The unit's commanding officer, Yehuda Ben-Horin, also signed up. In time, the section was to fulfill a vital role in the organization of unofficial immigration in Europe, as well as in its service in the brigade.

During that period important changes took place in the internal organization of the Palmakh. The Palmakh staff had its seat at Allonim under rather difficult conditions. Only in the summer of 1944 was it transferred to its own cottage in Kibbutz Mizra. Regular meetings of commanders and the staff were held. The staff included—in addition to instructional, administrative, and quartermaster officers—the chief medical officer and the information officer.

In the summer of 1944, the Palmakh staff people suggested to the General Staff that battalions be set up within the formation, to be composed of several companies each. This was a revolutionary proposal. Up till that time even the company, as an operative unit, was looked upon as a rather outstanding and bold achievement. There was not a single man within the entire Hagana who knew how to plan and execute combat operations at the battalion level. The General Staff feared the clumsiness of the larger apparatus and doubted whether, under the conditions prevailing in Palestine, there would be room for the employment of battalions, even in the distant future. The motivations of the Palmakh staff, which had made the original suggestion, were professional and organizational. The staff no longer had control of the nine or ten existing (or contemplated) companies and felt the necessity of studying the problems connected with the activation of larger units.

After deliberations, a General Staff committee approved the proposal. It accepted the Palmakh staff's reasoning—that the battalion commanders would learn their new functions by doing the job. Back in 1943, before the problem had been discussed in the General Staff, F and G Companies had been united as an experiment into a single battalion under the command of Shimon

Avidan. Now, C and D Companies were combined under the command of Uri Yoffe into the Third Battalion; A Company was added to Avidan's First Battalion, while B, E, and H Companies were merged into the Second Battalion under Uri Brenner. Thus the Palmakh blazed a trail toward the study of the military problems involved in the activation of larger units.

Toward the end of 1943, an additional company, the eighth, was founded in the Palmakh. It had its base in the Jerusalem area. Early in 1945, I Company in the eastern Upper Galilee and K Company, a special settlement outfit with its base in the Ginossar Valley, were also added. These companies were largely composed of people from the preparatory groups, and they readily combined agricultural pioneering with military training.

K Company was a first attempt at what later became a peculiarly Israeli phenomenon. Hakhshara groups that had ended their active service in the Palmakh ranks were not transferred to the ordinary reserves, but were called upon to found new kibbutzim in strategic areas. These kibbutzim were included in toto in the Palmakh membership, received additional training, and became pioneering-military outposts. In the course of 1945 five such settlements were founded, all of them in the Upper Galilee. They were officially released from the military framework only years later, and in them the original concept of Tabenkin—"Cossack" villages of builders and fighters—found a partial fulfillment. In the conditions of Mandatory rule, these settlements fulfilled a further important function: what appeared to the British to be just another agricultural collective, which would probably include Hagana men within its membership, was in fact a self-contained and independent Palmakh base. Agriculture was not simply camouflage—people were quite genuinely building their homes in the desolation of the Galilee mountains. But while they worked hard to make a living, they did in fact help in supporting not only themselves, but the Palmakh as well.

Apart from the ten companies mentioned, one company—J—

was set up to include Palmakh seamen. When in the fall of 1945 the Palmakh was redivided into three battalions, J Company remained separate. So did G Company which, in addition to scouts and demolition men, included the Germanist Section (until its enlistment in the Jewish Brigade), the Balkanist Section (which served as a reserve body for the recruitment of parachutists and was disbanded in 1944), and the Shahar Section. The last-named was created in the spring of 1943 from the members of the Arabist unit in Syria (which had been broken up at that time) and from new members who had joined up in Palestine. Special top secret courses were arranged for its people. Through 1944 its numbers grew by forty or fifty men, organized into three platoons. It was assigned to gather information among the Arab population and carried out its task with marked success.

A unique problem arose within the Palmakh with the enlistment of young people from the city neighborhoods and suburbs. First attempts to assimilate these youths had been made in several places back in the beginning of 1943. They were mostly without even an elementary education and were far removed from matters of settlement on the land and self-defense. One group, which won the nickname *Barhash* ("midges"), was at Givat-Hashelosha, within the framework of E Company, and under the instruction of a settler from Kibbutz Naan. As a result of the massive educational efforts which the best of the instructors and teachers of the company invested in it, the group's standards rose significantly from both the military and human points of view. It later founded its own kibbutz, Misgav-Am, in the mountains of the Galilee.

But this success remained one of a kind. Throughout 1943 other groups of the same type of youth came to the Palmakh, but the instruction given them bore no fruit. Sometimes not a single platoon remained out of an entire section.

Early in 1944 the Palmakh staff decided to concentrate its efforts in this field. An absorption camp was set up at Ayelet-

Hashahar in which the young people received an elementary education. They learned reading, writing, arithmetic, and the geography of Palestine. Resignations began to fall off, and the experiment turned out rather well. The pedagogic methods were initially different from those normally used by the Palmakh. Instructors insisted on harsh discipline. But in the course of time the regular Palmakh instructional approach, based on persuasion and the awakening of understanding, was introduced to these units. One of the most difficult problems with these young people was that of family allowances. In the slums of Tel Aviv or Jerusalem a boy of sixteen made an important contribution to the family budget. However, the Palmakh simply could not solve this problem within its small budget. That was the principal reason for resignations from these units.

In the end the young people were apportioned among the companies. They received various nicknames, among them *Yalmakh* ("assault children"), since their ages were generally much lower than was usual for the Palmakh. Finally, the name "Paratroops" (because they had just dropped in) stuck, and in time the appellation was accepted for all new people in the formation.

Ultimately, with the successful absorption of hundreds of youths from the slums, the Palmakh proved that it was a first-rate educator, which must be regarded as one of its most outstanding achievements. Those who claimed that the Palmakh was a formation solely of an "elite" composed of high school graduates, people from the agricultural settlements, and the like—and that any attempt to apply Palmakh methods to ordinary youth was bound to end in failure—were given the lie.

The agreement on the Hakhsharot in 1944 did not completely solve that question, and there was no lack of difficulties and arguments. At times, discouraging conclusions were drawn regarding the preparatory groups' terms of service in the formation. One publication noted that according to members' statements, various Hakhsharot are experiencing one crisis after another because of ceaseless friction with the Palmakh. . . . Our life is the straight Palmakh routine without the least measure of preparatory training. . . . In spite of the kibbutz promise to involve [our] members in estab:ished branches of skilled agricultural labor, we have not gotten satisfaction.[17]

But there were also other opinions. As more experience was accumulated on the problem of caring for the Hakhsharot, the results became more satisfactory.

It should be noted that the issue of the preparatory groups was in no small way connected with the development of the Palmakh way of life. This unique style of living, in both its military and social manifestations, was one of the most important and characteristic aspects of the Palmakh image. It had the nature of a spontaneous creation by hundreds of people in their various camps; but the intentional, conscious cultivation by the Palmakh leaders is also not to be overlooked. The accouterments and manners of that way of life were later made the subject of literary works: the *finjan* (coffee pot), the campfire, the songs, the freedom of expression, the naturalness, the friendly relationship between officers and men. But it seems that the primal roots of origin and nourishment of the Palmakh way of life have not yet been sufficiently studied. Of course, it was a continuation of a similar style that had prevailed in Hashomer, the Field Squads, and the Hagana generally. But its unique characteristics derived from the kibbutz as a result of the influence in the Palmakh of the kibbutz people, the trend-setters in its ranks. The relationship created in the Palmakh between officers and men was akin to the typical relationship of comrades in a collective society—adjusted, of course, to the military structure. It may be asked where the chief influences on the kibbutz movement which led it to its mode of life (which in turn, had such a deep effect on the Palmakh) came from—but that task would be beyond the scope of the present work.

From the first, classical forms and models of practice were taken by the Palmakh from the so-called popular armies. The leftist, socialist coloration, the fruit of kibbutz influence, was clearly discernible in this regard. *Palmakh Bulletin*s from the World War II years are full of stories, examples, and current events from the popular-revolutionary armies—in Spain, Titoist Yugoslavia, the Chinese Communist Army, the Irish Sinn Fein, and above all the Red Army. The erroneous impression might be created that the Palmakh simply copied the experience of such forces. But the truth is that it gleaned and adjusted to its own needs the aspects and values that conformed to its thinking—a Palestinian kibbutz way of thinking, for the most part. At the foundation of this approach was the sense that the Palmakh was a pioneering body, carrying out the tasks that fell on the shoulders of every young Jew with a conscience.

But in addition to the national task, there was a widespread awareness that this pioneering force had the obligation somehow to embody the vision of a labor society in which equality, brotherliness, comradeship, and self-sacrifice would hold sway. These feelings found expression mainly among the young people of the Hakhsharot, as a result of the kibbutz movement's influence over city youth. One girl from that background wrote:

> You suddenly felt with all your being that here, here among these flimsy shacks on the edge of the desert and in dozens of other camps scattered over the face of the land, something big and vital was being created. A pioneer creation was emerging out of struggles and suffering, failures and joys, subtle creative activity, and endless spiritual tension toward the imperative. Its beginnings were small, but concealed within it there were mighty forces and powerful potentialities.[18]

A more theoretical expression was given the same thoughts in Palmakh pamphlets (especially those of B Company) in which the nature of the Palmakh was discussed. Labor and training, which had initially been so much under attack, became the guiding slogan and ensign. The Palmakh model was the "fighting worker"; equivalent to that ideal was all the social pathos it connoted. The Palmakh staff, on its part, aided the creation of a shared way of life, culture, and ideals by laying down suitable patterns. In a series of directives in 1945, strong emphasis was placed on educational and cultural work, an active *elected* unit cultural committee, and rules that expressed an attitude of equality between officers and men.

The Palmakh strove from the beginning to foster both military discipline and freedom and naturalness of relationships. It was difficult to find the golden path that would suit the concepts of social life of the people from the collective settlements who were in the formation, and still be valid for a military unit. While striving for such a solution, however, the Palmakh crystallized a system of social relationships (in line with what prevailed in the Hagana, but more far-reaching) which became a source of pride to the formation in the course of time. There was never blind obedience or a chasm between officer and recruit, as is the practice in most armies of the world.

The equal material conditions shared by both and the informal, direct relationship between them did not run counter to the natural distance that separated officer and men, which was determined by the officer's personality and the authority given him by the community. Yitzhak Sadeh stated that "our people see their officers daily at work, during recreation, in his quarters, and in his relationships with male and female members. In every instance, he must set an example. He possesses no higher privileges in compensation for the higher duties imposed upon him: greater responsibility and, in battle, extra danger."[19] It was very difficult to attain this ideal, and there were most certainly deviations from the principles. Some officers even tried to revolt against them. But generally the Palmakh was successful in molding a popular unit, whose basis of discipline rested on freedom and personal understanding, without surrendering authority or battle readiness.

The result of all this was the "spirit" of the Palmakh. It was characterized in a contemporary Palmakh publication as "a wonderfully free spirit, happy, permeated with brotherliness among comrades; a spirit of courage and heroism, of love of the country . . . a spirit of audacity and sacrifice. These are no mere phrases. Every one of us has acquired that spirit."[20]

This success is explainable, to a great degree, by the inclusion of a large number of girls in the Palmakh. In the first year of the existence of the encampments, they contained about ninety girls, fifteen in each company. When the preparatory groups joined up, this wall was breached, the limitations were canceled, and the number of women members reached approximately three hundred by 1944. Their influence on the Palmakh was very great. It is to their credit that the Palmakh became a military community, while at the beginning it had been a military unit.

The problem of the woman member burdened the commanders of the formation heavily. At the start, the women themselves had sought to be equal to the men in every activity. That approach had resulted in injuries to their health, resignations, and despair. After awhile, it became clear that if basic training were given in separate units, the girls would accomplish the same achievements as the men—but the amount of time required for it would be greater. The idea gradually took shape that equal training must be given the women in separate units. Nevertheless, every new wave of girl recruits went back and repeated the experiences of its predecessors, with the same failures.

The question of special skills also came under discussion. At first, the girls opposed specialization for fear that they would be shunted into areas of service like cooking, laundry, and clothing stores; then they rebelled against the idea that such services should be placed in charge of men when most of the people working in them were women.

In September 1943 a meeting was held at Mishmar Haemek

to sum up the attempt at absorbing women into the Palmakh, with many of the formation's commanding officers taking part. The conclusions of this meeting, which were accepted by the Palmakh officers, were: to give training in separate platoons; to train women officers for women's platoons; and to train as many women as possible in skills of communication, first aid, driving, reconnaissance, administration, welfare, and culture. No one disputed the assumption that in times of emergency women would take part in activities connected with combat operations and that there would be women with the physical prowess to participate in actual battle.

The women themselves, of course, did not view their role and place in the Palmakh from exactly the standpoint we have presented here. "Social influence," said one female member, "is a *byproduct* of the woman's presence in our midst. But by no means can it serve as a standard for her service in the Palmakh. I did not join the Palmakh to keep the jokes clean at the staff meetings."[21] But it is a fact that the social role of the Palmakh woman was to have an effect even on the combat readiness and spirit of the men.

In summary, the Palmakh embodied, within a military context, the values and ideals, philosophies and life styles which were characteristic of the kibbutz movement. It was born directly out of that movement, and its city members were markedly influenced by it. From several points of view, the Palmakh was a "fighting kibbutz" or a military collective or, more simply, a collectivist army. The distinct cultural and sociological nature of the Palestinian kibbutz stamped its seal upon the unique character of the Palmakh. It is doubtful whether there has ever existed a military body in Europe—underground, organized, and standing—in which the principle of material equality between officers and men has attained such outstanding expression, in which such importance has been given to education in the area of formal discipline, and in which woman has achieved equal status with man. The character of the kibbutz was reflected in the character of the Palmakh. And, in fact, the Palmakh was true home, real friend, and—as far as the individual's sense of belonging was concerned—serious competitor of the kibbutz itself, from which it had drawn its inspiration.

⚔ At the Parting of the Ways

The year 1944 was the year of hopes for a political settlement of the Palestine problem in a Zionist spirit—with the aid of friends of Zionism in England and the United States; but 1945 witnessed a great increase in tension, a piling up of massive obstacles, and the multiplication of bitter disappointments.

One of the most important developments that burst forth during those two years was the growth of American influence in the Middle East in general, and in Palestine affairs in particular. Under the pressure of the American Zionist Emergency Council (and especially that of one of its chairmen, Rabbi Abba Hillel Silver), the draft of a bill was submitted to both Houses of Congress on February 1, 1944, which included the demand for the opening of the gates of Palestine to Jewish immigration so as "ultimately" to turn the country into a free and democratic commonwealth. Silver did not think it important to obtain President Roosevelt's advance support for the proposed bill. This gave the anti-Zionists in the War Department an opportunity to remove the bill from the docket for alleged security reasons (in General Marshall's testimony before the Senate Committee). The main argument was that if a bill such as this were to pass, it would be a threat to peace in the Middle East and would make military operations difficult.

To pacify the Emergency Council for this setback, Roosevelt received Rabbis Wise and Silver (March 9, 1944), reiterated his sympathy with the cause of a Jewish national home for their benefit, and expressed his happiness that the gates of Palestine were "at present open to Jewish refugees." This last phrase was an allusion to the British notice to the agency on July 16, 1943, that refugees from Europe who succeeded in reaching Turkey would be allowed to enter Palestine (and their number would be deducted from the White Paper quota!). According to facts in Sharett's possession, Secretary of State Cordell Hull had intervened back in October 1943 on behalf of the Jews, and the British had informed the agency that immigration—within the context of still unused White Paper certificates—would continue even after March 31, 1944 (the date on which Jewish immigration was to cease altogether).

The worth of Roosevelt's pronouncement is testified to by the fact that United States ambassadors in the Arab capitals immediately hastened to explain to Arab political leaders that the president had spoken of a "national home" and not of a "commonwealth" (a term taken from the Biltmore Program), and that the United States, though it had never expressed agreement to the White Paper, had also expressed no reservations in regard to it.[22]

During the summer of 1944, the conventions of the two major American political parties were held in preparation for the coming presidential elections. Both of them proclaimed their support for the aspirations of Zionism. In a letter (October 15, 1944) to the Democratic Convention, President Roosevelt also employed the explicit concept of "a free and democratic Jewish commonwealth."

In May and June of 1944, at the time of the London visit of the new secretary of state, Edward Stettinius, America intervened directly on the issues of Palestine. The British told him of the partition plan they had in the hopper and added that such a plan would be carried out after the war. Stettinius passed this information on to his Zionist friends in the United States. They, however, were not at all enthusiastic about the partition plan and remained loyal to the program of a commonwealth in the whole of Palestine.[23]

Relations between the Zionist leaders and Stettinius cooled during the winter of 1944. The bill that had been drafted on Rabbi Silver's initiative and rejected early in the year, supposedly for military reasons, was reintroduced into both Houses of Congress on November 29, 1944. Once again, Rabbi Silver refused to sound out the president and the secretary of state. The bill was rejected (December 11), this time because of Stettinius's opposition to it. After this failure, and some very angry personal arguments, both Rabbi Silver and his opponent, Rabbi Wise, resigned their positions on the Emergency Council.

On his way home from the Yalta Conference (February 1945), Roosevelt met with Ibn Saud and spoke with him about the Palestine problem, among other subjects. Ibn Saud apparently threatened an Arab uprising if the Zionist program were put into effect. After Roosevelt had "discovered" the intensity of Arab opposition to Zionism, he backed off somewhat from his pro-Zionist proclamations. On April 5, 1945, seven days before his sudden death, he wrote a letter to Ibn Saud promising that he would do nothing that might be interpreted as a hostile act toward the Arab nation and that no change in the status of Palestine would occur without prior consultation with the Jews and the Arabs. To Judge Joseph Proskauer he remarked that, "on account of the Arab situation, nothing could be done in Palestine."[24]

Roosevelt's death brought Harry Truman to the presidency of the United States. The new president's actions conformed with the traditional American position on the Jewish question— America was prepared to exert friendly pressure on Great Britain in favor of a Zionist solution, as long as that action did not obligate the United States to commit its military power to battle. Despite its limitations, this position gave great help to the Zionist cause.

Until the assassination of Lord Moyne, there was a widespread feeling in Britain that after the war some basis other that the White Paper would be needed to solve the Palestine problem. Although partition had not been finally decided on (the decision was postponed until after the victory), Churchill himself, as well as Colonial Secretary Stanley (a Conservative), favored that course. The Labour party proclaimed anew its full support of Zionism at the party conventions of 1943. At the 1944 convention, support was even voiced for the Biltmore Program as well as for a demand to remove the Arab population from Palestine. This last provision was introduced by initiative other than that of the Zionist Executive Office in London, which opposed that part of the Labour resolution.

An important achievement in the Zionist political battle was the creation of the Jewish Brigade. Sharett had striven for the founding of the brigade back in the autumn of 1942. His proposal had then been rejected by General H. M. Wilson. But Sharett did not slacken his efforts to bring about a Jewish participation of real weight in the anti-Nazi war. Those efforts were fruitless as long as the front line remained near the Arab countries, since the makers of British policy were still influenced by the same pro-Arab considerations as before. However, with the invasions of Sicily and Italy in the summer and fall of 1943, the situation at the front was drastically altered. It became easier to involve Jewish detachments in the liberation of Europe, where millions of Jews were being exterminated by the enemy.

On November 26, 1943, Weizmann and Professor Namier met with British War Secretary Grigg, who promised to carry the proposal for the creation of a Jewish fighting force to the war cabinet. In March 1944 Weizmann again met with Grigg and also wrote a memorandum on the subject of the brigade. On June 21 Grigg informed him that he himself had taken a stand and was now awaiting the decision of his fellow members of the government. Weizmann then addressed a letter to Churchill, who gave an encouraging reply (August 5, 1944) in which he even showed an interest in the proposal for the brigade's flag. On August 17 Grigg informed Weizmann that the program had been accepted—except that it was made clear that the Jews would be required to mobilize 3,500 men and 150 officers for the brigade.

This stipulation was a result of the pressure exerted by the command in Cairo, which opposed a Jewish force for many reasons. Chief among those reasons was its own reluctance to part with the small Jewish units scattered throughout the military zone of the Middle East which were fulfilling vital auxiliary roles. The command feared that creation of the brigade would lead to the concentration of all these Jews into the new unit. The agency pressed the British government to make a concession on this point, because the chances of an enlistment of such magnitude from the Yishuv were most slight. And the government finally agreed to establish the brigade mostly from existing units.

The establishment of the Jewish Brigade was received with mixed feelings in the Agency Executive. The well-known phrase "too little and too late" described the situation. Some members of the Agency Executive (Gruenbaum, for example) opposed the stationing of the brigade as an army of occupation in Europe. People of this opinion were moved by two reasons. They were revolted by the idea of Jewish contact, even as conquerors, with the Germans; and they feared that the English would intentionally remove the best of the Jewish youth from Palestine at the very moment when the political fate of the country was to be decided. The opinion was also expressed that the English had decided to set up a "fighting" force for the Jews only at the war's end, when the discharge of soldiers from the British Army was already under consideration, so that the force would take part in as few combat operations as possible. Gruenbaum and Rabbi Maimon viewed this as a typical English deception. Even Sharett himself, the chief sponsor and builder of the brigade, had his own doubts. But the political achievement was, nevertheless, great, and the weight of it overcame all the various doubts and fears.

The Jewish Brigade was, without a doubt, the greatest political accomplishment of the still basically pro-English Zionist diplomacy during the war years. Zionism was really not favored with a superabundance of achievements during that period.

But the value of the brigade as a political factor was seriously diminished by the assassination of Lord Moyne. That event brought about a change in the already cool attitude taken toward Zionism by the British government in general and even by Churchill himself. It must be reemphasized that Zionist policy was at that time built on the assumption that there was a chance to realize at least part of the Biltmore Program and to obtain concessions, like the cancellation of the White Paper, through various means of pressure; or, if worse came to worst, to achieve a "good" partition plan. But for that, the support of British political leaders was essential. The friendship of Winston Churchill, however, real or imagined, was undermined by the murder of his personal friend Lord Moyne.[25] Even the short period of the *Saison,* during which cooperation between the agency and the British in Palestine prevailed, did not change the situation fundamentally.[26]

With the end of the war and Labour's rise to power[27] (May–July 1945), Zionism found itself in a new situation. The full extent of the Holocaust in Europe became known; the remaining refugees began to crowd the displaced persons' camps, and their suffering was great. Theoretical questions, even those that had been foreseen, became very real, became burning issues. It was apparent that the reality was starker than the most dreadful nightmares could have portrayed. It became obvious that the White Paper had been the expression of a clearly thought-out political policy and not a chance accident caused by an appeasement policy whose time had passed. The activities of the breakaway groups in Palestine put an end to any chance— insofar as such still existed or could be created with the rise of Labour to power—to undermine the White Paper by means of negotiation.

The agency and its security arm, the Hagana, had argued as early as 1943, at the time of the crisis in relations with the British, that with the close of the war, Zionism would be confronted with two choices: a pro-Zionist solution for which Zionism would be called upon to fight with all its might; or a struggle against an anti-Zionist solution—the continuation of the White Paper in its original or in a revised form. Both possibilities were based on the desire to maintain the tie with the British.

Zionism reached that crossroads with the coming of the Labour party into power. Many factors—some that we have mentioned (like the empire's interests and security, the operations of the separatist organizations, and so forth) and some that we have not (because they were still not fully felt during the war years)—led the British government to a decision unfavorable to Zionism. At the same time, the problem of the Jewish refugees in Europe had greatly worsened. Redoubled urgency was added to the Zionist pressure for a positive solution. That pressure did not work. There remained only the possibility of battle to break down the bar that was closing the gates of Palestine.

The interlude of the war years, with its opportunities, its achievements, and its failures, had come to an end. Its most significant accomplishment—the jelling of military force in the Jewish Brigade, the Supernumerary Police Force, and above all in the independent internal force of the Palmakh—contributed immensely to the capability of the Zionist self-defense to conduct an anti-British battle. The war ended in 1945. At the same time, the limited, partial, and problematical cooperation with the British also ended. A bloody five-year episode had reached its conclusion. The struggle began.

Summary

During the World War II period, the leadership of the Zionist movement tried to reach an agreement with Great Britain on the future of Palestine. The White Paper of 1939 did not succeed in landing a death blow on the traditional conception of Zionist policy, which looked upon England fundamentally as an ally in the building of Jewish Palestine.

Hopes for such an agreement rested on several assumptions, some real, some imaginary. First, it was felt that England would need Palestinian Jewish manpower during the war to reinforce British strength in the Middle East. This manpower, nationalistic and well organized, would supposedly serve as a pressure factor in altering British policy. Second, it was assumed that the friends of Zionism in England, who had risen to high positions of power in the war period, would succeed—with the aid of constant political pressure on the part of the Jews—in undermining the foundations of the White Paper. Third, it would be possible to gain the sympathy of the United States, her Jewry, and her government to the Zionist cause. With the aid of the all-powerful lever of America's political influence, the direction of Britain's Palestine policy would be changed. Fourth, the pressure of the Jewish refugees during and after the war—and the pressure of the Holocaust, when details of it became known in November 1942—would influence British public opinion and lead to a change in British policy. Indeed, one could not deny some political effect to the Jewish war effort, or to highly placed pro-Zionist statesmen in England— to Churchill, for example; and the same is true of the influence of the United States.

One of the most interesting conclusions flowing from the material before us is that agreement to a pro-Jewish solution—or an approach to one—was sometimes closer than people supposed at the time. We have enumerated several instances where it was just a step from failure to significant success.

The first instance was at the time of the negotiations on the Jewish division between May 1940 and March 1941. There is no denying that the division was very close to realization— at any rate, the failure of that proposal was not a foregone conclusion. And if the agency had really succeeded at it, it would certainly have been a sizable political accomplishment.

The second opportunity came when the British Cabinet Committee on Palestine was set up, in the middle of 1943. The "good" partition plan proposed by that committee was an expression of the pro-Zionist component within the English government. Churchill's friendship was also a factor, in spite of all its reservations. On the eve of the Moyne assassination, the British statesman again took a sympathetic stand on Zionism. We cannot know, of course, whether promises of the type then given would have been put into effect at the proper time. But there is no doubt that when they were given, it was possible to see in them an opportunity for the future. British foreign policy was fraught with contradictions. The attempts of Zionist diplomacy to exploit those contradictions should not be judged as a lost cause from the start.

One other instance in which the chances for a British decision favorable to Zionism came to light was the plan for self-defense in the Diaspora in 1944. Large-scale assistance to the Diaspora would doubtless have affected the political situation. And it was only at the last minute that this further attempt to break through the wall of hostility failed.

But even considering all the favorable factors, Zionist policy also contained a basic measure of self-delusion. It drove its tent pegs into the sands of Anglo-American friendship to an extent which is hard to look upon as realistic, even in the best possible circumstances. The Biltmore-Jerusalem Program, in Ben-Gurion's understanding of it, was one result of this pipe dream. Transferring millions of Jewish refugees rapidly with the help of the great powers and the transformation of the whole of Palestine into a Jewish state by force of this act in a very short period—that kind of talk was not at all realistic in light of the actual international possibilities. The sole value of the Biltmore Program was psychological. It turned the powerful political desires of the people into a lofty banner, but it did not succeed in hastening their accomplishment.

The Zionist leadership could point to only one serious achievement in its favor in the political field: after 1943 the British government no longer disputed the proposition that the White Paper had given up the ghost. This partial success, at least, was mostly due to the unrelenting pressure of Zionist diplomacy. The only question was what would take its place: something similar or even worse, or a more positive solution from the Zionist point of view?

The practical result of the Zionist Executive's efforts to approach a solution to its political problems during the war was rather poor. The Jewish mobilization effort sent 26,000 Jewish men and women into the British Army as soldiers. It brought honor to the name of the Jewish people in the eyes of the non-Nazi world. It made it possible for Jewry as such to participate, though in modest proportions, in the struggle of the enlightened world against Hitler. But this mobilization bore no political fruit. At the most it may be said that if it had not been for the mobilization, worse things would have happened to the Yishuv than actually did. The enlistment of tens of thousands of Jews prevented the British administration and army from acting against the Jews as they, perhaps, wanted to do during 1943–1945.

The establishment of the Jewish Brigade—the outstanding event in the history of Yishuv mobilization—was chiefly a moral victory. The brigade's practical weight in the diplomatic area was not great, and we can find no effect on British policy from that direction. The value of the brigade came to the fore after the war, in plainly anti-British activities such as aiding Jews to separate themselves from the DP camps, unofficial immigration, and arms acquisition.

In the area of diplomatic negotiation and relations with the Palestine government and with British military bodies, the Zionist leadership was not successful in piercing the wall of enmity during the war years, despite manifold Jewish efforts. Moreover, there was a widespread feeling that the leadership stood utterly helpless before the disaster that struck European Jewry. All efforts came to nothing. The Allied governments did not want to offer any real help to the Jewish people, not even the possibility of helping themselves. Conditions did not allow the leadership of a small nation to surmount the wartime routine of the great powers.

As for internal relations, the separatists' operations during 1944 were able to frustrate any chance that still existed for altering the nature of British policy by peaceful means. It is true that those chances cannot be estimated. But if there were such chances before the separatist operations (particularly before the Moyne assassination), they were completely lost during 1944.

However, the Zionist leadership was diligent not only about nursing relations with the British along. Its concern was—to some extent or other, and accompanied by knotty problems—for the fostering of an independent security force for the Yishuv.

There is no doubt that the military training received by Jewish soldiers in the British Army was vital for the self-defense force. However, that training was not given within a Jewish-controlled framework; it was, therefore, impossible to employ it according to the wishes of the Jewish leadership. Years passed before the Second World War's military preparation was utilized within the structure of the Hagana. In the end it was the Hagana which exploited the soldiers' military training, rather than Hagana's simply being taken over by the returning British-trained veterans. The Hagana's development during the war, as we have seen, was not uniform. Here, too, the problematic partnership with the British in recruitment made it possible for the Hagana to realize plans and develop organization, administration, and skills which could not previously have been dreamt of.

The decisive period in this area was 1942, when Rommel threatened the conquest of the British Middle East. After that turning point, there was never a retreat to earlier patterns of organization and thought. From then on frameworks and patterns of life and organization were established, and they facilitated the strengthening of the independent defense force and the transformation of the entire Hagana into a substantial military power. That force was to serve as the security arm for a political line of action.

The Palmakh holds the chief and central position among the new branches developed during the war years. The creation of that body was the most outstanding and permanently valuable achievement of Zionist military policy. The founding of the Palmakh was the embodiment of the political leadership's fear that all attempts to reach a satisfactory agreement with the British government would come to naught. Were all else to fail, the leadership—or more correctly a part of the leadership (the entire Left and a part of the nonsocialist camp)—sought to have a force that would constitute a security arm to support diplomatic activity. In other words, leadership in both the agency and the Histadrut Actions Committee did not overlook the possibility of having to fight the British after the war. The Palmakh was established and reinforced in the light of three factors: the desire on the part of many (as far back as the 1936–1939 Arab rebellion) for an independent defense force that would be concentrated, mobilized, and ready for action; the possibility of participating in actual military actions at the side of the British (a hope that was, for the most part, frustrated); and consideration for the future, which held in store either the defense of some political gain, if such were attained, or the necessity of a battle with the English.

The establishment of the Palmakh was not a single act, nor did one man or one movement take part in it alone. Nevertheless, there is no doubt that Kibbutz Meuhad contributed the heaviest share to both the shaping of the framework itself and to the protection of the glowing coal, in times of crisis, from hostile elements. It is likewise beyond doubt that Hashomer Hatzair was a full partner in the building and maintenance of the structure. Eliyahu Golomb and the circle of officers around him also contributed a great deal to the rise of the Palmakh in its first stages of development.

On the other hand, there were right-wing circles in the Yishuv who either did not desire the enlargement of the Palmakh or did not ascribe importance to it—whether because they were not ready for a fight with the English or because they regarded the Palmakh as a rather leftist body. Within the Histadrut, the support for the Palmakh was also not homogeneous. The Palmakh, for all its stress on national unity and its emphasis on the duty of obedience to the national institutions, was nevertheless plainly leftist. Organizational patterns, style of life, cultural orientation, modes of existence, the very fact of being stationed in the collectives—everything lent the formation the air of a "kibbutz army." There was also no doubt about the political tendencies of the majority of its members.

The history of the Palmakh is pictured differently today from what may be gathered from earlier publications. Historical myths (like the participation in the invasion of Syria, the mystery of the disappearance of the Twenty-three, and the Arabist operation in Syria) emerge as minor operations whose influence on the course of events in the war was inconsequential, though they were carried out with great sacrifice. But that does not diminish the spiritual effect of those operations—their most important aspect was the strength and devotion of a few. We have already noted that this impression was more important for the history of the Palmakh and the molding of its power than were the dry facts of the operations themselves.

The renewal of the Palmakh in 1942 came when the structure was in danger of final disbandment. Partnership with the British was the factor which made possible the development of the Palmakh during and after the year of El Alamein.

The work-training camps also appear in a different light today. Most of the members of the Palmakh, and some of the political bodies which supported it, opposed the creation of those camps at the time. Only by large efforts at persuasion, and after grave crises, did the Palmakh accept the idea of the camps. The same is true of 1943, which was later to be remembered by the Palmakh members as a year of entrenchment and development, while in fact it was a period of profound and repeated crisis. All these facts, plus the debates about the Palmakh's future, point up the reality that the Palmakh passed through a difficult period during the years from 1941 through 1945. It was only then that the formation attained patterns which were never again qualitatively altered until the War of Independence, when it became the cornerstone for the building of the Israeli Army.

It was rescued from crisis, then, by these elements which worked in combination: surrender of the concept of a fighting elite in favor of a popular militia unit; acceptance of the rotation system, so that members would be replaced after two years of service; expansion of the role of women in the Palmakh; and the decision of the pioneering youth movements to send the members of their preparatory groups (Hakhsharot) into the Palmakh.

The establishment of the Palmakh and the strengthening of the Hagana enabled the Jewish leadership after World War II to pass from diplomatic attempts at regaining British support to a period of resistance and anti-British struggle and to the fight for an independent Jewish state in Palestine.

Appendix I

First segment of MacDonald's statements in the session of the Saint James Conference, February 14, 1939. From the Zionist Archives, S25-7632.

🖅 *Extract from the Minutes of the Saint James Conference*

14.2.1939. St. James.

Mr. MacDonald opened the proceedings at 4:30 P.M. by remarking that the subject for discussion at this meeting, which was the strategic issue, arose out of his reference at a previous meeting to the importance of maintaining generally friendly relations with the Arab States of the Middle East. He therefore thought it would perhaps be preferable for him to open this afternoon's discussion, which was unfortunately by no means an academic question. The security of British forces in the Middle East and lines of communication with India and the Far East depended to a considerable extent on our being able to persuade the Egyptian and other Governments in that part of the world to fulfill their treaty engagements where these were in existence, or otherwise to maintain a friendly neutrality. For example, Egypt commanded the air and sea route to the East and the air and land route to the Sudan and Africa, and contained the land base for the defence of the Suez Canal and the only naval base (Alexandria) suitable for the defence of the Eastern Mediterranean. Iraq commanded the air and land routes to the East and was the centre of important oil interests there and Iran. A hostile Saudi Arabia could threaten lines of communication through Trans-Jordan to Iraq, and the Aden Protectorate. His Majesty's Government's advice was that in the event of war Ibn Saud could without assistance cause us great embarrassment if he so desired, and with the support of a hostile Power could do very serious damage.

It was necessary not to exaggerate, and he wished to maintain a detached view, but he must emphasize that a great deal depended in the event of war on the active support of our allies in the Middle East and the friendship of the remaining States. The strength of the British forces in the Middle East and their dispositions were all made on this assumption. If this assumption were incorrect, and if we must contemplate even the risk that one or more of these States might be neutral or, at worst, hostile, our land, air and naval forces in the Middle East would have to be greatly increased as soon as possible.

According to His Majesty's Government's estimate, it would be necessary to reckon with this potential hostility, and to make this readjustment, if the States of the Middle East were tried too hard in the matter of British policy in Palestine. Their Governments, even if willing, would be inhibited from co-operating with us by the force of hostile public opinion which would be aroused.

Moreover, in the eventuality which he had just described it would be necesary to assume an extension of anti-British feeling beyond the Middle East. For example, there was the question of Northern Africa. In the event of war with a Mediterranean Power, valuable support could be looked for from the Moslem populations of Northern Africa, encouraged by Egypt, only if British-Moslem relations generally were good. This potentiality too would be destroyed by a continuation of the estrangement over Palestine. Similarly, it would be necessary to postulate a good deal of unrest among the Moslems of India which could be exploited by parties interested in preventing Indian cooperation with the rest of the British Empire in a crisis.

His Majesty's Government had received strong and unanimous warnings from all their sources of information in the Near and Middle East and in India as to the probable effects on public opinion in those countries of the pursuance of certain policies in

Palestine. The military advisers had in turn given a strong warning to the Cabinet.

He was well aware that there were other considerations. In the event of war, American feeling towards Great Britain was of great importance, and policy in Palestine was a considerable factor in the formation of that opinion. His Majesty's Government certainly kept this fact in mind. But it might be that the crucial moment would be in the early stages of a possible war, in which the theatre of war in the Near and Middle East would be as important, perhaps more important, than any. In certain circumstances this area might be the "Achilles' Heel." He had emphasized at an earlier meeting that the defeat of the British Empire would be, at least for a time, an equal disaster for the Jews.

Appendix II

A telegram from Wingate. For understandable reasons, it was sent over the signature of Dov Joseph. It came in response to Sharett's telegram of February 11, 1939, in which Wingate was requested to wire arguments favorable to the Zionist position in the negotiations with British military elements. From files of the Zionist Archives.

FEBRUARY 12, 1939

166

YOUR [TELEGRAM] 188 VIEW EVIDENTLY HELD BY MILITARY AUTHORI-TIES: (FIRST) EGYPT BEST BASE [FOR] PROTECTION [OF] BRITISH IN-TERESTS NEAR EAST; (SECOND) IMPOSSIBLE [TO] PROTECT PIPE LINE BY MILITARY MEANS; THEREFORE MUST RELY [ON] ARAB FRIENDSHIP; (THIRD) WAR MIGHT COME THIS YEAR, WOULD TAKE LONG TIME [TO] ESTABLISH JEWISH ARMY ADEQUATE [TO] PROTECT INTERESTS [IN] NEAR EAST; MOREOVER RELUCTANT [TO] TRUST JEWS OVERMUCH, FEAR MIGHT EVENTUALLY TURN AGAINST BRITISH. WE SHOULD ARGUE FOLLOWING: (FIRST) NO CERTAINTY WAR IMMINENT, HITLER NOT READY [TO] TACKLE EAST AND WEST; POLISH-RUSSIAN RAPPROCHE-MENT UPSET HIS PLANS; IN ANY EVENT WILL BE TIME [TO] ESTABLISH STRONG JEWISH FORCE BECAUSE DISTURBANCES PROVED JEWS CAN TRAIN QUICKER BRITISH SOLDIERS; MUCH SAFER [TO] RELY [ON] JEWS THAN UNTRUSTWORTHY FRIENDSHIP [WITH] ARABS PARTICULARLY [IN] VIEW [OF] JEWISH DEPENDENCE [ON] BRITAIN; (SECOND) JEWS [OF] PALESTINE BETTER FITTED ESTABLISH WAR INDUSTRY THAN EGYP-

TIANS, WHO LACK TECHNICAL EXPERTS, SCIENTIFIC ABILITY; (THIRD) JEWS CAN ESTABLISH AND MAN ARMS FACTORY [IN A] COUPLE [OF] MONTHS WITH BRITISH HELP, EGYPTIANS CANNOT; (FOURTH) JEWS WOULD PROVIDE LARGE FUNDS, ESTABLISH JEWISH ARMY IF GOVERN- MENT EMBARKED [ON] ZIONIST POLICY; EGYPTIANS UNWILLING [TO] PROVIDE CAPITAL [FOR] MILITARY PURPOSES; (FIFTH) EGYPT CANNOT PROVIDE MILITARY MANPOWER, PAST HISTORY PROVED EGYPTIANS NOT SOLDIERS; WAR OFFICE KNOWS THIS; RECENT DISTURBANCES PROVED JEWS EXCELLENT SOLDIERS, UNQUESTIONABLY SUPERIOR [TO] ARABS; JEWS HAVE VAST RESERVE MANPOWER CAPABLE [OF] HOLD[ING] NEAR EAST AFTER RAPID INSTRUCTION; (SIXTH) BRITISH MISTAKEN [TO] TRUST ARAB FRIENDSHIP, WHICH WILL DISAPPEAR MOMENT THINGS TURN AGAINST BRITISH; (SEVENTH) [IN] VIEW [OF] ATTITUDE [OF] TURKEY, UNITED STATES, H[IS] M[AJESTY'S] G[OVERN- MENT] CANNOT YIELD COMPLETELY; ARABS WHO WILL INEVITABLY REMAIN UNSATISFIED THEREFORE WILL BECOME DISLOYAL IF OP- PORTUNITY [OF] MOMENTARY BRITISH WEAKNESS PRESENTS ITSELF; (EIGHTH) PAN ARAB POLICY ANTAGONISES TURKEY, WHICH [IS] MORE IMPORTANT MILITARY FACTOR; (NINTH) ARABS ONLY NUISANCE NOT REAL MILITARY FORCE; IF BRITISH APPEAR STRONG, SUPPORTED BY ARMY [OF] 50,000 JEWS, ARABS WILL NOT DARE ATTACK BRITISH OR UNDERMINE INTERESTS NEAR EAST; OTHERWISE WILL.

[signed] JOSEPH

The second half of Weizmann's note to MacDonald of March 10, 1939 (Weizmann Archives, 1939). In its first three articles, the note mentioned the fact that the agency rejected the British proposals back on February 27, 1939. However, due to assurances by the British government that its proposals were not representative of a hard decision that had already been taken, the Jews were willing to continue the negotiations. In the meantime, British spokesmen had offered nothing new in the discussions and had only repeated their proposals to give Palestine independence with an Arab majority. However, the wording of the Palestine Mandate did not in the least obligate Britain to establish Palestine as an independent state.

The note continues:

4. Moreover, the injunction of Article 2 of the Mandate to develop self-governing institutions must be read in the light of the immediately preceding injunction to place the country "under such political, administrative, and economic conditions as will secure the establishment of the Jewish National Home." The Royal Commission stated that "unquestionably . . . the primary purpose of the Mandate, as expressed in its preamble and its articles, is to promote the establishment of the Jewish National Home" (Report, page 39). In the submission of the Jewish Delegation, this involves the positive obligation to facilitate Jewish immigration in accordance with the principle of absorptive capacity, as laid down by the Council of the

League of Nations, and the encouragement of close settlement by Jews on the land, without discriminatory or restrictive measures calculated to hinder such settlement and reduce the absorptive capacity.

5. The Jewish Delegation feel bound at this stage to formulate certain principles the acceptance of which they regard as an essential preliminary to the discussion of any concrete scheme:

(a) In any scheme for the government of Palestine effect shall be given to the obligations contained in the Balfour Declaration and the Mandate, and the continuation and growth of the Jewish National Home shall be secured. In particular, in pursuance of these obligations, facilities for Jewish immigration and land settlement shall be assured.

(b) The Mandate shall not be terminated save on conditions which would secure the promotion of the Jewish National Home as indicated above.

(c) No independent unitary Palestine State shall be set up without the consent of both Jews and Arabs.

6. If these principles are accepted, the Jewish Delegation would offer the following suggestions as a basis for discussion:

(a) During the Mandatory regime, self-governing institutions to be developed on a basis of parity as between Jews and Arabs, to ensure the non-domination of either race by the other. With regard to land settlement, while the Jewish Delegation could not agree to any negative policy of restriction and discrimination, they are anxious to co-operate with His Majesty's Government in a development scheme designed to promote the utilisation of the productive resources of Palestine in the interests of both Arabs and Jews.

(b) In the event of the termination of the Mandate otherwise than by the establishment, with the consent of both Jews and Arabs, of a unitary independent State, the following two alternatives might be explored:

(i) the establishment of a Jewish State in a part of Palestine with an area adequate to allow for further immigration and land settlement on a substantial scale;

(ii) the setting up of an administration for Palestine based on a federal arrangement with full Jewish control over immigration, and with federal institutions based on parity, always allowing for the adequate growth of the Jewish National Home.

7. It will be recalled that His Majesty's Government, in announcing, in the White Paper of July 1937, their acceptance in principle of the scheme proposed by the Royal Commission, stated that among the advantages of that proposal were:

  (i) that the National Home would be relieved "from any possibility of its being subjected in future to Arab rule";

  (ii) that "it would convert the Jewish National Home into a Jewish State with full control over immigration";

  (iii) that "the Jews would at last cease to live a minority life."

8. The Jewish Delegation would be glad to be informed whether the suggestions outlined above offer, in view of His Majesty's Government, a basis for further discussion.

I have the honour to be, Sir,
Your obedient Servant,
[signed] Ch. Weizmann

Appendix IV

The final British proposals of March 15, 1939 (Zionist Archives, 25-7631). For a comparison with the wording of the White Paper of May 17, 1939, see Chapter 1, "The Saint James Conference."

✄ Proposals Submitted by the British Government on March 15th, 1939

(1) His Majesty's Government's ultimate objective is the establishment of an independent Palestine State, possibly of a federal nature, in such treaty relations with Great Britain as would provide satisfactorily for the commercial and strategic interests of both countries. This would involve the termination of the Mandate.

(2) It is not the objective of His Majesty's Government that Palestine should become a Jewish State or an Arab State; nor do they regard their pledges to either Jews or Arabs as requiring them to promote either of these alternatives. It should be a State in which Arabs and Jews share in government in such a way as to ensure that the essential interests of each are safeguarded.

(3) The constitution of the independent State would be drafted in due course by a National Assembly of the people of Palestine, either elected or nominated as may be agreed. His Majesty's Government to be represented on the Assembly and to be satisfied as to the provisions of the constitution, and in particular as regards—

(a) the security of and access to the Holy Places;

(b) the protection of the different communities in Palestine in accordance with the obligations of His Majesty's Government to both Arabs and Jews, and as regards securing the special position in Palestine of the Jewish National Home.

His Majesty's Government would also require to be satisfied that the interests of certain foreign countries in Palestine, for the preservation of which the Government are at present responsible, were adequately safeguarded.

(4) The establishment of the independent State to be preceded by a transitional period throughout which His Majesty's Government, as the Mandatory Power, would retain responsibility for the government of the country.

(5) As soon as peace and order are sufficiently restored, the first steps are to be taken towards giving the people of Palestine, during the transitional period, an increasing part in the government of the country.

The first stage of this process would be as follows:

In the *legislative* sphere—The addition of a certain number of Palestinians, by nomination, to the Advisory Council; the numbers of Arab and Jewish representatives being fixed approximately in proportion to their respective populations, and so as to give a majority of Palestinian members.

In the *executive* sphere—The selection of Palestinian members of the Advisory Council to sit on the Executive Council; the numbers of Arab and Jewish representatives being fixed approximately in proportion to their respective populations, and so that half the members of the Council would be Palestinians.

The second stage would be:

In the *legislative* sphere—The conversion of the Advisory Council into a Legislative Council with an elected Palestinian element and with certain powers reserved to the High Commissioner.

In the *executive* sphere—Certain Departments would be placed in charge of Palestinian members of the Executive Council.

Then a third stage: Further advances towards self-government in the transitional period might be in the direction of increasing the powers of the Legislative Council and placing more Departments under the charge of Palestinian members of the Executive Council.

(6) His Majesty's Government would be prepared, if conditions in Palestine permit, to hold elections for a Legislative Council within two years. The composition and powers of the Council would be a

matter for consultation between the different parties. Beyond this no time limit can be fixed now for the advance from stage to stage of constitutional development in the transitional period; nor can a date be fixed for the end of the transitional period and the establishment of the independent State. His Majesty's Government would hope that the whole process could be completed in ten years, but this must depend upon the situation in Palestine and upon the success of the various constitutional changes during the transitional period, and the likelihood of effective co-operation in government by the people of Palestine. His Majesty's Government could not contemplate relinquishing all responsibility for the government of Palestine unless they were assured that the measure of agreement between the communities in Palestine was such as to make good government possible.

As regards immigration:

(1) Immigration during the next five years would be at a rate which, if economic absorptive capacity permits, would bring the Jewish population up to approximately one-third of the population. Taking into account the expected natural increase of the Arab and Jewish populations, and the number of illegal Jewish immigrants (estimated at 40,000) now in the country, this would entail the admission of some 75,000 immigrants over the next five years, who would be admitted as follows:

10,000 per year, and in addition 25,000 Jewish refugees (special consideration being given to refugee children and dependents). The refugees to be admitted as soon as the High Commissioner is satisfied that adequate provision is secured for them.

(2) The existing machinery for ascertaining economic absorptive capacity would be retained, and the High Commissioner would have the ultimate responsibility for deciding what the economic capacity allowed. Before a decision was reached, appropriate Jewish and Arab representatives would be consulted.

(3) After the period of five years further Jewish immigration would only be permitted subject to the acquiescence of the Arabs as well as of the Jews and the British authorities. The question to be discussed and settled through the medium of the appropriate constitutional organs functioning during the transitional period, or by means of consultation between His Majesty's Government and representatives of the Arabs and the Jews.

(4) His Majesty's Government are determined to check illegal immigration, and further preventive measures are being adopted and will be strictly enforced. The numbers of any Jewish illegal immi-

grants who, despite these measures, succeed in coming into the country and who cannot be deported would be deducted from the yearly quotas.

Finally, with regard to land sales, the High Commissioner would be given general powers to prohibit and regulate transfers of land. The High Commissioner would be instructed to fix areas in which transfer was to be permitted freely, regulated or prohibited, in the light of the findings of the Peel and Woodhead Reports. He would retain this power throughout the transitional period.

Appendix V

Conversation with Lt. Gen. Giffard, G. O. C., Palestine, June 14, 1940. From the Zionist Archives 82411, old numbering.

The General Officer Commanding, having welcomed the representatives, said that they had parted previously on the understanding that the representatives would again consult their organisations as a result of previous conversations, particularly with regard to his request to be given the numbers of illegal arms existing. He hoped that they would now be able to give him a favourable answer.

Mr. Shertok said that they had come to explain the position frankly. He wished to say first that he was extremely distressed that there should be any differences between the Jewish representatives and the G. O. C. at the present time. There were, however, certain things which must be cleared up. The question put to them regarding the numbers of illegal arms had placed them in a very difficult position. He had mentioned at the previous meeting the possibility of their being unable to discover the numbers. They were representatives of legal bodies, and as such, it was impossible for them to have any knowledge of an organisational connection with the subject. They realized that these were extraordinary times and that extraordinary measures might be necessary. It would be a quite unprecedented step for the official leaders of Jewish bodies to start enquiries about the numbers of illegal arms. They would have to appeal to settlements and individuals for the information, and ask them to trust the leaders as regards the use which was made of the information. They feared that their request might be met with refusal. Mr. Shertok reminded the G. O. C. what he had said previously, that he would make no promises as to how he would use the information if it was given him.

The G. O. C., intervening, said that he had promised that a reasonable and sensible proportion of the arms should be retained and that there should be no reduction in the Jewish Settlement Police. If arms were declared he would not, of course, search as the result of information, but the remainder of the arms must, however, be handed in, especially machineguns and bombs. He would adjust the distribution of arms as he thought fit. *Mr. Shertok* said that the disclosure of the number of arms held on such terms really brought them back to the original question, i.e., that of partial disarmament. They had already given the answer on this point. They could not accept the responsibility of asking their people to surrender arms. It was impossible for them to ask for figures on these conditions, and, if they did so, they would only meet with refusal and be faced with a disastrous deadlock between the leaders and the Jewish Community. *The G. O. C.* said that it had been impressed upon him that the Jews were a highly disciplined community and would follow their leaders, and that he did not see that such a deadlock must necessarily arise. *Mr. Shertok* said, that if they had an assurance that no searches would be made for the arms, and that no change in the position would be made, they could then ask for the numbers. *The G. O. C.* said that if the numbers were given, he would of course proceed to decide an allotment or reduction as he thought advisable. He was not going to give that up. *Mr. Shertok* said that in that case they were unable to help.

The G. O. C. said that he was most disappointed with the answer given. He had endeavoured to persuade the Jewish representatives by argument to help in this question, but had apparently failed entirely. What he really wanted to know was whether the Jewish representatives were genuinely anxious to help the Government and the Allies in the prosecution of the war. A great deal of lip-service was being paid to cooperation. It was impossible to pick up a paper in Palestine (for example, this morning's edition of "Palestine Post") without finding articles, statements and speeches by members of the Jewish community, saying that the Jews were ready to cooperate to defeat the Germans and of course now the Italians. What were the facts in Palestine? The Government had asked for assistance in forming the Auxiliary Pioneer Corps. Not only was there little assistance given, but a great deal of active propaganda made against the enlistment of Jews in this unit. If they were, as they said, a hundred percent out to help, they should have welcomed such an opportunity. Secondly, from the information at his disposal, Jews had made efforts to prevent Polish and Czechoslovakian nationals from enlisting in the armies those countries were trying to form from the relics of their forces. Thirdly, they had assured him the other day that there was no one in the Jewish community who would dream of taking part in fifth column activities, and if there was such a traitor in the midst, he would soon be discovered and eliminated. Yet illegal broadcasting with anti-Government tone (largely all its material was being used by German propagandists against us), remains active. He could not, in fact did not, believe that any real attempt had been made to stop it. The identity of those running it must be known to numbers of Jews. Did they think that he could have any confidence in their assurance regarding the fifth columnists? Now they refused to assist in the maintenance of the security of the country by disclosing the illegal hoards of arms they held, in spite of the promise that they should keep a sensible proportion of these arms, and settlement police should not be reduced. He was left with the strong impression that they were only prepared to help on conditions, and not to give a wholehearted unconditional assistance. To win the present war everyone who is really on the side of the Allies must put forward every ounce of energy regardless of all else. Those who did not were definitely hindering the prosecution of the war. He was certain that the rank and file of the Jewish community was really anxious to help in any way they could. From the present attitude of the representatives, it might appear to an outsider that the leaders were subordinating this urge to help and the wider issues of winning the war to their ambitions. He could not believe that they intended to give such an impression. He would tell them now that whereas hitherto he had only acted on such information as came in in the matter of searching for arms he would in future, for the sake of the security of the country, make every endeavour to get information and to search when there was the slightest indication of the presence of illegal arms.

Both *Mr. Shertok* and *Mr. Ben-Tsvi* wished to answer the G. O. C.'s final remarks, but the G. O. C. said that he wished to hear no more unless they could give some constructive answer to his proposals. *Mr. Shertok* asked that it should be recorded that certain points in the G. O. C.'s final remarks had remained unanswered.

We here present a section from Moshe Dayan's original report of the Iskenderun (Escandelion) operation (from the reports on the operation in Syria, Zionist Archives); compare Chapter 4, "The Twenty-three and the Syrian Operation":

6. At 0100 hours we reached the bridge twenty-one kilometers north of Iskenderun. According to information we had, this bridge was being guarded by sentries and was ready to be blown up. We left the main group of soldiers at some distance and crept up on the bridge with a group of four men; but, to our surprise, we found the bridge unguarded. After cutting the Beirut–Ras En-Naqoura telephone line at this point, a guard was left to prevent any damage to the bridge. The rest of the group turned south toward a second bridge which was at a distance of one kilometer north of Iskenderun. On examining this bridge, we found that it was also unguarded, though our men on patrol four days earlier had seen it guarded by two sentries.

7. We rested near this bridge and, at 0400 hours, decided to go to Iskenderun to assist in its capture by British forces which were to come from Ras En-Naqoura.

We also left a guard on this bridge; and the rest of us, about six Australians and four Jews, made for Iskenderun. When we approached village H* we noted a movement of French soldiers

---

* This and other such notations are references to a map which accompanied the original report.

in the orange groves and in the building (F). We turned east and continued moving forward through the orange groves. There we occasionally met French soldiers who fired at us and fled when we responded. When we reached the building (F), they opened fire on us from that building, which served as the command post for the French forces in Iskenderun. The French posted a machine gun on the building's porch (I) and opened fire on us from there. We decided to take the building. I threw a grenade at the machine gun, as a result of which the gun was abandoned, and those operating it withdrew inside the building. I regarded that as the proper moment for capturing the building and requested Clyfen and Allen, who had tommy guns, to put a continuous fire on the doors and windows of the building, so that those inside would not be able to shoot at us. The Australian officers and men opened strong fire from the stone wall (C). Two of my men and I bounded up to the porch (D), which was about one and one-half meters above ground level. From this protected point (D), I threw a grenade into the building through one of the open windows. When the grenade exploded, we burst into the building. A French officer and an English soldier were killed by the grenade, two other French soldiers were wounded, and the rest put their hands up. On entering the building, we took away the prisoners' arms, cut the building's telephone from its lines, and put all the prisoners in one room. We put the weapons and the machine gun on the roof of the building onto which one of my men and I climbed. One Australian soldier remained to guard the prisoners. The officers went out, with two of my men, to search the groves.

In a building east of the road (B), we found disassembled mines. They had, apparently, been laid earlier under the bridges north of Iskenderun. With the concentration of the army at Iskenderun, they were disassembled and left in the hands of the army, with the understanding that they would be used when needed. Inside the building, there were about fifty horses as well as a three-inch mortar with a French soldier guarding it. When the soldier guarding the mortar saw the Australian officers, he put his hands up. The weapon was brought to us and put on the roof. A motorcycle with a sidecar was also found at the side of the road. A R.E. officer, with one of my men, got into it to go to Ras En-Naqoura and contact the British Army there. But at the edge of village (G), they found the road blocked. Strong fire was poured on them by the French forces that were on the hill to the east (F); their object was to delay the English forces coming from Ras En-Naqoura.

The R.E. officer and my man were forced to leave the motor-cycle, which had been hit, and return to building (E) by way of the seashore. The other men who had gone out to explore the orange groves came back the same way and announced that a powerful French force was at the foot of the hill to the south (F). At that moment, the French began to fire on us from that point F. I turned the French machine gun, which was in my charge, on them and looked through my binoculars to fix their exact position. At that moment I was hit in the eye by a bullet from their fire and lost my capability for further action. Our entire unit concentrated near the building and returned fire. The officer, Clyfen, decided to summon the guards that had been left on the bridges, so as to strengthen our unit in Iskenderun. One of our men rode out on a French horse to call them. When he reached them, he found that they had captured several French motorcyclists who were traveling from Tyre to Iskenderun. The guard that was on the bridge moved to Iskenderun.

The Hagana order that sheds light on the reasons for the founding of the Palmakh:

The National Command
Lag Ba'omer 5701
15/5/1941

Order of the Day No. 8.

A period of relative quiet after years of troubles, the establishment of mutual relations with our neighbors, the stationing of a large army in the country, and the development of the war in Europe and the Middle East have fostered delusions among shortsighted people in the Yishuv as to the value of the role assigned the Organization* as an independent Jewish defensive force.

Many imagine that the "spear is only for when it's needed," as if it will automatically be there when the time comes. Many are misled and slight the Organization, get caught up in quarrels, resignation, and opposition.

The Kofer Hayishuv is weakened. The money shortage has caused skimping and cutting down on operations.

Even within the Organization's membership, the tension of personal effort has slackened.

Thanks to efforts mapped out and directed by the High Command, the Organization has succeeded in reinforcing its main force, even while going through this period of debilitation.

* Meaning Hagana.

The plan for dividing the Organization into regional commands has been carried through, preserving and even increasing the effectiveness of the work.

Defense plans have been worked out in detail, and brought up to a high standard.

The level of training has been elevated, progress has been accelerated along with the branching out into special skills.

Resources and equipment have developed and grown on a large scale.

Enlistments have been carried out which have strengthened the position of the Jewish soldier in the British Army.

Knowledge of conditions and events in the Arab community has been deepened, as has that on the neighboring states and everything pertaining to the Organization and its interests in general.

Systematic contact with members and officers of the Organization has been ramified and reinforced.

The approach of the front, the revolt in Iraq, the increased activity toward the rebirth of the Arab gangs in Palestine, the preparation for attack, the return of gang leaders and men specially trained in a military school in Iraq for the needs of the Palestine "revolt," the activity of a fifth column and of Nazi espionage, the increase of incidents where travelers are injured, shooting at guards and other objectives—all these factors obligate the Hagana to stand tensely prepared, to remain on guard, to be in a battle-ready state.

Additional means have now been placed at the call of the High Command, though late and on a still insufficient scale; but, considering our resources, large enough so as not to warrant any additional loss of time.

Increased mass training and the thorough acquisition of skills

Feverish labor to add to equipment and fortifications

Completion and execution of plans for local and national defense

Improvement of communications

Enlistment and training of units for special duties which may be needed

Redoubled activity to bring in the youth, intensify and prepare it

General enlargement of the Organization

Strengthening of the means of spreading information

—these are the urgent tasks laid out by the High Command as a plan of action for the coming months. Orders have been given to carry out this plan.

The High Command is depending on the members of the Organization, on the Jewish settlements, and on their official institutions to make a redoubled effort in the volunteering spirit and in sacrificial devotion to establish the Organization as a fortified wall for the Yishuv. Our strength depends upon it.

The Chief of the National Command

The following letter reflects the negotiations on the establishment of the radio network as the basis for the "Palestine Scheme" headed by Moshe Dayan. See the first section of Chapter 5. Source: ZA, P. S. file.

Jerusalem
Feb. 3, 1942.

Dear H.

This is in reference to your note No. 716/456 and in pursuance of our conversation with Squadron Leader R[oss] some time ago.

General.

Without underestimating what has been achieved in the few months since we started on our venture, I feel that we are not progressing satisfactorily considering the short time at our disposal. As I pointed out a number of times, our organisation will have to function, if ever, next spring, and I feel that at the present rate of progress our people will not be sufficiently trained by then to work efficiently.

Aim.

1. Our aim is to establish an organisation composed of four or more independent units who would be able, when the time comes, to collect the necessary information and transmit it. Each unit must be trained to act independently. During the preparatory stage, however, there should be a central staff to train and supervise these units. If possible some sort of central supervision of this

organisation should exist in the country or in the neighbourhood even later.

2. Each unit will be composed of a leader, his assistant, two operators and a collector of information. The leader is responsible for the work of the unit. He directs the collection of information, sifts it and prepares it for transmission. The operators are responsible for the actual transmission of messages by wireless. Their job, though technical only, is very difficult, considering the extremely difficult conditions under which they will have to work.

The collector of information will be responsible, under the direction of the unit leader, for the establishment of a network of informants and agents in his district.

Present Position.

As far as personnel for the units concerned, the position as described in your note 716/456 is more or less satisfactory (it may be necessary to replace somebody or add to the strength of some of the units). As to the training and general preparedness of the organisation, we feel that the present methods of training are insufficient. It is true that "the leaders have had lessons on various subjects and there are more to follow." These lessons however, are given very irregularly and the intervals between lessons are too long. To rectify this we suggest that in addition to lessons given by you or by officers whose services you may occasionally secure, a programme of studies should be worked out and that we should undertake to provide the instruction ourselves. As I have already mentioned to you orally, we have a number of men in Palestine who would be able to provide the necessary material.

Programme of training.

The training of leaders and others should, in our opinion, cover the following items:

1. General outline of the type of information which might be required (troop movements, description of military targets, industrial information, food position, political information, etc.).

2. Detailed instruction on the composition of enemy forces and equipment and of how to distinguish between various enemy formations.

3. Technical courses: map reading, topography, etc.

4. Means of communication other than wireless; these should be dealt with centrally though in contact with the unit leaders.

5. Thorough knowledge, topographical and other, of the district in which the unit will operate.

Both unit leaders and collectors of information have to be instructed in all these subjects. The unit leaders must, in addition, learn how to formulate messages and how to conduct their units under difficult circumstances. They must work out a system of communication between themselves and their operators on the one hand, and the collectors of information on the other hand.

The collector of information has to immediately begin preparing a list of potential informants in vital centres in his district. The operators have to be trained to work under difficult conditions. They have to learn, for instance, how to transfer their sets secretly and at short notice.

I also suggest that a number of men operators should be trained and held in reserve to fill the gap should there be a breakdown in any of the units. It is also necessary in order to enhance the efficiency of our organisation, to train a number of men who would be able to disguise themselves as Arabs, Germans or Italians, to act as messengers and agents. These could be trained separately and put in touch with unit leaders at the last moment.

Equipment.

It is essential to begin preparing now all the equipment that the organisation might need as well as secret hiding places for such equipment. The following is some of the equipment I have in mind:

Batteries, battery charges, spare parts for wireless sets, simple tools for the repairs of sets, camera and films, money in various currencies, maps of the districts, Arab clothing, German and Italian uniforms, arms (for use in self-defence in case of discovery), etc.

The above is a general outline of what we think must be done. I believe that subject to certain modification this is the only way to ensure efficient and effective working of the machinery we are trying to set up.

To achieve the above we suggest that in addition to M. D. [Moshe Dayan] we should be authorised to appoint a full-time instructor who, in conjunction with M. D. should be responsible for the training of the unit leaders and collectors of information. It is essential that each unit leader should be visited by M. D. or the instructor at least once a week. I enclose an estimate of the budget necessary to carry out this scheme. I should be very grateful if you could discuss it and come to a decision as soon as possible.

Yours,
[unsigned copy]

Appendix IX

Speech by Yitzhak Sadeh at Mishmar Haemek, April 16, 1942.

No one sent me here. And no one invited me either. I am a soldier and, as such, I want to say a few words. I have been in service since 1936. I was jealous of other members. The time has come when I am no longer jealous. You have probably been talking about important things. But how have you done that? Could people in Russia get together and discuss such things? There is no healthy anxiety here. Today, things do not have to be pondered over. Everything is needed for defense only. There is only one means, and that is arms with which to fight for the blue and white flag and the red flag. You ask whether we are going to be able to do anything. Yes, we will. The whole war is not mechanized. Men have value. Mikhailovitch in Yugoslavia is not fighting with machines, but with men. There is a war of men. Men have value, and all our effort is going toward that. Have we prepared better than Chamberlain—the one we criticized? There is almost nothing more for me to say. We can mobilize 100,000 in Palestine; the arms are there, but where are the men? You don't get a feeling of awareness of what is coming. We are enthusiastic about Russia's courage, but here I have been busy with recruitment for the Palmakh—and every place I go, they start bargaining; it's amazing. If this is what happens right now—all the words are worthless. We are not free in this war. We have a partner who has power, but he has no talent, that's why all the exertion is necessary. We have the ability to defend the country, and the English see that. The Yishuv must emerge in full force. Therefore, I want *you* to prod *us* so that we won't be the ones making demands—*you* make the demands. We, for our part, are ready with thought and plans to call on everybody for the defense of our land.

Notes

📓 *Introduction*

1. Statistics are taken from I. Cohen. *The Zionist Movement.* London: 1946, pp. 238–252, 359–362.

    In November of 1935 the representatives of five Arab parties (with the exception of Istihlal), under the chairmanship of Hajj Amin el-Husseini, presented the following demands to the high commissioner: (a) a democratic regime in Palestine; (b) cessation of land sales to Jews; and (c) immediate cessation of immigration. See John Marlow. *Seat of Pilate.* London: 1959, p. 134.

2. Yehuda Slutsky. *Sefer Toldot Hahagana.* (STH), vol. 2, book 2. Tel Aviv: 1963, pp. 736–737.

3. Marlowe, in *Seat of Pilate,* p. 145.

4. Great Britain. Parliament. Cmd. 5513.

5. Great Britain. Parliament. *Hansard's Parliamentary Debates* (House of Lords), vol. 106, no. 94, coll. 626–643, 7/20/37.

6. ESCO Foundation. *Palestine: British, Jewish and Arab Policies.* New Haven: 1947, p. 882.

7. Ibid. p. 886; *Seat of Pilate,* p. 203.

8. *Seat of Pilate,* p. 153.

9. Christopher Sykes. *Orde Wingate.* London: 1959, pp. 202–4.

10. STH, ibid., p. 849.

✎ Chapter 1

1. Hansard. *House of Lords,* vol. 3, no. 13, coll. 463, 12/8/38. In his letter to the Agency Executive (3/7/39), Ben-Gurion wrote that MacDonald had declared the government was bound by the Balfour Declaration, rejected the "idea of an Arab state," and rejected the notion of a stoppage of Jewish immigration. The government was to renege on all three promises.

2. Weizmann-MacDonald conversation, 12/14/38, in General Zionist Archives, Jerusalem (ZA), S25-7642. The idea of an Arab veto was brought up in R. A. Butler's talk with Weizmann, 1/24/39, ibid.

3. Ben-Gurion in the Jewish Agency Executive meeting (JAE), 2/1/39.

4. Maj. Gen. I. S. O. Playfair. *The Mediterranean and the Middle East,* vol. 1. London: 1956, p. 17.

5. Royal Institute of International Affairs. *The World in March, 1939.* Oxford: 1952, p. 138.

6. See Appendix I.

7. *Mediterranean and Middle East,* p. 15.

8. See Appendix II.

9. ZA, S25-7642. Protocols of the conference will be found in ZA, S25-7632-7642. Further quotations from these protocols, unless otherwise stated, are taken from these files.

10. *Orde Wingate,* p. 209.

11. JAE, 2/1/39.

12. For a summary of the talk, see Weizmann Archive, (WA), Rehovot. Files there are arranged chronologically.

13. Panel session of 2/27 (see note 9). Lord Rothschild opposed the exploitation of the incident for political ends and emphasized that "a study of the so-called proposals shows that the document is nothing more than a summary of those proposals as presented at the meeting [2/25] without going beyond them." See also JAE.

14. It is important to remember that unity did not prevail among the Arab representatives. The chief Egyptian representative, Ali Maher Pasha, recognized (3/6) the special position of the Jews in Palestine and was ready to grant them "extraordinary rights" in keeping with the British request. Azzam Pasha took a similar position. In contrast, George Antonius stated that the

Jews were "asking for the moon in demanding rights beyond those of an ordinary minority; if they are fewer, they must submit" (3/4).

15. ZA, S25-7643a; the quotations following are from the same source.

16. Cf. Appendix III. According to Sharett's diary (ZA) on 3/6/39, Ben-Gurion demanded "an independent Jewish state or a federal state with Jewish control over immigration." On 3/7, Sharett notes Ben-Gurion's words in an unofficial meeting with Arab representatives, as follows: "On a wider range it is possible that a way might be found to satisfy the national aspirations of both the Arabs and the Jews. . . . We must strive not for the domination of one element over the other, but for their mutual harmony."

17. In the Arabs' rejection of the British proposals, differences within the Arab mission were discernible. The mufti's representatives rejected the proposals in a very sharp manner. But the representatives of the Arab states, particularly Ali Maher, hinted that they were making such a definite rejection of the proposals for the sake of Arab solidarity alone. Ali Maher announced that the atmosphere of the talks was not right for obtaining agreement. He added that there was a chance for an understanding with the British, if the length of time until the turning over of Palestine to its inhabitants could be set. It appears further that during the war, the Arab states accepted the White Paper solution *de facto*.

18. Weizmann. *Masa Vamaas (Trial and Error)*. Jerusalem: 1963 (Hebrew), p. 407; George Kirk. *The Middle East in the War*. London: 1953, p. 239n.

19. On the threat of determined Jewish resistance, see for example, p. 36 and Weizmann's telegram to Chamberlain, 4/18/39, in the Zionist Archives.

20. The principal differences between the two versions are: (1) deletion of the federative solution as a possible final arrangement at the close of the transition period; (2) deletion of the sentence stating that the state should be neither Jewish nor Arabic; and (3) deletion of the passage explicitly stating that the realization of the new policy would be subject to the consent of both the parties.

21. ZA, 5/24/39. "Guidelines" and meeting of the Smaller Zionist Actions Committee, ibid.

22. For the Twenty-first Zionist Congress caucus meeting, see Hashomer Hatzair Archive, Internal Bulletin No. 86, 3/23/39; for the 7/5/39 Mapai meeting, see Mapai Central Committee Bulletin No. 150, ZA.

23. Cmd. 6019.

24. ZA, Smaller Zionist Actions Committee, 5/3/39, 5/10/39, 6/26/39; and JAE 5/14/39.

25. In passing, we may note that Menachem Begin introduced a similar idea at a Revisionist meeting in Warsaw in the fall of 1938: "The Jewish national movement began with Practical Zionism; then came Political Zionism; now we stand on the threshold of Military Zionism."

26. JAE, 5/21/39.

27. See Note 21: "All our steps, crash programs, and sacrifices are only a means to the end: a land for Israel, Israel for its land. This was the political mission that was cast upon the Mandatory government. That regime has now openly and knowingly betrayed the mission, and we must prepare to take its place. By agreement and alliance, if possible—by force, if there is no choice. For this purpose, we must mobilize our youth, to train and equip them—in the country and outside it—so that they will be ready when the decisive moment comes. We can no longer depend only on negotiation, publicity, and propaganda; though we shall continue our political exposition in England and America, within the Jewish people and the European nations. But we shall be able to count only on our own power. The creation of a Jewish force, sufficient to tip the balance at the proper moment—let that be the directing, guiding path for all our labors in and outside Palestine" (JAE, 5/8/39, p. 21).

28. The question of immigration without government certificates (Aliyah Bet) has still not been examined in methodical historical fashion. We are confining ourselves here to only the most general description. For some details, see STH, vol. 2, book 2, pp. 1032–1052 and Chaim Lazar-Litai. *Af Al Pi*. Tel Aviv: 1957, pp. 85–134.

29. STH, ibid.

30. See the proceedings of the Twenty-first Zionist Congress, speeches by Silver and Katznelson. Sharett supported unofficial immigration, even in a letter to Ralph Butler (Weizmann Archives, 5/3/39).

The reader will not, perhaps, grasp this theoretical division of the fabric of *aliyah* into a political aspect and a justification in the name of the sanctity of human life. But it is a fact that one of the most frequent arguments in the British debate with Zionism, both at the time and in historical analysis, was the assumption that Zionism was exploiting the suffering of persecuted Jews in search of a refuge for the sake of attaining political ends. To the British, the European Jewish problem was a humanitarian one; the Palestine issue was, as far as they were concerned, first and foremost a painful political question. The entire British line from the time of the White Paper until the rise of Israel was based on an attempt to separate these two aspects of the problem.

The contradiction in the British position seems to be this: No one saw to the opening of the gates to the countries of the free world for the Jewish refugees while there was time. Palestine stood alone, as a matter of course, as the only practical solution for those few for whom flight was at all possible. Therefore, there was no escaping the organic combination of the humanitarian and political problems. The Zionist movement— and in this there was no division of opinion among its various branches—looked upon the closing of the nations' doors in the face of persecuted Jews as a confirmation of the correctness of the Zionist analysis. Political pressure for the opening of the gates of Palestine was, perforce, the only path to the rescue of masses of Jews. Certainly not a few Jews were saved by flight to Western countries, also. But for the Jews of eastern and central-eastern Europe, even this partial means was closed off.

31. During the period of the struggle, March–September 1939, nine ships of the Mosad and one which the Hagana took under its protection (*Assimi*) arrived. They contained 4,700 immigrants. The fate of private ships, which were organized from time to time on the authority of bodies or political parties in the lands of origin, was very grave. The *Assando* (arrived in March) was driven off and returned to Rumania. The *Aspia* (arrived 4/2) was driven off; the *Hagios Nikoloros* (6/1), *Las Perlas* (7/2), and *St. Nicholas* (3/7) were captured. It is still not known which ships were "private" and which organized by various parties. At any rate, thousands of immigrants arrived in them.

32. In all, from 1936 to 1939 about fifteen thousand "illegal" immigrants entered.

33. On 5/24 Lord Dufferin informed the House of Lords, in the

name of the government, that if the Mandates Commission did not approve the White Paper, England would demand that the League Council emend the mandate. Jewish Agency. *Documents Relating to the Palestine Problem.* London: 1945, pp. 60–65.

34. In Ireland, during the years 1919–1921, a similar attempt was made at noncooperation with the government. However, we have found no use of it as a precedent. Cf. R.I.I.A. *Survey of British Commonwealth Affairs,* vol. 1, *Problems of Nationality,* ch. 3.

35. The Vaad Leumi Executive decided, on 5/21, to propose the stoppage of tax payments to the government treasury. This was not accepted by other elements.

36. *Davar* (Hebrew) and *Palestine Post* from May 17–22, 1939. On 5/17 an act of sabotage prevented the broadcast of the contents of the White Paper for two hours. On the same day, Revisionist demonstrations were organized in Tel Aviv, which turned against the government offices in Allenby Street. In Jerusalem the government immigration offices were attacked by the Hagana. On 5/18 gigantic organized demonstrations took place under the official bodies in Tel Aviv, while the Revisionists were burning Rokakh's car and trying to set fire to Arlosoroff's house. In Jerusalem a demonstration of about four thousand persons took place. It ended with the slaying of a British policeman. Further demonstrations continued until 5/21.

37. On 5/19 the commander of the army in Palestine, General Haining, received the representatives of the Jewish community and warned them that in case of disruption of public order, the responsibility would be on them. This notice was given to the Jews in a very insulting manner—they were not permitted to sit or to reply. But it seems that there was no premeditated intent in this instance, but rather thoughtlessness and disorganization. In the correspondence file of the Zionist Archives, POL/ 47/39, is Ben-Gurion's answer to Haining, also dated 5/19. In this letter Ben-Gurion wrote that the demonstrations were the beginning of the Jewish struggle. Responsibility for the results of this struggle would rest upon the government and its new policy. In order to reinforce his words, Ben-Gurion quoted Weizmann's telegram to Chamberlain (4/18), already cited here (see note 19). From Ben-Gurion's remarks at the Agency Executive session of 5/21/39, page 1, it appears that the general also upbraided the British policemen for their behavior

toward the Jews. Haining was by no means an anti-Zionist; with the start of the implementation of the White Paper, he was transferred from Palestine (see Weizmann Archives, letter to Amery, 5/3).

According to a letter by A. H. Cohen to Dov Joseph (ZA, 7/7/39), it seems that British policemen carried on anti-Jewish propaganda among the Arabs.

The Hagana instructed its members to participate in the demonstrations. Nonetheless, one directive of 5/16 (one day *before* the riots) stated: "Since we have been asked, we herewith reply. We absolutely forbid use of firearms against British security forces at the demonstrations, no matter what the circumstances" (Hagana Archive, Tel Aviv, ATH, file 1335–9, General Staff).

✠ Chapter 2

1. *Middle East in the War,* p. 230, and material in Mrs. Dugdale's diary, December 1939. This position remained unaltered even after Italy's entry into the war and the fall of France. Nuri Said, who was the foreign minister of Iraq in the first government of Rashid Ali, a friend of the Axis, sought to press the British for a speedup in the implementation of the White Paper, in exchange for an Iraqi declaration of war on Italy. A proposal of this nature was transmitted to London through Colonel S. P. Newcombe in July 1940. But Churchill, who had come to power in June, refused to yield to that pressure. He gave a negative answer to the Iraqi proposal on August 29, 1940. The opponents of Zionism in British public life claimed that this rejection of Iraqi offers was the start on the road to the war between Britain and Iraq under the leadership of Rashid Ali (since, because of her protection of Jewish rights, Britain risked the Iraqi betrayal). It is difficult to know what truth there is to this argument. One can look upon the whole affair as merely a convenient excuse for the Iraqi government to approach Germany and Italy.
2. The Halifax-Weizmann conversation took place on 10/23/39. Two further notes were sent by Weizmann to Halifax to make sure that there would be no land laws (WA, 10/16 and 11/30/39). The letters mentioned subsequently are also in the Weizmann Archives.

3. JAE, 2/4/40, 4/1/40; Israel State Archives, C.I.D. reports (2/2/40), and a report by Abba Eban, "Notes on the work of the political department," February 1940 (ZA).

4. File 8242 (old registration, ZA) and (WA) two letters by Joseph (3/4 and 3/8/40).

5. *Middle East in the War,* p. 236, note 2.

6. Above, note 3. Another possible way for the Jews to attack the land law was to mobilize the opinions of those Arabs who were opposed to it. Indeed, attempts were made in that direction, based on the severe economic crisis that prevailed in Palestine in 1939/40 and on the interests of Arabs who would receive cash for land. A memorandum was handed the government by Arab notables on this issue, but without results.

7. The Weizmann program is first mentioned in the archives on October 6, 1939 (Sharett's diary, ZA). Sharett's initial reaction was, despite various reservations, positive. Of course, Weizmann himself was not ready for thorough consistency in the matter. In a conversation with Brendan Bracken, Churchill's friend, Weizmann responded in the negative to the suggestion that the Arabs be transferred out of Palestine and that it be turned into a Jewish state, a prop for the empire. Weizmann drew Bracken up short by stating that he would be happy if the program would take on the form indicated by the Peel plan, with several alterations. Sharett's reaction to this inconsistency was sharp.

8. JAE, 10/22/39.

9. JAE, 11/26; Ben-Gurion explicitly puts the program forth as that of Dr. Weizmann. "In Dr. Weizmann's opinion, we must demand all of western Palestine."

10. JAE, 4/8/40.

11. May 9, letters of Ben-Gurion (ZA). In a session of the Arab Affairs section of the Agency (2/40), one of the discussants states, ". . . if friendly relations prevailed, the high commissioner and MacDonald would point to the good relations as proof that the White Paper policy was right. I did not suggest that we should do anything positive to spoil good Arab-Jewish relations, but our policy should be to devote our political efforts to other aspects of our task, to defeating the White Paper policy. This is not the time to improve Arab-Jewish relations."

12. Agency Executive, 4/8/40.

13. Katznelson's speech at Afikim, 12/16/40, ATH.
14. Hashomer Hatzair Executive session 5/7/40, HH Archive.
15. Ben-Gurion's letter to the JAE, 7/15/40, ZA.
16. Sharett's letter to Maj. Gen. H. R. Pownall, 8/25/39, WA; interview of Joseph and Hos with Gen. Barker, 8/29/39, ZA. In his talk with Ironside (8/25/39, WA), Sharett suggested Wingate as commander of the Jewish unit.
17. The program, in its original form, is in a letter from Sharett to Barker (9/27/39). Wingate's influence on defense policy was, at the time, at its height. Weizmann asked him for the memo to Churchill in their conversation on September 19, but it was not handed in at that time because of various fears. Wingate's influence on Sharett was great, and Sharett often followed his advice. The cabinet discussed the battalions plan in the middle of October, but no final motion was accepted. A memo on the subject of the cadre was handed in on October 23, and a meeting between Sharett and Ironside took place the next day.

    On the inside discussion: Victor Cazalet (Conservative M.P. and one of Zionism's greatest friends) and Wingate were present at a Zionist leadership meeting at the Dorchester Hotel on November 1 (ZA). When Wingate suggested a division from Palestine for general service, Sharett asked: "Will you take fifteen thousand of the best of our youth out of Palestine now?" Wingate replied: "Of course not, at present the main thing is to make the proposal. By the time it is carried out, the Middle East will have become a battlefield, and the division will fight there." The final Jewish decision to ask for a division was taken on November 14, in a meeting at which Wingate's and Sharett's proposals were accepted.

    By the way, it may be pointed out that Ben-Gurion made no objection to the executive's concession on publicity in behalf of the division. That is interesting in light of his later criticism of the matter.
18. Wavell opposed a division that would fight in the Middle East, but not one for the west (WA). MacLeod's answer, 12/4/39, is in WA.
19. Lloyd's letter to Weizmann 6/15/40, WA. A summary of the negotiations up to that point was presented by Dov Hos at the JAE, 7/5/40. Hos was sure that one of the positive influences was Bevin, with whom Hos had negotiated. Lloyd, on the other

hand, apparently, did not understand the division proposal. He requested Weizmann to agree to two conditions: (a) inclusion of the unit within the British Army (!) and obligation for general service; and (b) "that for this purpose Jews should be recruited, subject to War Office requirements, in any country where such enlistment was permissible and practicable, and should be organized as units of the British Army and trained at the most convenient military centers, though not in Palestine."

20. W. S. Churchill. *History of the Second World War*, vol. 2, pp. 163–4. Churchill charged, correctly, that because of the anti-Zionist policy, Britain was forced to keep more than twenty thousand troops in Palestine. See *Mediterranean and the Middle East*, p. 93.

21. Chaim Weizmann. *Trial and Error*, pp. 521–2. In the end, Wingate was sent to Wavell and charged with operations in Ethiopia but was forbidden to visit Palestine. On Jews in Middle East commando units, see Gordon Landsborough. *Tobruk Commando*. London: 1956.

22. The commander was to be Brigadier L. A. Hawes. The correspondence will be found in ZA, s25-5092.

23. *History of Second World War*, vol. 3, p. 658.

24. Telegram of Oliver Lyttelton to Eden (ZA, S25-1555), 8/9/41, states that employment of Jewish forces would reawaken Arab fear of Jewish expansionist tendencies, and that the division plan would have no military worth for Britain. It was Lyttelton who suggested postponing the program for several months more and telling Weizmann that the reason for the delay was involved with problems of supply. Lyttelton added that Ben-Gurion visited him and, when told of the difficulties of supply, appeared to accept this explanation! British faith in Jewish naïveté, apparently, knew no bounds.

25. ZA, S25-5092.

26. 7/1/40, 9/12/40, 10/15/41, WA.

27. On 12/10/41, WA.

28. Quotations from HH Executive meeting, 7/7/40, HH Archive; and Histadrut Executive (HE), 7/4/40, Histadrut Archive (HA).

29. Quoted from Mapai Central Committee Bulletin No. 158, 8/27/40.

30. HE, 7/4/40 (HA).

31. All the material mentioned in the text will be found in ATH.
32. As early as 11/27/39 it was reported (by Gordon to Ben-Gurion) that the police wished to decrease the number of rifles in the hands of Jewish policemen and halt the movement of Hebrew armored cars, out of "fear that, one fine day, they will be used against us."
33. Daphne Trevor. *Under the White Paper.* Jerusalem: 1948, ch. 3; Ben-Gurion's report on negotiations on issue in London to JAE, 11/26. Ironside's intervention (according to Ben-Gurion on 11/15) came when the general heard that the prisoners included some of Wingate's trainees. "Fancy, they have condemned one of Wingate's lads to life imprisonment—he ought to have been given the D.S.O." He added that, in his opinion, the sentence was "wildly foolish" (ZA).
34. See JAE meetings for May–June, 1940; HE—5/23, 6/13, HA; and Noah Dagoni's diary, ATH. Aaron Zisling states that Golomb agreed with the idea of turning in five hundred rifles as a token (ATH—oral statement). But this is unconfirmed from any other source.
35. See Appendix V. Sharett replied to the general in a detailed letter on 6/20/40 (POL 66/40-ZA). Giffard, in his remarks, mentioned the existence of a secret radio broadcasting station, Kol Israel, which had been broadcasting under the Hagana since the land law—a symbol of resistance to the White Paper. But this station stopped broadcasting on June 11 because of Italy's entry into the war.
36. John Marlowe. *Rebellion in Palestine.* London: 1946, p. 239.
37. The C.I.D. reports are at the Israel State Archives.

✌ Chapter 3

1. Sources for the above and for subsequent details will be found in Zerubavel Gilead. *Magen Beseter.* Jerusalem: 1948, pp. 39–89; *Sefer Hapalmakh,* vol. 1. Tel Aviv: 1953, pp. 79–84, 102; and oral testimonies, ATH, as well as Hacohen's report (no date), ZA.
2. Christopher Sykes. *Orde Wingate,* p. 225.
3. The quotation is from *Magen Beseter,* p. 42; further material on the above in Gideon Raphael. *The Secret War Effort of the Yishuv* (Hebrew), 8/30/45, ZA.

4. *Under the White Paper,* pp. 9–11; Braha Habas, *Portsei Ha-shearim,* Tel Aviv: 1957, pp. 287–302; and oral testimonies of Shind (ATH) and Braginsky (Hebrew University).

5. Quoted from Y. Allon's "Report on the Syrian Operations," ZA (no date). Cf. also ZA, PS file, and oral testimonies by R. Shiloah, Y. Allon, Y. Rattner (ATH).

6. Hacohen's report (see note 1), p. 13.

7. Shiloah's report, 1949 (ZA).

8. Hacohen's report, p. 29.

9. *Orde Wingate,* p. 232.

10. *Middle East in the War,* p. 64.

11. H. M. Wilson. *Eight Years Overseas.* London: 1946, p. 106.

12. In a speech (4/29/41, ATH) Golomb asserted that "not long ago, there were dreams of a merger in Palestine between certain [right-wing] people in the private villages and the Etzel. For some reason, that deal went sour for a while, because Etzel began to extort money in a village. But they, the Etzel, now seem to understand that a deal [with the rightists] is better than squeezing out some money. So they promise to be good little boys, and the process starts all over again." The extortion occurred in Petah Tiqva. There a bomb was thrown into the house of one citizen who did not agree to respond to the collection. A policeman was wounded in the skirmish.

In another speech (8/11), Golomb declared that Rabbi Berlin had informed him that, in the event of a split, the rabbi still had to decide with whom to go. Golomb explained the differences of opinion: "We look upon the Hagana as a Zionist force for the protection of our settlements, our rights, and our future in the land. They say that the question of rights and future are not in the province of the Hagana."

The approaching split is also mentioned in C.I.D. reports, whose terminology throughout is identical with that of the Revisionists.

13. "Bulletin of the Political Central Committee of the NZO," 1941, p. 2.

14. It appears that by early 1942, 1,157 people had enlisted through the NZO recruiting offices, out of some 10,900 Jewish soldiers. The NZO (which in Palestine was identical with the Revisionist party) allowed its members to enlist and recruit others, without itself taking a clear-cut position on the issue. Etzel, on the other hand, declared that it would agree to a recruiting campaign

only if the government set up Jewish units. When that happened, "the Government will be interested . . . in introducing into them a majority of national elements [i.e., Etzel members] and entrust the central positions to them" (1940 Etzel material, ATH).

15. German Federal Archives, Koblenz, Auswärtiges Amt, E234158; also Otto von Hentig, *Mein Leben, eine Dienstreise,* pp. 377–8. I am indebted to Mr. David Hadar for having discovered the Sternist proposal to the Germans and directed my attention to it. On the setting up of the Stern group, apart from material in ATH, see also Yaakov Weinshall. *Hadam Asher Basaf.* Tel Aviv: 1956.

16. The Revisionist party was opposed in principle to the Histadrut because of the latter's left-wing tendencies. Workers who belonged to the party, and put national before "class" interests, founded an independent National Workers' Organization.

   The Revisionists had left the World Zionist Organization in 1935 to found their own New Zionist Organization. They therefore abandoned their former support of the Jewish National Fund and the Jewish Foundation Fund (Keren Hayesod) and established their own settlement fund, the Tel-Hai Fund, which, however, did not become significant.

   The C.I.D. appears to have continued its friendship with the Revisionists, and arrived at an agreement with the Etzel on 8/9/41; in its report of 8/21, it even went so far as to suggest to its own superiors in the government an overall settlement with the NZO. Pritzker's cooperation with the C.I.D. is amply documented in material at the ATH.

17. From Galili's deposition, ATH.

18. On April 22, a long letter was sent from Namier to Lord Moyne (ZA) with a vigorous demand that the parity be canceled and the Jewish units in Palestine be expanded. In this regard, he writes: "Cooperation is an offer, self-defence is a human right and a claim. . . . There are ways of dying: defenceless Jews have perished in pogroms in the Dispersion, or had to fly for life; the Jews will not evacuate Palestine (even were this possible), nor will they let themselves be slaughtered like sheep in a shambles. Their manner of meeting their doom would count for all future in Jewish history, and their claim to self-defence raises a moral problem which the Jewish Agency submit for the consideration of His Majesty's Government."

19. Namier-Moyne interview, 5/6/41, ZA.
20. The agency had far-reaching plans for the use of Supernumeraries in case of war. The Zionist Archives contain an undated, unsigned plan for the mobilization of thirty thousand citizens at lookout points scattered over the entire country; their function was to be to give warning of enemy landings or parachute drops. The civilians were to watch voluntarily on a rotating basis. In the vicinity of the lookout posts, there were to be thirty guards, bases, organized in "assault companies"—the term was very common at the time!—recruited from the Settlement Police Mobile Guards.

    Internal evidence places the date of the plan in the spring of 1941. An echo of it appears, perhaps, in the Membership Order of 1941. See next note.
21. In addition to the Principles the ATH archives also contain the 1941 Hagana Membership Order, which states, among other things, that a function of the border posts was to impede an (Arab) attack initially, until the Field Force could be mobilized. Sadeh noted, in the margin of that order, that the Field Force must be kept in reserve and employed later at weak points. Service in the Field Force was set at two to three years and included two weeks of concentrated training a year. Other evidence indicates that the commanding officers were ordered to speed up their preparations on Plan A (5/22/41 ATH).
22. Deposition of Yosef Avidar, and Moshe Sneh, ATH.
23. Golomb at HE, 5/11/41, HA.
24. Ben-Gurion: "Work and Defence," in *Geulim,* 1949 (ATH).
25. Sharett in *Davar,* 1/27/50, and his oral deposition, ATH.
26. Galili, oral deposition, ATH.

✠ Chapter 4

1. *Eight Years Overseas,* pp. 104–134.
2. M. Dayan: "From the Days of the Syrian Invasion," *Palmakh Bulletin,* No. 20, July 1944.
3. G. Lang. *Australia in the War of 1939–45.* Series 1, vol. 2, p. 346.
4. See note 2 above.
5. The Syrian episode became a legend. Various stories circulated

among the Palmakh people about the defense of Metulla by
the Palmakh against a French counterattack. These stories contained a small grain of truth.

The Australians and their allies were unsuccessful in breaking
the French lines at Merj Uyun, and the enemy began a counterattack. On June 9 Metulla was shelled, and most of its inhabitants ran for their lives. The army wished to evacuate the
residents of Kefar Giladi also, but the people there were against
that. Tsvi Kroll, a Hashomer veteran, went up to Metulla and
organized a watch with the help of six Supernumeraries, three
men from Kefar Giladi, and two local men (after most of the
village's guards had run off). The group guarded the area until
June 16, when an English police officer came to Metulla, wish-
ing to take the guards out. Kroll persuaded him to leave them
there along with several Supernumeraries who had come with
the officer. By June 17, after another bombardment, Kroll remained with twelve men, and later with only seven. The guards
drove out several Arabs who had come to loot.

On June 19 a Palmakh platoon of ten to fifteen men arrived
and remained at Metulla with nine other men (Supernumeraries,
men of Kefar Giladi, and local residents) until June 25. On
June 20 the attack on Merj Uyun was executed, and the French
were driven out. During the entire time, Metulla was never attacked by infantry, but it was shelled.
6. Giora Shinan diary, ATH.
7. In the spring of 1942, the girls were court-martialed by the
Jerusalem regional commander for "illegal entry into the Palmakh." They achieved "legalization" on May 3, 1942, by decision of the National Command.

◪ Chapter 5

1. ZA, S25-359, Dayan, 10/20/41; agency letter, 2/3/42; Dayan,
8/5/42.
2. Galili lecture (probably in 1940), lectures file, ATH.
3. Smaller Zionist Actions Committee (SZAC), 1/14/41, ZA.
4. ZA, S25-6056.
5. Golomb at SZAC, 8/26/41.
6. Hazan at the Fifth Histadrut Convention, 4/19–23/42, HA.
7. Ben-Gurion, HE, 4/6/41, HA.

8. Israel Galili, at the Thirteenth Convention of Kibbutz Meuhad, October 1941, Labor Archive, Tel Aviv.
9. Golomb, HE, 4/24/41, HA.
10. In a passage in his book, (on p. 129), General Wilson says that when the situation in the western desert had become difficult, he felt that "any transfer of divisions to Syria would be exceedingly difficult, and without extra divisions it would be impossible to hold Lebanon; the defence lines had, therefore, to be drawn to northern Palestine, the Jebel Druze and the lava belt; luckily the occasion never arose; with the German Air Force established in Syria [sic!] the situation in Egypt and on the Suez Canal would have been most serious." However, Wilson was consoled by the offer of the Ruallas, a Bedouin tribe in Syria, to help him against the Germans (ibid., p. 130). Is it surprising that Britain almost lost the Middle East?

In the session of the Agency Executive of 7/5/42, when Auchinleck was also planning a retreat from Egypt, Sharett commented that there was still the assumption that "the enemy, concentrating his forces in Crete, and perhaps in other islands, could stage a sea-air invasion of Syria and, after concentrating there and throwing back the local forces, reach the northern border of Palestine. He might then turn east to Damascus and from there to Transjordan, reaching Jericho and attacking Jerusalem from that direction. We have not only heard the views that are widely held among the [British] Command, but we have seen with our own eyes the lines of fortifications, in the preparation of which our troops, Jewish troops, took part, and a very active part. . . . And we do not witness any preparations for fortification activities in southern Palestine. Rafa bears testimony to the earlier plan. If they thought the front would be in the north, they considered Rafa the rear, and there they built central workshops. . . . And if they considered a line of fortifications in the south, they thought of it as being turned northward, to prepare a line of retreat. . . . After the fall of Tobruk, we have not witnessed a practical reorientation, but the stagnation of military thought. . . . They even assumed that an invasion by way of the Sinai Desert is not possible; the area is vast, there is no water; all those factors that had their place in the last war bear witness as if people are visualizing an army that has to cross the desert, some on foot and some riding; and this at a time when you can drive from Ismailia to Jerusalem in six hours, bringing your water along in the car."

11. In ATH.
12. B. T. Wilson was an interesting personality. Shiloah (ATH) tells the following about him: "He was a rather extreme person. He called MacMichael and his people 'the Malaya generals.' He asserted that Jewish youth must be armed to the teeth. He fought tenaciously for the survival of the Mishmar Haemek camp and created scandals for the MacMichael group on this matter. His approach was not always simple. For example, he came to the Mishmar Haemek camp and stood at attention when the Zionist flag was raised. But then he wrote a letter to Sharett [actually to Avigur] in which he complained about the chauvinism of our youth. He had more than a few problems because of his fresh manner, but the story that he was almost court-martialed because of us is false. He was involved in scandals, but against a different background. After a time, he was transferred to the Gold Coast."
13. Oral depositions of Y. Rattner and I. Galili, ATH.
14. Oral deposition of S. Avidan, ATH.
15. Oral deposition of Y. Avidar, ATH.
16. Y. Allon: "Report on the Syrian Operations," ZA, S25-7902.
17. Ibid.
18. Ibid.
19. Galili deposition (ATH).
20. Tabenkin at Givat-Brenner, 5/16/42, Labor Archive, and ibid., Kibbutz Meuhad Bulletin No. 128.
21. JAE, 6/30/42, 7/5/42.
22. Sharett, 4/19/42 and 9/17/42 at Histadrut meetings, HA.
23. Tabenkin, Histadrut Convention, 4/19/42, (HA).
24. Peled, HH Executive, 8/11/42 (HH Archive).
25. Several things indicate that Auchinleck was more friendly toward the Jewish cause than were other generals. We may suppose that he recommended the acceptance of some of the provisions included in the memorandum: the formation of battalions and the stepping up of the training for the Supernumerary Police Force, for example. It was remarked to Sharett, both in Auchinleck's letters and in conversations with McConnell (the commander in Palestine) that the memorandum's contents were discussed in London. It is clear that the changes announced on August 6 (see below) were considered by the British as the fulfillment of those demands of the memorandum which could be honored.

⚑ Chapter 6

1. See Weizmann's article "The Jewish Problem in the Coming Reconstruction," *New York Times,* 8/13/41, hinting at a solution within the framework of a federation. In a speech to Zionist leaders at the Astor Hotel in New York (7/17/41) the federation was also mentioned. Weizmann went on to say there: "I would say that I would like western Palestine, with the possible cutting off of the triangle Nablus-Jenin-Tulkarem."

   The above items are in the Weizmann Archives, which also contain the interview with Lord Moyne of 7/28/41. Weizmann there sharply attacked the partition plan and spoke of a Jewish state within the structure of an Arab federation. In April of the same year, Weizmann had granted an interview to the American publication *Zionist Record,* where he said that after the war an Arab federation would surely arise from Persia to Libya, and that therefore there was also a place for a Jewish commonwealth that would live in peace with that federation.

2. Sharett's diary (ZA) 10/6/39; and Philby's memorandum to Weizmann, 11/17/43, in Weizmann Archives.

3. Lord Cranbourne, who in 1942 was colonial secretary, tried to obtain his colleagues' approval of immigration into Palestine by Jewish refugees from the Balkans, but failed (March 1942). In May 1942 (letter to Locker, 5/22/42) he finally succeeded, but by then it had become impossible to get ships to go from the Balkans to Turkey.

4. The high commissioner's plan for the determination of Palestine's future (September 1942, WA) reached the agency. He had suggested the establishment of a federation of Palestine, Transjordan, Syria, and Lebanon under British protection; and a proclamation of the continuation of White Paper policy until the creation of the federation. In his proposal the commissioner praised the position of Dr. Magnes and his group (the Ihud movement), which was prepared to reach a compromise with the Arabs on the basis of a federation and a Jewish minority in Palestine.

   Among programs of this type, one must also number that of Amir Abdullah for a union of Transjordan and Syria, with the intention of including Palestine at a later stage. This suggestion was offered the British (7/2/41), but their reply (7/14)

was rather cool. It was emphasized that this was an internal
Arab affair, and it was even said that one must wait for more
convenient circumstances for the program's enactment. The
British set little store by Abdullah and preferred to come to an
agreement with Iraqi representatives, particularly with Nuri
Said Pasha. See Majid Kadouri's article in R. N. Frye. *The
Near East and the Great Powers.* Cambridge, Mass.: 1951, p.
138 ff.

5. Ben-Gurion's memo, 5/14/40, WA.
6. JAE, 2/9/41.
7. Ibid., 3/16/41 and 3/23/41.
8. Ibid., 5/16/41.
9. Ibid., 2/16/41.
10. On the UPA Convention, see the *New York Times* (1/27/41).
    In March, Weizmann himself employed the commonwealth
    terminology in a speech in Chicago (3/29). He expressed the
    wish that such a commonwealth should rise within the frame-
    work of an Arab federation stretching from the Euphrates to
    Libya. In September 1941, the Zionist Organization of America
    decided to accept the commonwealth program. A similar resolu-
    tion was passed in South Africa in May, although there the
    desire that the commonwealth be included within the British
    Commonwealth of Nations was openly voiced. Cf. also the
    resolutions of the Hadassah Convention (Pittsburgh, October
    1941). The formulation also occurs in correspondence between
    Joseph and Weizmann in March 1941. The term appears in
    Zionist correspondence as far back as World War I. But it now
    served to allude to the democratic nature of the Jewish state
    which was to arise (since the connotation of the word "state"
    in English smacked of the German-Nazi *Staat* during the war
    period). It also hinted at the inclusion of the new political
    entity with the British *Commonwealth* of Nations. Ben-Gurion
    expounded the matter at length in the Smaller Zionist Actions
    Committee (10/15/42).
11. The members of the Agency Executive in Jerusalem hesitated,
    even after the article's publication was known in Palestine, to
    voice the commonwealth demand publicly. Even in March
    1942, Sharett, Kaplan, and Arthur Ruppin opposed the publi-
    cation of this demand.
12. At the SZAC, 10/15/42, ZA.
13. Weizmann to Namier, 10/21/42, WA.

14. "Not in the distant future, not in the course of generations, as we thought before the present disaster [meaning World War II, not the extermination of the Jews]; but immediately," said Ben-Gurion in a speech (2/26/41). Ben-Gurion never used the word "immediately" again and even tried to deny it. But once employed, the word stuck.

15. Sharett at the Histadrut Convention, 5/19/42, HA.

16. Hazan, SZAC, 10/15/42.

17. Riftin, 5/19/42, HA.

18. See Nuri Said's "blue book," in which are included his proposals of January 1943 on the union of the lands of the Fertile Crescent, along with the granting of autonomy to the Jews within the Arab state; and also Casey's reply. (I have not had access to the original, but there exists a Hebrew translation by E. Sasson in ZA, 9/24/43, G-01142.) The Egyptians had earlier advanced a program for the unification of the Nile countries (the Sudan, Eritrea, Uganda, and Egypt) over that for the Arab lands. They offered the latter plan in November 1942 (through Nahas Pasha at the Wafd Convention) even before the Iraqi program was presented; and see *Middle East in the War,* pp. 335 ff.

⚑ *Chapter 7*

1. The most authoritative description thus far of the Levantine episode, from a distinctly British point of view, is found in *Middle East in the War,* pp. 272–306.

2. Cf. Mrs. Dugdale's diary, WA. Sir Llewellyn Woodward. *British Foreign Policy in the Second World War.* London: 1962, pp. 385–395. Oliver Stanley, the colonial secretary in 1943, declared in 1946 (Hansard, *House of Commons,* vol. 426, colls. 983–5, 7/31/46) that he had been in favor of partition during the war and was sorry that his advice had not been followed. British representatives in the Middle East brought pressure to bear on Arab and Jewish statesmen alike to accept a partition resolution. Sharett reported on these developments at the JAE, 8/22/43 (see below, in the text, on his conversations with Rucker).

3. Interesting in this regard is Churchill's outburst at a press conference in Cairo on his way home from the Teheran meeting,

as reported by Dov Joseph in the Agency Executive (12/19/ 43). According to this version, Churchill stated: "Well, I have always been a Zionist. In my opinion there is room for all of them there [in Palestine]. If things are handled correctly, I feel that we can arrive at a satisfactory arrangement with the Arabs. We are not setting a high enough value on the Jewish contribution to the war effort—they are rendering a truly great service —nor on the great benefit which the Jewish endeavor has brought to Palestine. They have turned a desert into a blossoming garden," and so on, on that line. At the end, he added: "We have fulfilled our obligation to the Arabs by enthroning Faisal in Iraq and Amir Abdullah in Transjordan; and we shall keep —even if slowly—our promise to the Jews."

4. In a letter (8/30/43) to Goldmann, Sharett stated that partition had grown out of "our uncompromising opposition to the White Paper." He continued: "The line we should take is not to rush to its welcome but to keep coldly aloof and go on pressing for the 'whole loaf.' It will be disastrous, externally as well as internally, if at this stage partition became, or if the impression were created that it had become, our slogan. Internally, because a very violent controversy would then be revived—the last thing that we need today. Externally, because the chances of any further political headway would thereby be destroyed."

   In a private letter (to Moshe Medzini, 6/25/44, ZA) he said that "whatever we declare to be a favorable solution will immediately become a political 'maximum,' and the practical outcome will be considerably less than that. It is therefore better to ask for what really is a maximal demand, both because of the hope that we may after all attain it and because we should not be accused of having willingly renounced our historic rights. They can, of course, force us to accept partition, but why should we appear to choose it of our own free will?"

5. In his meeting with Smuts, Joseph took an extreme position (8/24/44, ZA). Only a Jewish state in all of Palestine could guarantee Britain a canal from the Mediterranean to Aqaba, a port for the British navy in Haifa, an oil pipeline, and an air base.

6. Yisrael Bar-Yehuda in the session of the Smaller Zionist Actions Committee (9/1/43).

7. Aaron Zisling in the Fifty-first Histadrut Convention, HA.

8. Reports by E. Sasson on talks with Abdullah and Nuri Said, 1/30/44 and 6/29/44, ZA.

9. Weizmann, in a letter to Lady Dugdale (1/8/43, WA): "The Biltmore resolution is just a resolution like the hundred and one resolutions usually passed at great meetings in this country, or in any other country. It embodies, in somewhat solemn tones, the chief points as laid down in my article in *Foreign Affairs*. But Ben-Gurion . . . injected into it all his extreme views, such as an immigration of two million people in three years, or something to that effect; and the building of a great defense force to fight either the Arabs or the British or both or goodness knows whom, and many more adornments of that kind, of which the Biltmore conference never thought and would certainly have rejected." Yet with all Weizmann's opposition to the Ben-Gurion "adventurism," he too sometimes was not reluctant to talk of grandiose numbers. Thus, for example, in a conversation (12/3/42) with Secretary of the Treasury Henry Morgenthau, Jr., and Judge Rosenman, he advocated the "immediate" immigration of three to five million Jews (letter to Weisgal, 1/8/43, WA).

10. Kaplan, in the Agency Executive (6/20/43 and 11/7/43), openly opposed Ben-Gurion's position, while Sharett and Locker mainly tried to prevent the resignation. The others, except for Rabbi Maimon, did not accept his assertions against Weizmann. After the resignation, his fellow Mapai members and various personages (like the South African Zionist leader Kirschner) brought serious pressure to bear so as to dissuade him from that step.

11. *Sefer Hapalmakh*, pp. 22–23.

12. In his letter of 4/29, in which he announced the closing of the centers, Sharett stated that the authorities had abundantly demonstrated by their acts that they were not interested in a continuation of Jewish recruitment. Sergeant Lebedanski's complaint about his beating was submitted on 5/2, but no public hearing was set up. See also Macpherson's letter to Sharett (5/3) and the latter's reply (5/5). After the closing of the centers, Sharett went to Egypt for talks. During that visit, when General Morehead asked why Jewish enlistment had ceased after the closing of the centers, Sharett answered that it was because they had not told people to enlist.

" 'Imagine recruiting in England without the call of the English government.'

" 'But you are no government.'

"I replied," Sharett continued, " 'from a legal standpoint, you are right. There is no similarity between us. But from a moral-psychological point of view, it is exactly the same thing' " (JAE, 5/2/43).

13. Sirkin and Reichlin were released in 1946. For the trials, see *Middle East in the War,* pp. 307 ff., which presents all the official matter; *Eight Years Overseas,* p. 172; and the Hebrew press. The creating of a Police Mobile Force at the end of 1943 was connected with fears of the outbreak of a Jewish revolt (see Sir Charles Jeffries. *The Colonial Police.* London: 1952). The British fear of a Jewish revolt continuously grew. Thus, for example, the governor of the Jerusalem District, Keith-Roach, in a report of 1/31/43 (ATH), warned that the Jews had no safety valve and might revolt in the middle of the war. Wilson wrote in Dispatch 2: Operations in the Middle East from 16th February 1943 to 16th January 1944—Supplement to the *London Gazette,* 11/12/46 (quoted in *Middle East in the War,* pp. 310 f.): "The Jewish Agency was in some respects arrogating to itself the powers and status of an independent Jewish government. It no longer attempted to deny the existence of arms caches, but claimed the right not only to hold arms for self-defense but to resist any attempt on the part of lawful authority to locate them. It was, in fact, defying the government, and to that extent rebellion could be said to exist."

The pretence of British authorities that they never knew the Jews had arms and that this was quite a new discovery on their part was of course part of the diplomatic game. The agency on its part pretended that it did not know of an organization called the Hagana. If it had admitted its knowledge, it would have undermined its position as a legal body.

The Palestine administration failed in the trials: American newsmen and American public opinion, insofar it was interested at all, was pro-Jewish.

14. In the search at Hulda, some weapons were discovered, including hand grenades of Hebrew manufacture. That made a deep impression on the English and confirmed their fears of the danger of a Jewish revolt. *Middle East in the War,* p. 311, note 1.

15. Kirk, *Middle East in the War,* p. 310, says that the high commissioner intervened with the army people and stopped anti-Hagana actions. Sharett's report on his meeting with Mac-Michael, JAE, 11/17/43.

16. The I.S.L.D. was a branch of (M.I.1) Central British Intelligence. In contrast, the S.O.E. (M.O.4) and its offshoot, the A Force, were young services which had been set up during the war; they were administered, not by professional intelligence people, but by civilians who had been drafted for the armed services like other Britishers. These intelligence and resistance services competed, and even fought, with one another. This was well known to the agency people.

17. Original material on the parachutists is concentrated at the Zionist Archives, where each parachutist's mission has a separate file. See also *Magen Beseter* and *Secret War Effort of Yishuv,* ZA, 8/30/45.

18. See "Self-Defense" file, ATH.

✍ Chapter 8

1. The words of a Palmakh officer during the debate over the work-training camps. (Y. Allon's deposition, ATH.)

2. *Palmakh Bulletin,* Nos. 2, 4, and 5, ATH.

3. Letters by David Idlin, ATH. Palmakh soldiers' letters of this period are scarce because it was strictly forbidden to write letters mentioning the formation or its affairs.

4. Peled, 1/6/43, at HH Executive, HH Archive.

5. The song of the sweater that was sung in the camps at a later time was also a fitting anthem for 1943: "Get it through your head pal/ A sweater you won't get—so what!/ Get out of the Palmakh/ And join up with HEESH—so what!" The song is unpublished and quoted from the author's memory. (Translator's note: HEESH is an acronym from the initials of the Hebrew for Field Force.)

6. Galili, oral deposition, ATH.

7. HH Archive, Merhavya.

✍ Chapter 9

1. *Bamakhane* (Hagana paper), No. 80, 3/10/44, ATH.

2. Golomb's speech on "Ways of Defence," 1943, in: *Khevyon,* vol. 2. Tel Aviv: 1954, p. 58.

3. Sharett's lecture, no title, 1943, ATH.

4. Ya'ari at the HE, 12/9/43, HA.
5. Galili's lecture, "Facing the Future," *Palmakh Bulletin,* No. 16, March 1944.
6. In *Palmakh Bulletin,* No. 30, June 1945.
7. *Lamadrikh,* Hagana instruction booklet, August 1945, p. 70.
8. *Palmakh Bulletin,* No. 25, December 1944.
9. In the spring of 1942 Etzel offered its cooperation to the British, but nothing came of it.
10. The above is based on material in ATH, a number of oral testimonies and the booklet *Am Lohem,* published 11/1/43, ATH.
11. For the above, see M. Begin. *The Revolt.* London: 1951; also Begin. *Bamakhteret,* 3 vols. Tel Aviv: 1959–62, and material in ATH. His talk with Sneh took place on 10/8/44, and Sneh's notes on it are deposited in ZA.
12. JAE, 2/27/44.
13. JAE 2/27/44, 3/26/44, 4/2/44. The most determined opponent of the antischismatic operation was Gruenbaum, who resigned because of it from the Agency Executive. Talks were held between Dov Joseph and the Revisionists, with the object of persuading them to influence Etzel to cease operations (2/18/44, 2/20/44, 2/27/44, 2/28/44, 4/3/44). In this last session, the Revisionists announced, in contradiction to their previous statements, that they no longer had any influence over Etzel. In passing, Joseph notes on 2/28 that one of the Revisionist representatives related that a C.I.D. officer had asked them what they would take in exchange for halting their acts of terror.
14. JAE 4/9/44, and talks with the chief of police inspector (3/9) and the government secretary (3/27), conducted by Dov Joseph (ZA).
15. Statements by Sharett and Ben-Gurion in the Agency Executive session, 11/7/44. In a proclamation agreed upon at that same session, it was stated: "The Yishuv must spew forth from its midst all the men of this destructive gang, deny the terrorists all protection and refuge, not give in to threats, and extend all aid necessary to the authorities to prevent acts of terror and to wipe out its organization; for our lives depend on it."
16. JAE, 10/20/44, 11/7/44, 11/12/44, 11/20/44, 12/10/44. See also the minutes of the Sixth Histadrut Convention, opening session (11/20/44). Statements of Sharett, Ben-Gurion, Hazan, and Moshe Erem assert that the choice is between terrorist

organizations and an organized community, an organized workers' movement; as Ben-Gurion worded it at that session: "A community which does not have self-rule must resort for the purpose [war against saboteurs] to the existing regime and power of others. . . . It is they or we."

17. From the publication *Yahdav,* Kibbutz Nirim.
18. *Palmakh Bulletin,* No. 1, October 1942.
19. *Palmakh Bulletin,* No. 1413, December 1943. The concept of the Palmakh officer's role drew sustenance from Hagana tradition. The problems connected with the officer's position in that regimen were explored in a discussion of some officers with Golomb in the summer of 1944. Only one officer favored an increase in the officer's formal authority, while it was Golomb who defended the traditional position of the Hagana and Palmakh officer as a Histadrut heritage. He stated that if the officer depended "only on the power structure, there is danger of killing the soldier's will power. We must, therefore, seek the proper mix between formal authority and the soldier's power of thought. . . . He must be a *friend* who has great knowledge and, at the same time, authority as well over all matters of command" (*Palmakh Bulletin,* No. 24).
20. D Company bulletin, February 1945, ATH.
21. *Palmakh Bulletin,* No. 6.
22. Cordell Hull. *Memoirs,* vol. 2, pp. 1535–6.
23. Goldmann in JAE, 9/28/44. In Goldmann's vivid language, the conversation with Stettinius went as follows: " 'Goldmann,' said Stettinius, 'everything's O.K., you will get a Jewish state under an Anglo-American protectorate. We'll give you everything you need, even money, it'll all be all right.' I told him it all sounded too good to be true. He answered: 'I have spoken with everyone in a very free manner, and that is the decision.' I said: 'Stettinius, if they said there will be a Jewish state, they might have meant partition,' to which he responded: 'Say that word again, what's that partition, never heard of it, isn't that good?' "
24. Rabbi Heller's report in JAE, 5/28/45 (after the president's death).
25. Moyne was among the supporters of partition, and he also tried to come to an agreement with the Arabs on the basis of their consent to an influx of 25,000 Jews per year. Weizmann's attitude toward Moyne was expressed in the Agency Executive,

on 12/16/44, when he noted, "I know that, in the Cairo Conference, in a meeting between Roosevelt and Churchill, Lord Moyne suggested a partition plan. When Roosevelt heard that, he said nothing at first. Later he said: 'Gentlemen, what do you want, that little country . . . you want to divide that little country down even further?' Thus the matter was rejected and taken off the agenda."

26. During the *Saison,* the pro-British Zionist policies were re-emphasized. For instance, Ben-Gurion told Lord Gort on 3/13/45 that "the state would come—and I stressed that I was giving my opinion—if I had my choice it would have a connection with the British Commonwealth of Nations; a tie like that of Australia is not possible, that is, of the same race, but some kind of a tie." In the future state, the navy and air force would have to remain in British hands (Agency Executive, 3/15/45). However, even during the *Saison,* the agency's friendship was, at times, repugnant to the British. Gort went into a rage over Jewish demands for a policy of lower taxes, larger appropriations for health and education, and enlargement of the Jewish Settlement Police, "for which, in his opinion, there is no military justification; and, with unconcealed anger, he rejected the argument that the Jewish Settlement Police were necessary for protection against Arab troubles" (Agency Executive, 6/3/45).

27. On the eve of Labour's ascent to power, the party's pro-Zionist policies were proclaimed again in a resolution of its Executive Committee, 4/25/45. Labour party resolutions from 1940 to 1945 are contained in a booklet published by the Jewish Agency: *Documents Relating to the Palestine Problem.* London: 1945, pp. 79–82.

Glossary

AGENCY. See JEWISH AGENCY FOR PALESTINE.

AGENCY EXECUTIVE. See JEWISH AGENCY FOR PALESTINE.

AGUDATH ISRAEL. Extremist orthodox non-Zionist group.

AHDUT AVODAH. Left-wing political party, based on the "B" Faction. It split off from Mapai in 1944. The core of Ahdut Avodah was a majority of Kibbutz Meuhad; its main leaders were Yitzhak Tabenkin and Israel Galili.

ALIYAH. Immigration.

ALIYAH BET. Illegal or clandestine immigration by those not holding official certificates.

"B" FACTION. Left-wing group based mainly on a majority of Kibbutz Meuhad members. It was a factional element within Mapai at the beginning of World War II. It had an activist-Zionist, anti-British, and somewhat pro-Soviet orientation.

BETAR. Youth movement of the Jabotinsky group. See REVISIONISTS.

DAVAR. Daily newspaper of the Histadrut, actually of Mapai.

ETZEL. Generally known in English as the Irgun. It was a military group much smaller than the Hagana and began active anti-British operations in 1944. Originally affiliated with the Revisionists, it became independent later.

FIELD FORCE (HEESH). Mobile Hagana units, first founded 1939 by Yitzhak Sadeh. They were controlled by district commanders and served as the starting point for recruitment in the 1948 War of Independence.

FIELD SQUADS (FOSH). Mobile Hagana units during the Arab rebellion, 1936–1939.

GENERAL ZIONISTS. Moderate, centrist Zionist party, deriving its main strength before the war from Poland, the U.S., and Britain. During World War II there were two groups: "A" General Zionists, identified with Weizmann, Stephen Wise, Yitzhak Gruenbaum, and Professor Selig Brodetsky; and "B" General Zionists, who had a more right-wing hue and were much stronger in Palestine than the more liberal prolabor "A" wing. The "B" group was led in Palestine by the mayor of Tel Aviv, Yitzhak Rokakh, and Dr. Emil Shmorak, Agency Executive member.

GUARD FORCE (HIM). Main reserve of the Hagana (numbered 29,000 members in 1944). The Guard Force was rather poorly trained and was really in the nature of a home guard. Its main purpose was the defense of Jewish settlements and towns.

HAGANA. The main military underground arm of Palestinian Jewry.

HANODEDET. Mobile Hagana group, founded in 1936 by Sadeh.

HASHOMER. Precursor of the Hagana; founded in 1909, its aim was to provide defense for Jewish settlements and at the same time to found new villages, mostly of the kvutza, kibbutz or moshav type. Officially it was dissolved in 1920 when the Hagana was founded, but in fact it maintained a clandestine existence until 1929.

HASHOMER HATZAIR. Marxist Zionist youth movement, founded in 1914. It created Kibbutz Artzi, which became its parent body in the twenties. In 1942 Kibbutz Artzi founded a political party, also using the name Hashomer Hatzair. Its political orientation was antiactivist and pro-Soviet. It favored a peaceful arrangement with the Arabs through the establishment of Palestine as a binational state.

HEVER HAKVUTZOT. Non-Marxist grouping of collectivist settlements. It was the original basis of Hapoel Hatzair (Young Worker) party that joined with Ahdut Avodah to form Mapai in 1930. Hever Hakvutzot setlements tended to be small. They relied on "organic" growth. They remained intimate and were permeated with a Tolstoian ideology of return to agriculture and the "religion of labor." The first kvutzot in Palestine—Degania, Ayelet Hashahar, and so on—belonged to the Hever Hakvutzot.

HISTADRUT. General Federation of Jewish Labor in Palestine, founded in 1920. It wielded a decisive political and economic influence in the Yishuv.

HITYASHVUT.   Settlement on the land.

IHUD (Union).   Political movement centered around a group of Jerusalem University people and led by Judah L. Magnes; the only Zionist group willing to accept a minority status for Jews in Palestine. Its small numbers were somewhat offset by the outstanding personalities who were its members: Professors Buber, Bergmann, and others.

JEWISH AGENCY FOR PALESTINE.   Set up in 1929 as the central representative of Jews vis-à-vis the Mandatory government on all questions affecting Palestine. Originally, Zionists and non-Zionists were to be equally represented. However, not enough interested non-Zionists could be found to undertake work in the agency. By 1939 the agency and the World Zionist Organization were to all intents and purposes identical. The only non-Zionist on the Agency Executive was Dr. Werner Senator, a German Jew. From then on, the terms "agency" and "Zionist movement" were interchangeable. Ben-Gurion was chairman of the Agency Executive, and Weizmann was president.

KIBBUTZ ARTZI HASHOMER HATZAIR.   Kibbutz organization of Hashomer Hatzair.

KIBBUTZ MEUHAD.   During World War II this was the largest kibbutz organization (about nine thousand members as against six thousand in Kibbutz Artzi). It contained a Mapai minority and a "B" Faction majority.

KOFER HAYISHUV.   Financial body set up in 1938 to levy voluntary contributions for security expenditures, mainly for the Hagana. It was largely under the influence of the Middle-Class Union.

KOL ISRAEL.   Hagana broadcasting station.

KVUTZA.   Kibbutz; collective settlement. Means of production are owned in common, and distribution of products is done on a collective basis. The difference between kvutza and kibbutz was, during the pre-1948 period, one of size and atmosphere rather than one of organization. Kvutza (pl., kvutzot) tended to be a small settlement engaged solely in agriculture; kibbutz (pl., kibbutzim) was identified with a tendency to constant growth and a striving for industrial as well as agricultural development. These differences later disappeared.

LEHI.   (Fighters for the Freedom of Israel). Popularly known in English as the Stern group. Lehi was a very small extreme anti-British military underground group which broke off from Etzel in 1940. It was founded by Avraham Stern.

MAGEN DAVID ADOM. Jewish aid organization equivalent to the Red Cross.

MAHANOT HA-OLIM. Left-wing youth movement of high school youths in Palestine organized and aided by Kibbutz Meuhad.

MAPAI. Palestine labor party, a moderate socialist grouping. Led by Berl Katznelson and David Ben-Gurion, it was the dominant political force in the Yishuv. It was founded in 1930.

MATKAL. General Staff of Hagana, headed by the chief of General Staff (Ramatkal).

MIDDLE-CLASS UNION (Ihud Ezrahi). Founded in 1940, it was an attempt to form a representation of middle-class and rightist circles in the Yishuv, especially on economic and security matters. It was composed largely of industrialists, merchants, shopkeepers, and private farmers (as opposed to members of farming cooperatives or collectives).

MIZRAHI. Religious party of middle-class outlook. Its main aim was establishment of a Jewish state guided by the laws of the Torah. A labor group by the name of Hapoel Hamizrahi was established in the twenties and set up a number of kibbutzim. By the Second World War, Hapoel Hamizrahi became the dominant faction in religious Zionism. Its leader, Moshe Haim Shapira, and the Mizrahi leader, Rabbi Yehuda L. Maimon, were both members of the Agency Executive.

MOSAD LE'ALIYAH BET ("B" Immigration Bureau). Originally a Histadrut, later a general underground organization set up in 1938/9 under Shaul Avigur (Meirov) to organize unofficial, or "illegal," immigration, i.e., immigration without government permit.

MOSHAV. Smallholders' cooperative village, where every settler owns a private plot and manages his own household, but the larger portion of the lands are cooperatively worked and profits divided according to labor days invested.

NASHASHIBI. One of the most influential Arab families in Palestine. Ragheb bey al-Nashashibi was once mayor of Jerusalem and head of the Palestine Defence Party, a moderate and pro-British group.

NEW ZIONIST ORGANIZATION. Rival organization to the World Zionist Organization. It was set up by Jabotinsky in 1935 and was based almost exclusively on the Revisionist party.

NOAR OVED. Youth section of the Histadrut, looking after employment conditions and educational facilities for working youths.

At the same time it also had an active youth movement section whose members tended to join Kibbutz Meuhad settlements.

NODEDET. See HANODEDET.

PALMAKH. Commando units, the strategic reserve of the Hagana.

POLICE. Jewish police formations in Palestine, controlled by the Mandatory government, were the Jewish Settlement Police (which included special Mobile Guards with armored cars or "tenders"); the so-called Notrim (Supernumerary Police Force), who were special policemen for the defense of specific objects (railway, electric lines, refineries); and the Temporary Auxiliary Policemen (TAP). The TAPs wore no uniforms and received no pay, and their training and equipment were poor. Those in the villages (over fourteen thousand) were more organized than those in the towns (some two thousand). However, they carried special cards and were allowed to bear arms under certain conditions.

REVISIONISTS. Political party founded by Jabotinsky in 1925. Its policy demanded the establishment of a Jewish state on both sides of the Jordan. It was largely lower middle class in composition and antisocialist in outlook. It supported Etzel (the Irgun) from 1933 until early in 1944. At that time, Etzel became an independent entity.

RIGHT WING. All the political groupings to the right of Mapai; specifically the General Zionists, the Mizrahi, and the Revisionists.

SAISON. The name given to the bitter struggle of the Hagana against Etzel in 1944/5, in the course of which some one hundred Etzel members were handed over to the British police. "Little *Saison*" was the name given, after the event, to a similar action of Hagana against Lehi in 1942.

SOLEL BONEH. Histadrut construction company engaged in building roads and housing. In 1938 it built a defensive barrier in northern Palestine under British direction to prevent Arab guerrillas from entering the country. During World War II its engineers did construction work at Abadan in Iran and in northern Syria.

SPECIAL SQUADS (POM). Small groups of Hagana men organized outside the Hagana framework at the initiative of Ben-Gurion to act against Arab guerrillas and British authorities in 1939.

UNITED KIBBUTZ. See KIBBUTZ MEUHAD.

VAAD LEUMI. National executive, the elected quasi-government of the Yishuv.

YISHUV. The Jewish community in Palestine.

Bibliography

◪ Works in English

Abcarius, M. *Palestine through the Fog of Propaganda*. London: 1946.

Abdullah, Amir. *Memoirs*. London: 1950.

Alpert, C. *Palestine between Wars*. Washington: 1944.

Antonius, G. *Arab Awakening*. London: 1938.

Barbour, N. *Nisi Dominus*. London: 1946.

Bonne, A. *The Economic Development of the Middle East*. New York: 1945.

Boveri, M. *Mediterranean Cross-Currents*. London: 1938.

Broido, E. *Jews, Arabs and the Middle East*. New York: 1944.

Churchill, W. S. *History of the Second World War*. London: 1953.

ESCO Foundation. *Palestine* (2 vols.). New Haven: 1947.

Fink, R. *America and Palestine*. New York: 1945.

Friedrich, C. J. *American Policy towards Palestine*. Washington: 1944.

Frye, R. N. (ed.). *The Near East and the Great Powers*. Cambridge, Mass.: 1951.

Gass, O.; Nathan, R. *Problem and Promise*. Washington, D.C.: 1946.

Glubb Pasha. *The Story of the Arab Legion*. London: 1948.

Great Britain. Parliament. Command 6019 (The White Paper of 1939). London: 1939.

Great Britain. Parliament. Command 6180 (The 1940 Land Transfer Regulations). London: 1940.

Gwynn, Sir Charles. *Imperial Policy*. London: 1939.

Hanna, P. C. *British Policy in Palestine*. Washington: 1942.

Harris, Sir Douglas. *Supplies in Wartime*. Jerusalem: 1942.

Hirschmann, I. *Life-line to the Promised Land*. New York: 1946.

Histadrut. *Palestine Agricultural Economy under Wartime Conditions*. Tel Aviv: 1946.

Hurewitz, J. C. *Diplomacy in the Near and Middle East*. Princeton: 1956.

———. *The Struggle for Palestine*. New York: 1950.

Hyamson, A. *Palestine under the Mandate*. London: 1950.

Jeffries, Sir Charles. *The Colonial Police*. London: 1952.

Jewish Agency. *Activities in Palestine during the War*. London: 1945.

———. *Documents Relating to the Palestine Question*. London: 1945.

———. *The Economic War Effort of Jewish Palestine*. London: 1945.

Kaplan, E. *A Report on Seven Years of Palestine, 1939–1946*. New York: 1947.

Kimche, J. *Seven Fallen Pillars*. London: 1950.

Kirk, G. *The Middle East in the War*. London: 1953.

Koestler, A. *Promise and Fulfilment*. London: 1949.

Lang, G. *Australia in the War of 1939–1945* (series one, vols. 1 & 2). Melbourne: 1950.

Manuel, F. *The Realities of American-Palestine Relations*. Washington: 1949.

Marlowe, J. *Rebellion in Palestine*. London: 1946.

———. *Seat of Pilate*. London: 1959.

Meinertzhagen, R. *Middle East Diary*. London: 1959.

Morton, G. J. *Just the Job*. London: 1955.

Moseley, G. *Gideon Goes to War*. London: 1955.

Orenstein, M. *A Plea for Arab-Jewish Unity*. London: 1936.

Paassen, P. van. *The Forgotten Ally*. New York: 1943.

Palestine Government Statistical Office. *Statistical Abstracts, 1939–1946*. Jerusalem: 1947.

Philby, St. J. A. *Arabian Jubilee*. London: 1952.

Playfair, I. S. O. *The Mediterranean and the Middle East*. London: 1956.

Rabinowitz, L. *Soldiers from Judea*. London: 1945.

Royal Institute of International Affairs. *Great Britain and Palestine, 1915–1945*. London: 1946.

————. *Survey for 1939–1946: The World in March, 1939*. Oxford: 1952.

————. *Survey of British Commonwealth Affairs*, vol. 1. Oxford: 1952.

Sidebotham, H. *The Problem of Palestine*. London: 1937.

Stark, F. *East Is West*. London: 1945.

Stein, L. *Promises and Afterthoughts*. London: 1939.

Storrs, Sir Ronald. *Orientations*. London: 1937.

Sykes, C. *Crossroads to Israel*. London: 1965.

Trevor, D. *Under the White Paper*. Jerusalem: 1948.

U.S. Congress. House. *Jewish National Home*, Hearing in the House of Representatives, 1944.

Warriner, D. *Land and Poverty in the Middle East*. London: 1948.

Weizmann, C. *Palestine's Role in the Solution of the Jewish Question*. New York: 1942.

Woodward, Sir Llewellyn. *British Foreign Policy in the Second World War*. London: 1962.

🔖 *Works in Hebrew*

GENERAL LITERATURE

Assaf, Michael. *Hatenua Haaravit Beerets Yisrael Umekoroteha*. Tel Aviv: 1947.

Ben-Gurion, David. *Bamaarakha*. Tel Aviv: 1957.

————. *Mimaamad Leam*. Tel Aviv: 1955.

Cohen, Aharon. *Hamizrakh Haaravi*. Tel Aviv: 1955.

Horowitz, David. *Hakimum Uvayotav Baolam Uveerets Yisrael*. Tel Aviv: 1948.

Weizmann, Chaim. *Am Yisrael Veerets Yisrael*. Jerusalem: 1936.

————. *Masa Vamaas*. Jerusalem: 1963.

ZIONIST POLICY

Abbady, Isaac A. *Benenu Leven Haanglim*. Jerusalem: 1948.

Abramovich, Z. *Bemaarakhot Hitabkutenu*. Tel Aviv: 1939.

Jabotinsky, Zeev (Vladimir). *Ketavim*. Jerusalem: 1959.

Kaplansky, Shelomo. *Khazon Vehagshama*. Merhavya: 1950.

Liebenstein, A. *Im Havikuakh Hatsioni*. Tel Aviv: 1944.

Lubianker (Lavon), Pinhas. *Bavikuakh Hamedini*. Tel Aviv: 1945.

Remez, David. *Turim*. Tel Aviv: 1952.

Tornovsky, V. *Tokhnit Hayishuv Baarets Lizeman Hamilkhama.* Tel Aviv: 1941.
Ya'ari, Meir. *Befetakh Tekufa.* Merhavya: 1942.
Yerubaal (Katznelson). *Begabenu El Hakir.* Tel Aviv: 1940.
———. *Hitbonenut Bematsavenu.* Tel Aviv: 1940.

HAGANA, PALMAKH, ETZEL, AND LEHI

Banay, Jacob. *Khayalim Almonim.* Tel Aviv: 1958.
Begin, Menachem. *Bamakhteret.* Tel Aviv: 1959–1962.
———. *Hamered.* Jerusalem: 1950.
Ben-Avraham, Y. *Haheavkut Al Tsava Yehudi.* Tel Aviv: 1946.
Dekel, Ephraim. *Alilot Shai.* Tel Aviv: 1953.
Friedmann, A. *Lokhame Khofesh Beyisrael.* Tel Aviv: 1959.
Gilead, Zerubavel, ed. *Magen Beseter.* Jerusalem: 1948.
Golomb, Eliyahu. *Khevyon Oz.* Tel Aviv: 1954.
Habas, Braha. *Portsei Hashearim.* Tel Aviv: 1957.
———, ed. *Sefer Meorot Tartsav.* Tel Aviv: 1937.
Hadani, Ever. *Am Bemilkhamto,* Tel Aviv: 1948.
———. *Beruakh Uvekhayil.* Tel Aviv: 1952.
Hanoter Haivri. Tel Aviv: 1957.
Halperin, Y., ed. *Sefer Hagevura.* Tel Aviv: 1941.
Kovets Lehi (anthology). Tel Aviv: 1959.
Lamdan, Isaac. *Kovets Sefer Hahitnadvut.* Tel Aviv: 1946.
Landsborough, T. *Hakomando Shel Tobruk.* Tel Aviv: 1959.
Lazar-Litai (Lazar), Chaim. *Af Al Pi.* Tel Aviv: 1957.
Lifshitz, Y., ed. *Sefer Habrigada.* Tel Aviv: 1957.
Mardor, Meir. *Shelikhut Aluma.* Tel Aviv: 1957.
Meirov, Sh. *Im Dor Hahagana.* Tel Aviv: 1951.
Raanan, Tsvi, ed. *Tsava Umilkhama* (anthology). Tel Aviv: 1955.
Sadeh, Yitzhak. *Ma Khidesh Hapalmakh.* Merhavya: 1950.
Scheib, Israel. *Maaser Rishon.* Tel Aviv: 1950.
Sefer Hapalmakh. Tel Aviv: 1953.
Sefer Toldot Hahagana, vol. 2, bks. 1 & 2. Tel Aviv: 1960–63.
Shamir, A. *Yehudim Okhazim Beneshek.* Tel Aviv: 1946.
Shmulevitz, M. *Beyamim Adumim.* Tel Aviv: 1949.
Sykes, Christopher. *Wingate.* Tel Aviv: 1961.
Weinshall, Yaakov. *Hadam Asher Basaf.* Tel Aviv: 1956.
Wingate, Charles Orde. *Yalkut Devarim.* Tel Aviv: 1945.
Yakobovits, M. *Mipalmakh Ad Tsahal.* Tel Aviv: 1953.
Zalitsky (Carmel), Moshe. *Ben Hakhomot.* Tel Aviv: 1949.

Index